Ōoku

☯ THE INNER CHAMBERS

by **Fumi Yoshinaga**

VOL.**3**

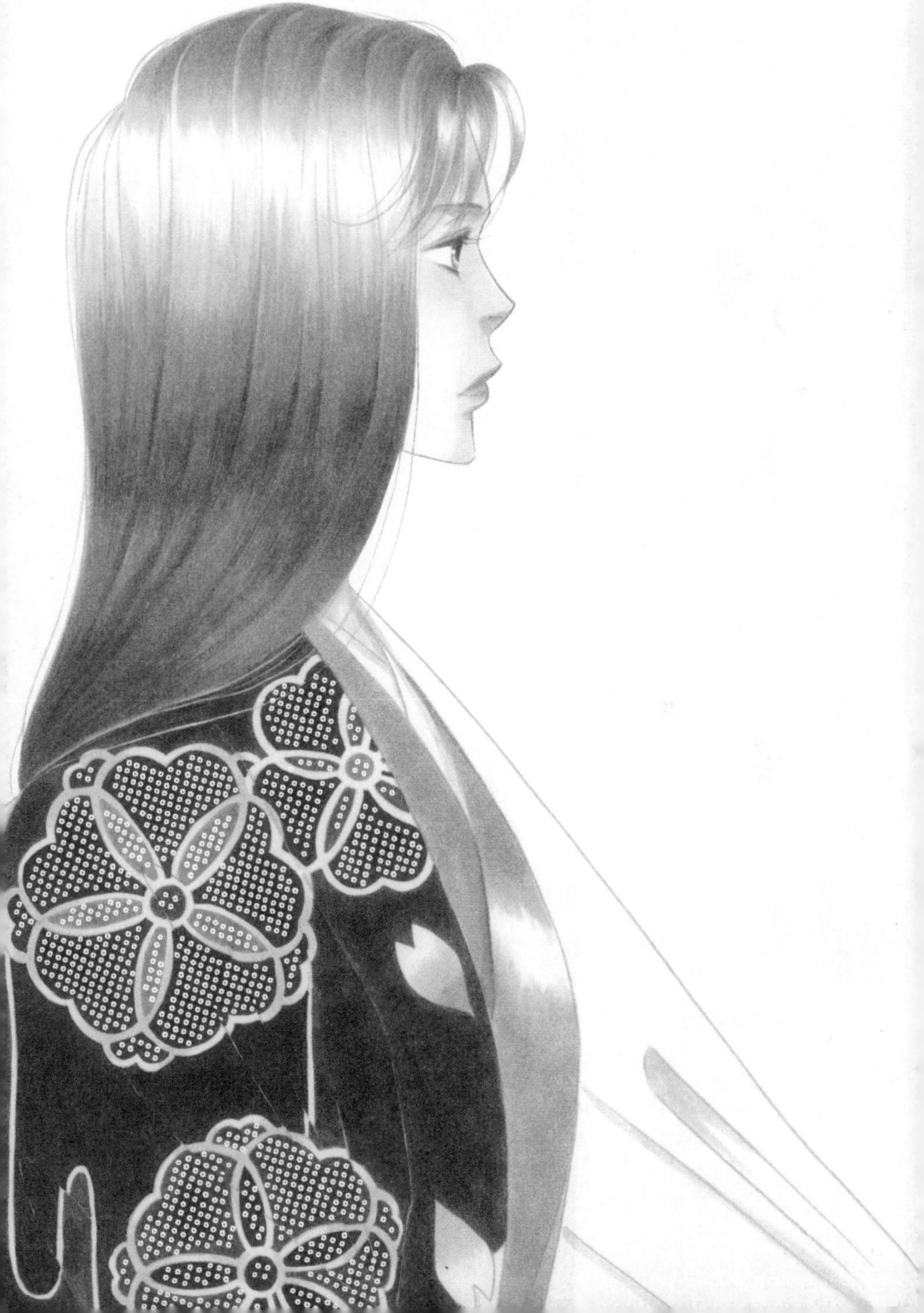

TABLE *of* CONTENTS

Ōoku

THE INNER CHAMBERS

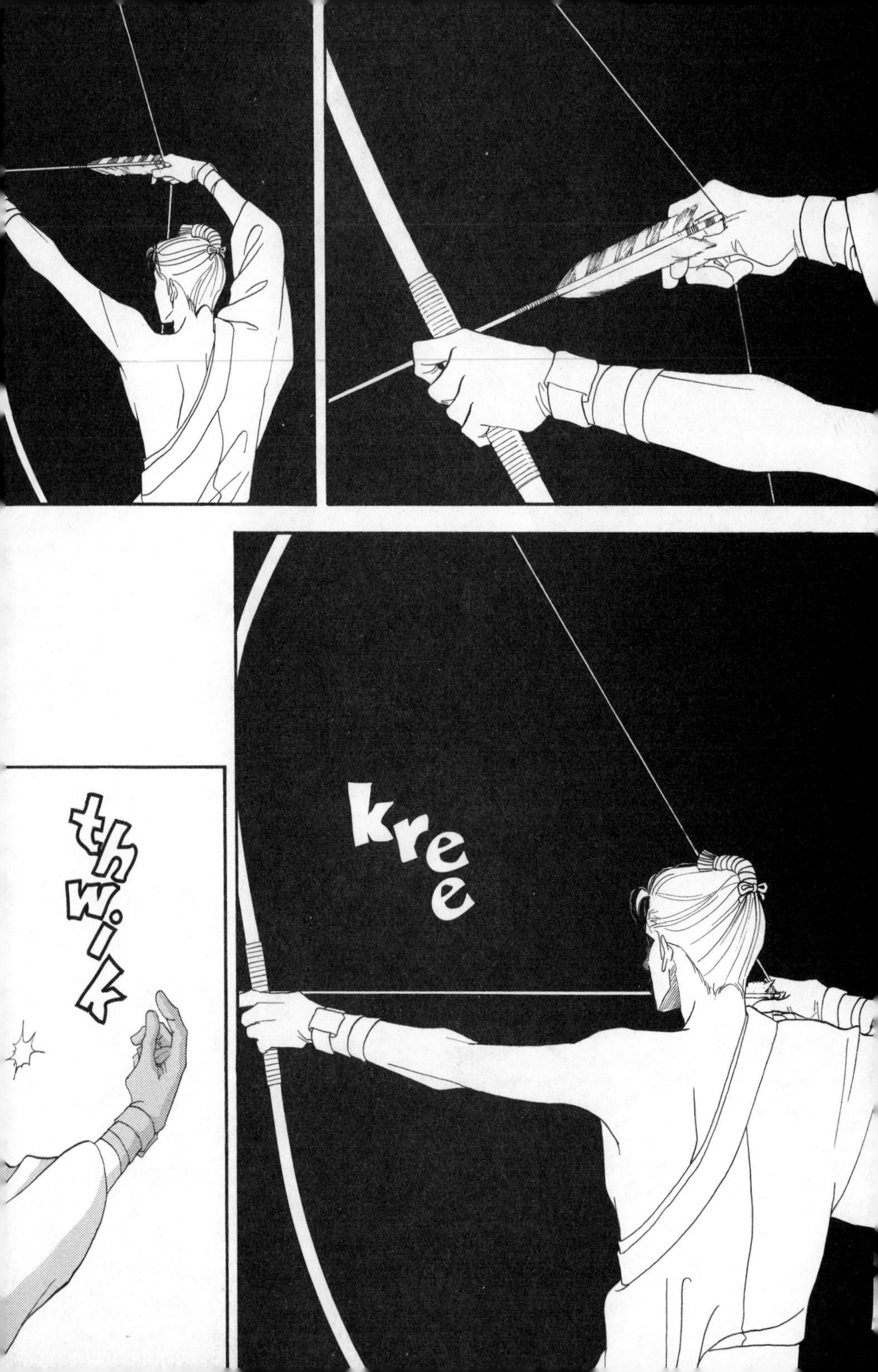
kree
thwik

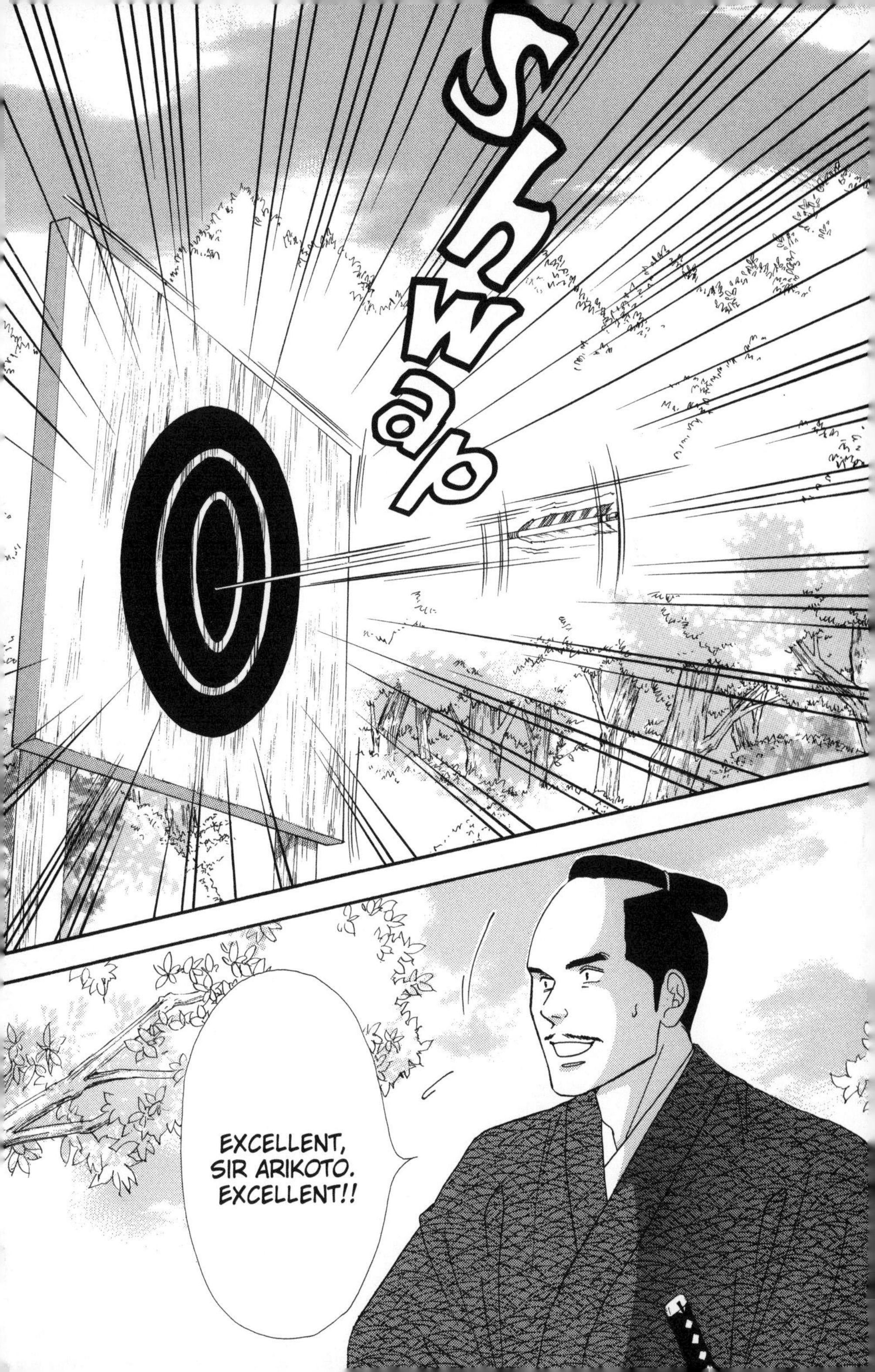
Shwap
EXCELLENT, SIR ARIKOTO. EXCELLENT!!

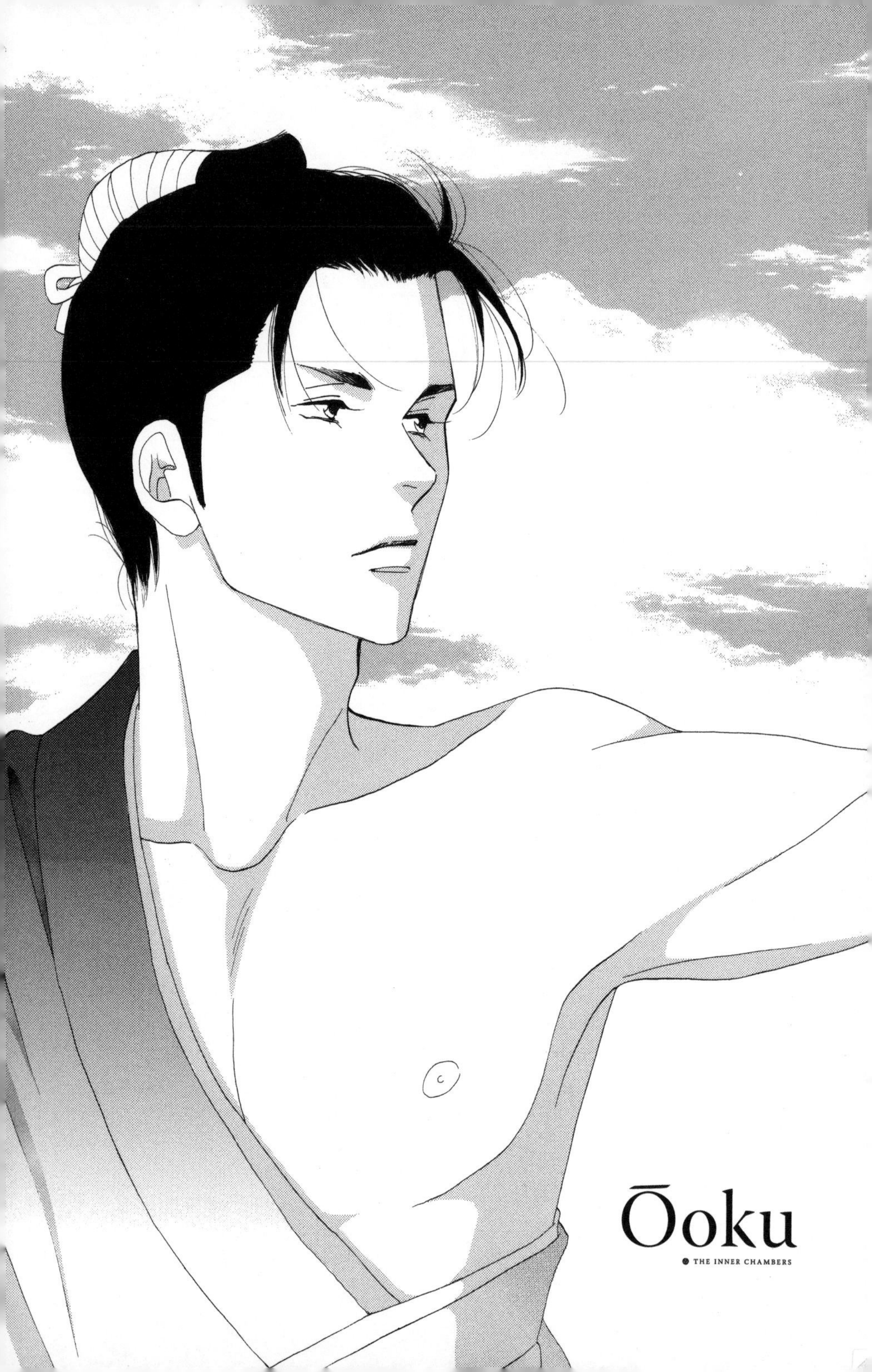
Ōoku
THE INNER CHAMBERS

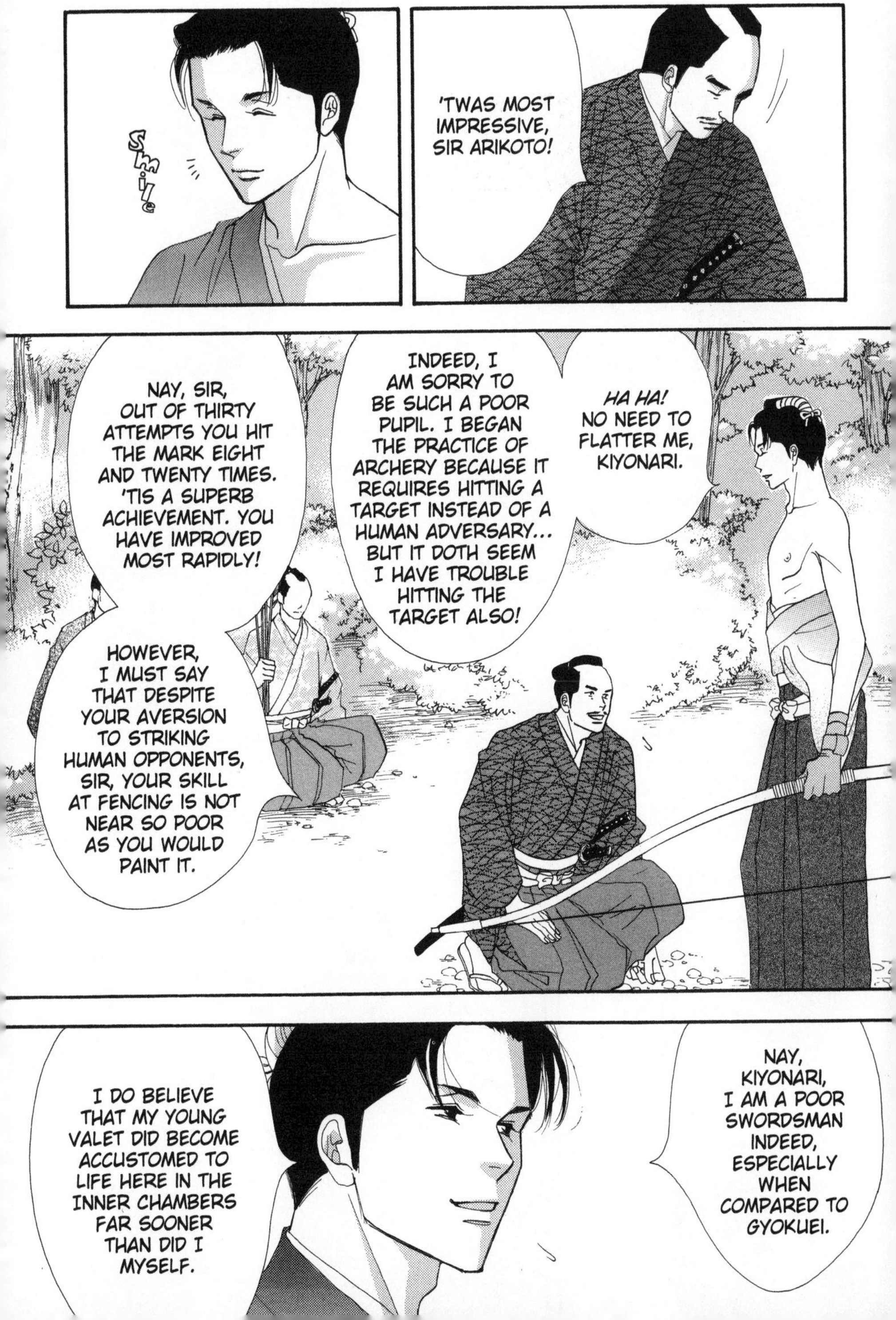
'TWAS MOST IMPRESSIVE, SIR ARIKOTO!
Smile
HA HA! NO NEED TO FLATTER ME, KIYONARI.
INDEED, I AM SORRY TO BE SUCH A POOR PUPIL. I BEGAN THE PRACTICE OF ARCHERY BECAUSE IT REQUIRES HITTING A TARGET INSTEAD OF A HUMAN ADVERSARY... BUT IT DOTH SEEM I HAVE TROUBLE HITTING THE TARGET ALSO!
NAY, SIR, OUT OF THIRTY ATTEMPTS YOU HIT THE MARK EIGHT AND TWENTY TIMES. 'TIS A SUPERB ACHIEVEMENT. YOU HAVE IMPROVED MOST RAPIDLY!
HOWEVER, I MUST SAY THAT DESPITE YOUR AVERSION TO STRIKING HUMAN OPPONENTS, SIR, YOUR SKILL AT FENCING IS NOT NEAR SO POOR AS YOU WOULD PAINT IT.
NAY, KIYONARI, I AM A POOR SWORDSMAN INDEED, ESPECIALLY WHEN COMPARED TO GYOKUEI.
I DO BELIEVE THAT MY YOUNG VALET DID BECOME ACCUSTOMED TO LIFE HERE IN THE INNER CHAMBERS FAR SOONER THAN DID I MYSELF.

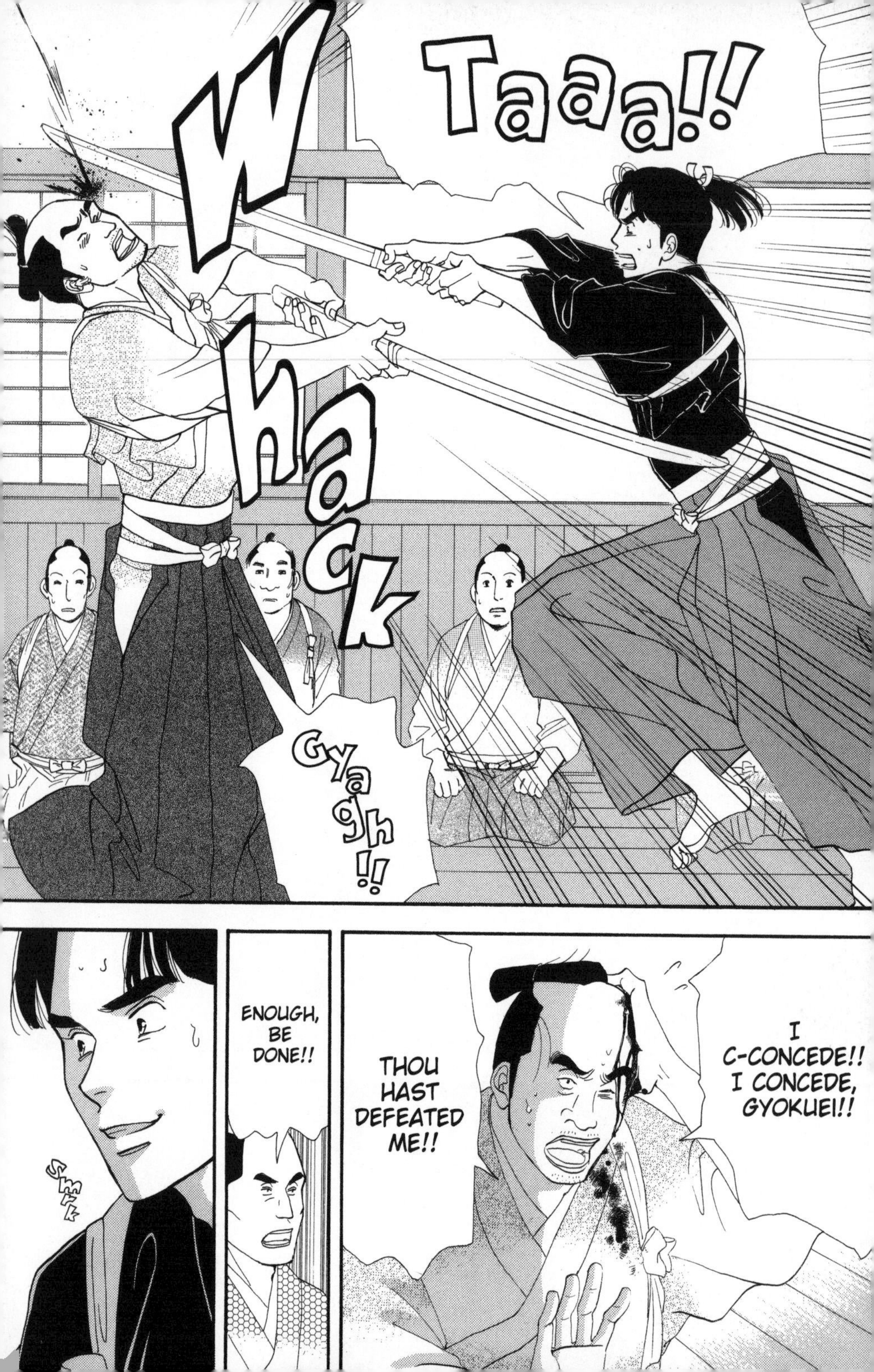
Taaaa!!
Whack
Gyagh!!
I C-CONCEDE!! I CONCEDE, GYOKUEI!!
THOU HAST DEFEATED ME!!
ENOUGH, BE DONE!!
Smrk

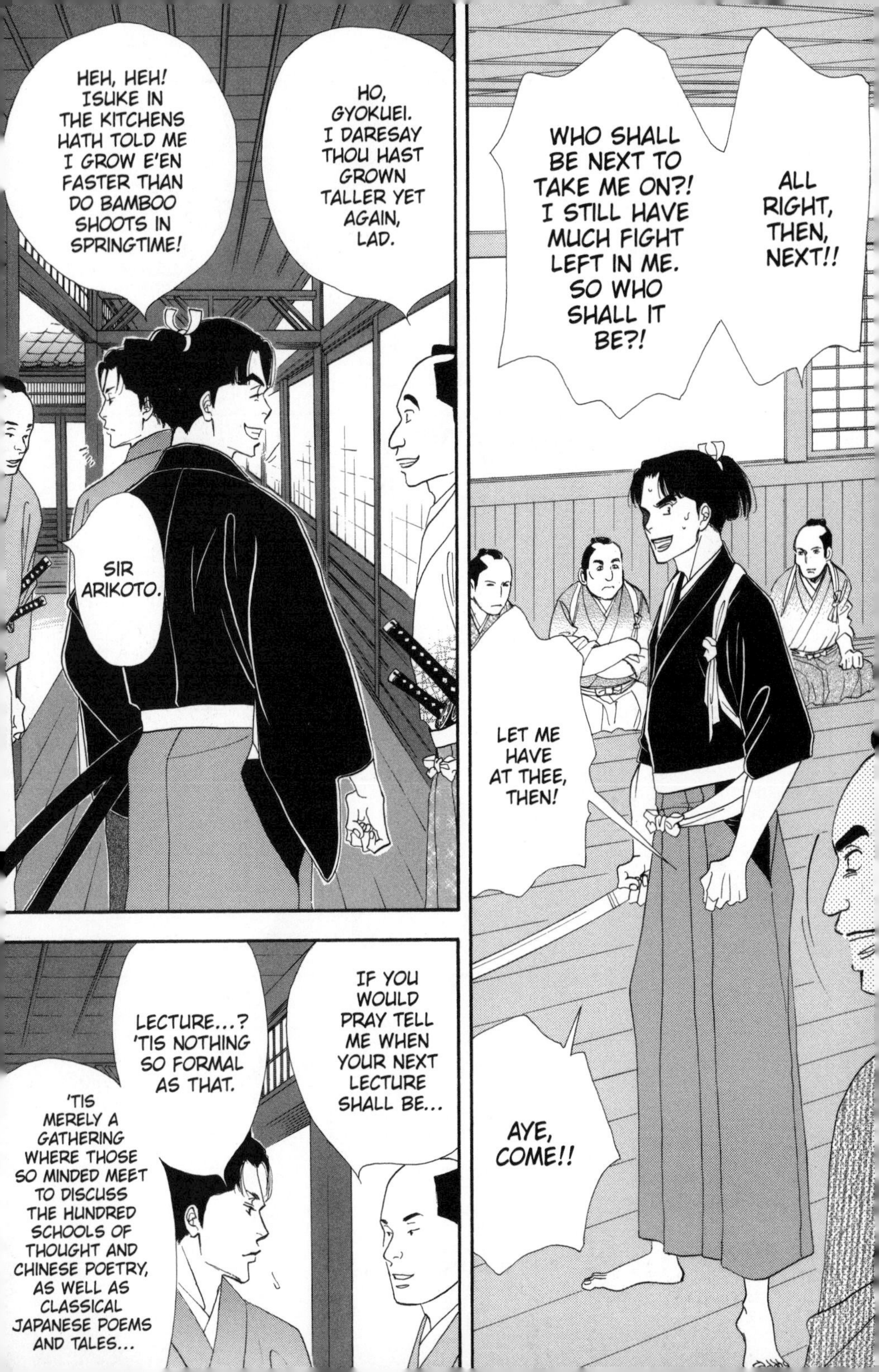
ALL RIGHT, THEN, NEXT!!
WHO SHALL BE NEXT TO TAKE ME ON?! I STILL HAVE MUCH FIGHT LEFT IN ME. SO WHO SHALL IT BE?!
LET ME HAVE AT THEE, THEN!
AYE, COME!!
HO, GYOKUEI. I DARESAY THOU HAST GROWN TALLER YET AGAIN, LAD.
HEH, HEH! ISUKE IN THE KITCHENS HATH TOLD ME I GROW E'EN FASTER THAN DO BAMBOO SHOOTS IN SPRINGTIME!
SIR ARIKOTO.
IF YOU WOULD PRAY TELL ME WHEN YOUR NEXT LECTURE SHALL BE...
LECTURE...? 'TIS NOTHING SO FORMAL AS THAT.
'TIS MERELY A GATHERING WHERE THOSE SO MINDED MEET TO DISCUSS THE HUNDRED SCHOOLS OF THOUGHT AND CHINESE POETRY, AS WELL AS CLASSICAL JAPANESE POEMS AND TALES...

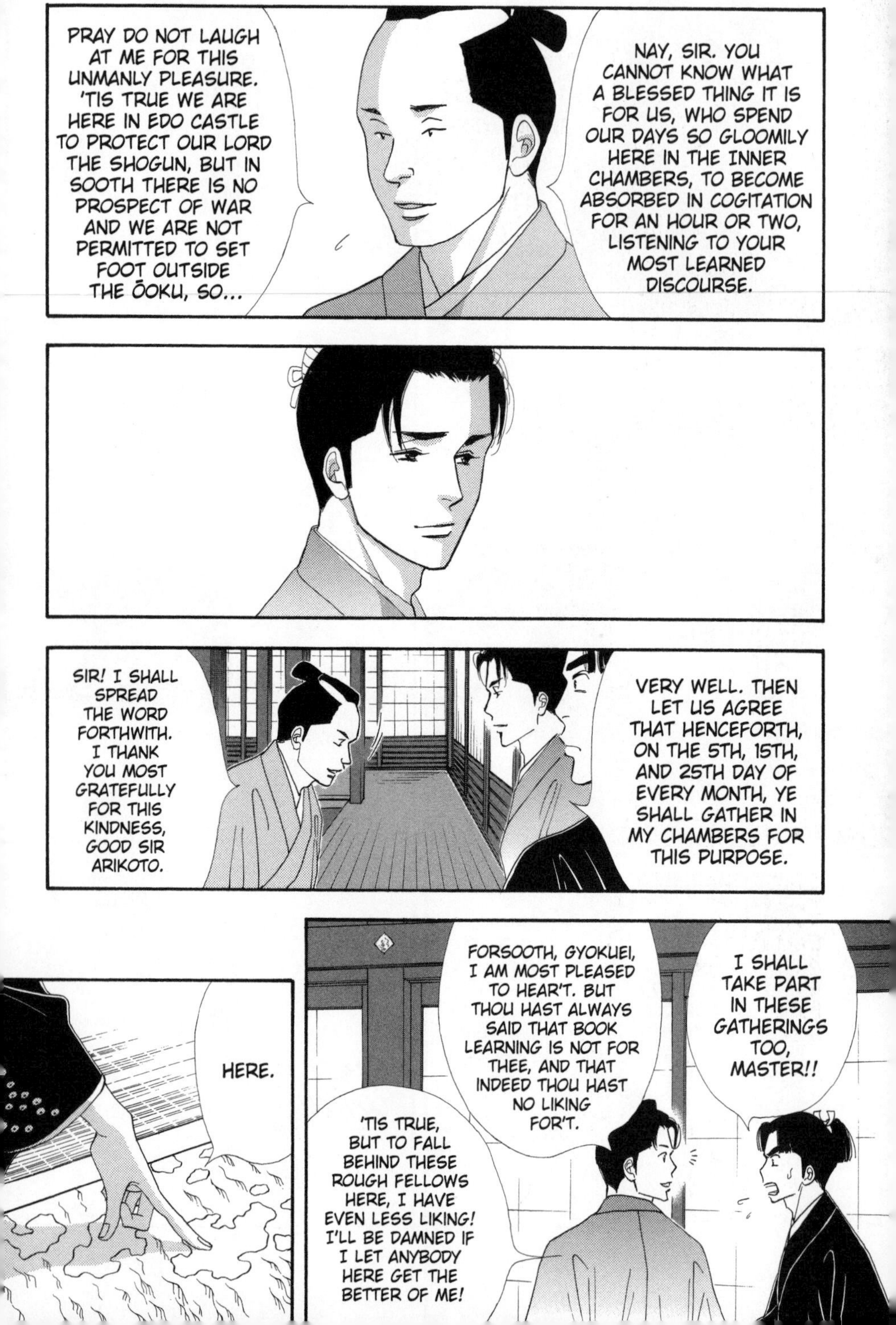
NAY, SIR. YOU CANNOT KNOW WHAT A BLESSED THING IT IS FOR US, WHO SPEND OUR DAYS SO GLOOMILY HERE IN THE INNER CHAMBERS, TO BECOME ABSORBED IN COGITATION FOR AN HOUR OR TWO, LISTENING TO YOUR MOST LEARNED DISCOURSE.
PRAY DO NOT LAUGH AT ME FOR THIS UNMANLY PLEASURE. 'TIS TRUE WE ARE HERE IN EDO CASTLE TO PROTECT OUR LORD THE SHOGUN, BUT IN SOOTH THERE IS NO PROSPECT OF WAR AND WE ARE NOT PERMITTED TO SET FOOT OUTSIDE THE ŌOKU, SO...
VERY WELL. THEN LET US AGREE THAT HENCEFORTH, ON THE 5TH, 15TH, AND 25TH DAY OF EVERY MONTH, YE SHALL GATHER IN MY CHAMBERS FOR THIS PURPOSE.
SIR! I SHALL SPREAD THE WORD FORTHWITH. I THANK YOU MOST GRATEFULLY FOR THIS KINDNESS, GOOD SIR ARIKOTO.
I SHALL TAKE PART IN THESE GATHERINGS TOO, MASTER!!
FORSOOTH, GYOKUEI, I AM MOST PLEASED TO HEAR'T. BUT THOU HAST ALWAYS SAID THAT BOOK LEARNING IS NOT FOR THEE, AND THAT INDEED THOU HAST NO LIKING FOR'T.
'TIS TRUE, BUT TO FALL BEHIND THESE ROUGH FELLOWS HERE, I HAVE EVEN LESS LIKING! I'LL BE DAMNED IF I LET ANYBODY HERE GET THE BETTER OF ME!
HERE.

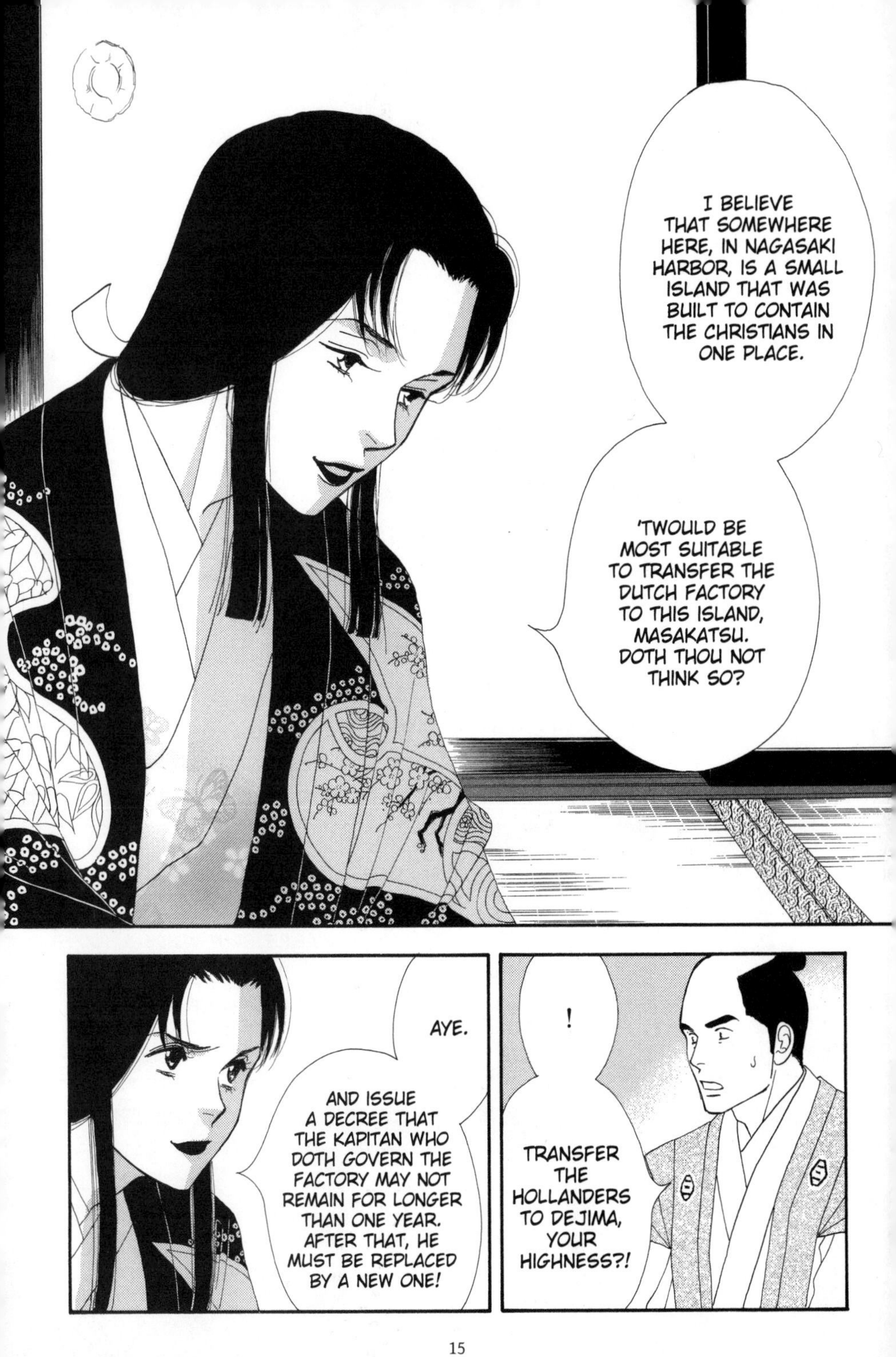
I BELIEVE THAT SOMEWHERE HERE, IN NAGASAKI HARBOR, IS A SMALL ISLAND THAT WAS BUILT TO CONTAIN THE CHRISTIANS IN ONE PLACE.
'TWOULD BE MOST SUITABLE TO TRANSFER THE DUTCH FACTORY TO THIS ISLAND, MASAKATSU. DOTH THOU NOT THINK SO?
!
TRANSFER THE HOLLANDERS TO DEJIMA, YOUR HIGHNESS?!
AYE.
AND ISSUE A DECREE THAT THE KAPITAN WHO DOTH GOVERN THE FACTORY MAY NOT REMAIN FOR LONGER THAN ONE YEAR. AFTER THAT, HE MUST BE REPLACED BY A NEW ONE!

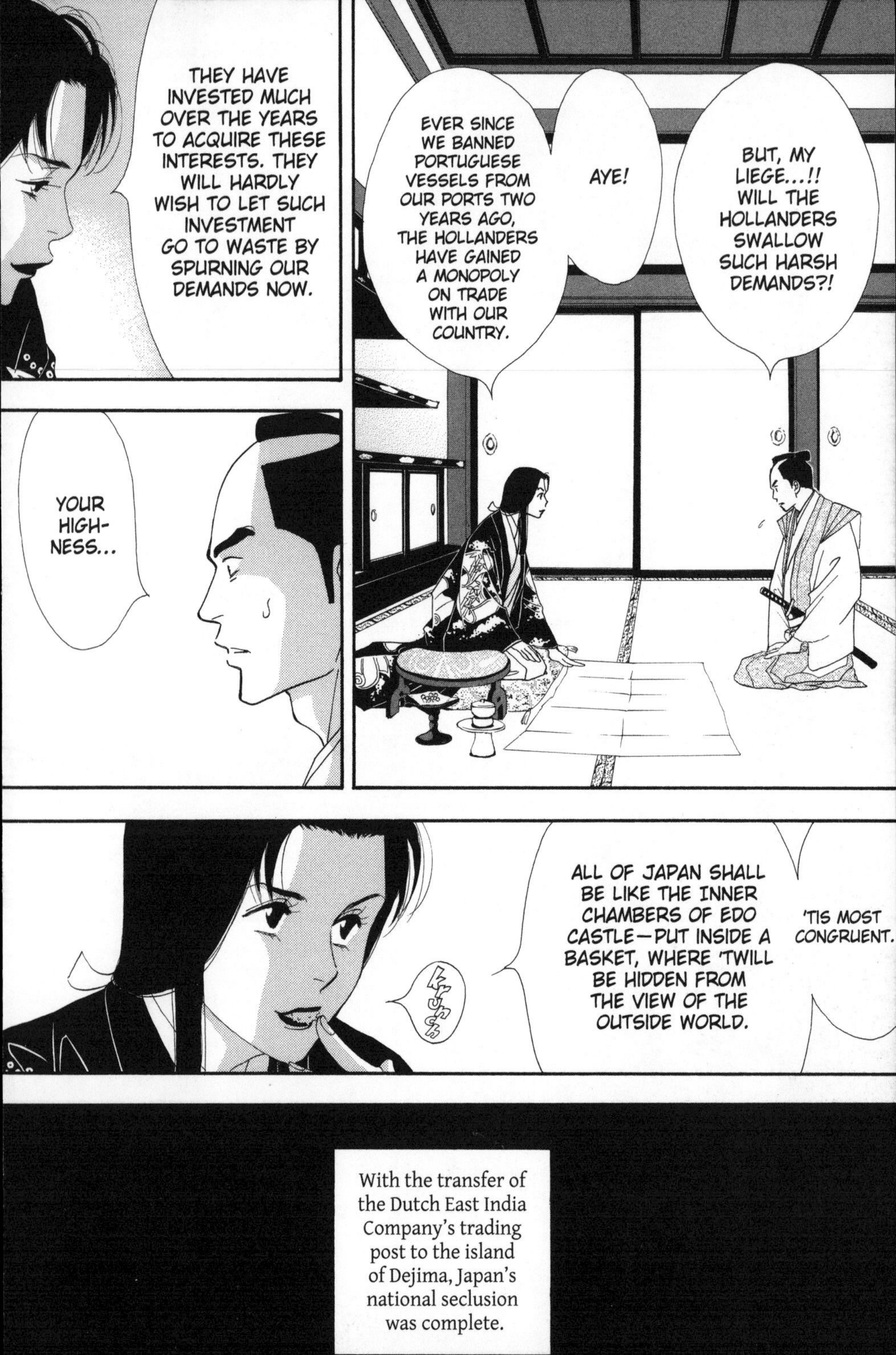
BUT, MY LIEGE...!! WILL THE HOLLANDERS SWALLOW SUCH HARSH DEMANDS?!
AYE!
EVER SINCE WE BANNED PORTUGUESE VESSELS FROM OUR PORTS TWO YEARS AGO, THE HOLLANDERS HAVE GAINED A MONOPOLY ON TRADE WITH OUR COUNTRY.
THEY HAVE INVESTED MUCH OVER THE YEARS TO ACQUIRE THESE INTERESTS. THEY WILL HARDLY WISH TO LET SUCH INVESTMENT GO TO WASTE BY SPURNING OUR DEMANDS NOW.
YOUR HIGH-NESS...
'TIS MOST CONGRUENT.
ALL OF JAPAN SHALL BE LIKE THE INNER CHAMBERS OF EDO CASTLE—PUT INSIDE A BASKET, WHERE 'TWILL BE HIDDEN FROM THE VIEW OF THE OUTSIDE WORLD.
krunch
With the transfer of the Dutch East India Company's trading post to the island of Dejima, Japan's national seclusion was complete.

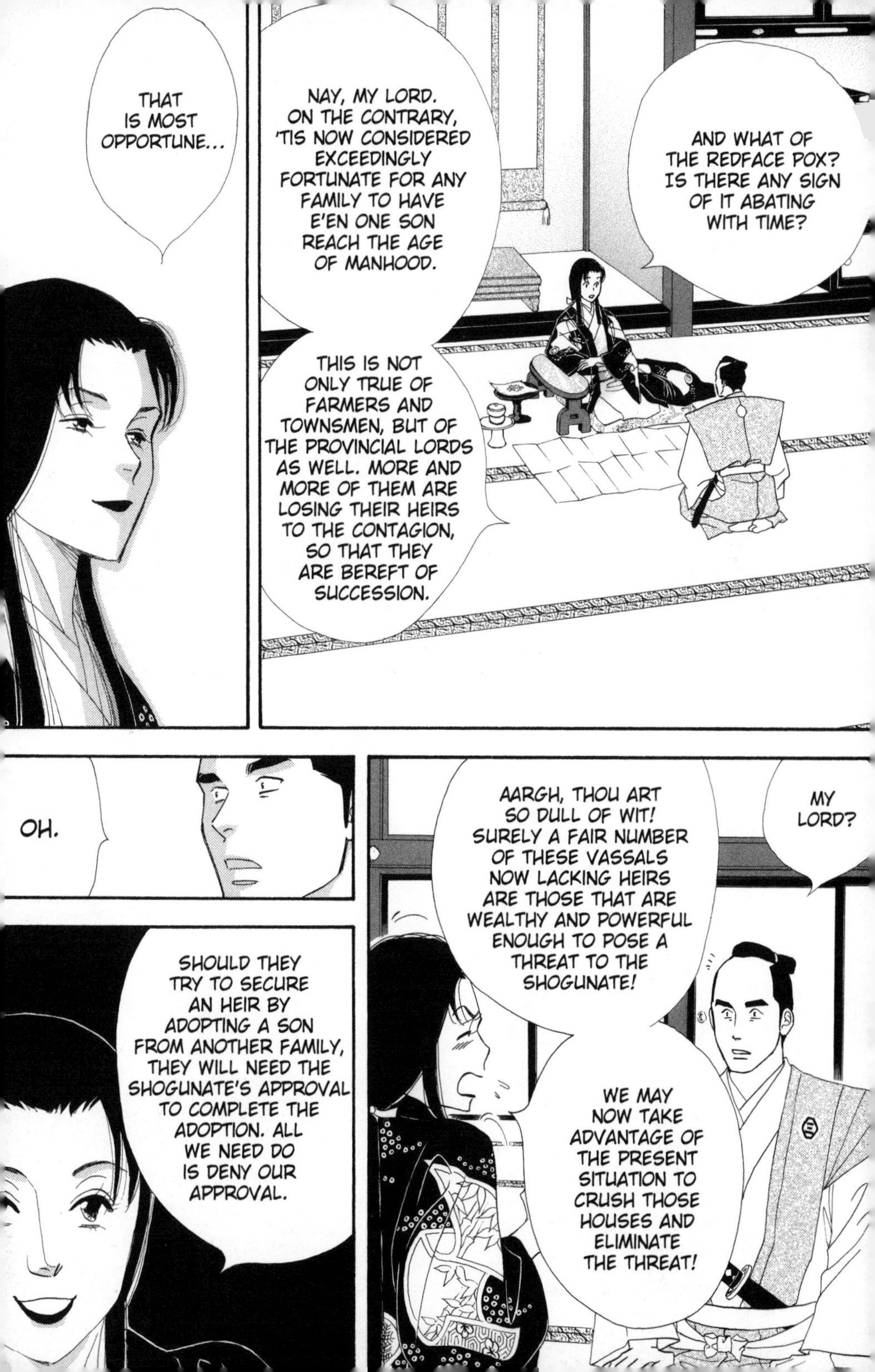
AND WHAT OF THE REDFACE POX? IS THERE ANY SIGN OF IT ABATING WITH TIME?
NAY, MY LORD. ON THE CONTRARY, 'TIS NOW CONSIDERED EXCEEDINGLY FORTUNATE FOR ANY FAMILY TO HAVE E'EN ONE SON REACH THE AGE OF MANHOOD.
THIS IS NOT ONLY TRUE OF FARMERS AND TOWNSMEN, BUT OF THE PROVINCIAL LORDS AS WELL. MORE AND MORE OF THEM ARE LOSING THEIR HEIRS TO THE CONTAGION, SO THAT THEY ARE BEREFT OF SUCCESSION.
THAT IS MOST OPPORTUNE...
MY LORD?
AARGH, THOU ART SO DULL OF WIT! SURELY A FAIR NUMBER OF THESE VASSALS NOW LACKING HEIRS ARE THOSE THAT ARE WEALTHY AND POWERFUL ENOUGH TO POSE A THREAT TO THE SHOGUNATE!
WE MAY NOW TAKE ADVANTAGE OF THE PRESENT SITUATION TO CRUSH THOSE HOUSES AND ELIMINATE THE THREAT!
OH.
SHOULD THEY TRY TO SECURE AN HEIR BY ADOPTING A SON FROM ANOTHER FAMILY, THEY WILL NEED THE SHOGUNATE'S APPROVAL TO COMPLETE THE ADOPTION. ALL WE NEED DO IS DENY OUR APPROVAL.

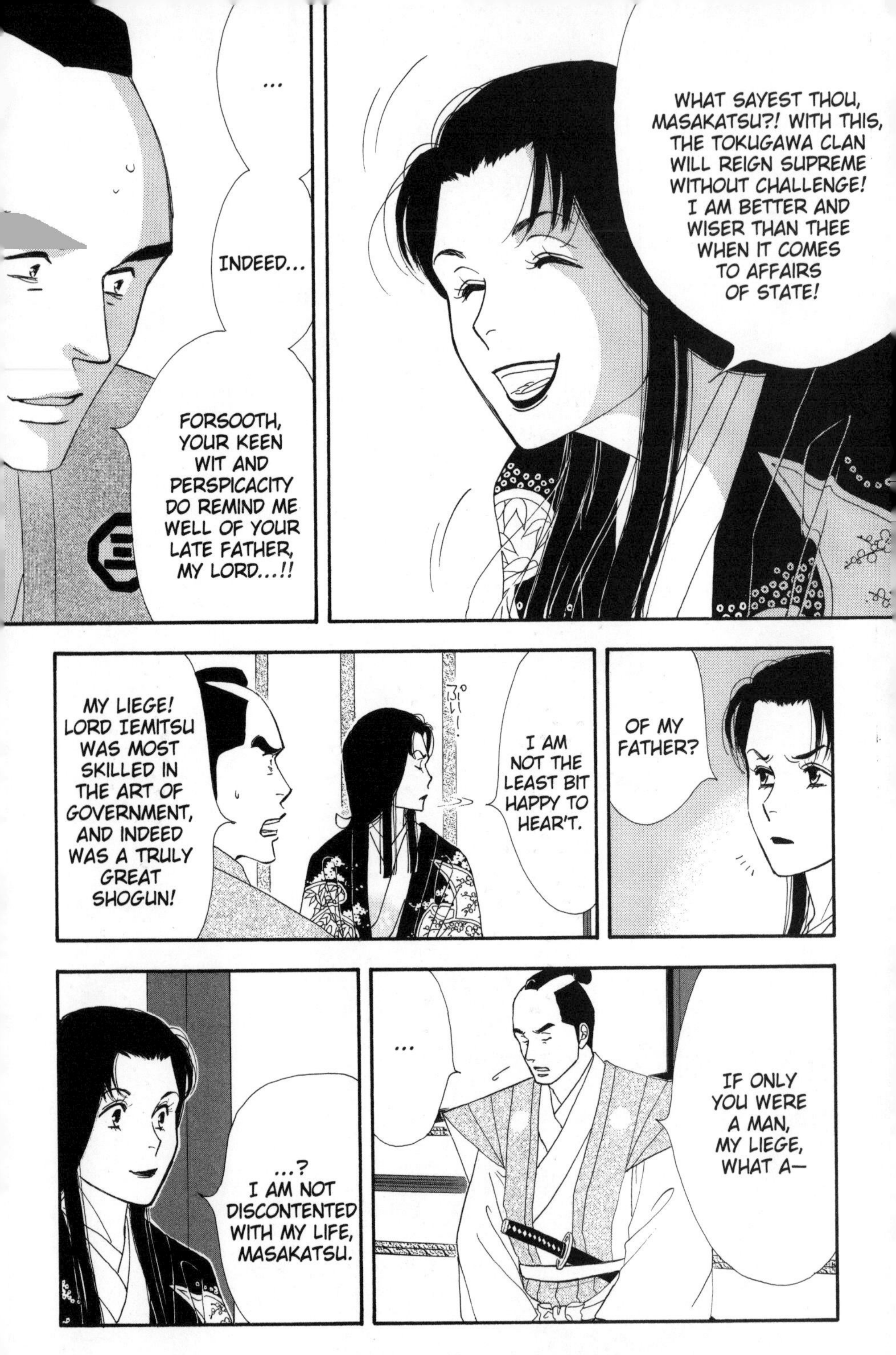
WHAT SAYEST THOU, MASAKATSU?! WITH THIS, THE TOKUGAWA CLAN WILL REIGN SUPREME WITHOUT CHALLENGE! I AM BETTER AND WISER THAN THEE WHEN IT COMES TO AFFAIRS OF STATE!
...
INDEED...
FORSOOTH, YOUR KEEN WIT AND PERSPICACITY DO REMIND ME WELL OF YOUR LATE FATHER, MY LORD...!!
OF MY FATHER?
I AM NOT THE LEAST BIT HAPPY TO HEAR'T.
MY LIEGE! LORD IEMITSU WAS MOST SKILLED IN THE ART OF GOVERNMENT, AND INDEED WAS A TRULY GREAT SHOGUN!
IF ONLY YOU WERE A MAN, MY LIEGE, WHAT A—
...
...? I AM NOT DISCONTENTED WITH MY LIFE, MASAKATSU.

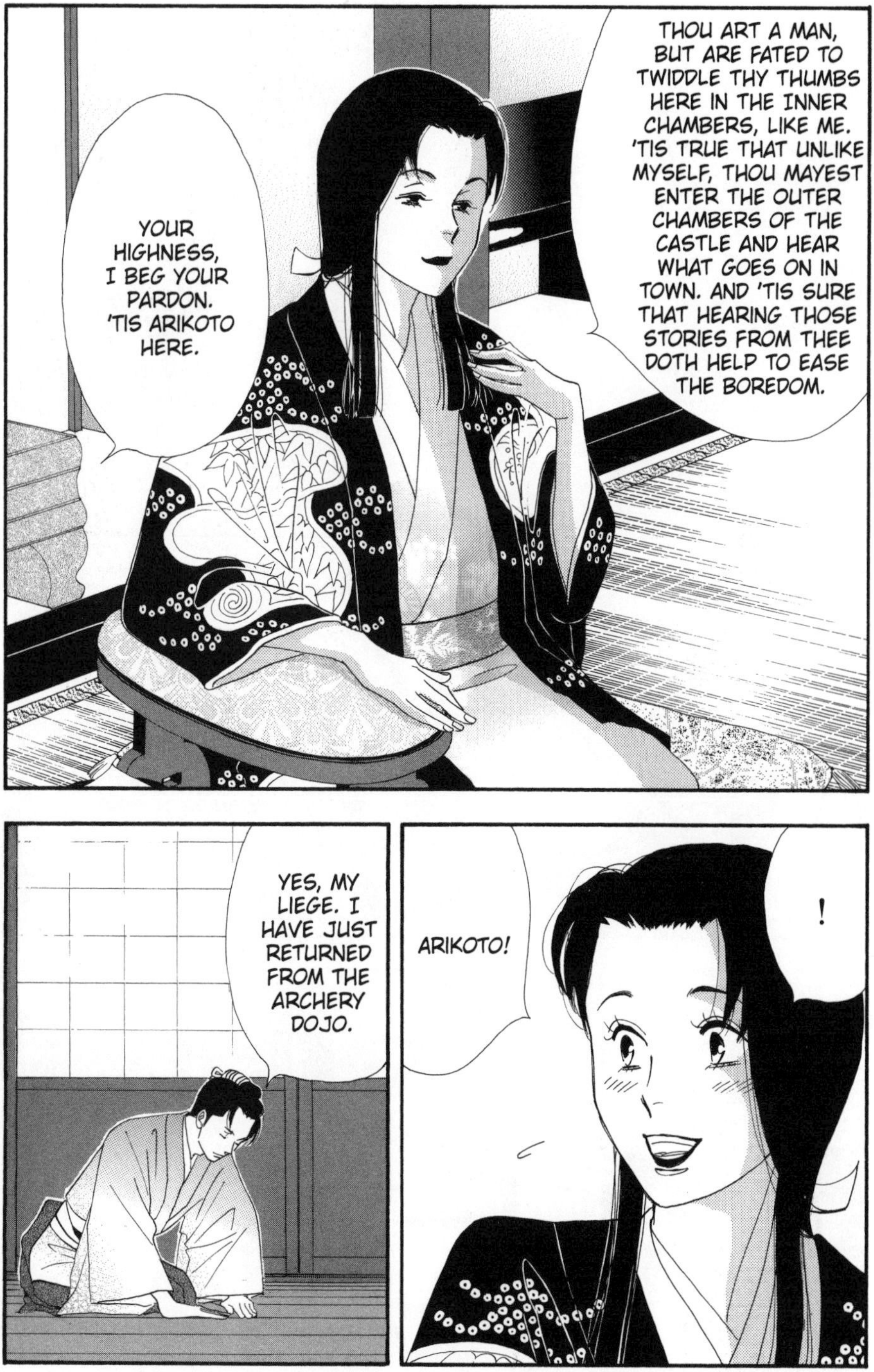
THOU ART A MAN, BUT ARE FATED TO TWIDDLE THY THUMBS HERE IN THE INNER CHAMBERS, LIKE ME. 'TIS TRUE THAT UNLIKE MYSELF, THOU MAYEST ENTER THE OUTER CHAMBERS OF THE CASTLE AND HEAR WHAT GOES ON IN TOWN. AND 'TIS SURE THAT HEARING THOSE STORIES FROM THEE DOTH HELP TO EASE THE BOREDOM.
YOUR HIGHNESS, I BEG YOUR PARDON. 'TIS ARIKOTO HERE.
!
ARIKOTO!
YES, MY LIEGE. I HAVE JUST RETURNED FROM THE ARCHERY DOJO.

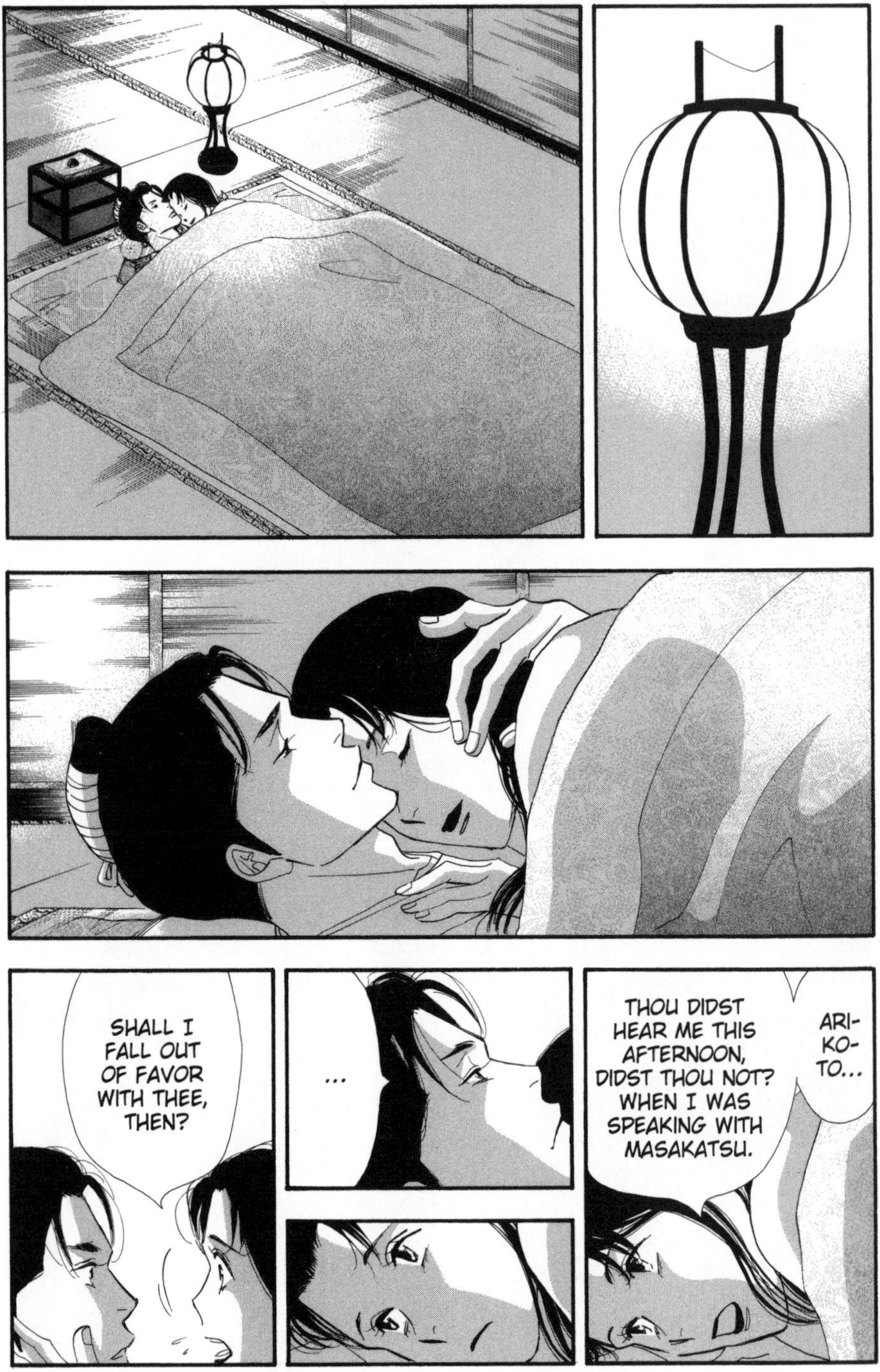
ARI-KO-TO...
THOU DIDST HEAR ME THIS AFTERNOON, DIDST THOU NOT? WHEN I WAS SPEAKING WITH MASAKATSU.
...
SHALL I FALL OUT OF FAVOR WITH THEE, THEN?

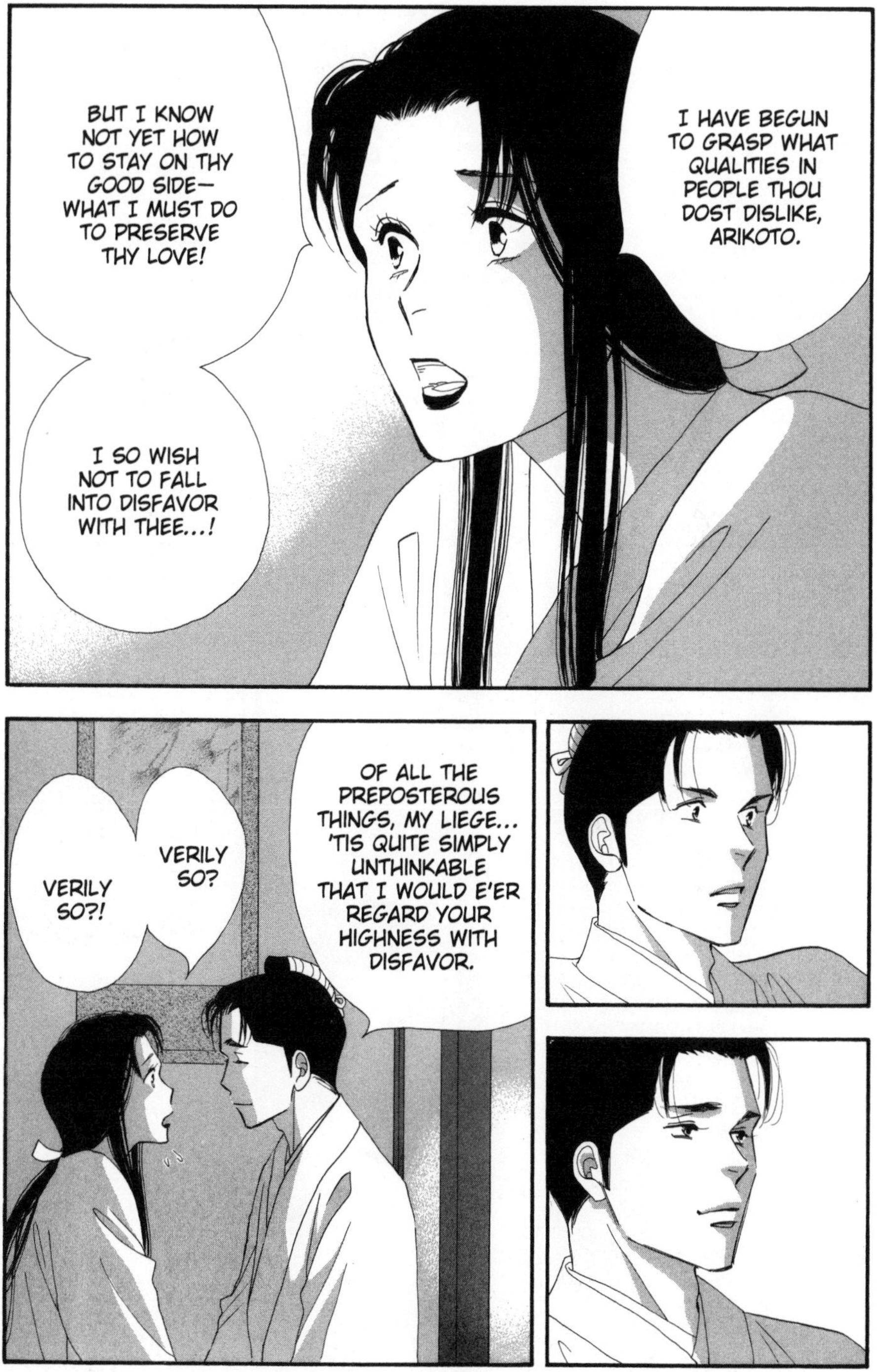
I HAVE BEGUN TO GRASP WHAT QUALITIES IN PEOPLE THOU DOST DISLIKE, ARIKOTO.
BUT I KNOW NOT YET HOW TO STAY ON THY GOOD SIDE—WHAT I MUST DO TO PRESERVE THY LOVE!
I SO WISH NOT TO FALL INTO DISFAVOR WITH THEE...!
OF ALL THE PREPOSTEROUS THINGS, MY LIEGE... 'TIS QUITE SIMPLY UNTHINKABLE THAT I WOULD E'ER REGARD YOUR HIGHNESS WITH DISFAVOR.
VERILY SO?
VERILY SO?!

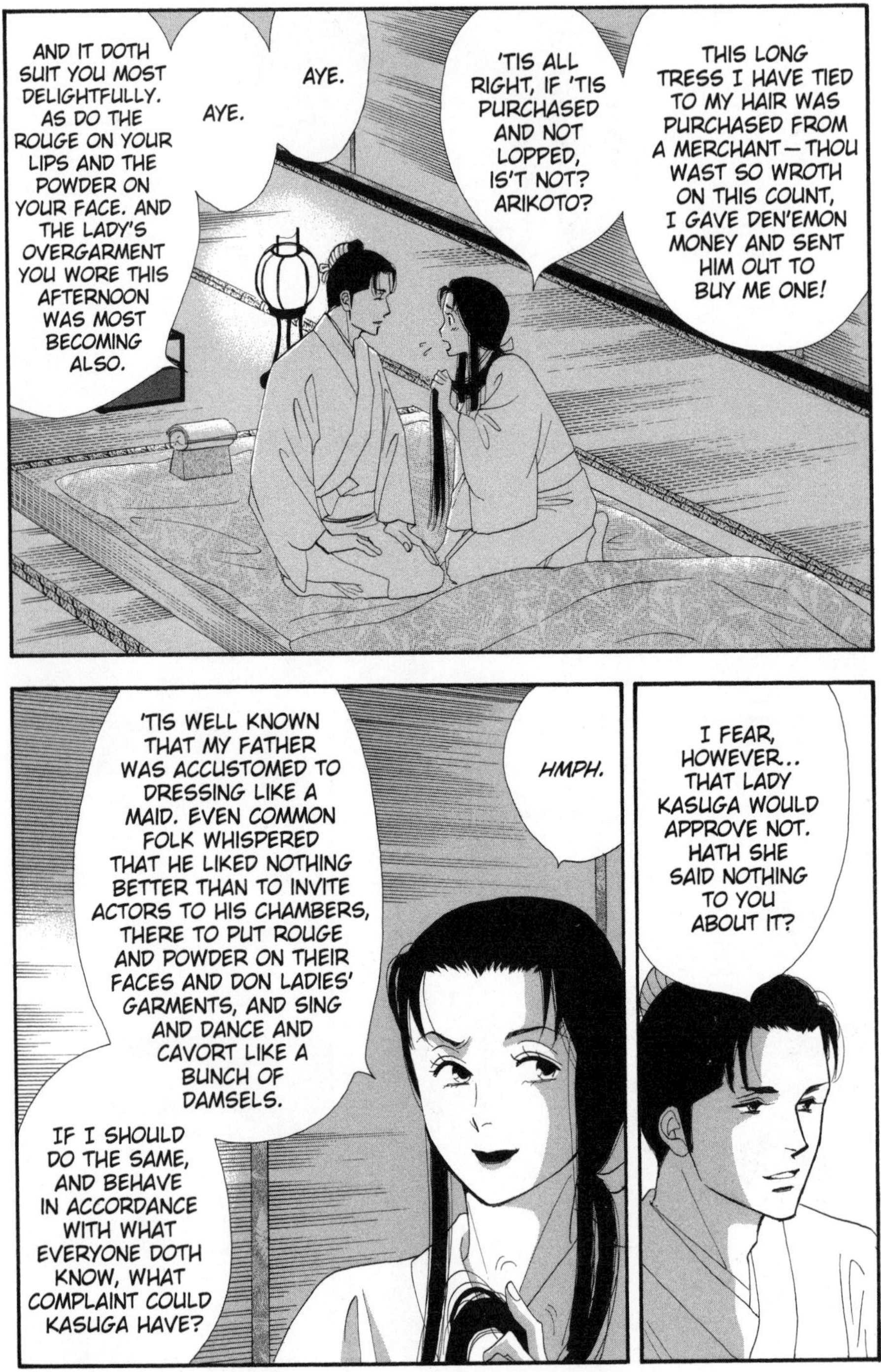
THIS LONG TRESS I HAVE TIED TO MY HAIR WAS PURCHASED FROM A MERCHANT—THOU WAST SO WROTH ON THIS COUNT, I GAVE DEN'EMON MONEY AND SENT HIM OUT TO BUY ME ONE!
'TIS ALL RIGHT, IF 'TIS PURCHASED AND NOT LOPPED, IS'T NOT? ARIKOTO?
AYE.
AYE.
AND IT DOTH SUIT YOU MOST DELIGHTFULLY. AS DO THE ROUGE ON YOUR LIPS AND THE POWDER ON YOUR FACE. AND THE LADY'S OVERGARMENT YOU WORE THIS AFTERNOON WAS MOST BECOMING ALSO.
I FEAR, HOWEVER.. THAT LADY KASUGA WOULD APPROVE NOT. HATH SHE SAID NOTHING TO YOU ABOUT IT?
HMPH.
'TIS WELL KNOWN THAT MY FATHER WAS ACCUSTOMED TO DRESSING LIKE A MAID. EVEN COMMON FOLK WHISPERED THAT HE LIKED NOTHING BETTER THAN TO INVITE ACTORS TO HIS CHAMBERS, THERE TO PUT ROUGE AND POWDER ON THEIR FACES AND DON LADIES' GARMENTS, AND SING AND DANCE AND CAVORT LIKE A BUNCH OF DAMSELS.
IF I SHOULD DO THE SAME, AND BEHAVE IN ACCORDANCE WITH WHAT EVERYONE DOTH KNOW, WHAT COMPLAINT COULD KASUGA HAVE?

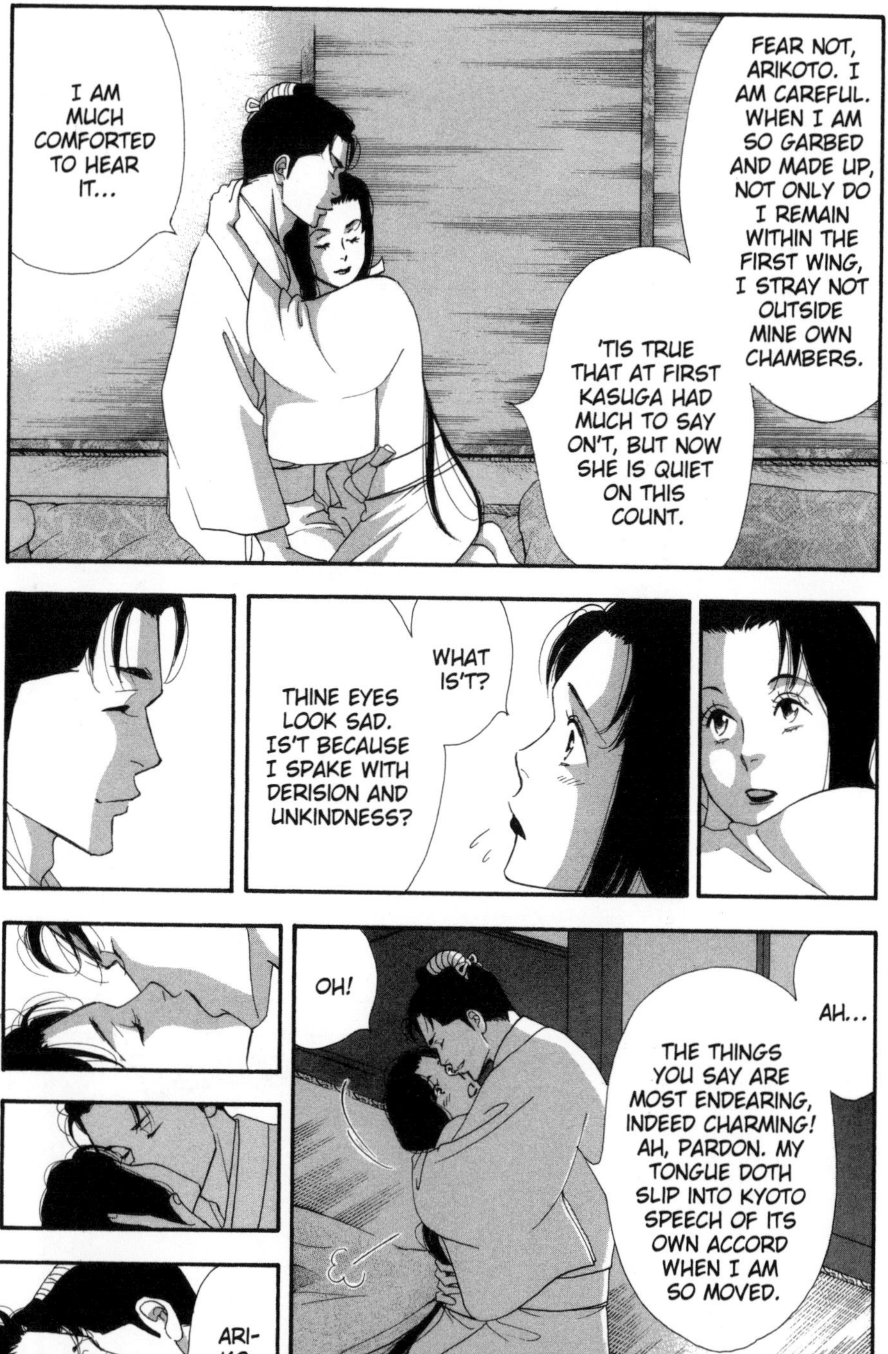
FEAR NOT, ARIKOTO. I AM CAREFUL. WHEN I AM SO GARBED AND MADE UP, NOT ONLY DO I REMAIN WITHIN THE FIRST WING, I STRAY NOT OUTSIDE MINE OWN CHAMBERS.
'TIS TRUE THAT AT FIRST KASUGA HAD MUCH TO SAY ON'T, BUT NOW SHE IS QUIET ON THIS COUNT.
I AM MUCH COMFORTED TO HEAR IT...
WHAT IS'T?
THINE EYES LOOK SAD. IS'T BECAUSE I SPAKE WITH DERISION AND UNKINDNESS?
AH...
THE THINGS YOU SAY ARE MOST ENDEARING, INDEED CHARMING! AH, PARDON. MY TONGUE DOTH SLIP INTO KYOTO SPEECH OF ITS OWN ACCORD WHEN I AM SO MOVED.
OH!
ARI-KO-TO...

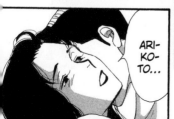

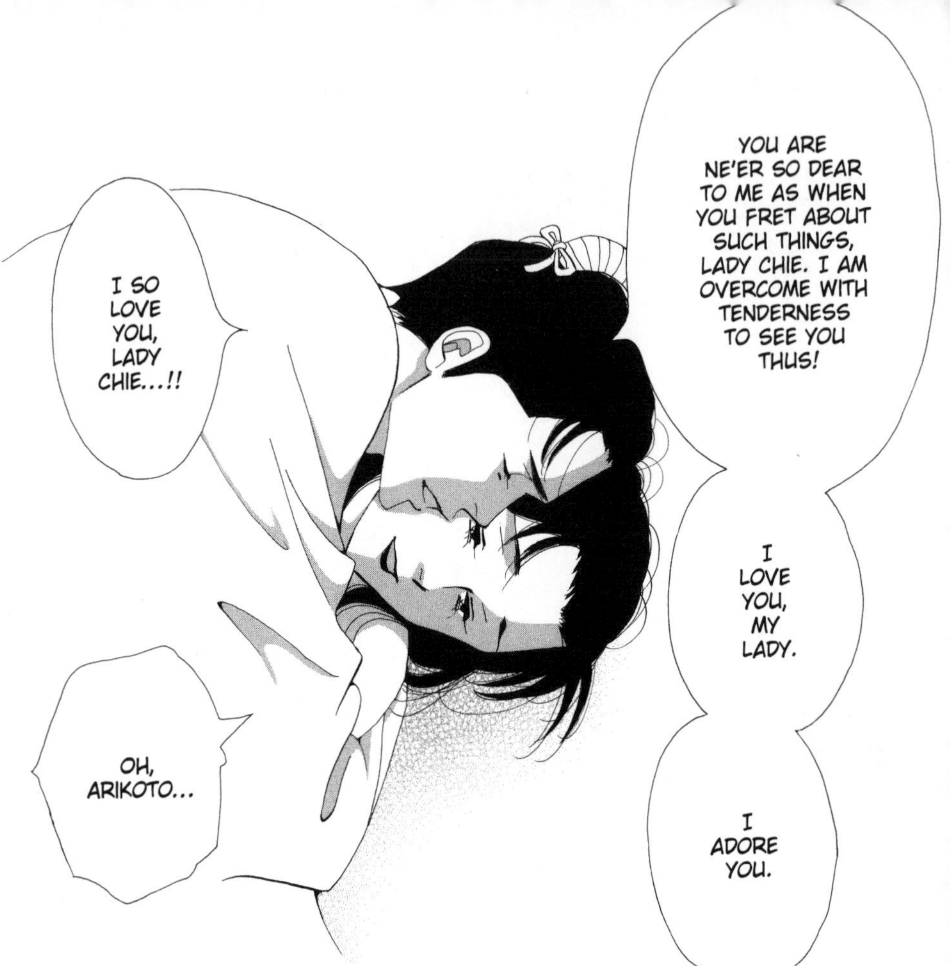
YOU ARE NE'ER SO DEAR TO ME AS WHEN YOU FRET ABOUT SUCH THINGS, LADY CHIE. I AM OVERCOME WITH TENDERNESS TO SEE YOU THUS!
I LOVE YOU, MY LADY.
I ADORE YOU.
I SO LOVE YOU, LADY CHIE...!!
OH, ARIKOTO...

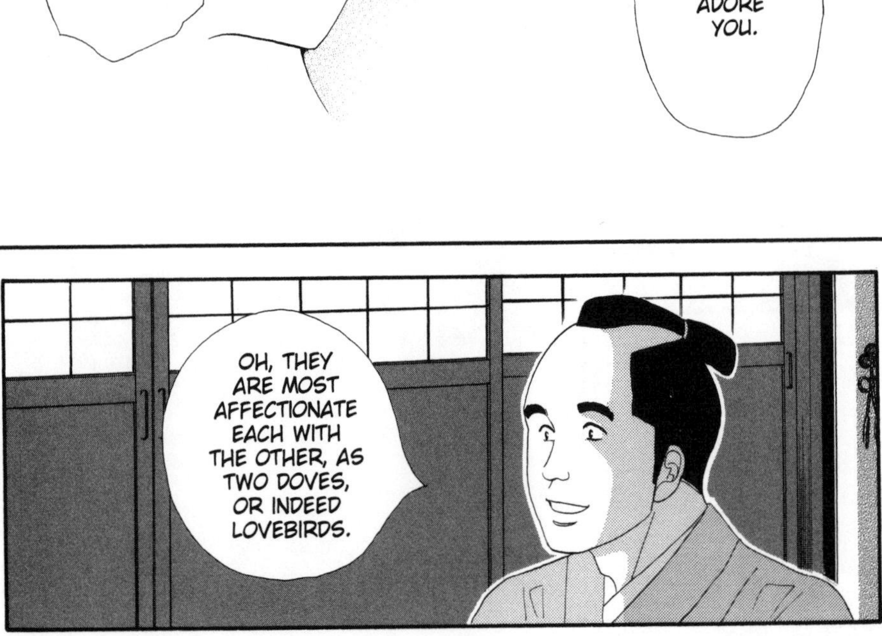
OH, THEY ARE MOST AFFECTIONATE EACH WITH THE OTHER, AS TWO DOVES, OR INDEED LOVEBIRDS.

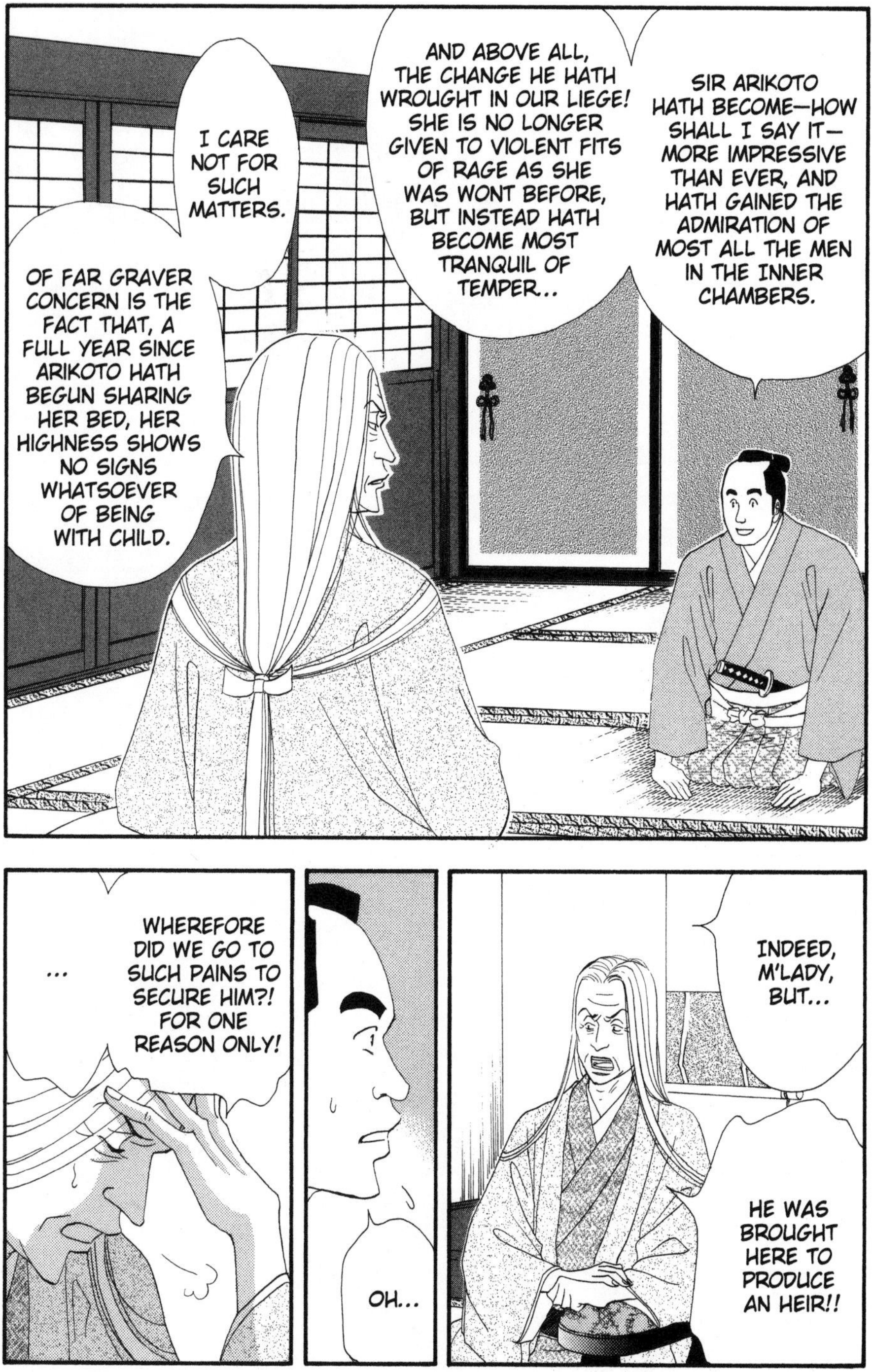
SIR ARIKOTO HATH BECOME—HOW SHALL I SAY IT—MORE IMPRESSIVE THAN EVER, AND HATH GAINED THE ADMIRATION OF MOST ALL THE MEN IN THE INNER CHAMBERS.
AND ABOVE ALL, THE CHANGE HE HATH WROUGHT IN OUR LIEGE! SHE IS NO LONGER GIVEN TO VIOLENT FITS OF RAGE AS SHE WAS WONT BEFORE, BUT INSTEAD HATH BECOME MOST TRANQUIL OF TEMPER...
I CARE NOT FOR SUCH MATTERS.
OF FAR GRAVER CONCERN IS THE FACT THAT, A FULL YEAR SINCE ARIKOTO HATH BEGUN SHARING HER BED, HER HIGHNESS SHOWS NO SIGNS WHATSOEVER OF BEING WITH CHILD.
INDEED, M'LADY, BUT...
HE WAS BROUGHT HERE TO PRODUCE AN HEIR!!
OH...
WHEREFORE DID WE GO TO SUCH PAINS TO SECURE HIM?! FOR ONE REASON ONLY!
...

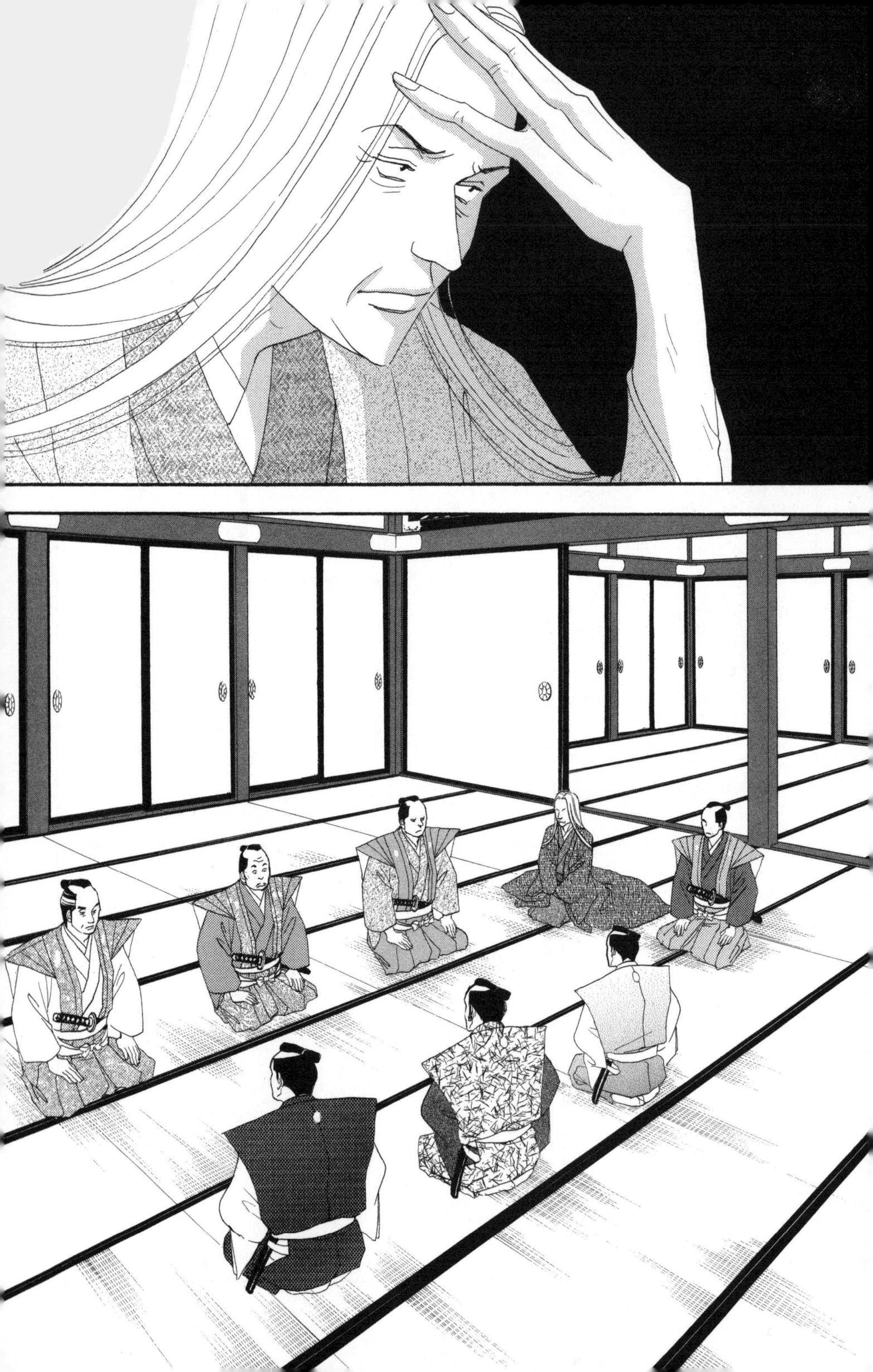

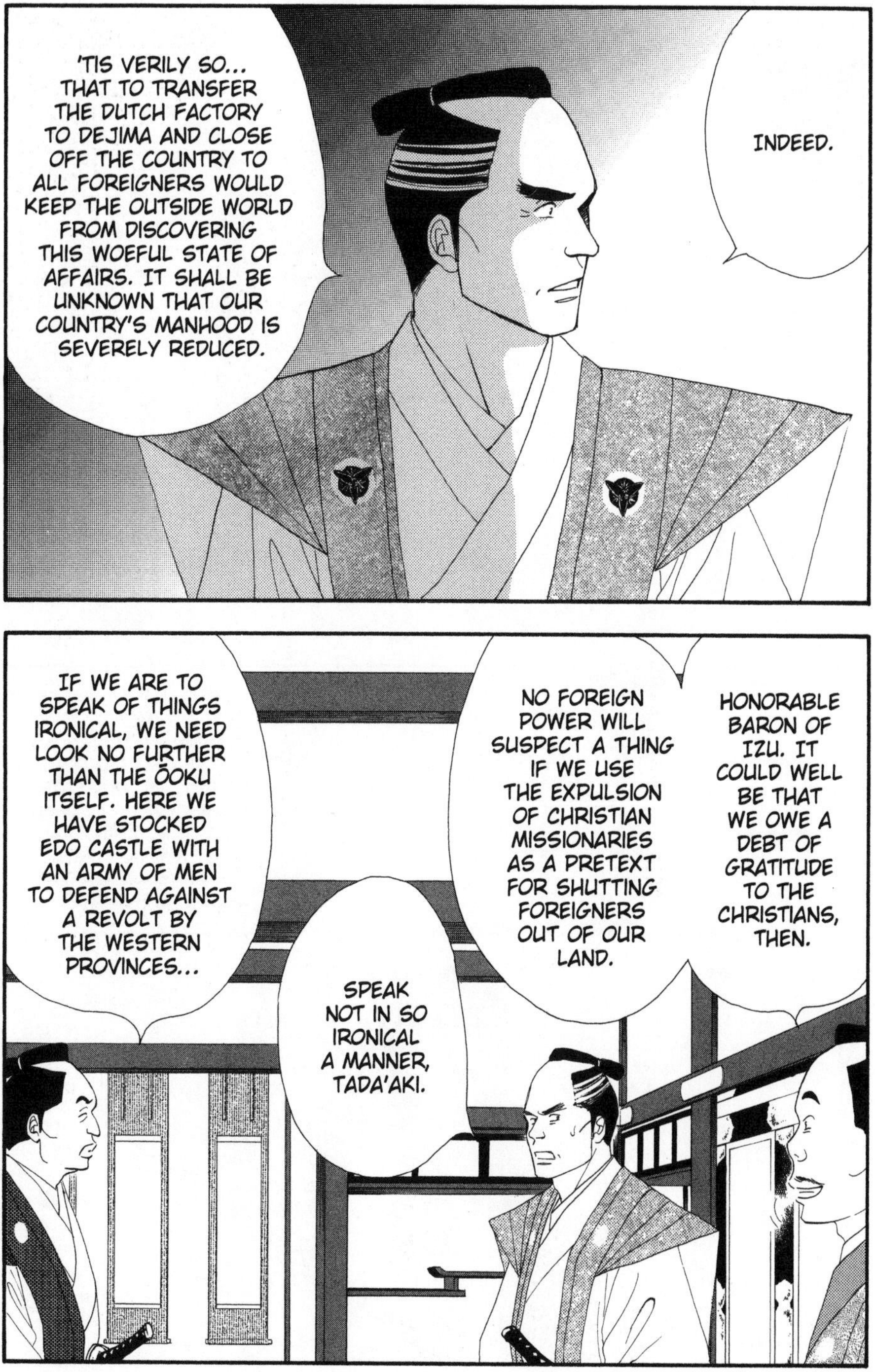
INDEED.
'TIS VERILY SO... THAT TO TRANSFER THE DUTCH FACTORY TO DEJIMA AND CLOSE OFF THE COUNTRY TO ALL FOREIGNERS WOULD KEEP THE OUTSIDE WORLD FROM DISCOVERING THIS WOEFUL STATE OF AFFAIRS. IT SHALL BE UNKNOWN THAT OUR COUNTRY'S MANHOOD IS SEVERELY REDUCED.
HONORABLE BARON OF IZU. IT COULD WELL BE THAT WE OWE A DEBT OF GRATITUDE TO THE CHRISTIANS, THEN.
NO FOREIGN POWER WILL SUSPECT A THING IF WE USE THE EXPULSION OF CHRISTIAN MISSIONARIES AS A PRETEXT FOR SHUTTING FOREIGNERS OUT OF OUR LAND.
SPEAK NOT IN SO IRONICAL A MANNER, TADA'AKI.
IF WE ARE TO SPEAK OF THINGS IRONICAL, WE NEED LOOK NO FURTHER THAN THE ŌOKU ITSELF. HERE WE HAVE STOCKED EDO CASTLE WITH AN ARMY OF MEN TO DEFEND AGAINST A REVOLT BY THE WESTERN PROVINCES...

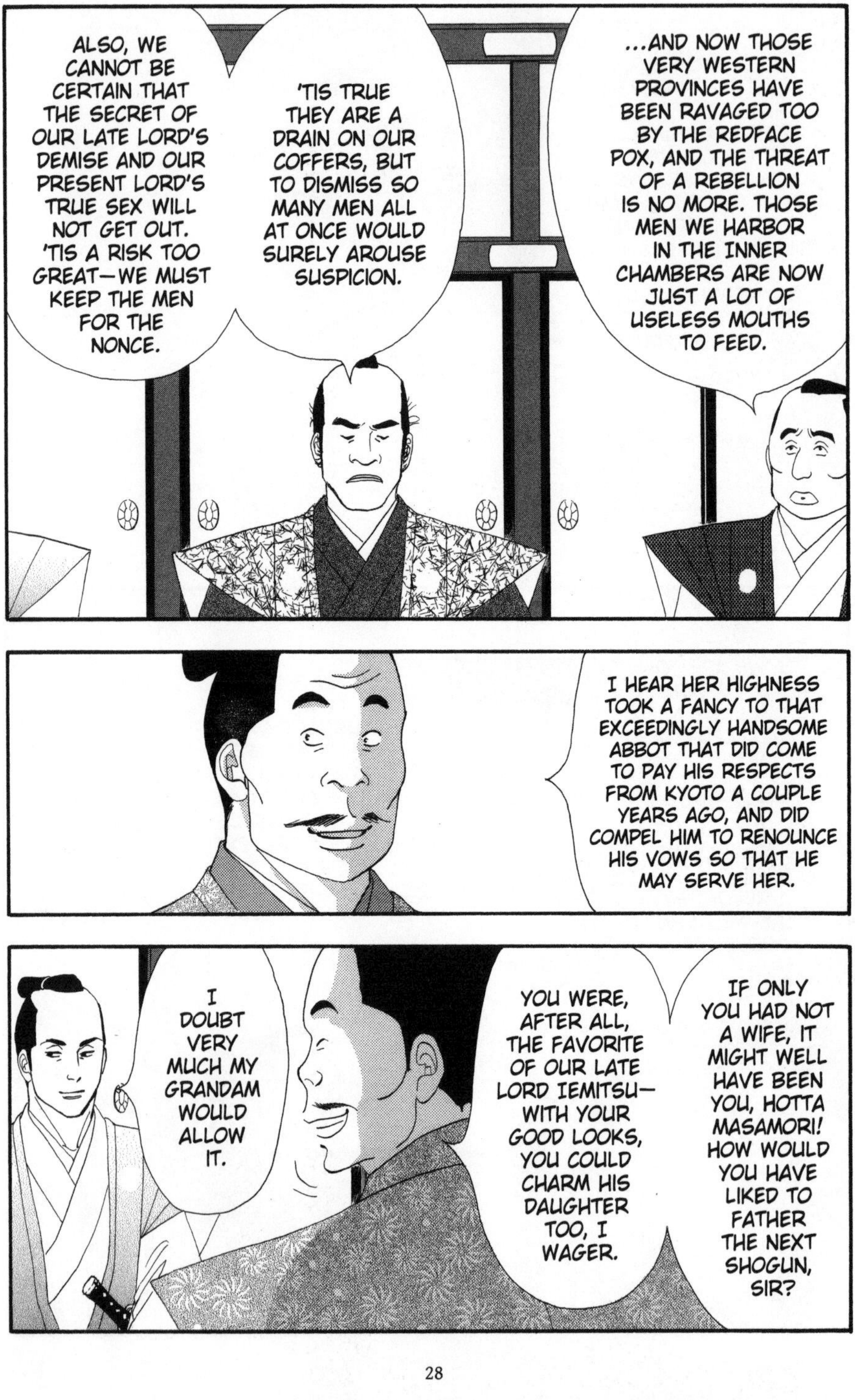
...AND NOW THOSE VERY WESTERN PROVINCES HAVE BEEN RAVAGED TOO BY THE REDFACE POX, AND THE THREAT OF A REBELLION IS NO MORE. THOSE MEN WE HARBOR IN THE INNER CHAMBERS ARE NOW JUST A LOT OF USELESS MOUTHS TO FEED.
'TIS TRUE THEY ARE A DRAIN ON OUR COFFERS, BUT TO DISMISS SO MANY MEN ALL AT ONCE WOULD SURELY AROUSE SUSPICION.
ALSO, WE CANNOT BE CERTAIN THAT THE SECRET OF OUR LATE LORD'S DEMISE AND OUR PRESENT LORD'S TRUE SEX WILL NOT GET OUT. 'TIS A RISK TOO GREAT—WE MUST KEEP THE MEN FOR THE NONCE.
I HEAR HER HIGHNESS TOOK A FANCY TO THAT EXCEEDINGLY HANDSOME ABBOT THAT DID COME TO PAY HIS RESPECTS FROM KYOTO A COUPLE YEARS AGO, AND DID COMPEL HIM TO RENOUNCE HIS VOWS SO THAT HE MAY SERVE HER.
IF ONLY YOU HAD NOT A WIFE, IT MIGHT WELL HAVE BEEN YOU, HOTTA MASAMORI! HOW WOULD YOU HAVE LIKED TO FATHER THE NEXT SHOGUN, SIR?
YOU WERE, AFTER ALL, THE FAVORITE OF OUR LATE LORD IEMITSU—WITH YOUR GOOD LOOKS, YOU COULD CHARM HIS DAUGHTER TOO, I WAGER.
I DOUBT VERY MUCH MY GRANDAM WOULD ALLOW IT.

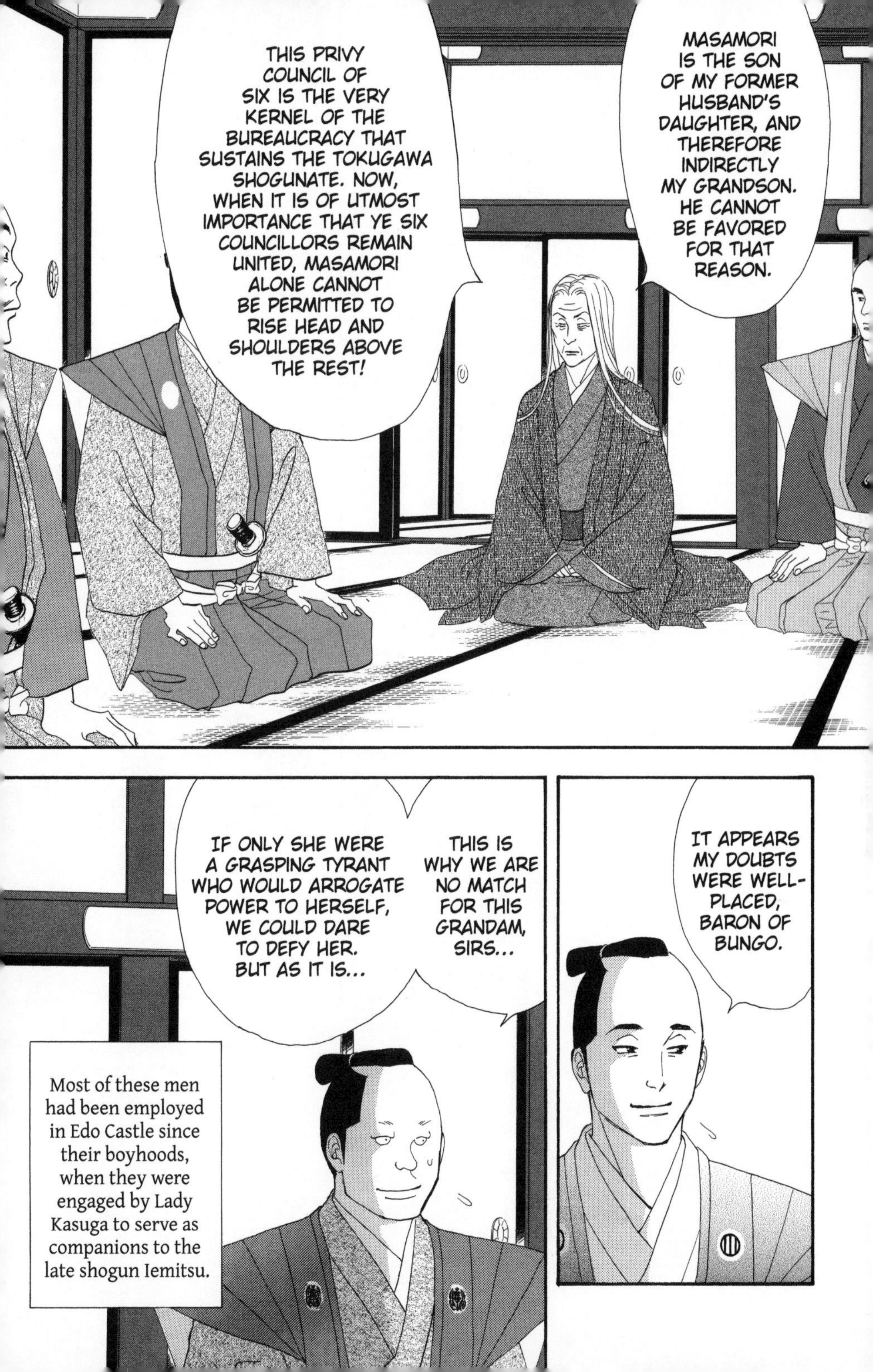
MASAMORI IS THE SON OF MY FORMER HUSBAND'S DAUGHTER, AND THEREFORE INDIRECTLY MY GRANDSON. HE CANNOT BE FAVORED FOR THAT REASON.
THIS PRIVY COUNCIL OF SIX IS THE VERY KERNEL OF THE BUREAUCRACY THAT SUSTAINS THE TOKUGAWA SHOGUNATE. NOW, WHEN IT IS OF UTMOST IMPORTANCE THAT YE SIX COUNCILLORS REMAIN UNITED, MASAMORI ALONE CANNOT BE PERMITTED TO RISE HEAD AND SHOULDERS ABOVE THE REST!
IT APPEARS MY DOUBTS WERE WELL-PLACED, BARON OF BUNGO.
THIS IS WHY WE ARE NO MATCH FOR THIS GRANDAM, SIRS...
IF ONLY SHE WERE A GRASPING TYRANT WHO WOULD ARROGATE POWER TO HERSELF, WE COULD DARE TO DEFY HER. BUT AS IT IS...
Most of these men had been employed in Edo Castle since their boyhoods, when they were engaged by Lady Kasuga to serve as companions to the late shogun Iemitsu.

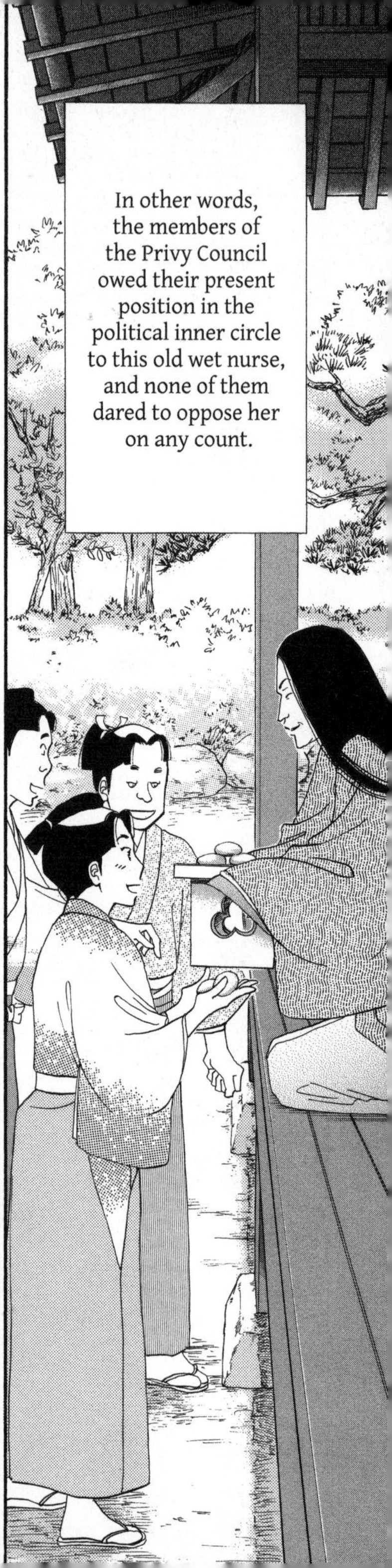
In other words, the members of the Privy Council owed their present position in the political inner circle to this old wet nurse, and none of them dared to oppose her on any count.

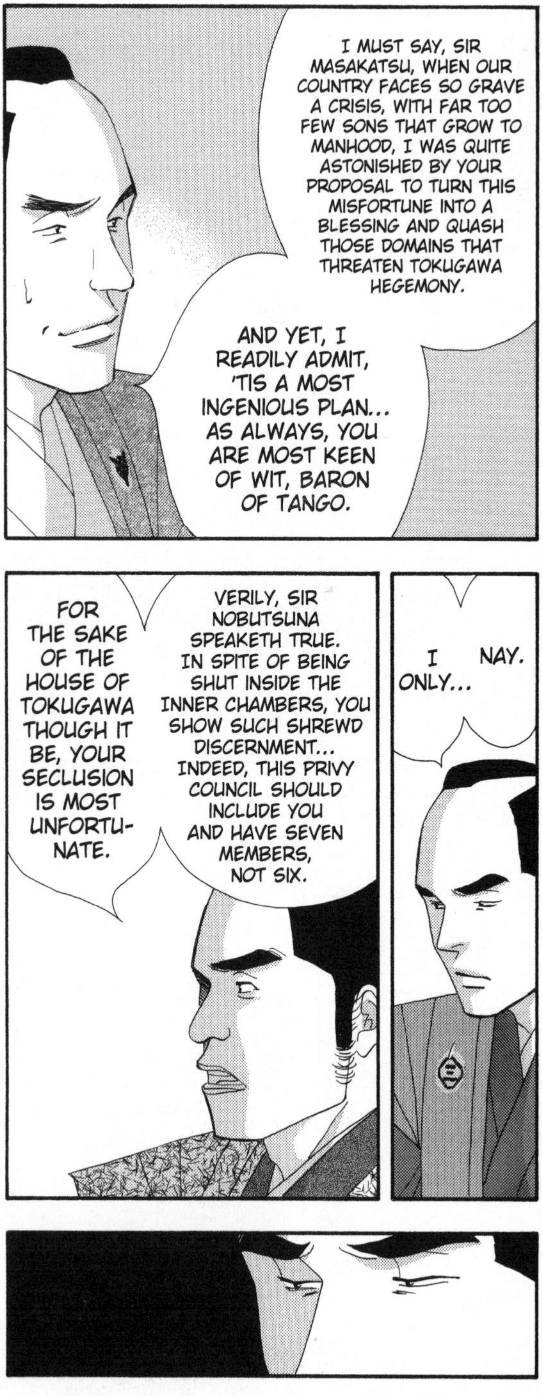
I MUST SAY, SIR MASAKATSU, WHEN OUR COUNTRY FACES SO GRAVE A CRISIS, WITH FAR TOO FEW SONS THAT GROW TO MANHOOD, I WAS QUITE ASTONISHED BY YOUR PROPOSAL TO TURN THIS MISFORTUNE INTO A BLESSING AND QUASH THOSE DOMAINS THAT THREATEN TOKUGAWA HEGEMONY.
AND YET, I READILY ADMIT, 'TIS A MOST INGENIOUS PLAN... AS ALWAYS, YOU ARE MOST KEEN OF WIT, BARON OF TANGO.
NAY. I ONLY...
VERILY, SIR NOBUTSUNA SPEAKETH TRUE. IN SPITE OF BEING SHUT INSIDE THE INNER CHAMBERS, YOU SHOW SUCH SHREWD DISCERNMENT... INDEED, THIS PRIVY COUNCIL SHOULD INCLUDE YOU AND HAVE SEVEN MEMBERS, NOT SIX.
FOR THE SAKE OF THE HOUSE OF TOKUGAWA THOUGH IT BE, YOUR SECLUSION IS MOST UNFORTUNATE.

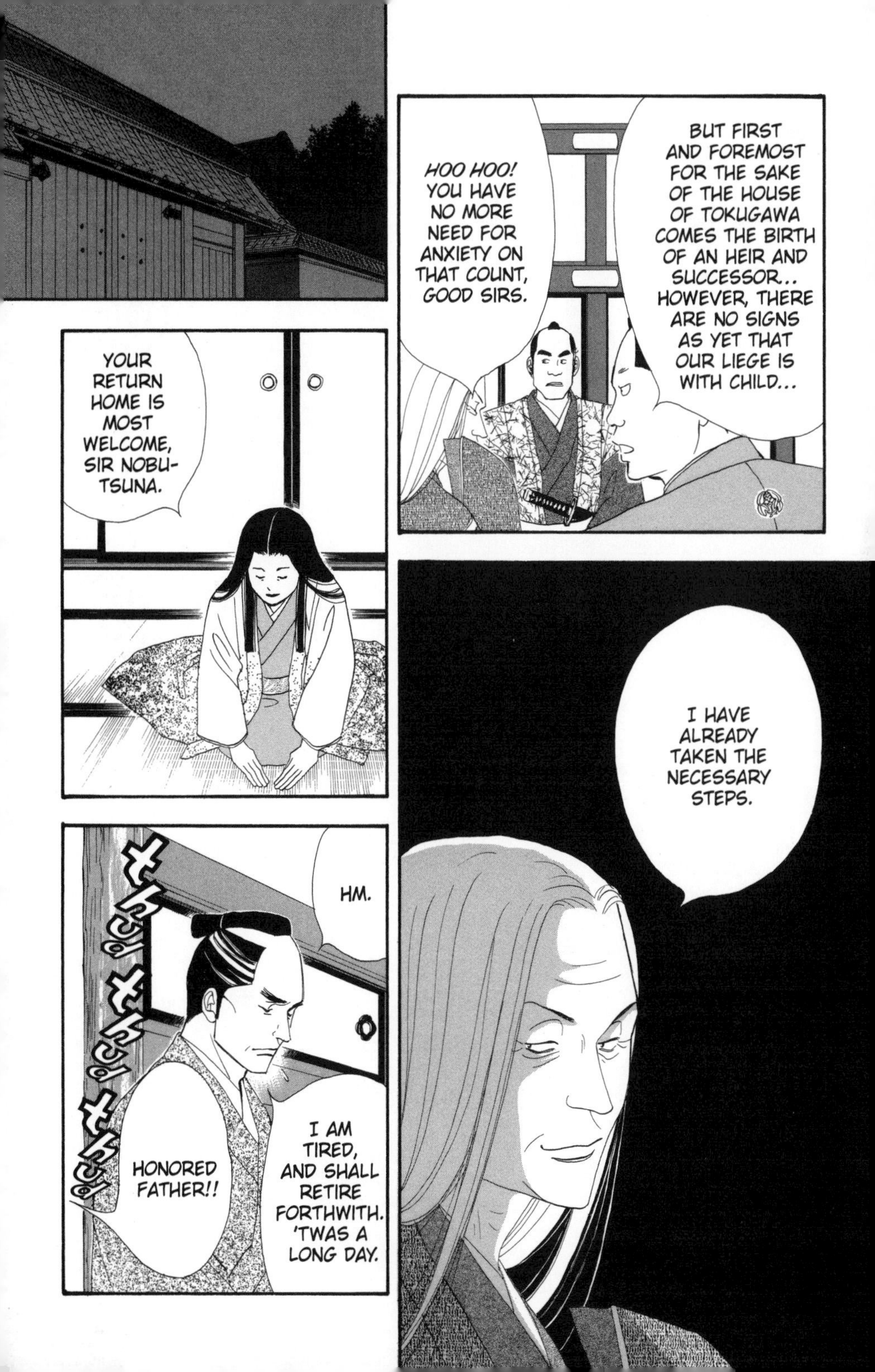
BUT FIRST AND FOREMOST FOR THE SAKE OF THE HOUSE OF TOKUGAWA COMES THE BIRTH OF AN HEIR AND SUCCESSOR... HOWEVER, THERE ARE NO SIGNS AS YET THAT OUR LIEGE IS WITH CHILD...
HOO HOO! YOU HAVE NO MORE NEED FOR ANXIETY ON THAT COUNT, GOOD SIRS.
I HAVE ALREADY TAKEN THE NECESSARY STEPS.
YOUR RETURN HOME IS MOST WELCOME, SIR NOBU-TSUNA.
HM.
I AM TIRED, AND SHALL RETIRE FORTHWITH. 'TWAS A LONG DAY.
HONORED FATHER!!

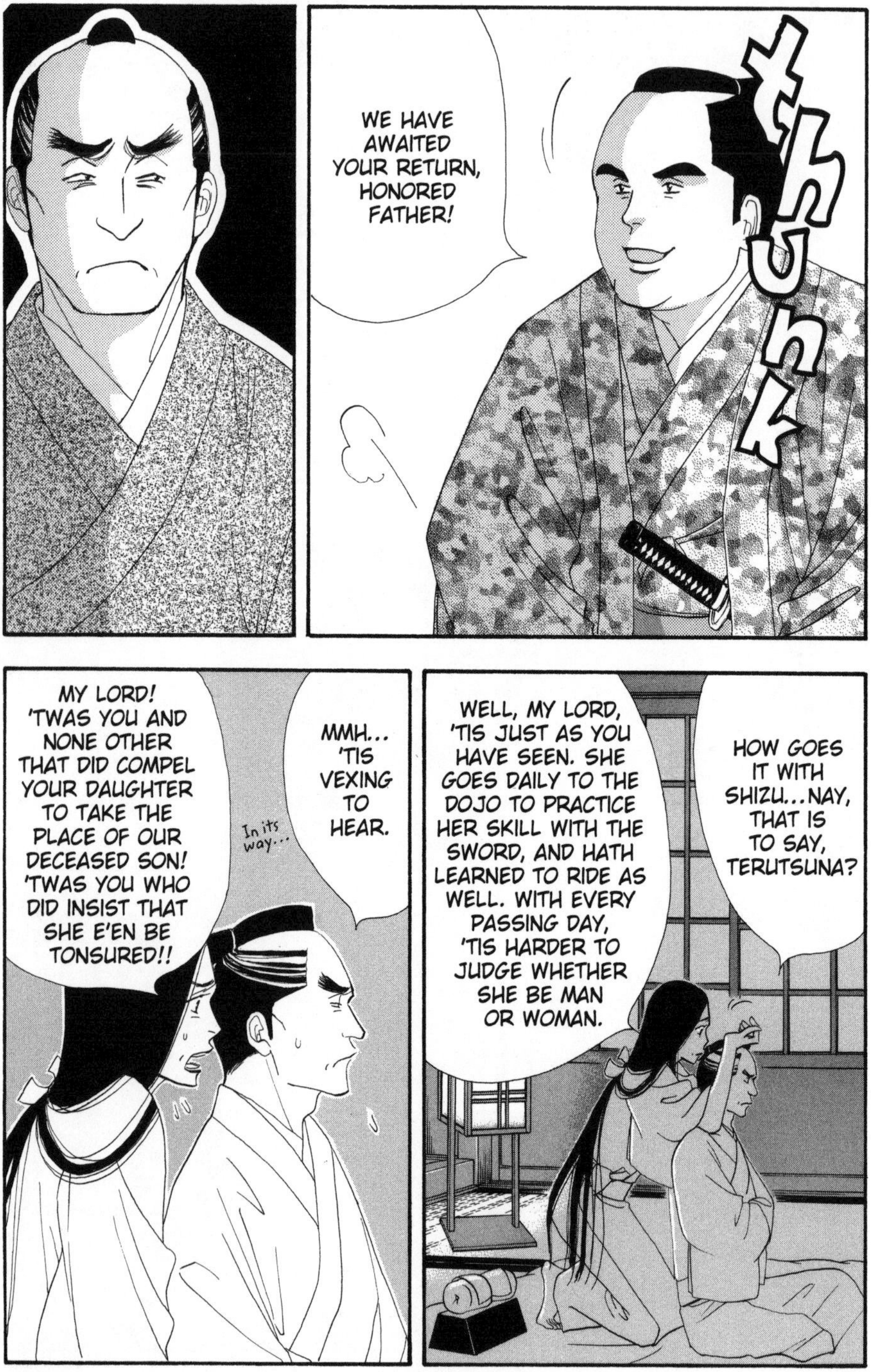
WE HAVE AWAITED YOUR RETURN, HONORED FATHER!
thhunk
HOW GOES IT WITH SHIZU...NAY, THAT IS TO SAY, TERUTSUNA?
WELL, MY LORD, 'TIS JUST AS YOU HAVE SEEN. SHE GOES DAILY TO THE DOJO TO PRACTICE HER SKILL WITH THE SWORD, AND HATH LEARNED TO RIDE AS WELL. WITH EVERY PASSING DAY, 'TIS HARDER TO JUDGE WHETHER SHE BE MAN OR WOMAN.
MMH... 'TIS VEXING TO HEAR.
In its way...
MY LORD! 'TWAS YOU AND NONE OTHER THAT DID COMPEL YOUR DAUGHTER TO TAKE THE PLACE OF OUR DECEASED SON! 'TWAS YOU WHO DID INSIST THAT SHE E'EN BE TONSURED!!

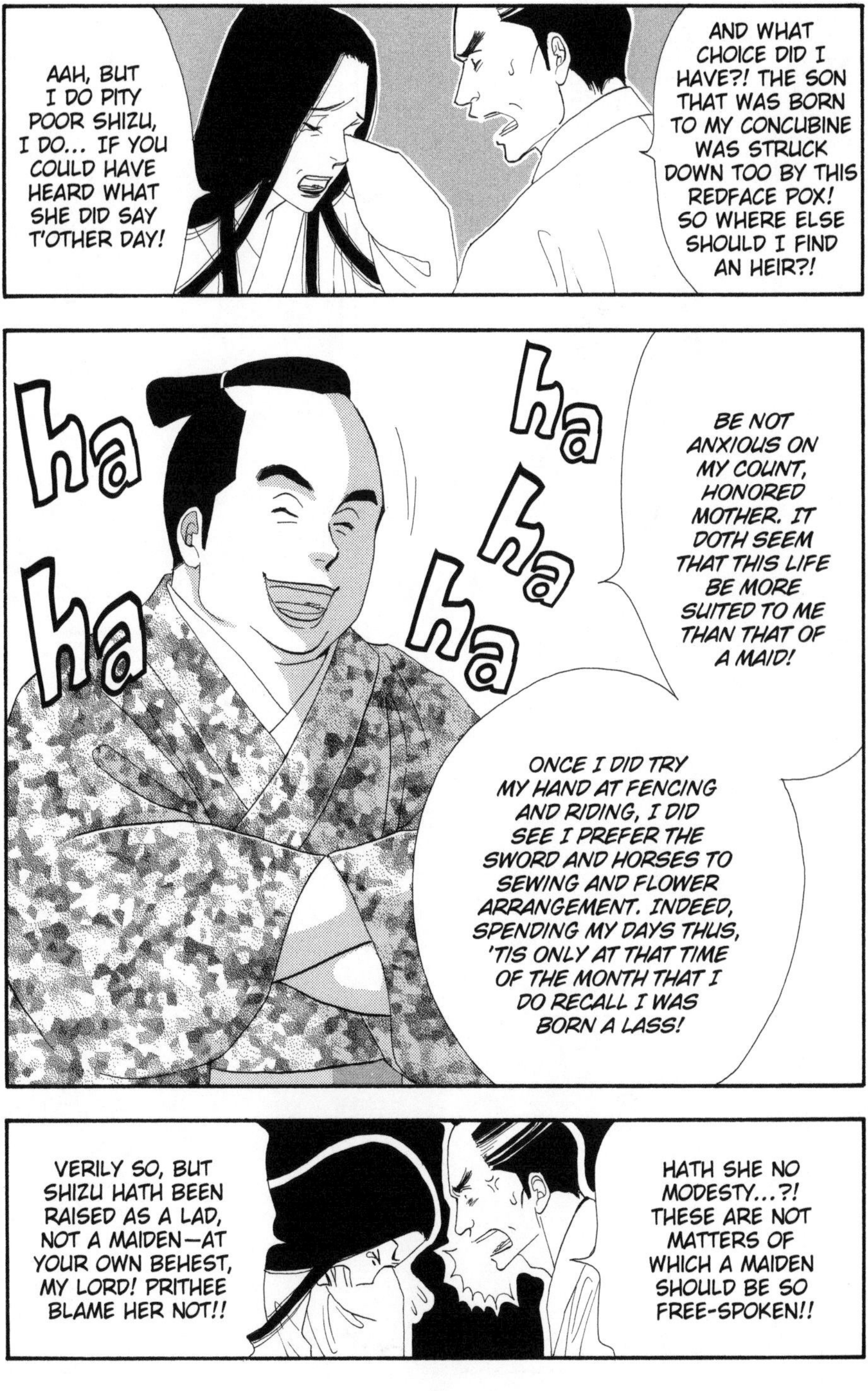
AND WHAT CHOICE DID I HAVE?! THE SON THAT WAS BORN TO MY CONCUBINE WAS STRUCK DOWN TOO BY THIS REDFACE POX! SO WHERE ELSE SHOULD I FIND AN HEIR?!
AAH, BUT I DO PITY POOR SHIZU, I DO... IF YOU COULD HAVE HEARD WHAT SHE DID SAY T'OTHER DAY!
BE NOT ANXIOUS ON MY COUNT, HONORED MOTHER. IT DOTH SEEM THAT THIS LIFE BE MORE SUITED TO ME THAN THAT OF A MAID!
ha ha ha ha
ONCE I DID TRY MY HAND AT FENCING AND RIDING, I DID SEE I PREFER THE SWORD AND HORSES TO SEWING AND FLOWER ARRANGEMENT. INDEED, SPENDING MY DAYS THUS, 'TIS ONLY AT THAT TIME OF THE MONTH THAT I DO RECALL I WAS BORN A LASS!
ha ha
HATH SHE NO MODESTY...?! THESE ARE NOT MATTERS OF WHICH A MAIDEN SHOULD BE SO FREE-SPOKEN!!
VERILY SO, BUT SHIZU HATH BEEN RAISED AS A LAD, NOT A MAIDEN—AT YOUR OWN BEHEST, MY LORD! PRITHEE BLAME HER NOT!!

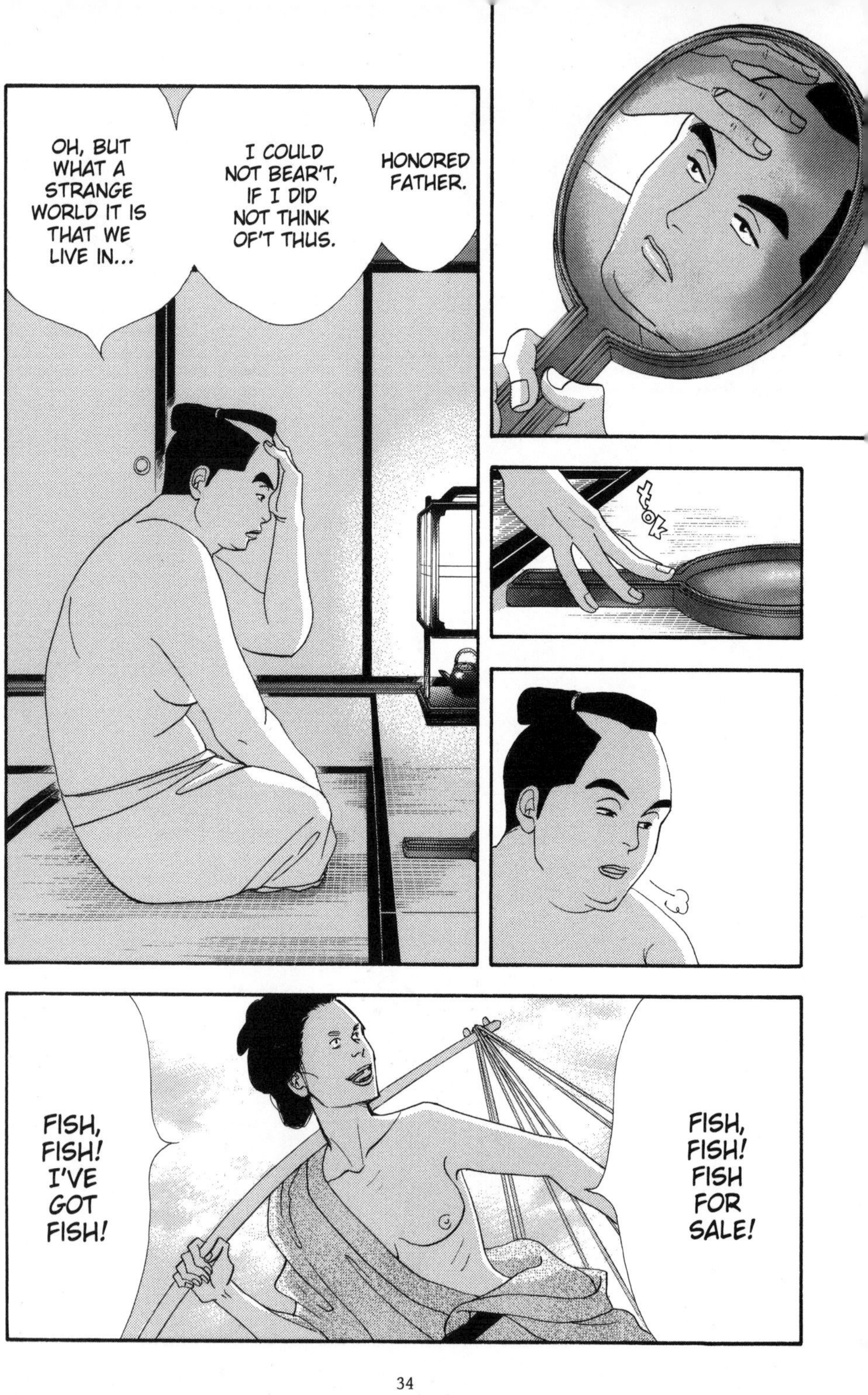
tok
HONORED FATHER.
I COULD NOT BEAR'T, IF I DID NOT THINK OF'T THUS.
OH, BUT WHAT A STRANGE WORLD IT IS THAT WE LIVE IN...
FISH, FISH! FISH FOR SALE!
FISH, FISH! I'VE GOT FISH!

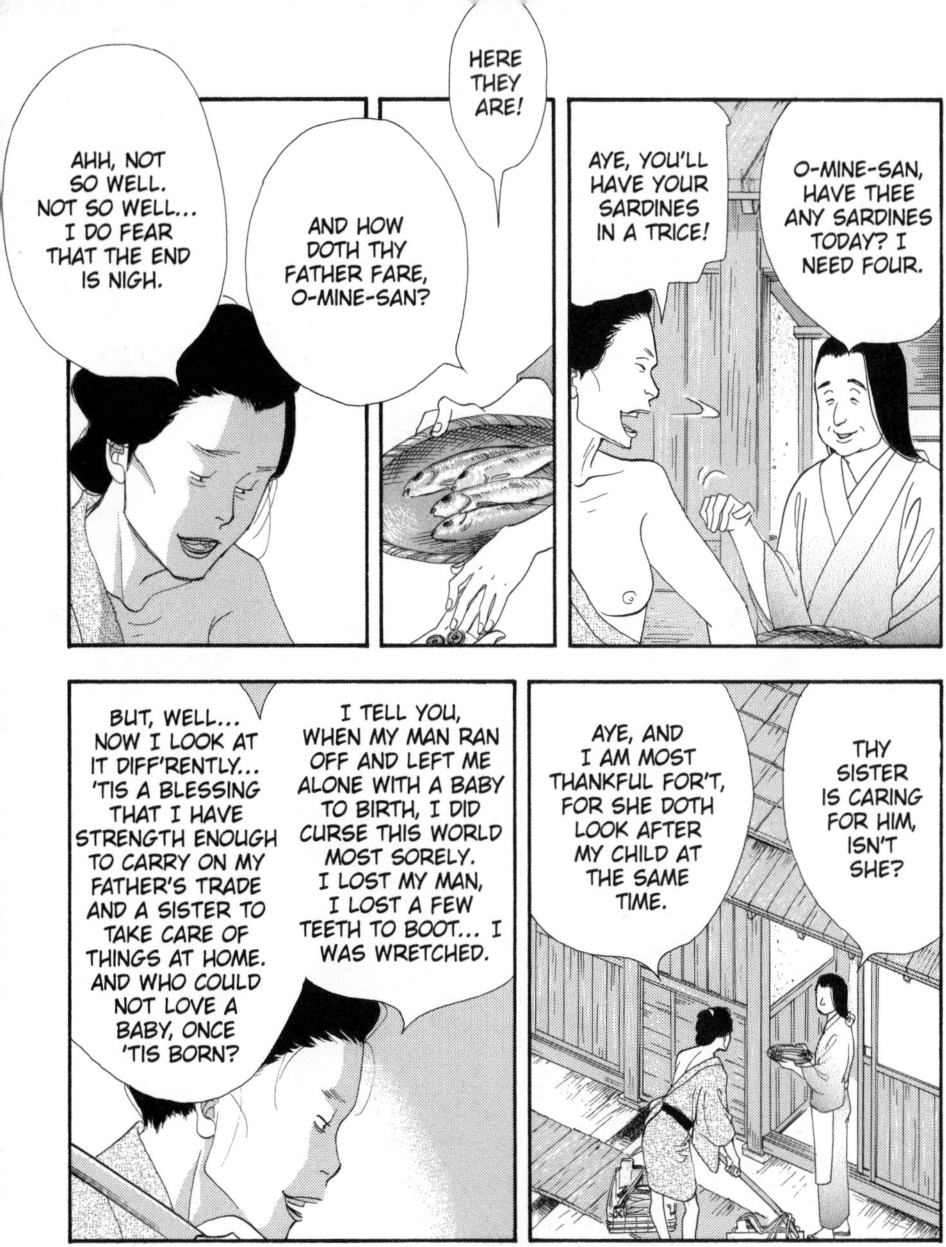
O-MINE-SAN, HAVE THEE ANY SARDINES TODAY? I NEED FOUR.
AYE, YOU'LL HAVE YOUR SARDINES IN A TRICE!
HERE THEY ARE!
AND HOW DOTH THY FATHER FARE, O-MINE-SAN?
AHH, NOT SO WELL. NOT SO WELL... I DO FEAR THAT THE END IS NIGH.
THY SISTER IS CARING FOR HIM, ISN'T SHE?
AYE, AND I AM MOST THANKFUL FOR'T, FOR SHE DOTH LOOK AFTER MY CHILD AT THE SAME TIME.
I TELL YOU, WHEN MY MAN RAN OFF AND LEFT ME ALONE WITH A BABY TO BIRTH, I DID CURSE THIS WORLD MOST SORELY. I LOST MY MAN, I LOST A FEW TEETH TO BOOT... I WAS WRETCHED.
BUT, WELL... NOW I LOOK AT IT DIFF'RENTLY... 'TIS A BLESSING THAT I HAVE STRENGTH ENOUGH TO CARRY ON MY FATHER'S TRADE AND A SISTER TO TAKE CARE OF THINGS AT HOME. AND WHO COULD NOT LOVE A BABY, ONCE 'TIS BORN?
THOU ART A GOOD DAUGHTER, THOU ART.
IF ONLY MINE OWN DAUGHTER WOULD GIVE ME A GRANDCHILD, I WOULD DO ALL THE FUSSING AND CARING IT NEEDED.
BUT THE SAUCY LASS SAYETH THAT SHE WILL TAKE ONLY A HANDSOME SWAIN TO GIVE HER A CHILD...

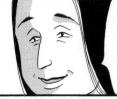

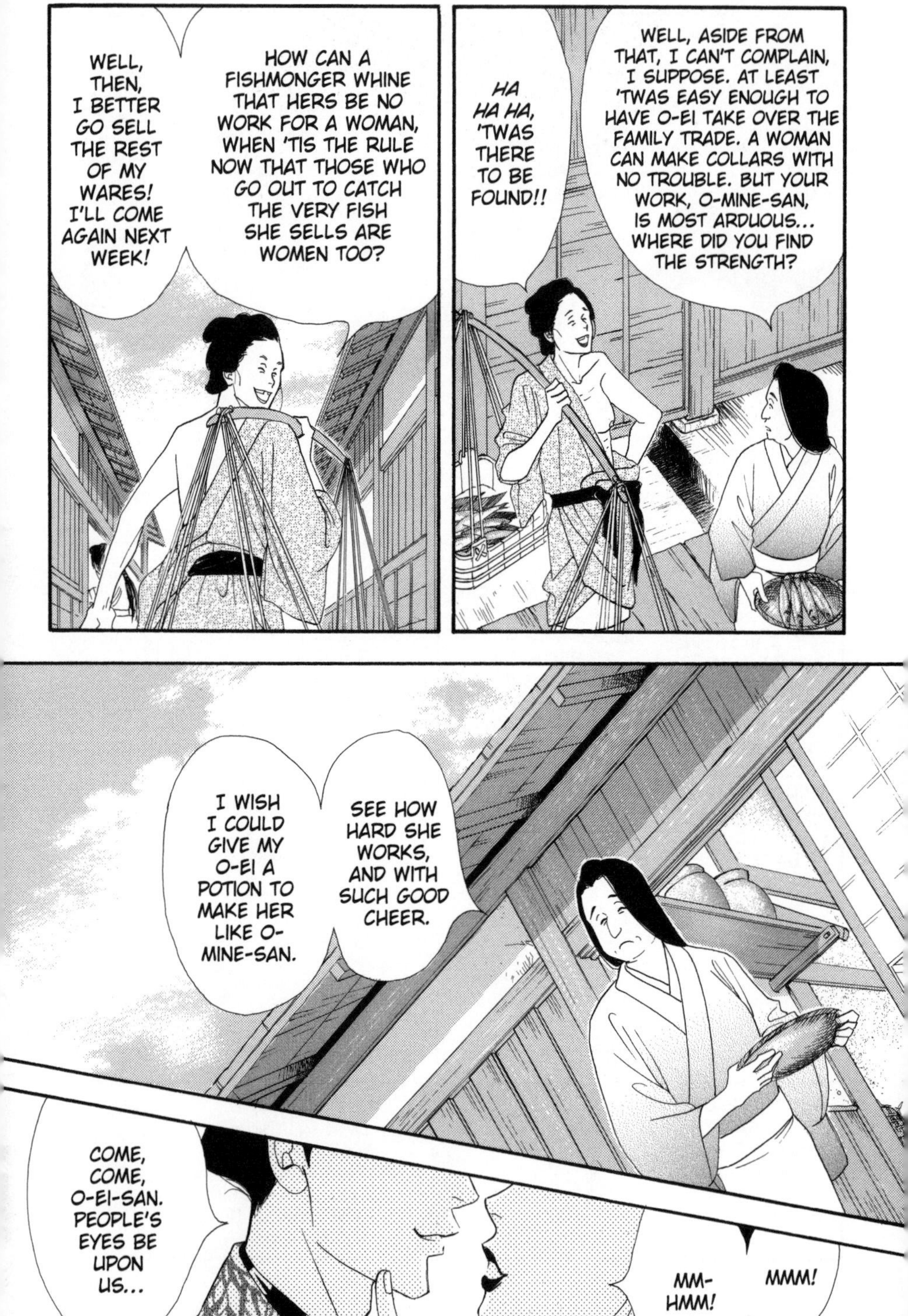
WELL, ASIDE FROM THAT, I CAN'T COMPLAIN, I SUPPOSE. AT LEAST 'TWAS EASY ENOUGH TO HAVE O-EI TAKE OVER THE FAMILY TRADE. A WOMAN CAN MAKE COLLARS WITH NO TROUBLE. BUT YOUR WORK, O-MINE-SAN, IS MOST ARDUOUS... WHERE DID YOU FIND THE STRENGTH?
HA HA HA, 'TWAS THERE TO BE FOUND!!
HOW CAN A FISHMONGER WHINE THAT HERS BE NO WORK FOR A WOMAN, WHEN 'TIS THE RULE NOW THAT THOSE WHO GO OUT TO CATCH THE VERY FISH SHE SELLS ARE WOMEN TOO?
WELL, THEN, I BETTER GO SELL THE REST OF MY WARES! I'LL COME AGAIN NEXT WEEK!
SEE HOW HARD SHE WORKS, AND WITH SUCH GOOD CHEER.
I WISH I COULD GIVE MY O-EI A POTION TO MAKE HER LIKE O-MINE-SAN.
MMM!
MM-HMM!
COME, COME, O-EI-SAN. PEOPLE'S EYES BE UPON US...

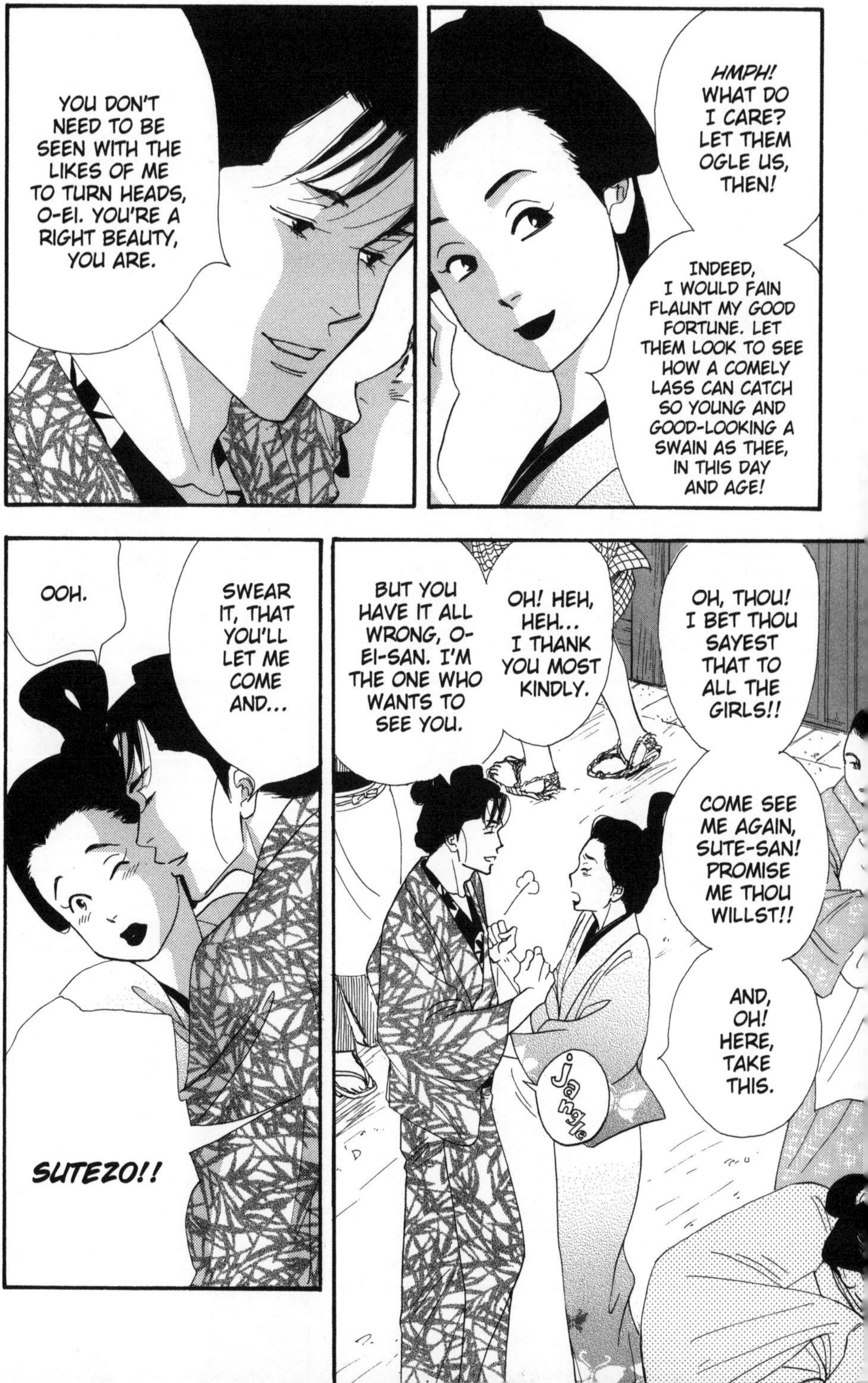
HMPH! WHAT DO I CARE? LET THEM OGLE US, THEN!
INDEED, I WOULD FAIN FLAUNT MY GOOD FORTUNE. LET THEM LOOK TO SEE HOW A COMELY LASS CAN CATCH SO YOUNG AND GOOD-LOOKING A SWAIN AS THEE, IN THIS DAY AND AGE!
YOU DON'T NEED TO BE SEEN WITH THE LIKES OF ME TO TURN HEADS, O-EI. YOU'RE A RIGHT BEAUTY, YOU ARE.
OH, THOU! I BET THOU SAYEST THAT TO ALL THE GIRLS!!
OH! HEH, HEH... I THANK YOU MOST KINDLY.
BUT YOU HAVE IT ALL WRONG, O-EI-SAN. I'M THE ONE WHO WANTS TO SEE YOU.
COME SEE ME AGAIN, SUTE-SAN! PROMISE ME THOU WILLST!!
AND, OH! HERE, TAKE THIS.
jangle
SWEAR IT, THAT YOU'LL LET ME COME AND...
OOH.
SUTEZO!!

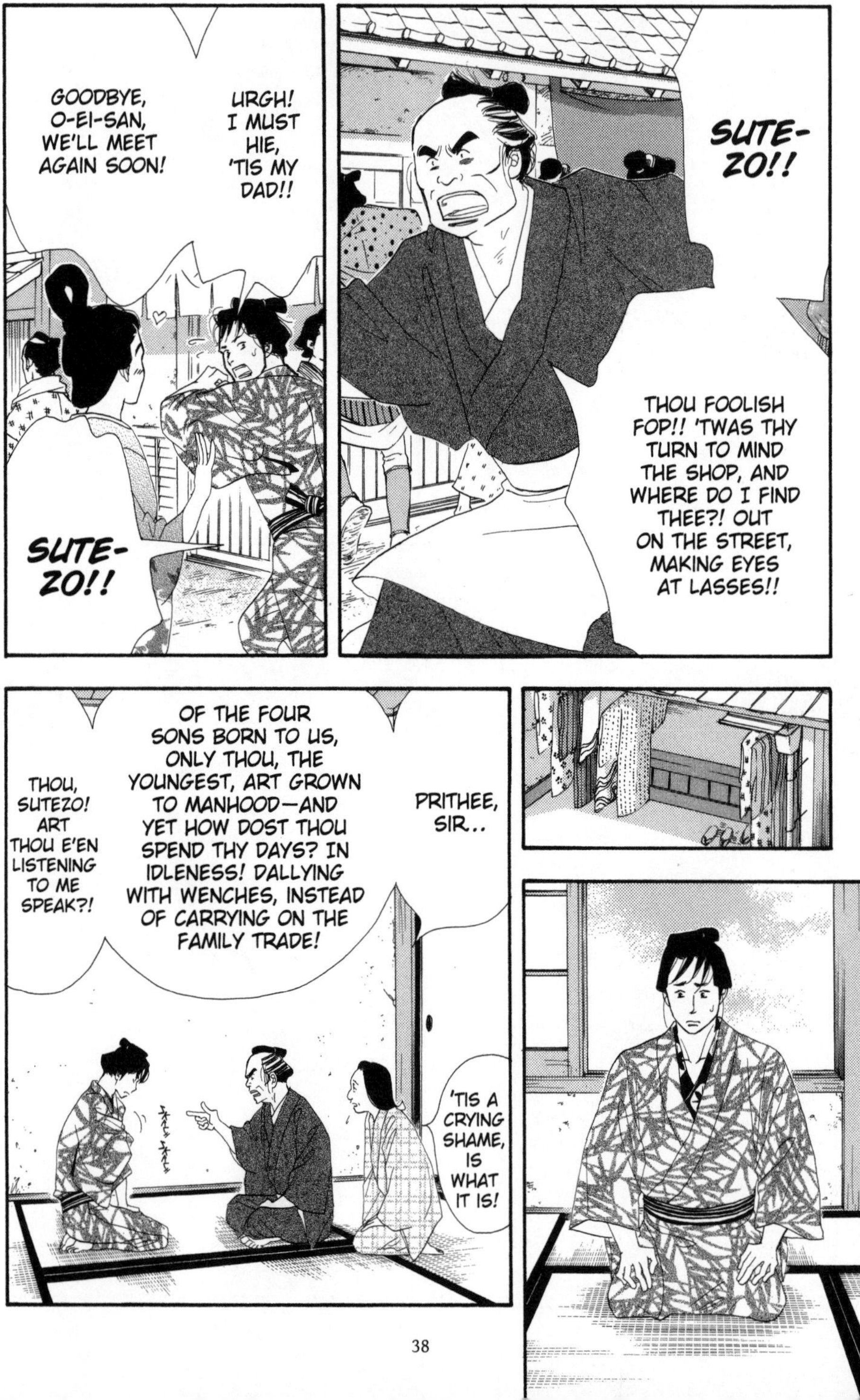
SUTE-ZO!!
THOU FOOLISH FOP!! 'TWAS THY TURN TO MIND THE SHOP, AND WHERE DO I FIND THEE?! OUT ON THE STREET, MAKING EYES AT LASSES!!
URGH! I MUST HIE, 'TIS MY DAD!!
GOODBYE, O-EI-SAN, WE'LL MEET AGAIN SOON!
SUTE-ZO!!
PRITHEE, SIR..
OF THE FOUR SONS BORN TO US, ONLY THOU, THE YOUNGEST, ART GROWN TO MANHOOD—AND YET HOW DOST THOU SPEND THY DAYS? IN IDLENESS! DALLYING WITH WENCHES, INSTEAD OF CARRYING ON THE FAMILY TRADE!
THOU, SUTEZO! ART THOU E'EN LISTENING TO ME SPEAK?!
'TIS A CRYING SHAME, IS WHAT IT IS!

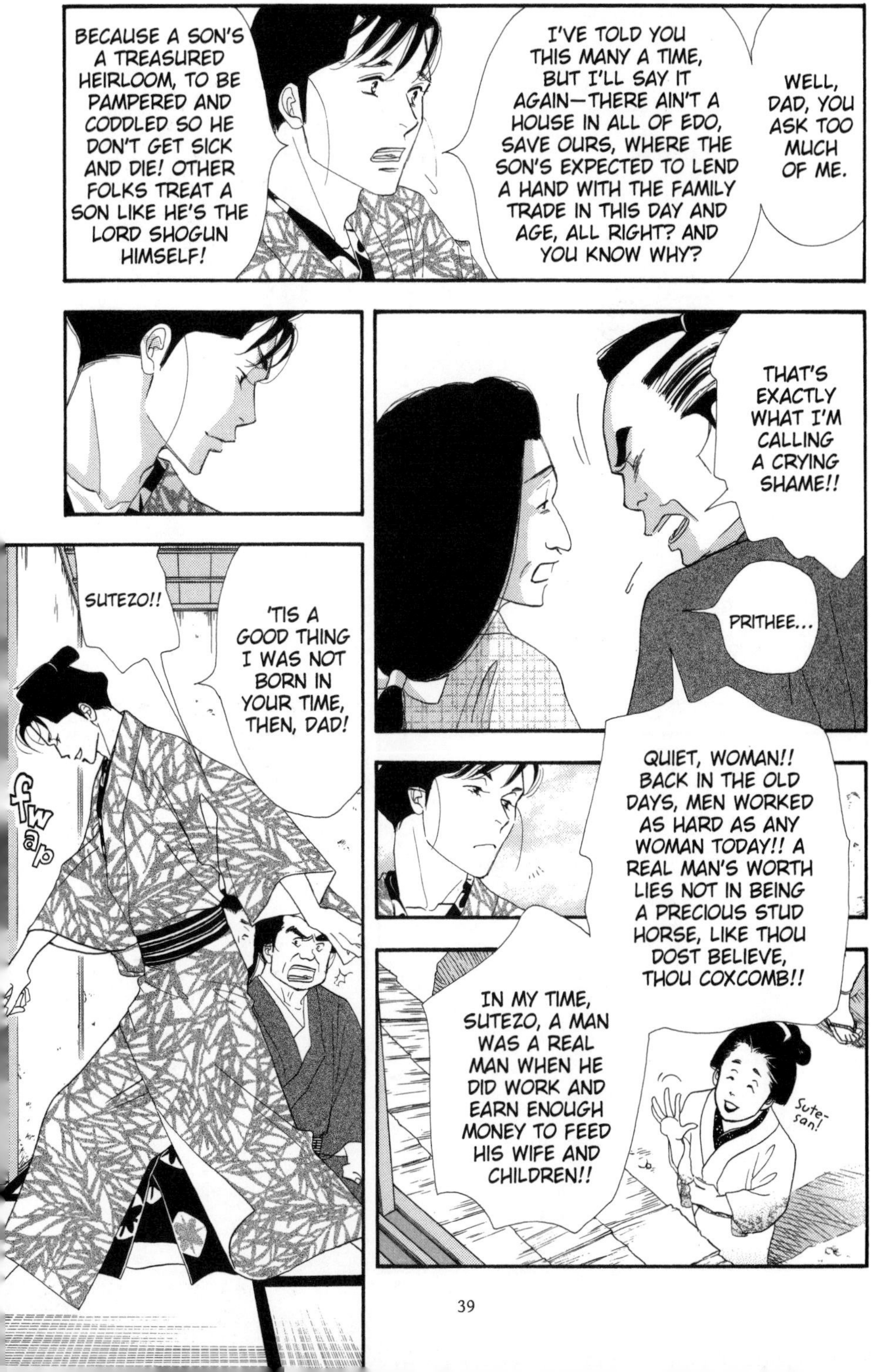
WELL, DAD, YOU ASK TOO MUCH OF ME.
I'VE TOLD YOU THIS MANY A TIME, BUT I'LL SAY IT AGAIN—THERE AIN'T A HOUSE IN ALL OF EDO, SAVE OURS, WHERE THE SON'S EXPECTED TO LEND A HAND WITH THE FAMILY TRADE IN THIS DAY AND AGE, ALL RIGHT? AND YOU KNOW WHY?
BECAUSE A SON'S A TREASURED HEIRLOOM, TO BE PAMPERED AND CODDLED SO HE DON'T GET SICK AND DIE! OTHER FOLKS TREAT A SON LIKE HE'S THE LORD SHOGUN HIMSELF!
THAT'S EXACTLY WHAT I'M CALLING A CRYING SHAME!!
PRITHEE...
QUIET, WOMAN!! BACK IN THE OLD DAYS, MEN WORKED AS HARD AS ANY WOMAN TODAY!! A REAL MAN'S WORTH LIES NOT IN BEING A PRECIOUS STUD HORSE, LIKE THOU DOST BELIEVE, THOU COXCOMB!!
IN MY TIME, SUTEZO, A MAN WAS A REAL MAN WHEN HE DID WORK AND EARN ENOUGH MONEY TO FEED HIS WIFE AND CHILDREN!!
Sute-san!
'TIS A GOOD THING I WAS NOT BORN IN YOUR TIME, THEN, DAD!
SUTEZO!!
fwap

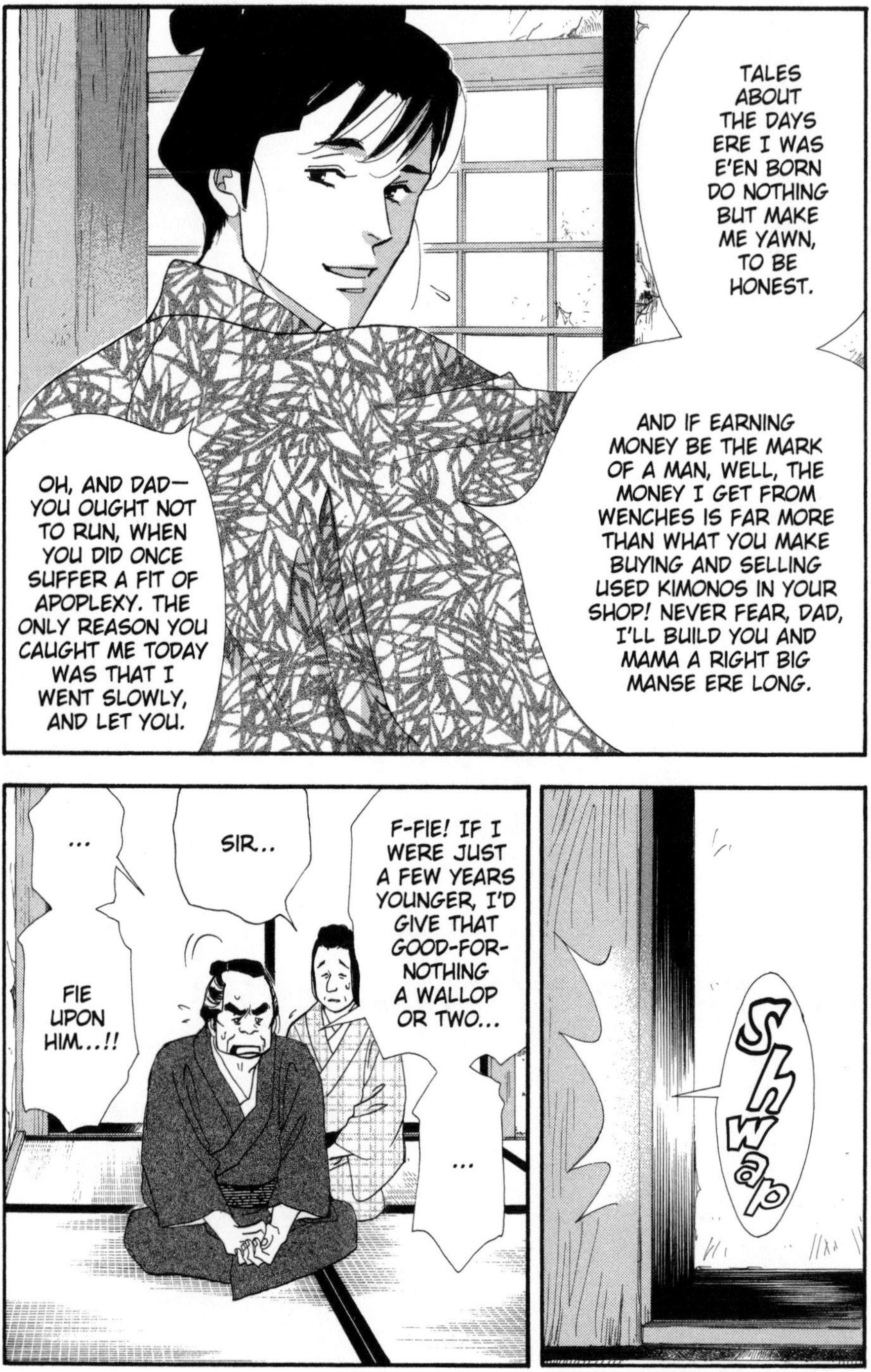
TALES ABOUT THE DAYS ERE I WAS E'EN BORN DO NOTHING BUT MAKE ME YAWN, TO BE HONEST.
AND IF EARNING MONEY BE THE MARK OF A MAN, WELL, THE MONEY I GET FROM WENCHES IS FAR MORE THAN WHAT YOU MAKE BUYING AND SELLING USED KIMONOS IN YOUR SHOP! NEVER FEAR, DAD, I'LL BUILD YOU AND MAMA A RIGHT BIG MANSE ERE LONG.
OH, AND DAD—YOU OUGHT NOT TO RUN, WHEN YOU DID ONCE SUFFER A FIT OF APOPLEXY. THE ONLY REASON YOU CAUGHT ME TODAY WAS THAT I WENT SLOWLY, AND LET YOU.
Shwap
F-FIE! IF I WERE JUST A FEW YEARS YOUNGER, I'D GIVE THAT GOOD-FOR-NOTHING A WALLOP OR TWO...
SIR...
...
...
FIE UPON HIM...!!

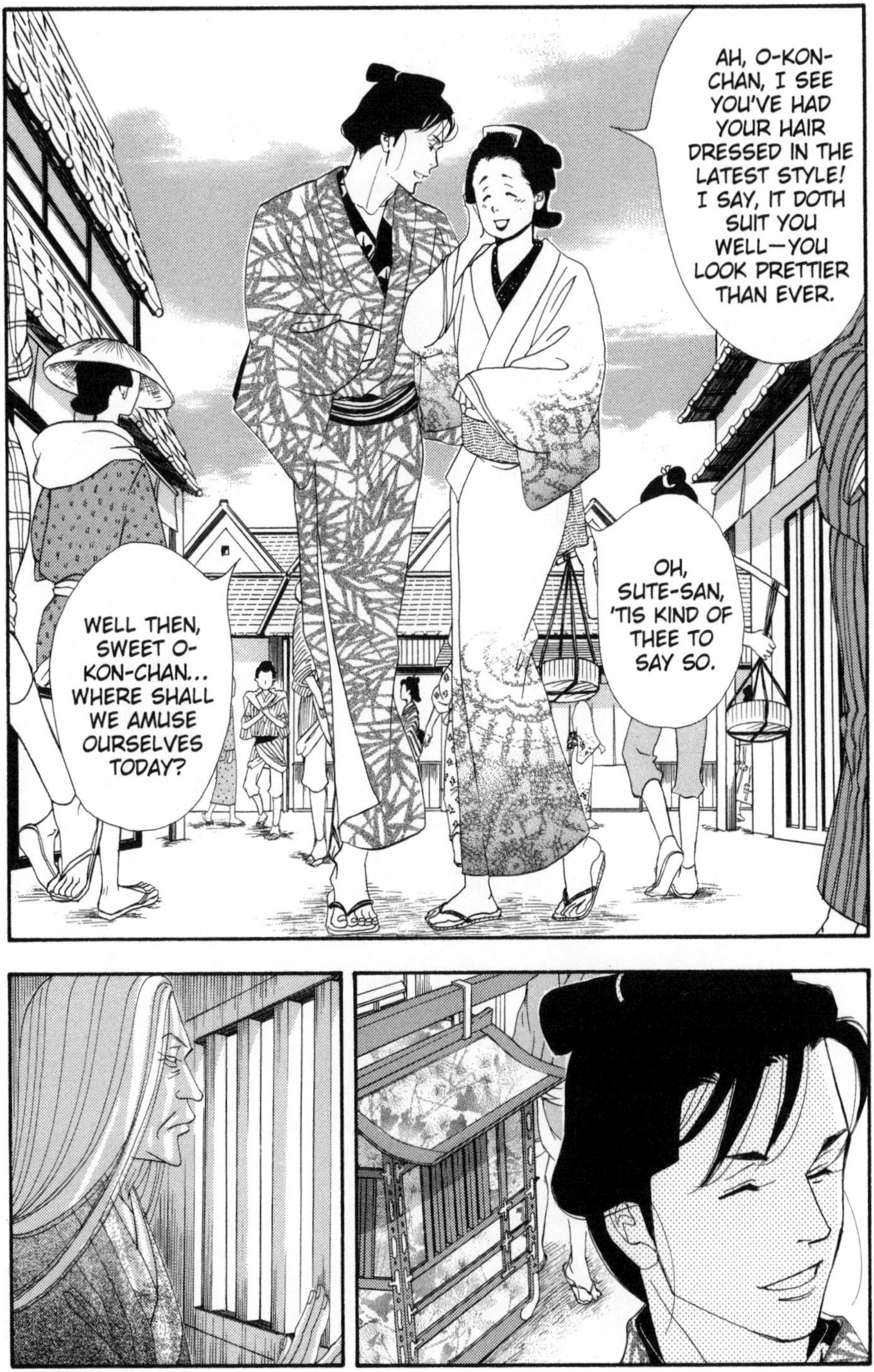
AH, O-KON-CHAN, I SEE YOU'VE HAD YOUR HAIR DRESSED IN THE LATEST STYLE! I SAY, IT DOTH SUIT YOU WELL—YOU LOOK PRETTIER THAN EVER.
OH, SUTE-SAN, 'TIS KIND OF THEE TO SAY SO.
WELL THEN, SWEET O-KON-CHAN... WHERE SHALL WE AMUSE OURSELVES TODAY?

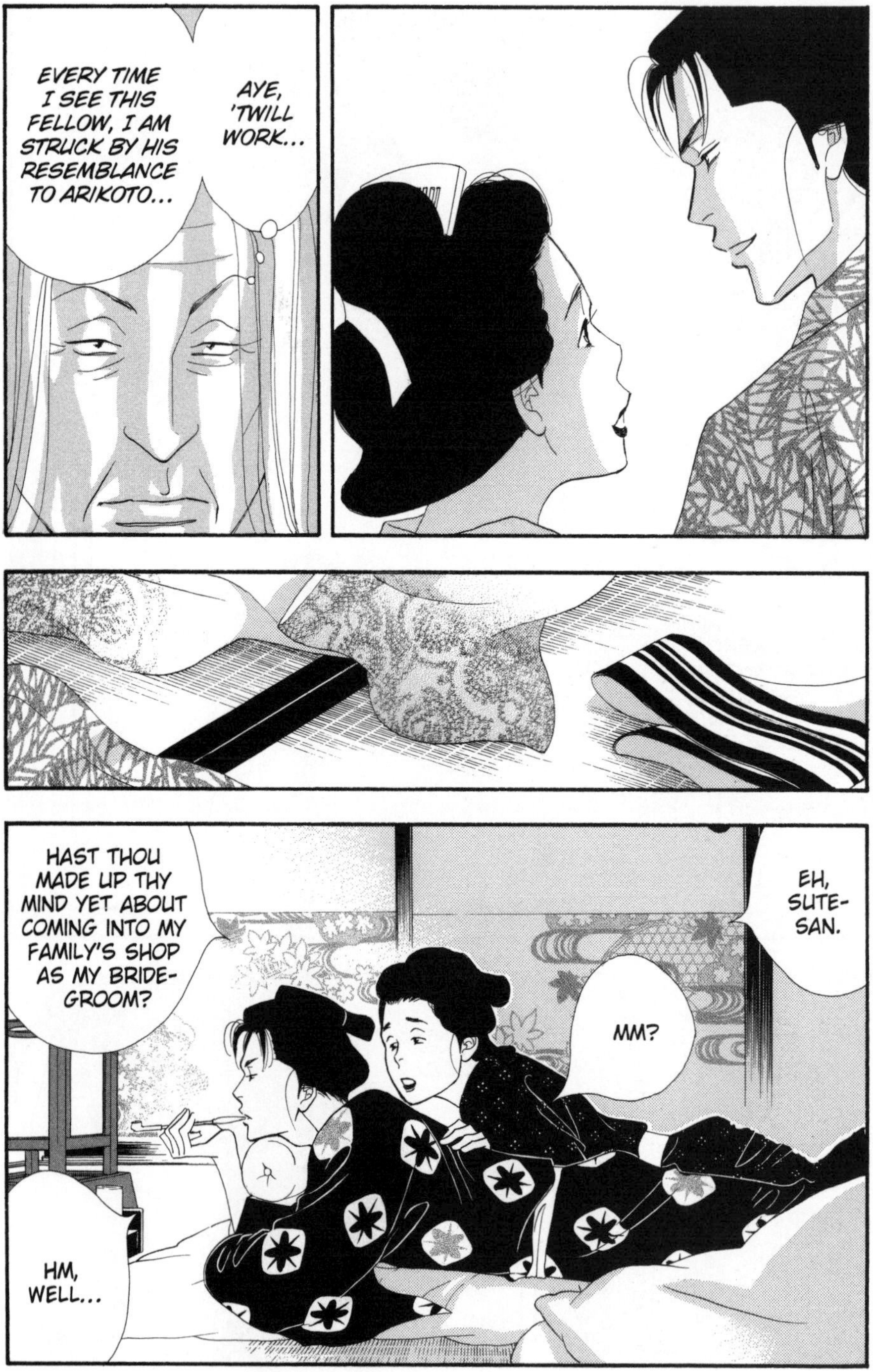
AYE, 'TWILL WORK...
EVERY TIME I SEE THIS FELLOW, I AM STRUCK BY HIS RESEMBLANCE TO ARIKOTO...
EH, SUTE-SAN.
MM?
HAST THOU MADE UP THY MIND YET ABOUT COMING INTO MY FAMILY'S SHOP AS MY BRIDE-GROOM?
HM, WELL...

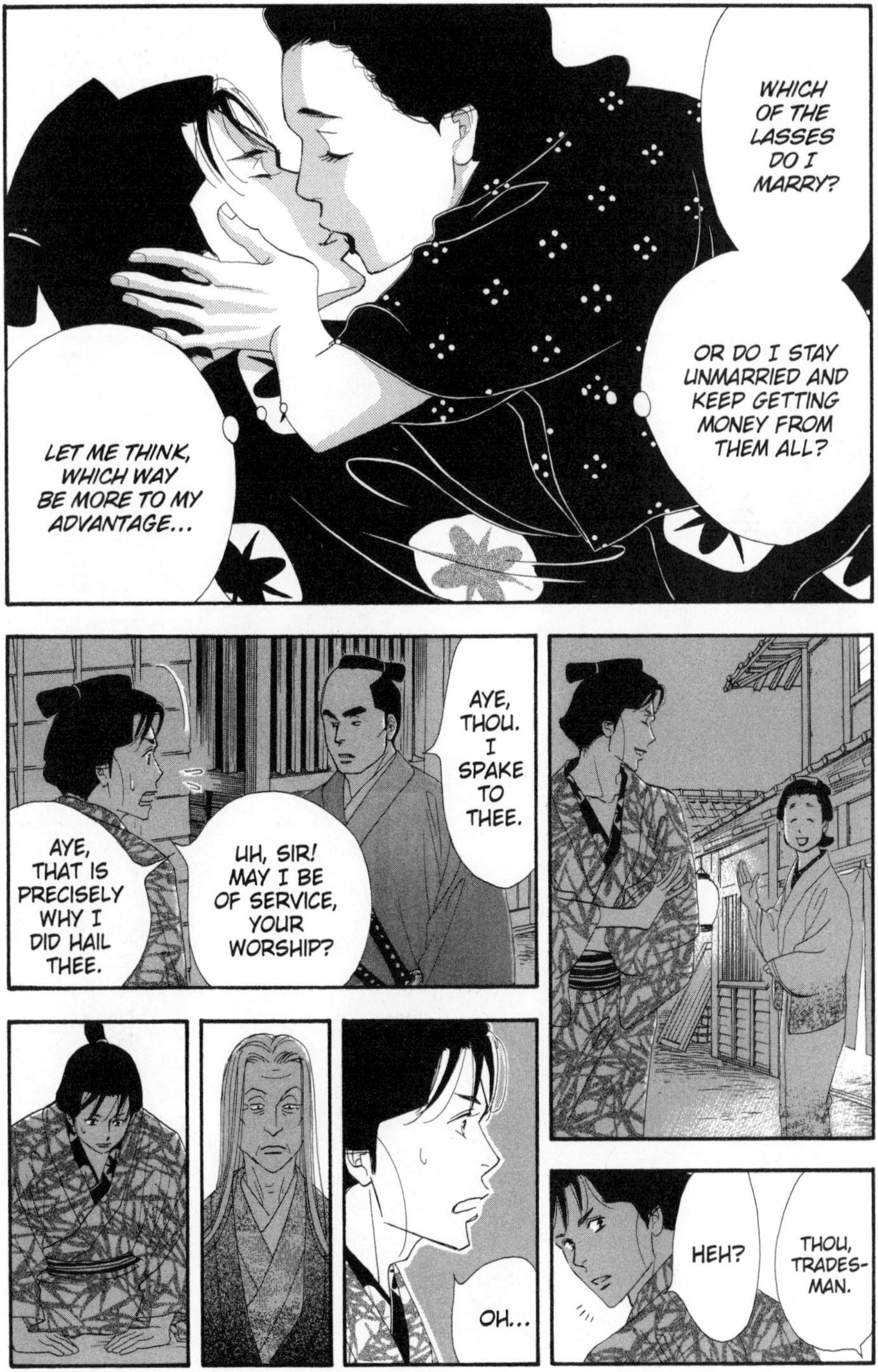
WHICH OF THE LASSES DO I MARRY?
OR DO I STAY UNMARRIED AND KEEP GETTING MONEY FROM THEM ALL?
LET ME THINK, WHICH WAY BE MORE TO MY ADVANTAGE...
THOU, TRADES-MAN.
HEH?
AYE, THOU. I SPAKE TO THEE.
UH, SIR! MAY I BE OF SERVICE, YOUR WORSHIP?
AYE, THAT IS PRECISELY WHY I DID HAIL THEE.
OH...

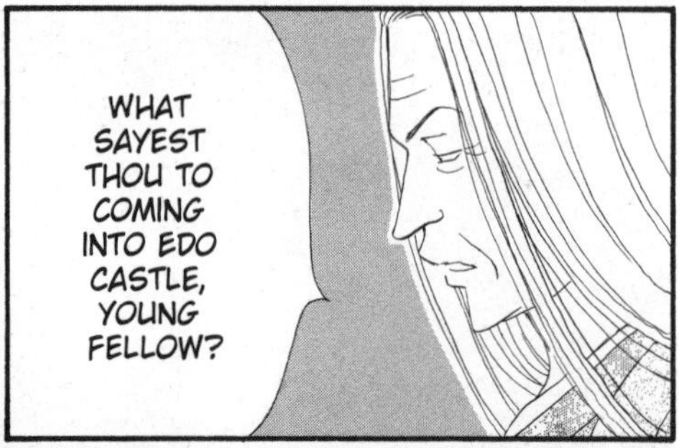
WHAT SAYEST THOU TO COMING INTO EDO CASTLE, YOUNG FELLOW?
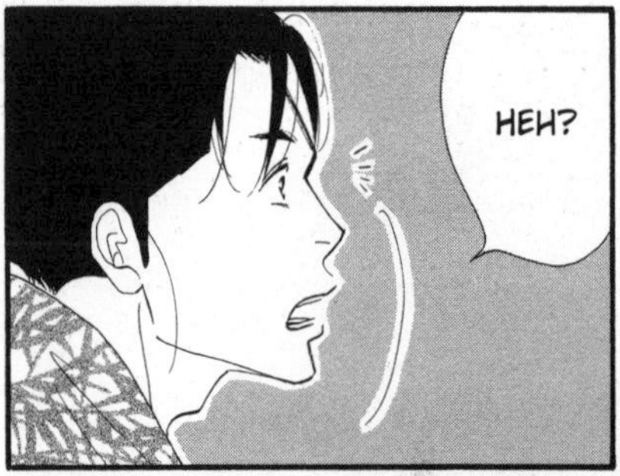
HEH?
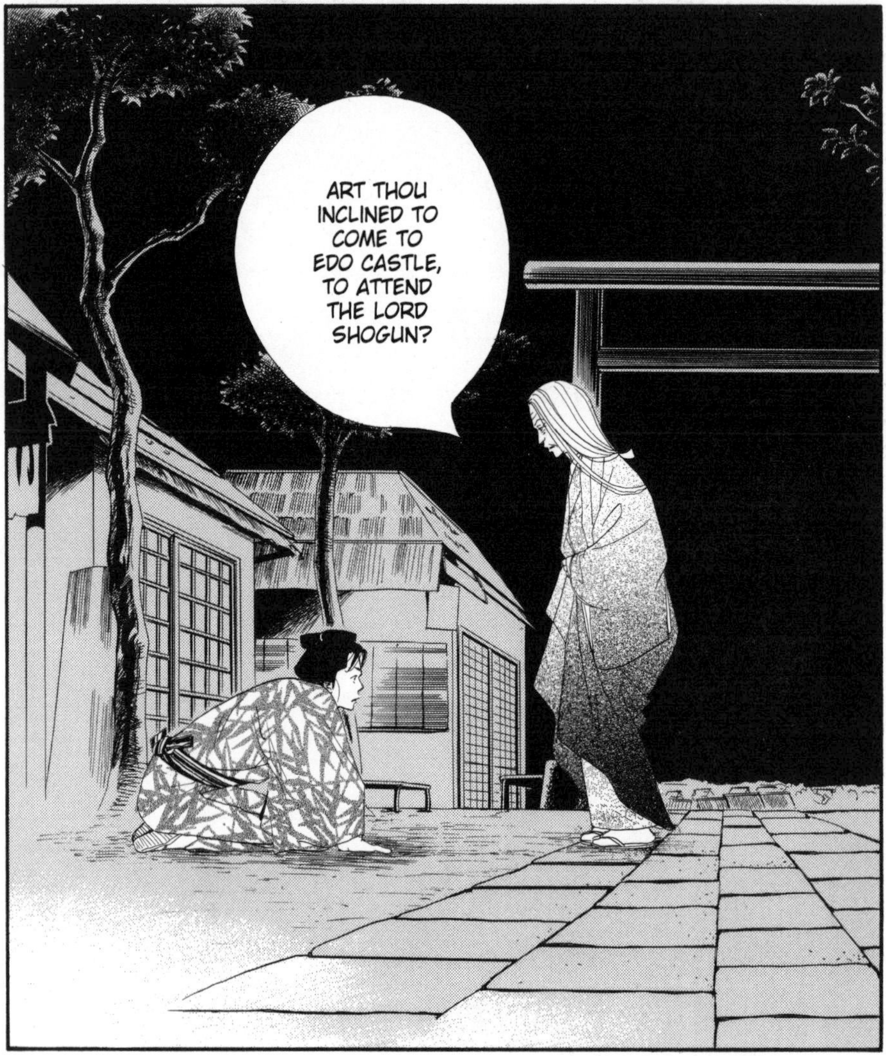
ART THOU INCLINED TO COME TO EDO CASTLE, TO ATTEND THE LORD SHOGUN?

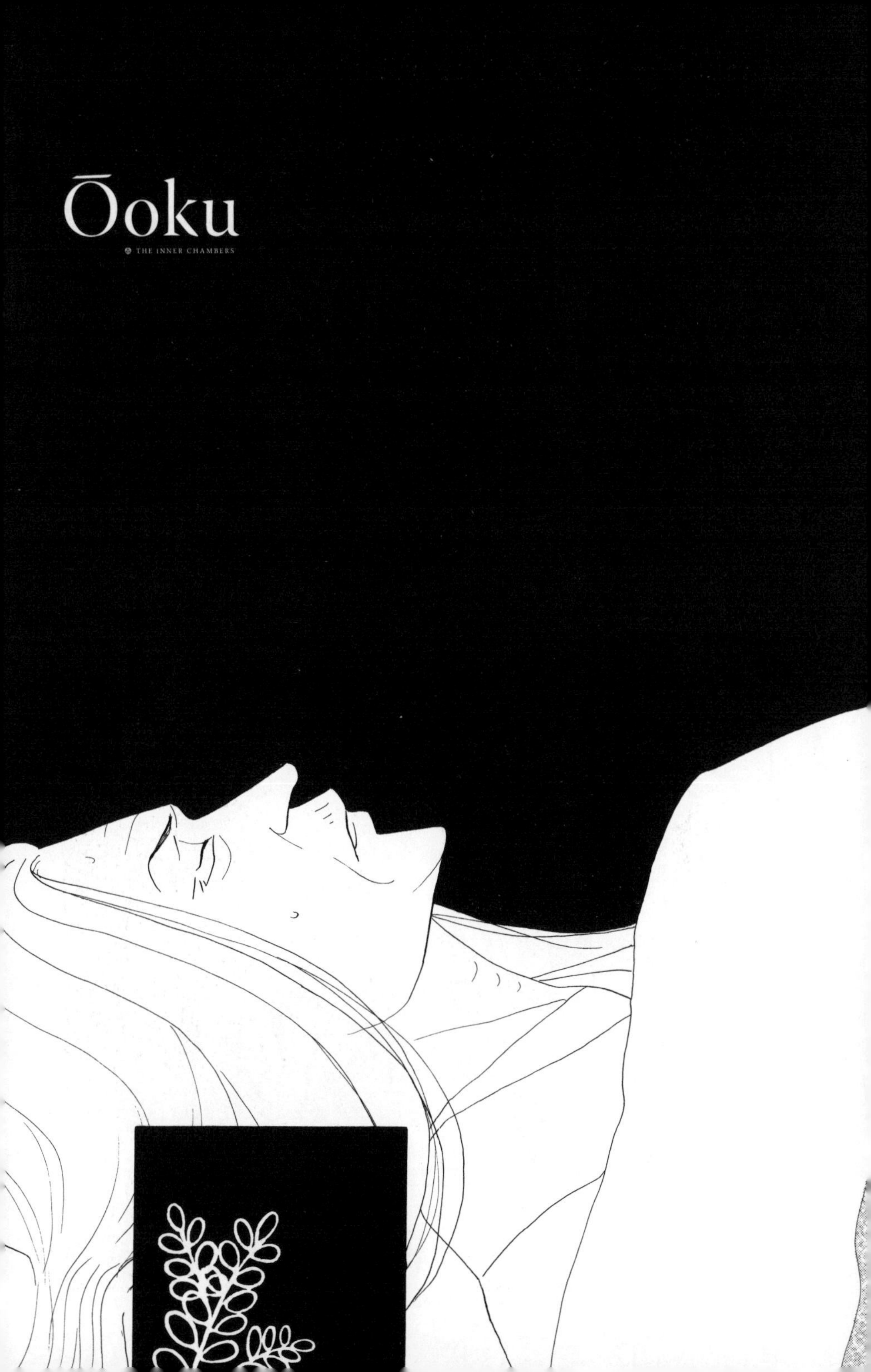
Ōoku
THE INNER CHAMBERS

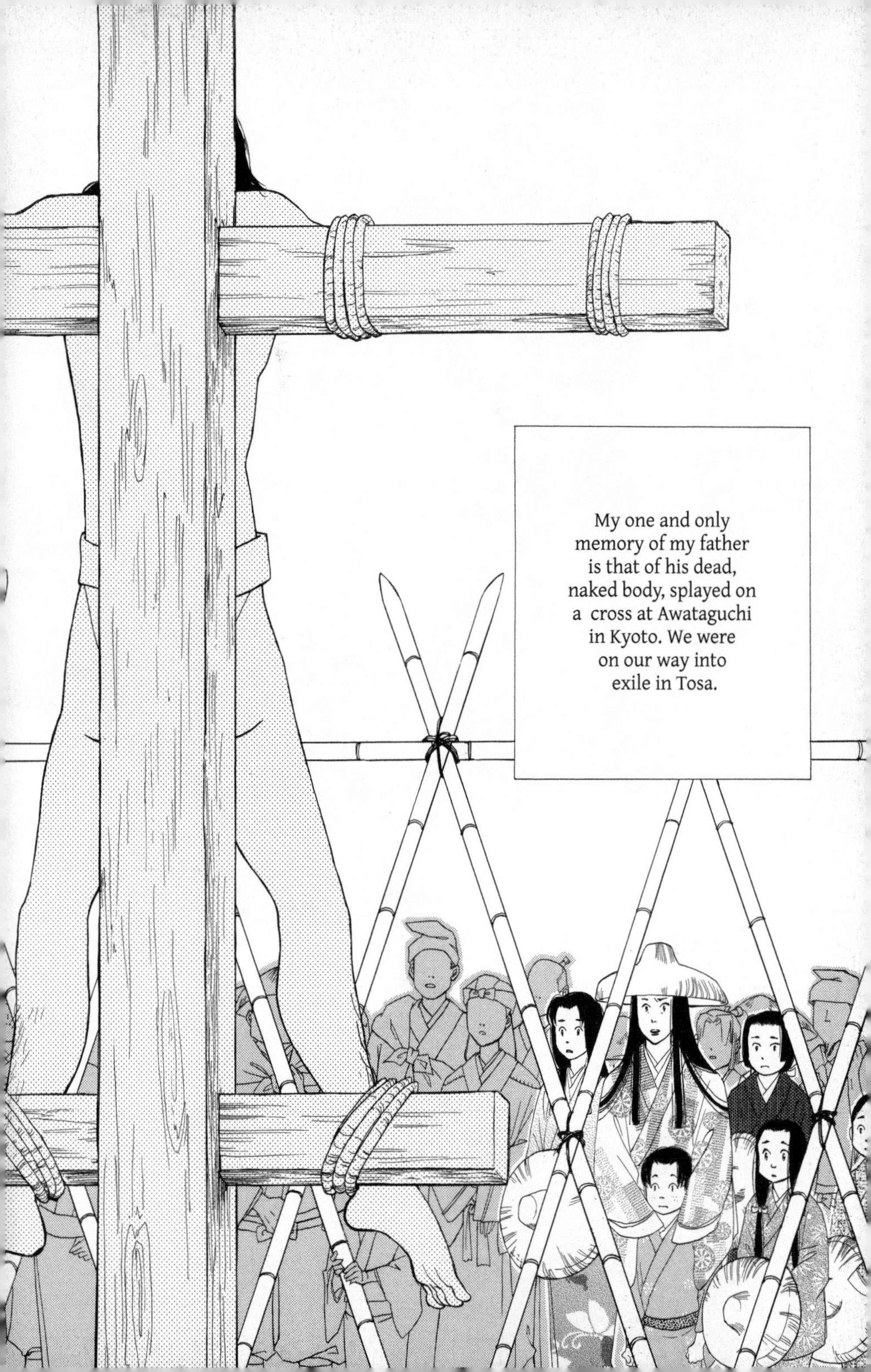
My one and only memory of my father is that of his dead, naked body, splayed on a cross at Awataguchi in Kyoto. We were on our way into exile in Tosa.

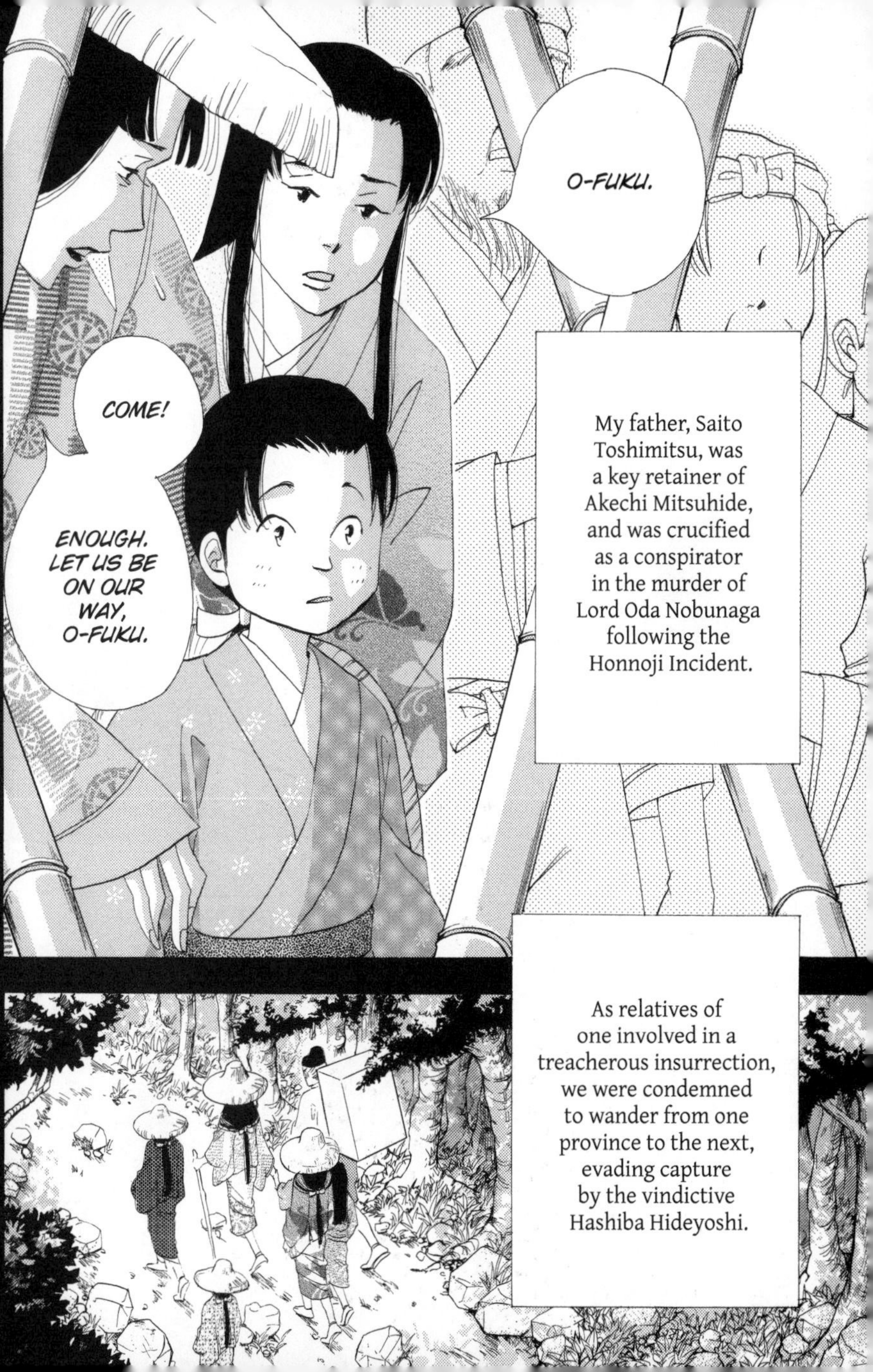
O-FUKU.
My father, Saito Toshimitsu, was a key retainer of Akechi Mitsuhide, and was crucified as a conspirator in the murder of Lord Oda Nobunaga following the Honnoji Incident.
COME!
ENOUGH. LET US BE ON OUR WAY, O-FUKU.
As relatives of one involved in a treacherous insurrection, we were condemned to wander from one province to the next, evading capture by the vindictive Hashiba Hideyoshi.

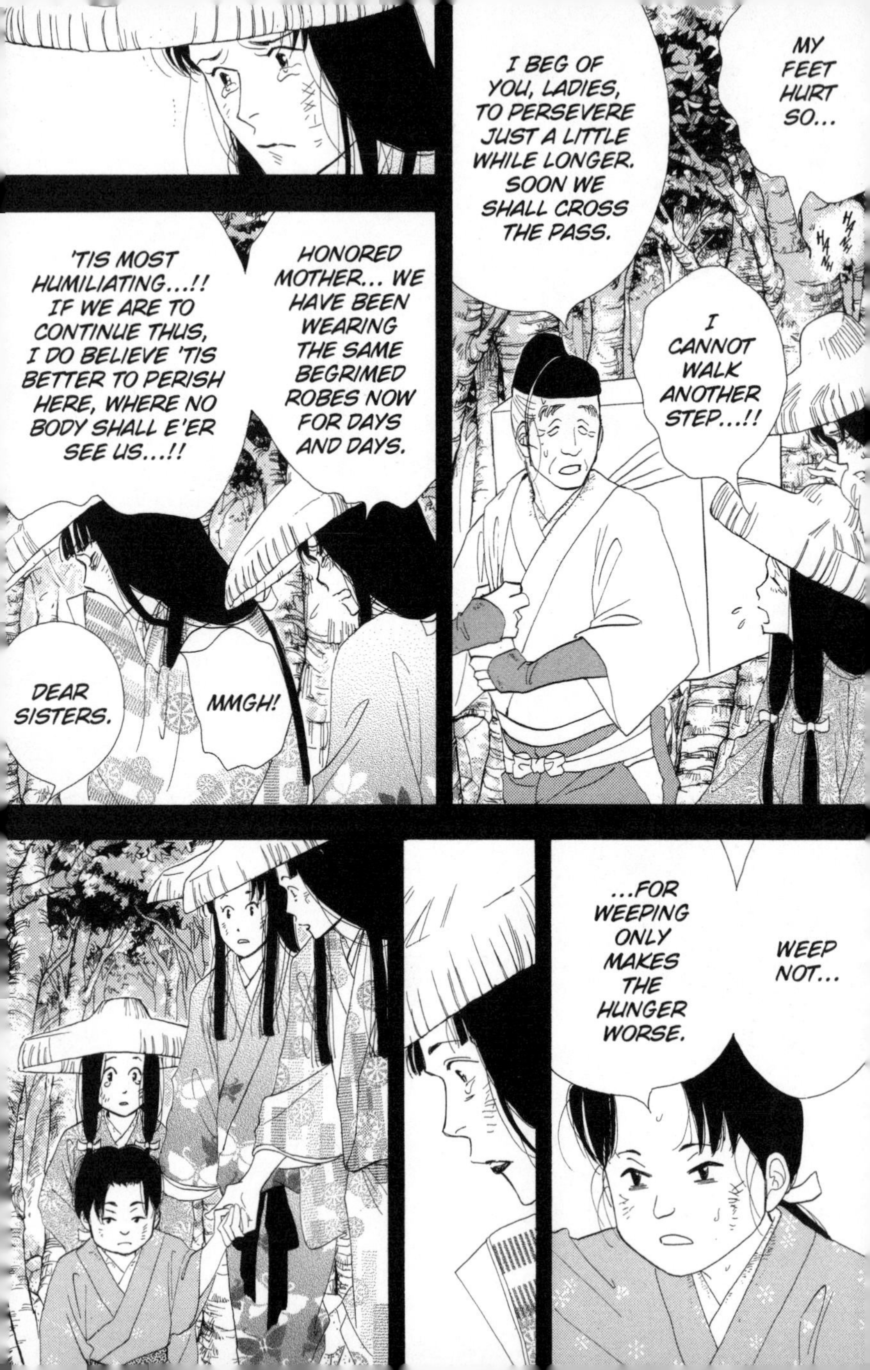
MY FEET HURT SO...
I BEG OF YOU, LADIES, TO PERSEVERE JUST A LITTLE WHILE LONGER. SOON WE SHALL CROSS THE PASS.
HA NH HA NH
I CANNOT WALK ANOTHER STEP...!!
HONORED MOTHER... WE HAVE BEEN WEARING THE SAME BEGRIMED ROBES NOW FOR DAYS AND DAYS.
'TIS MOST HUMILIATING...!! IF WE ARE TO CONTINUE THUS, I DO BELIEVE 'TIS BETTER TO PERISH HERE, WHERE NO BODY SHALL E'ER SEE US...!!
MMGH!
DEAR SISTERS.
WEEP NOT...
...FOR WEEPING ONLY MAKES THE HUNGER WORSE.

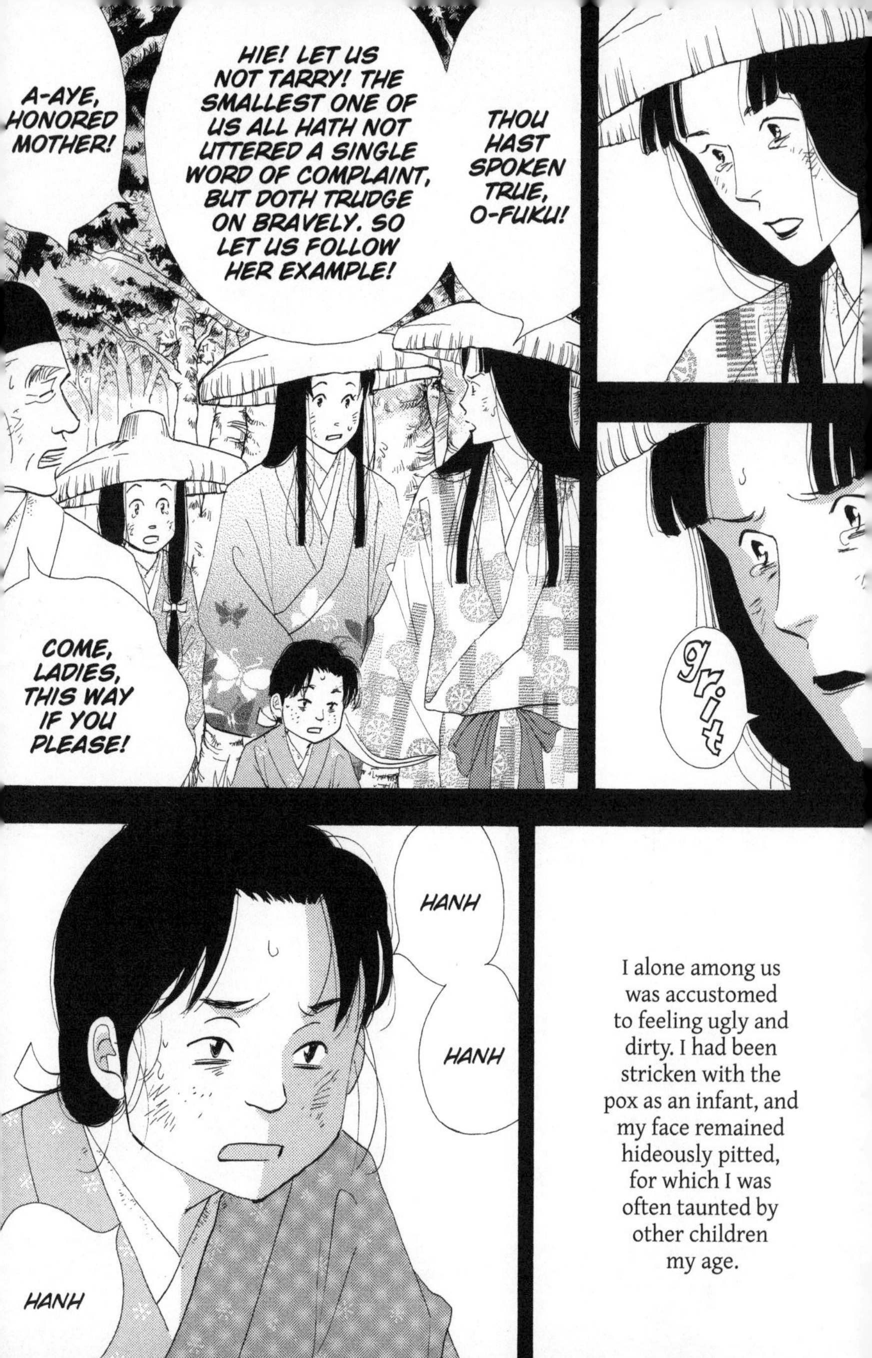
HIE! LET US NOT TARRY! THE SMALLEST ONE OF US ALL HATH NOT UTTERED A SINGLE WORD OF COMPLAINT, BUT DOTH TRUDGE ON BRAVELY. SO LET US FOLLOW HER EXAMPLE!
THOU HAST SPOKEN TRUE, O-FUKU!
A-AYE, HONORED MOTHER!
COME, LADIES, THIS WAY IF YOU PLEASE!
grit
HANH
HANH
HANH
I alone among us was accustomed to feeling ugly and dirty. I had been stricken with the pox as an infant, and my face remained hideously pitted, for which I was often taunted by other children my age.

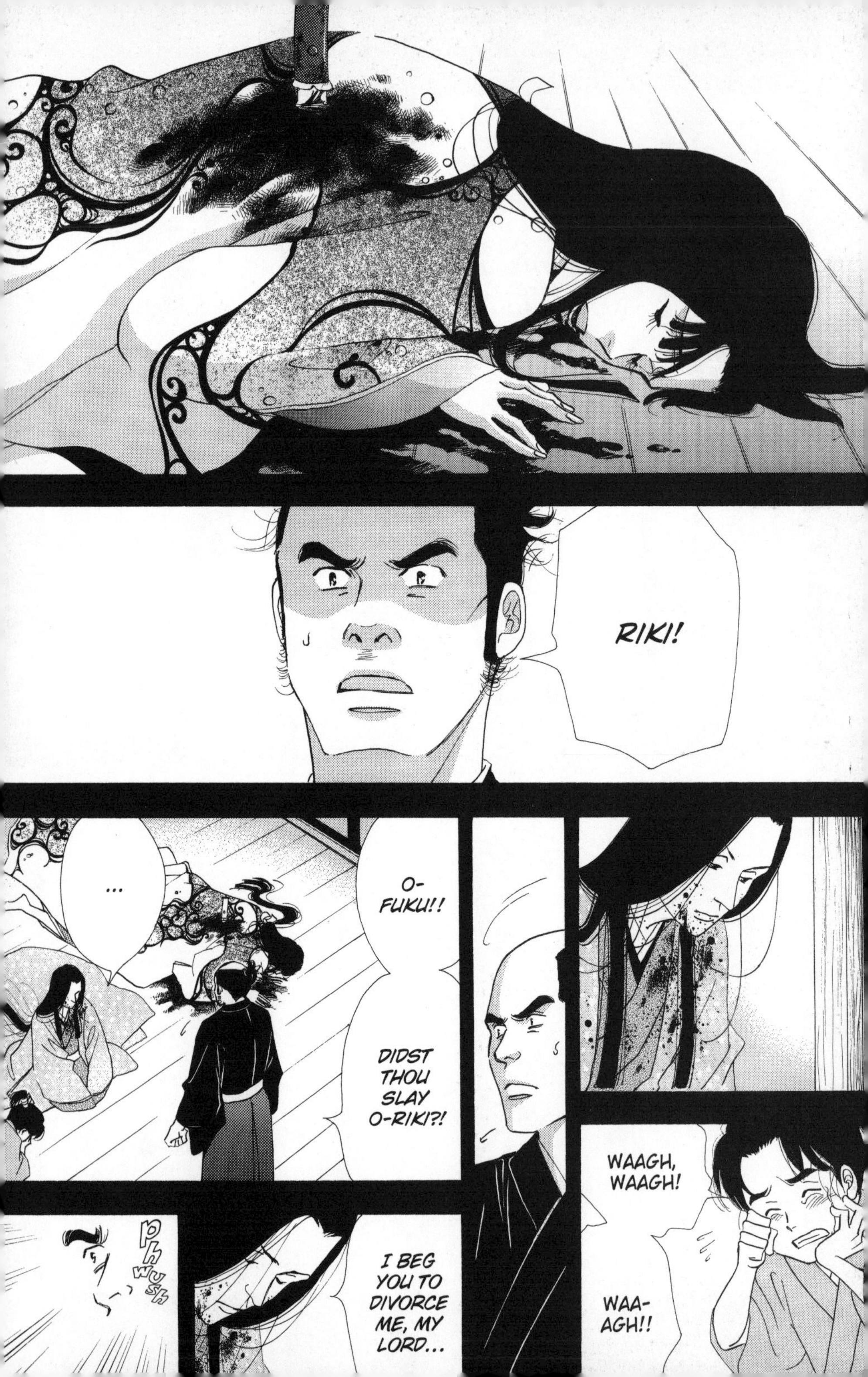
RIKI!
WAAGH, WAAGH!
WAA-AGH!!
O-FUKU!!
DIDST THOU SLAY O-RIKI?!
...
I BEG YOU TO DIVORCE ME, MY LORD...
phwush

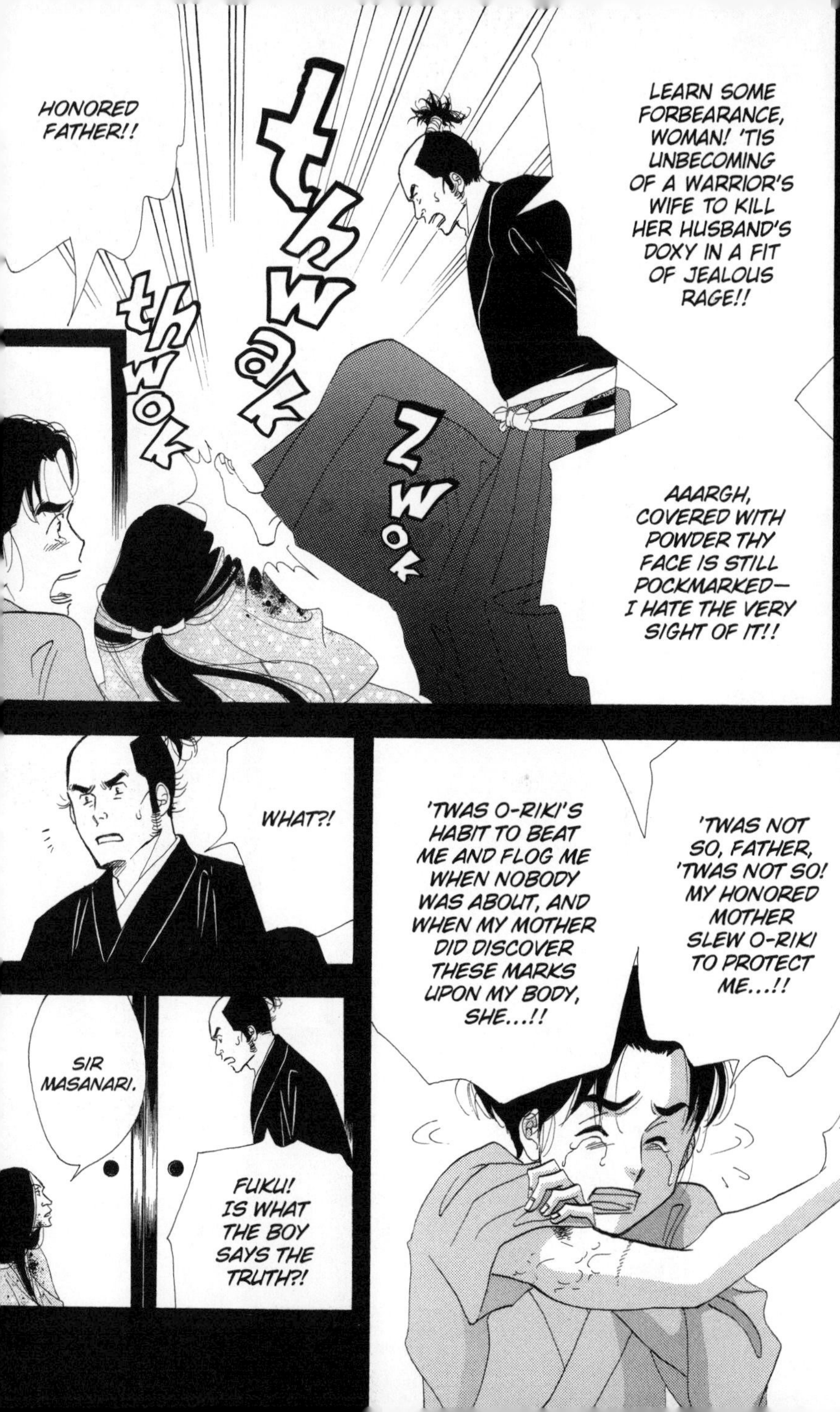
LEARN SOME FORBEARANCE, WOMAN! 'TIS UNBECOMING OF A WARRIOR'S WIFE TO KILL HER HUSBAND'S DOXY IN A FIT OF JEALOUS RAGE!!
HONORED FATHER!!
thwak
thwok
AAARGH, COVERED WITH POWDER THY FACE IS STILL POCKMARKED— I HATE THE VERY SIGHT OF IT!!
zwok
'TWAS NOT SO, FATHER, 'TWAS NOT SO! MY HONORED MOTHER SLEW O-RIKI TO PROTECT ME...!!
'TWAS O-RIKI'S HABIT TO BEAT ME AND FLOG ME WHEN NOBODY WAS ABOUT, AND WHEN MY MOTHER DID DISCOVER THESE MARKS UPON MY BODY, SHE...!!
WHAT?!
FUKU! IS WHAT THE BOY SAYS THE TRUTH?!
SIR MASANARI.

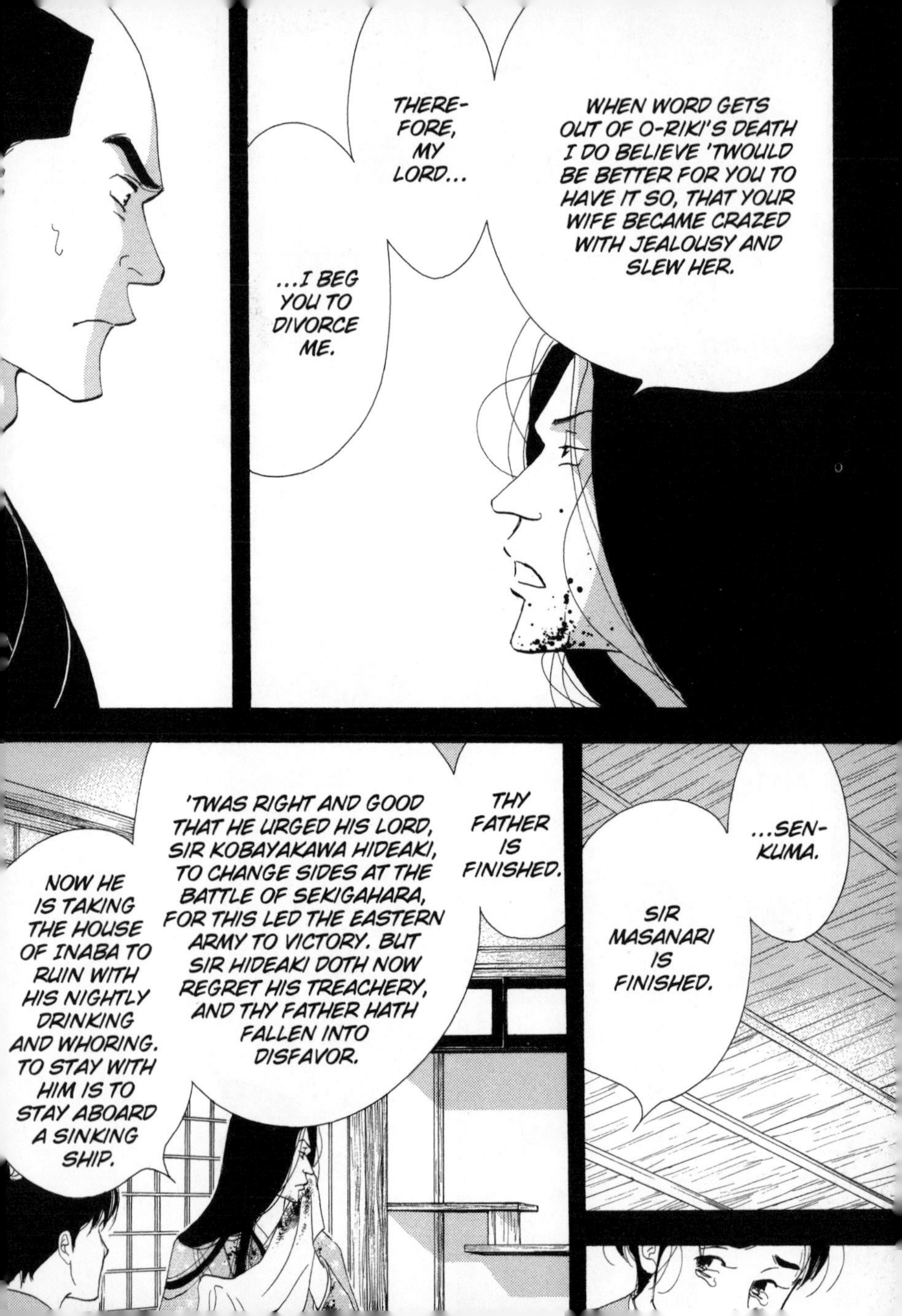
WHEN WORD GETS OUT OF O-RIKI'S DEATH I DO BELIEVE 'TWOULD BE BETTER FOR YOU TO HAVE IT SO, THAT YOUR WIFE BECAME CRAZED WITH JEALOUSY AND SLEW HER.
THERE-FORE, MY LORD...
...I BEG YOU TO DIVORCE ME.
...SEN-KUMA.
SIR MASANARI IS FINISHED.
THY FATHER IS FINISHED.
'TWAS RIGHT AND GOOD THAT HE URGED HIS LORD, SIR KOBAYAKAWA HIDEAKI, TO CHANGE SIDES AT THE BATTLE OF SEKIGAHARA, FOR THIS LED THE EASTERN ARMY TO VICTORY. BUT SIR HIDEAKI DOTH NOW REGRET HIS TREACHERY, AND THY FATHER HATH FALLEN INTO DISFAVOR.
NOW HE IS TAKING THE HOUSE OF INABA TO RUIN WITH HIS NIGHTLY DRINKING AND WHORING. TO STAY WITH HIM IS TO STAY ABOARD A SINKING SHIP.

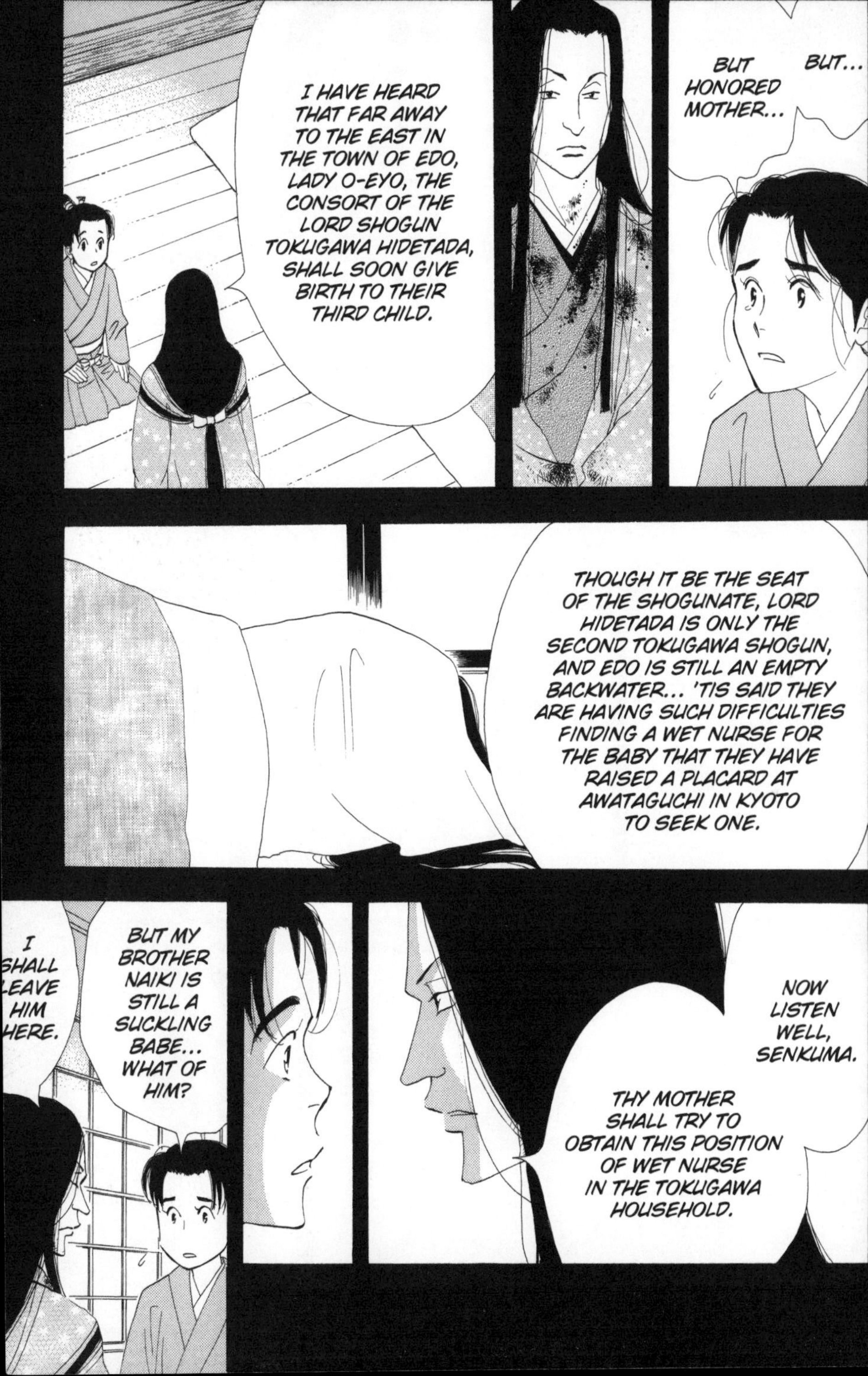
BUT...
BUT HONORED MOTHER...
I HAVE HEARD THAT FAR AWAY TO THE EAST IN THE TOWN OF EDO, LADY O-EYO, THE CONSORT OF THE LORD SHOGUN TOKUGAWA HIDETADA, SHALL SOON GIVE BIRTH TO THEIR THIRD CHILD.
THOUGH IT BE THE SEAT OF THE SHOGUNATE, LORD HIDETADA IS ONLY THE SECOND TOKUGAWA SHOGUN, AND EDO IS STILL AN EMPTY BACKWATER... 'TIS SAID THEY ARE HAVING SUCH DIFFICULTIES FINDING A WET NURSE FOR THE BABY THAT THEY HAVE RAISED A PLACARD AT AWATAGUCHI IN KYOTO TO SEEK ONE.
NOW LISTEN WELL, SENKUMA.
THY MOTHER SHALL TRY TO OBTAIN THIS POSITION OF WET NURSE IN THE TOKUGAWA HOUSEHOLD.
BUT MY BROTHER NAIKI IS STILL A SUCKLING BABE... WHAT OF HIM?
I SHALL LEAVE HIM HERE.

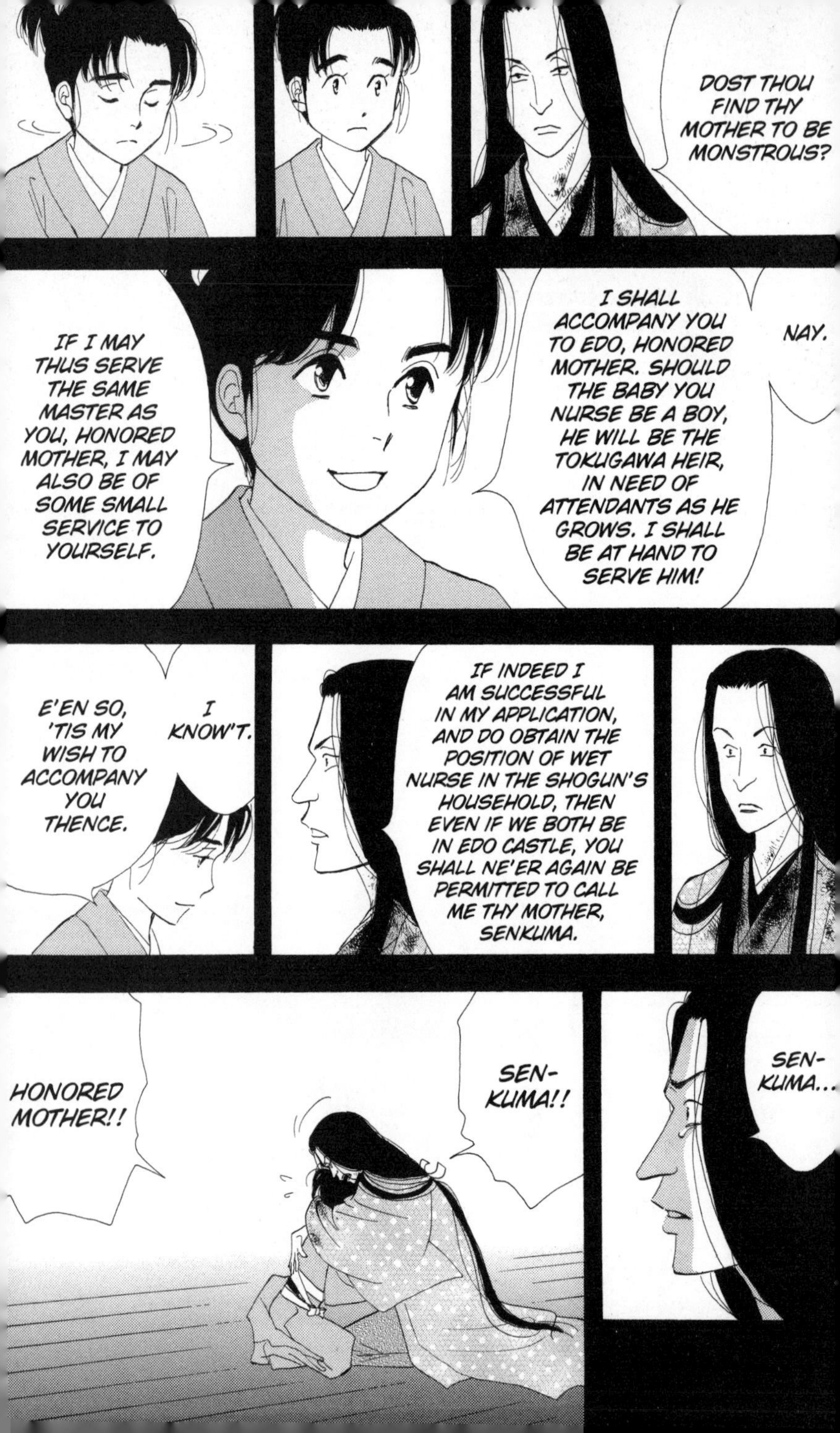
DOST THOU FIND THY MOTHER TO BE MONSTROUS?
NAY.
I SHALL ACCOMPANY YOU TO EDO, HONORED MOTHER. SHOULD THE BABY YOU NURSE BE A BOY, HE WILL BE THE TOKUGAWA HEIR, IN NEED OF ATTENDANTS AS HE GROWS. I SHALL BE AT HAND TO SERVE HIM!
IF I MAY THUS SERVE THE SAME MASTER AS YOU, HONORED MOTHER, I MAY ALSO BE OF SOME SMALL SERVICE TO YOURSELF.
IF INDEED I AM SUCCESSFUL IN MY APPLICATION, AND DO OBTAIN THE POSITION OF WET NURSE IN THE SHOGUN'S HOUSEHOLD, THEN EVEN IF WE BOTH BE IN EDO CASTLE, YOU SHALL NE'ER AGAIN BE PERMITTED TO CALL ME THY MOTHER, SENKUMA.
I KNOW'T.
E'EN SO, 'TIS MY WISH TO ACCOMPANY YOU THENCE.
SEN-KUMA...
SEN-KUMA!!
HONORED MOTHER!!

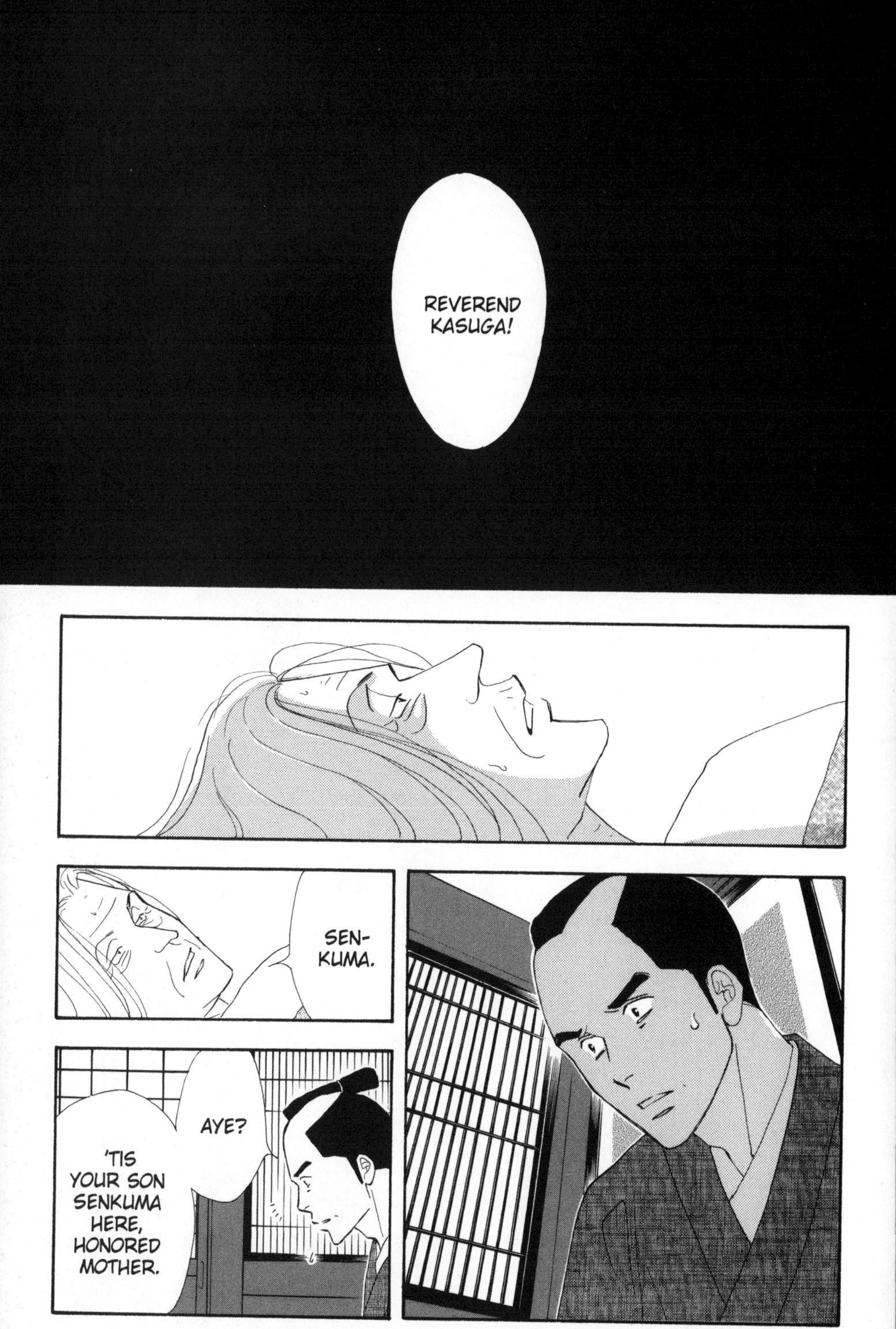
REVEREND KASUGA!
SEN-KUMA.
AYE?
'TIS YOUR SON SENKUMA HERE, HONORED MOTHER.

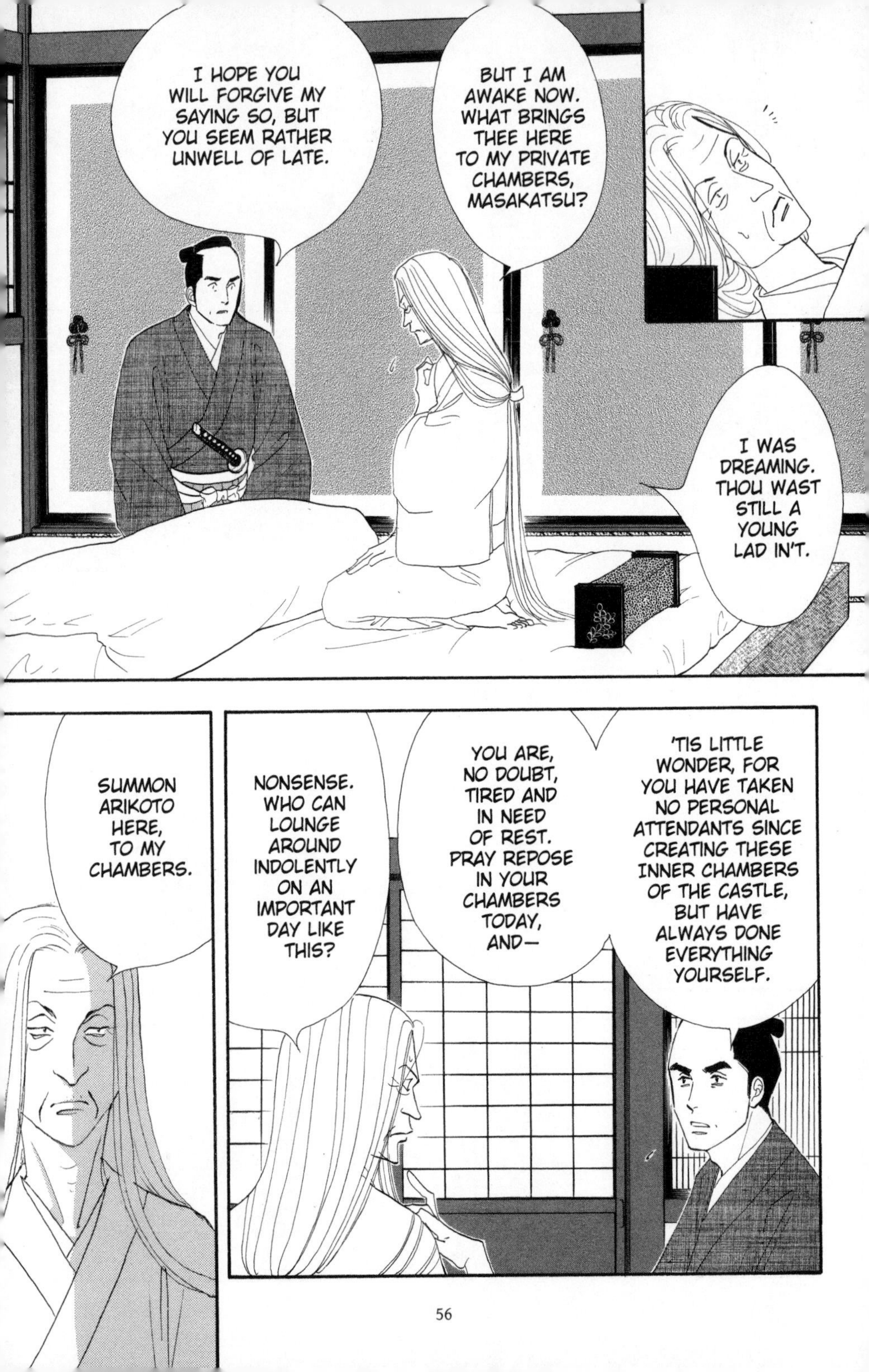
I WAS DREAMING. THOU WAST STILL A YOUNG LAD IN'T.
BUT I AM AWAKE NOW. WHAT BRINGS THEE HERE TO MY PRIVATE CHAMBERS, MASAKATSU?
I HOPE YOU WILL FORGIVE MY SAYING SO, BUT YOU SEEM RATHER UNWELL OF LATE.
'TIS LITTLE WONDER, FOR YOU HAVE TAKEN NO PERSONAL ATTENDANTS SINCE CREATING THESE INNER CHAMBERS OF THE CASTLE, BUT HAVE ALWAYS DONE EVERYTHING YOURSELF.
YOU ARE, NO DOUBT, TIRED AND IN NEED OF REST. PRAY REPOSE IN YOUR CHAMBERS TODAY, AND—
NONSENSE. WHO CAN LOUNGE AROUND INDOLENTLY ON AN IMPORTANT DAY LIKE THIS?
SUMMON ARIKOTO HERE, TO MY CHAMBERS.

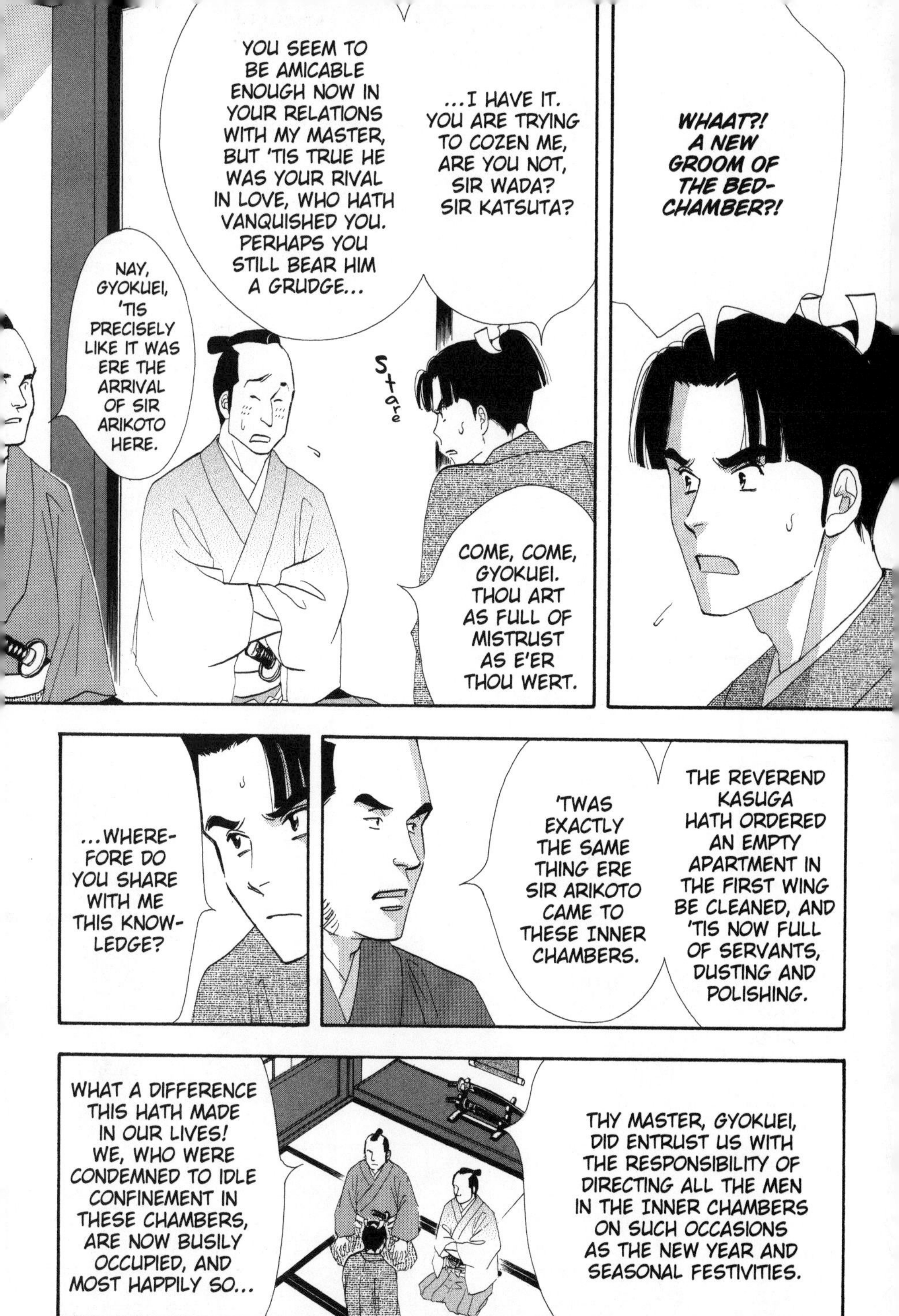
WHAAT?! A NEW GROOM OF THE BED-CHAMBER?!
...I HAVE IT. YOU ARE TRYING TO COZEN ME, ARE YOU NOT, SIR WADA? SIR KATSUTA?
YOU SEEM TO BE AMICABLE ENOUGH NOW IN YOUR RELATIONS WITH MY MASTER, BUT 'TIS TRUE HE WAS YOUR RIVAL IN LOVE, WHO HATH VANQUISHED YOU. PERHAPS YOU STILL BEAR HIM A GRUDGE...
Stare
COME, COME, GYOKUEI. THOU ART AS FULL OF MISTRUST AS E'ER THOU WERT.
NAY, GYOKUEI, 'TIS PRECISELY LIKE IT WAS ERE THE ARRIVAL OF SIR ARIKOTO HERE.
THE REVEREND KASUGA HATH ORDERED AN EMPTY APARTMENT IN THE FIRST WING BE CLEANED, AND 'TIS NOW FULL OF SERVANTS, DUSTING AND POLISHING.
'TWAS EXACTLY THE SAME THING ERE SIR ARIKOTO CAME TO THESE INNER CHAMBERS.
...WHEREFORE DO YOU SHARE WITH ME THIS KNOWLEDGE?
THY MASTER, GYOKUEI, DID ENTRUST US WITH THE RESPONSIBILITY OF DIRECTING ALL THE MEN IN THE INNER CHAMBERS ON SUCH OCCASIONS AS THE NEW YEAR AND SEASONAL FESTIVITIES.
WHAT A DIFFERENCE THIS HATH MADE IN OUR LIVES! WE, WHO WERE CONDEMNED TO IDLE CONFINEMENT IN THESE CHAMBERS, ARE NOW BUSILY OCCUPIED, AND MOST HAPPILY SO...

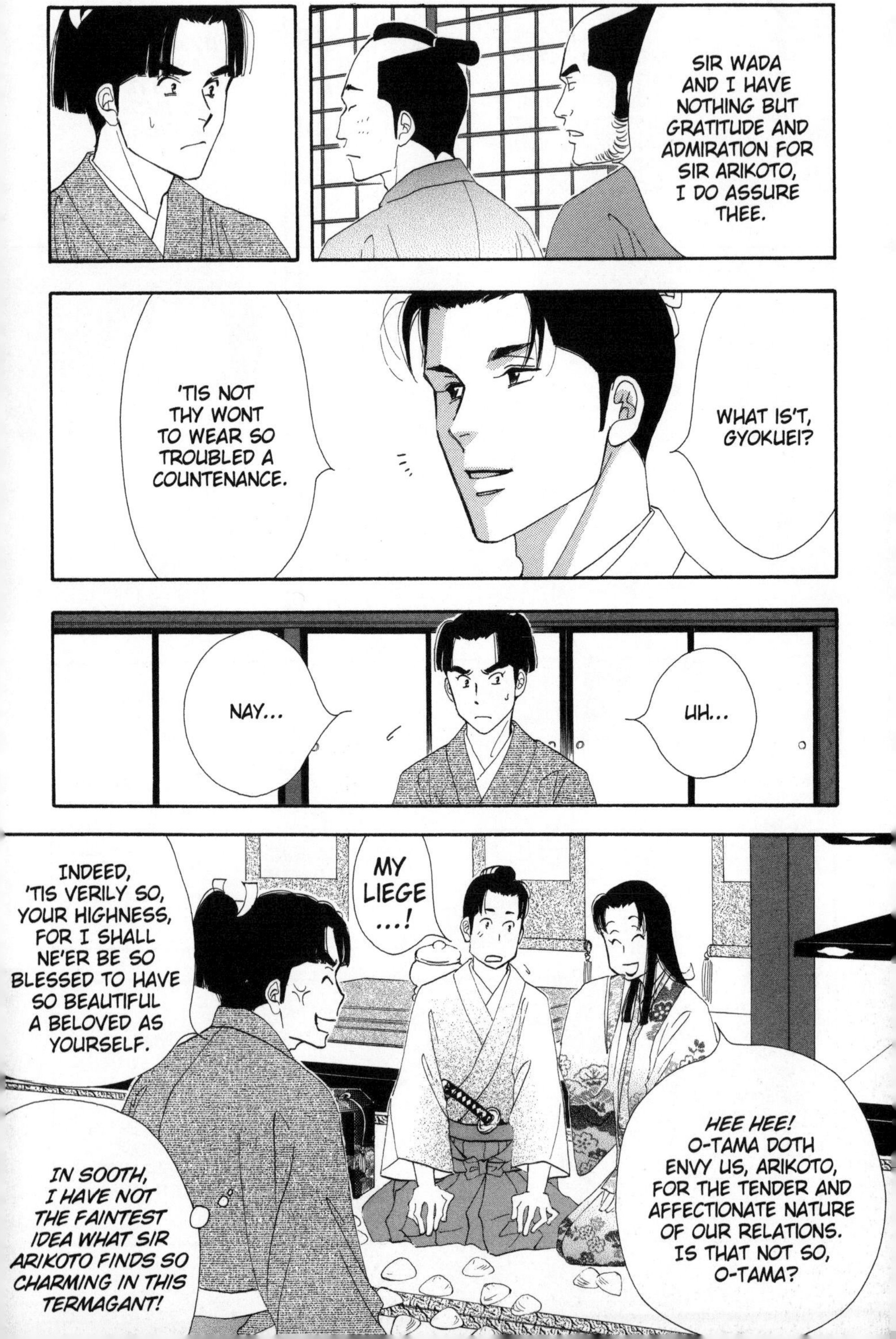
SIR WADA AND I HAVE NOTHING BUT GRATITUDE AND ADMIRATION FOR SIR ARIKOTO, I DO ASSURE THEE.
WHAT IS'T, GYOKUEI?
'TIS NOT THY WONT TO WEAR SO TROUBLED A COUNTENANCE.
UH...
NAY...
HEE HEE! O-TAMA DOTH ENVY US, ARIKOTO, FOR THE TENDER AND AFFECTIONATE NATURE OF OUR RELATIONS. IS THAT NOT SO, O-TAMA?
MY LIEGE ...!
INDEED, 'TIS VERILY SO, YOUR HIGHNESS, FOR I SHALL NE'ER BE SO BLESSED TO HAVE SO BEAUTIFUL A BELOVED AS YOURSELF.
IN SOOTH, I HAVE NOT THE FAINTEST IDEA WHAT SIR ARIKOTO FINDS SO CHARMING IN THIS TERMAGANT!

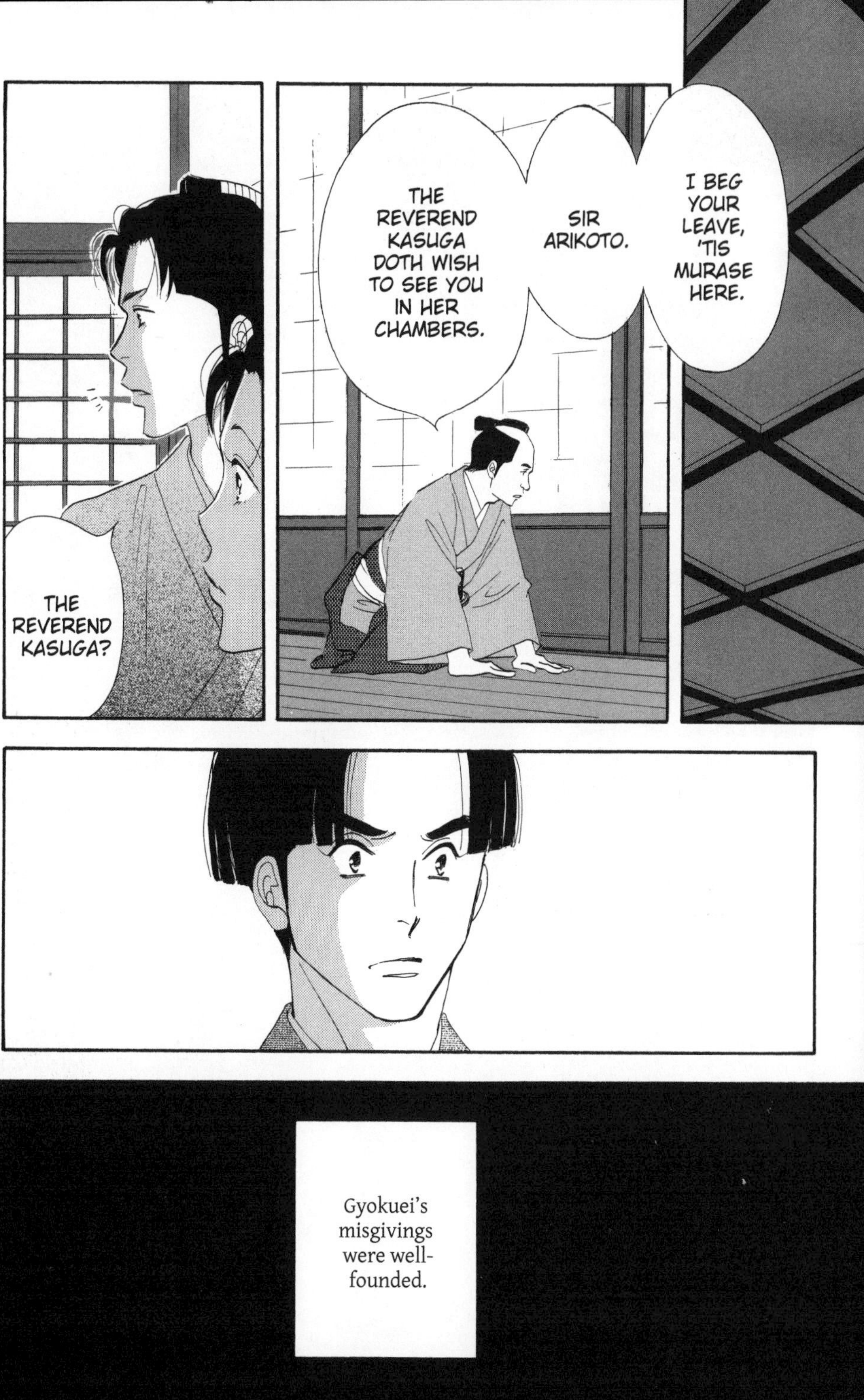
I BEG YOUR LEAVE, 'TIS MURASE HERE.
SIR ARIKOTO.
THE REVEREND KASUGA DOTH WISH TO SEE YOU IN HER CHAMBERS.
THE REVEREND KASUGA?
Gyokuei's misgivings were well-founded.

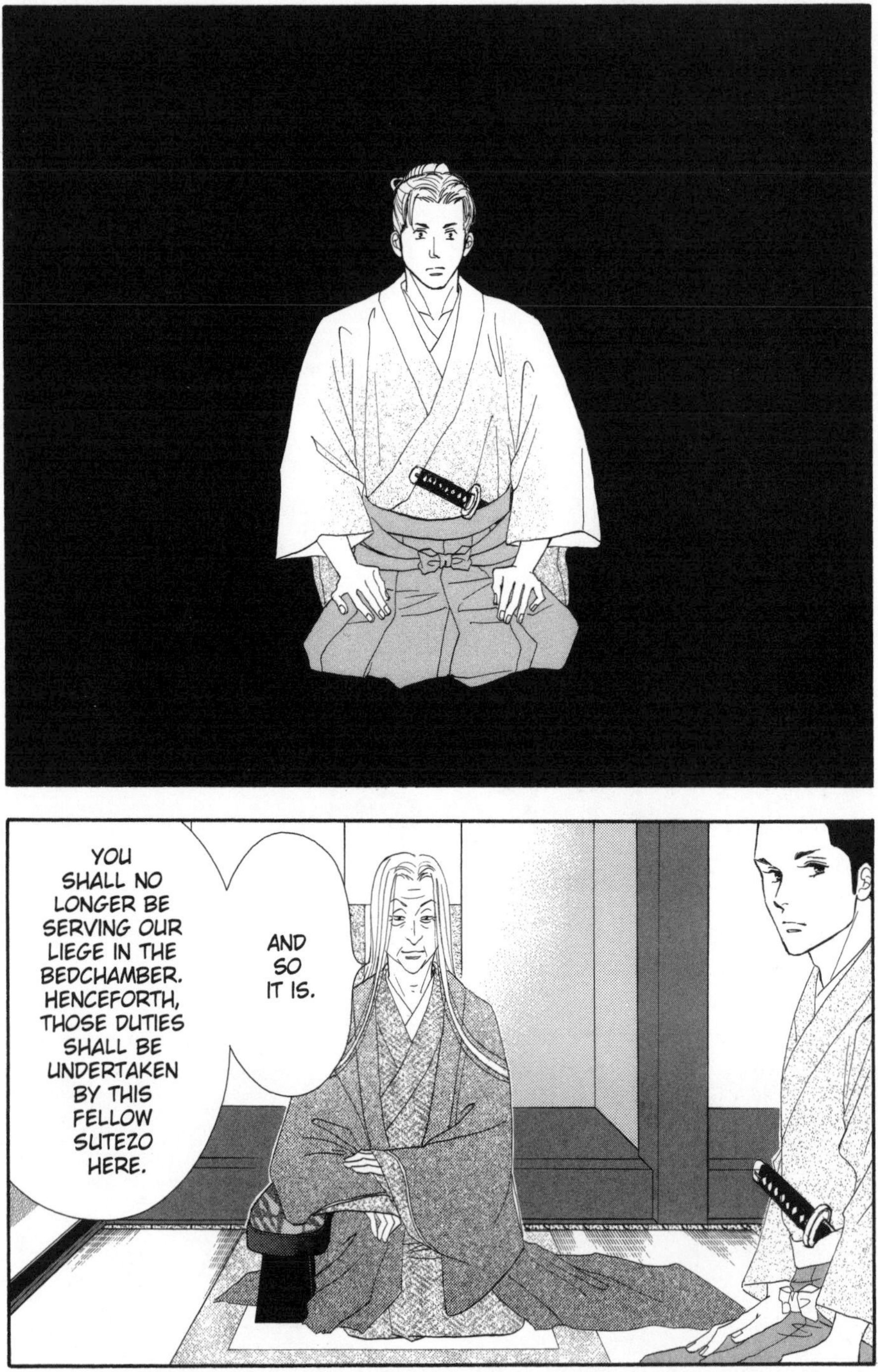
AND SO IT IS.
YOU SHALL NO LONGER BE SERVING OUR LIEGE IN THE BEDCHAMBER. HENCEFORTH, THOSE DUTIES SHALL BE UNDERTAKEN BY THIS FELLOW SUTEZO HERE.

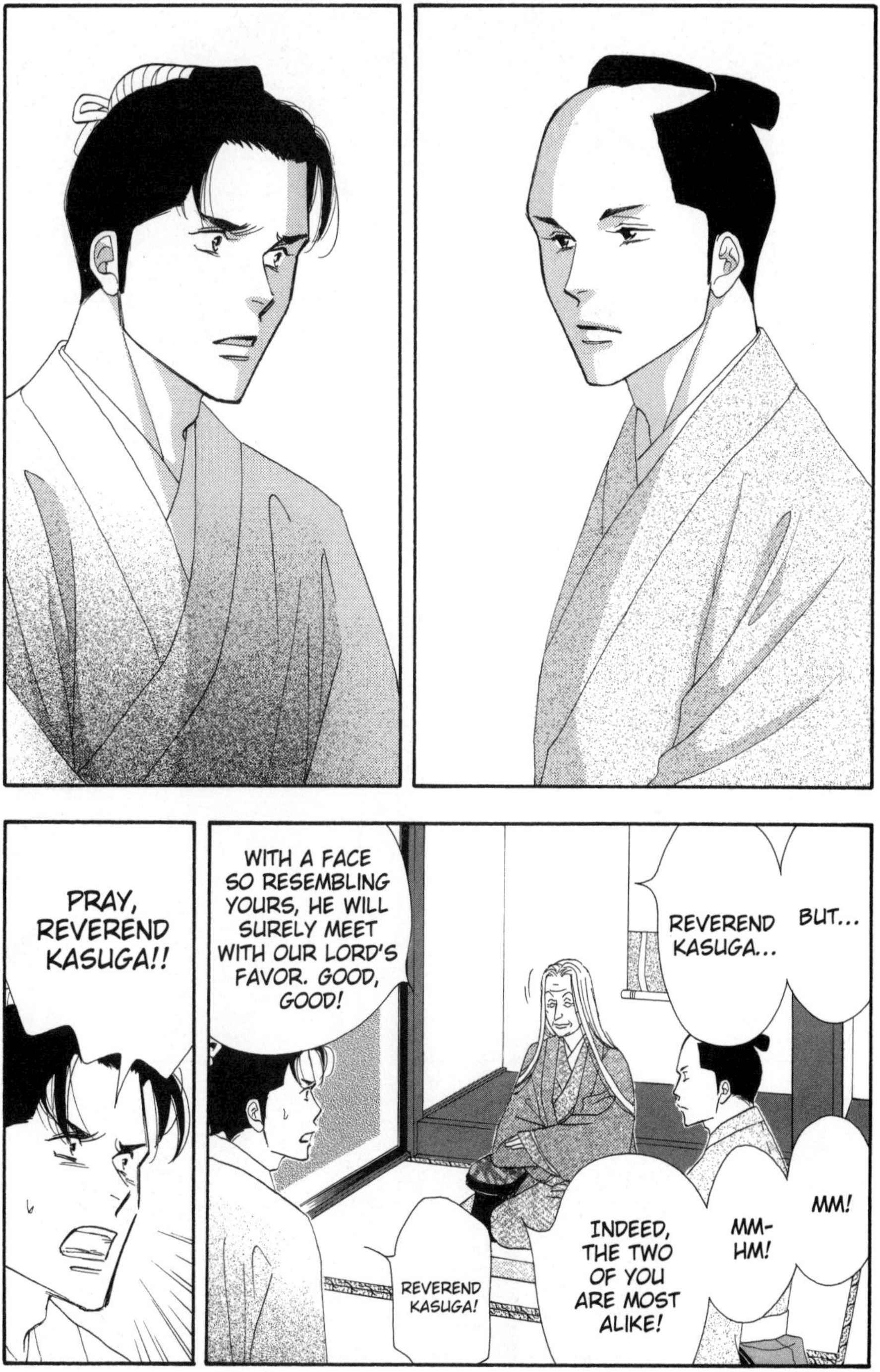
BUT...
REVEREND KASUGA...
WITH A FACE SO RESEMBLING YOURS, HE WILL SURELY MEET WITH OUR LORD'S FAVOR. GOOD, GOOD!
MM!
MM-HM!
INDEED, THE TWO OF YOU ARE MOST ALIKE!
REVEREND KASUGA!
PRAY, REVEREND KASUGA!!

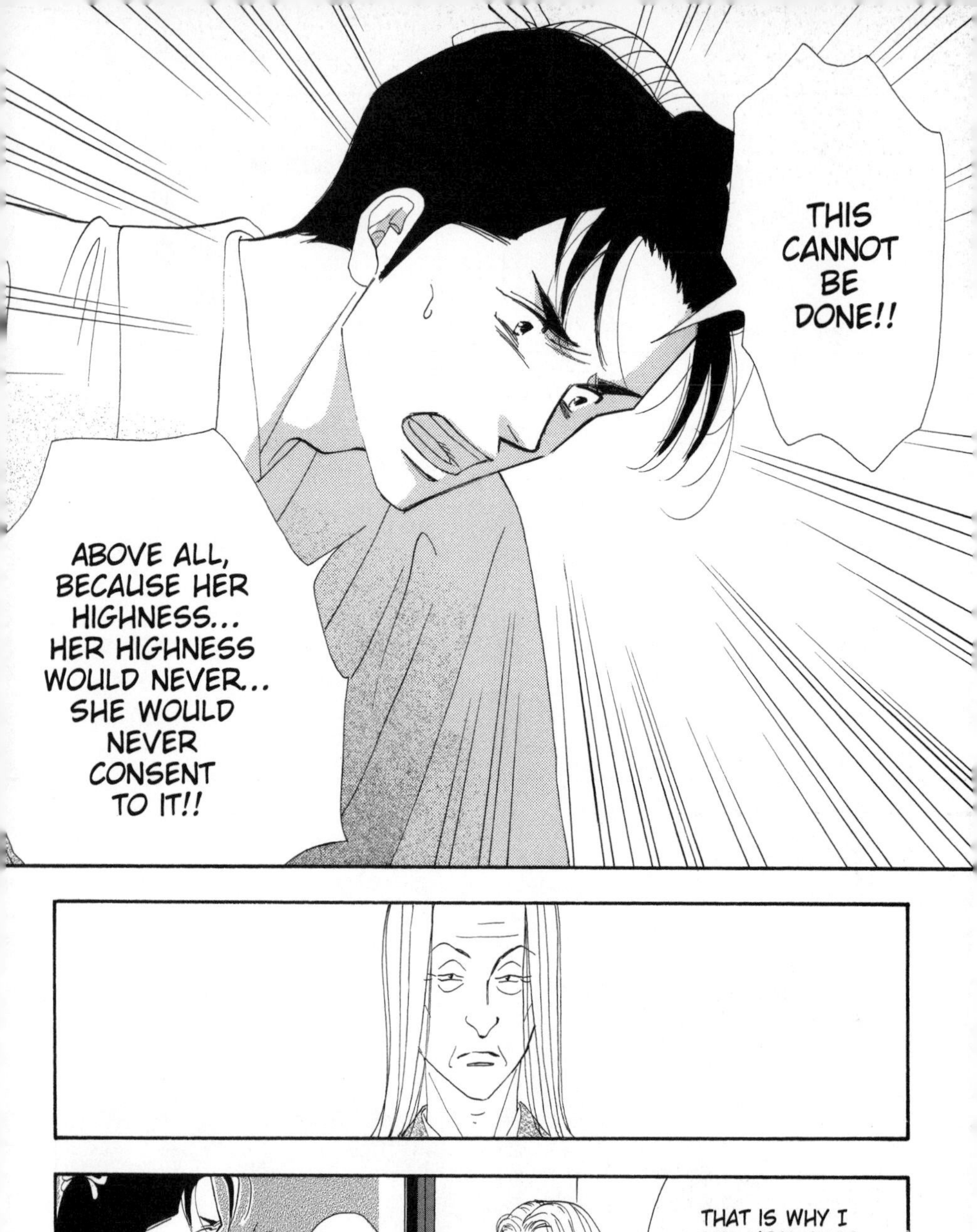
THIS CANNOT BE DONE!!
ABOVE ALL, BECAUSE HER HIGHNESS... HER HIGHNESS WOULD NEVER... SHE WOULD NEVER CONSENT TO IT!!
THAT IS WHY I SAID *YOU* MUST PETITION HER TO BE EXCUSED FROM NIGHTTIME INTIMACIES WITH HER. *YOU* MUST BEG TO BE REPLACED.
!!

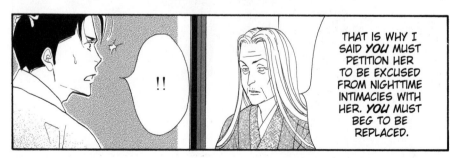

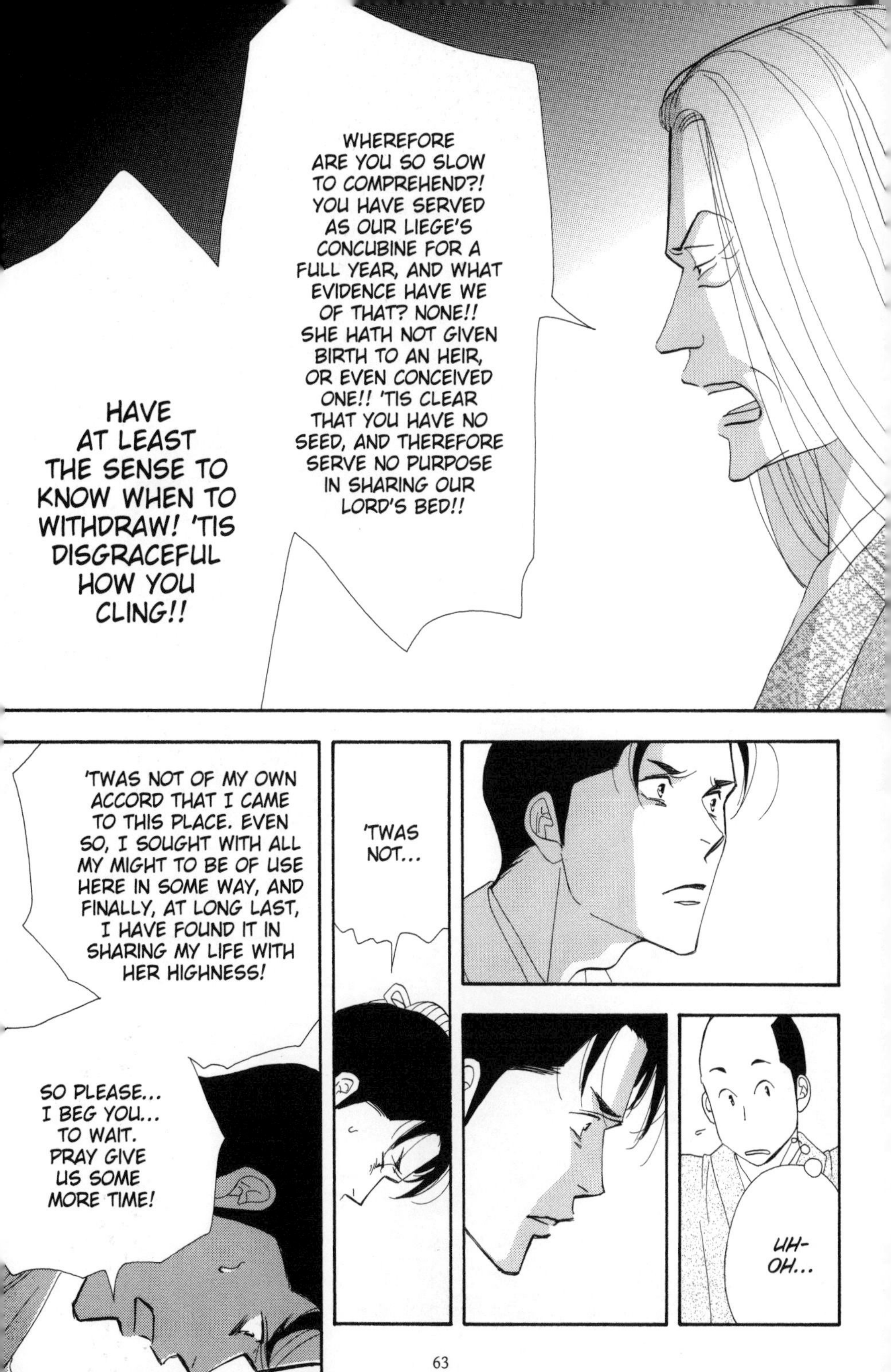
WHEREFORE ARE YOU SO SLOW TO COMPREHEND?! YOU HAVE SERVED AS OUR LIEGE'S CONCUBINE FOR A FULL YEAR, AND WHAT EVIDENCE HAVE WE OF THAT? NONE!! SHE HATH NOT GIVEN BIRTH TO AN HEIR, OR EVEN CONCEIVED ONE!! 'TIS CLEAR THAT YOU HAVE NO SEED, AND THEREFORE SERVE NO PURPOSE IN SHARING OUR LORD'S BED!!
HAVE AT LEAST THE SENSE TO KNOW WHEN TO WITHDRAW! 'TIS DISGRACEFUL HOW YOU CLING!!
'TWAS NOT...
UH-OH...
'TWAS NOT OF MY OWN ACCORD THAT I CAME TO THIS PLACE. EVEN SO, I SOUGHT WITH ALL MY MIGHT TO BE OF USE HERE IN SOME WAY, AND FINALLY, AT LONG LAST, I HAVE FOUND IT IN SHARING MY LIFE WITH HER HIGHNESS!
SO PLEASE... I BEG YOU... TO WAIT. PRAY GIVE US SOME MORE TIME!

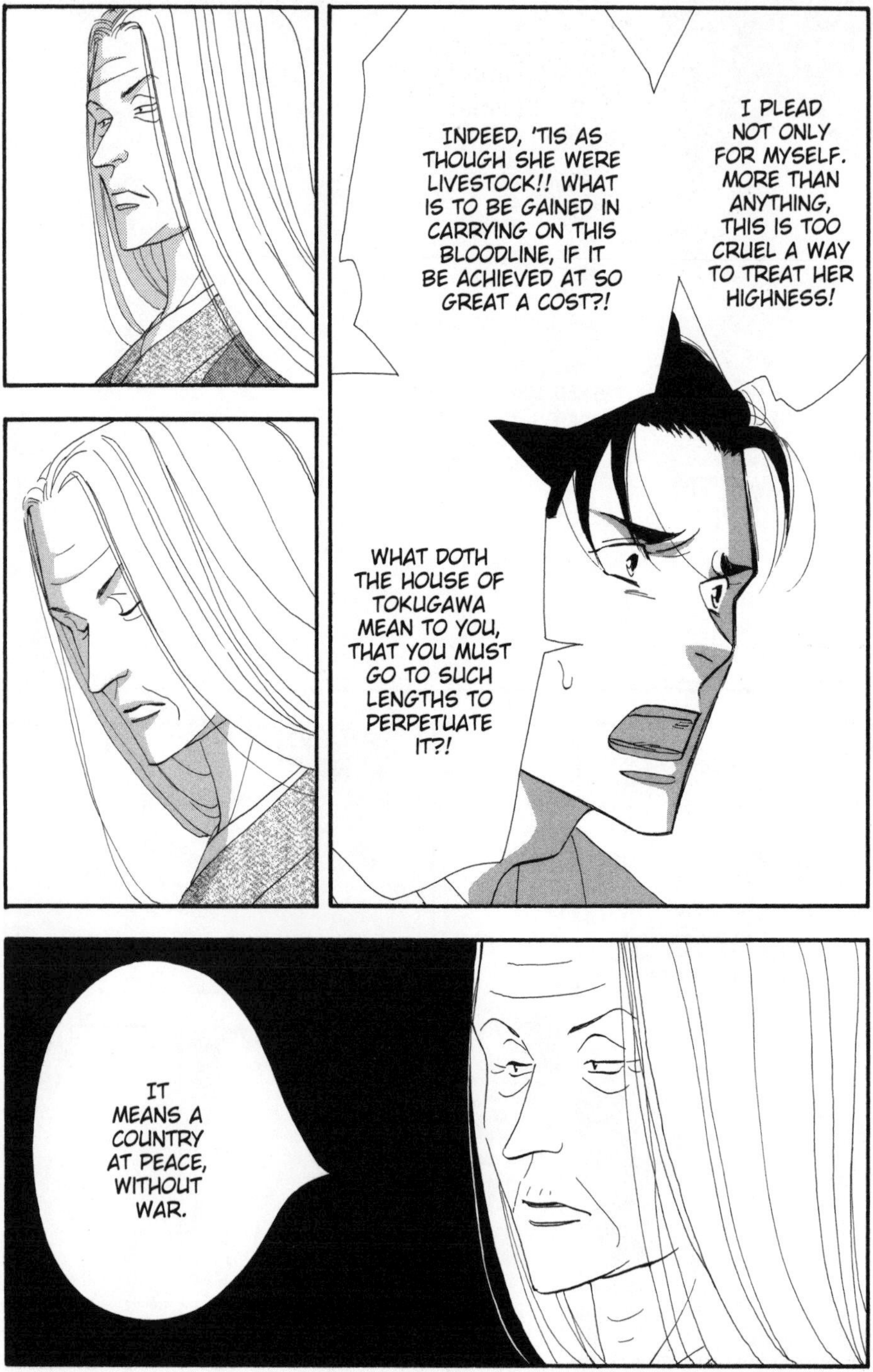
I PLEAD NOT ONLY FOR MYSELF. MORE THAN ANYTHING, THIS IS TOO CRUEL A WAY TO TREAT HER HIGHNESS!
INDEED, 'TIS AS THOUGH SHE WERE LIVESTOCK!! WHAT IS TO BE GAINED IN CARRYING ON THIS BLOODLINE, IF IT BE ACHIEVED AT SO GREAT A COST?!
WHAT DOTH THE HOUSE OF TOKUGAWA MEAN TO YOU, THAT YOU MUST GO TO SUCH LENGTHS TO PERPETUATE IT?!
IT MEANS A COUNTRY AT PEACE, WITHOUT WAR.

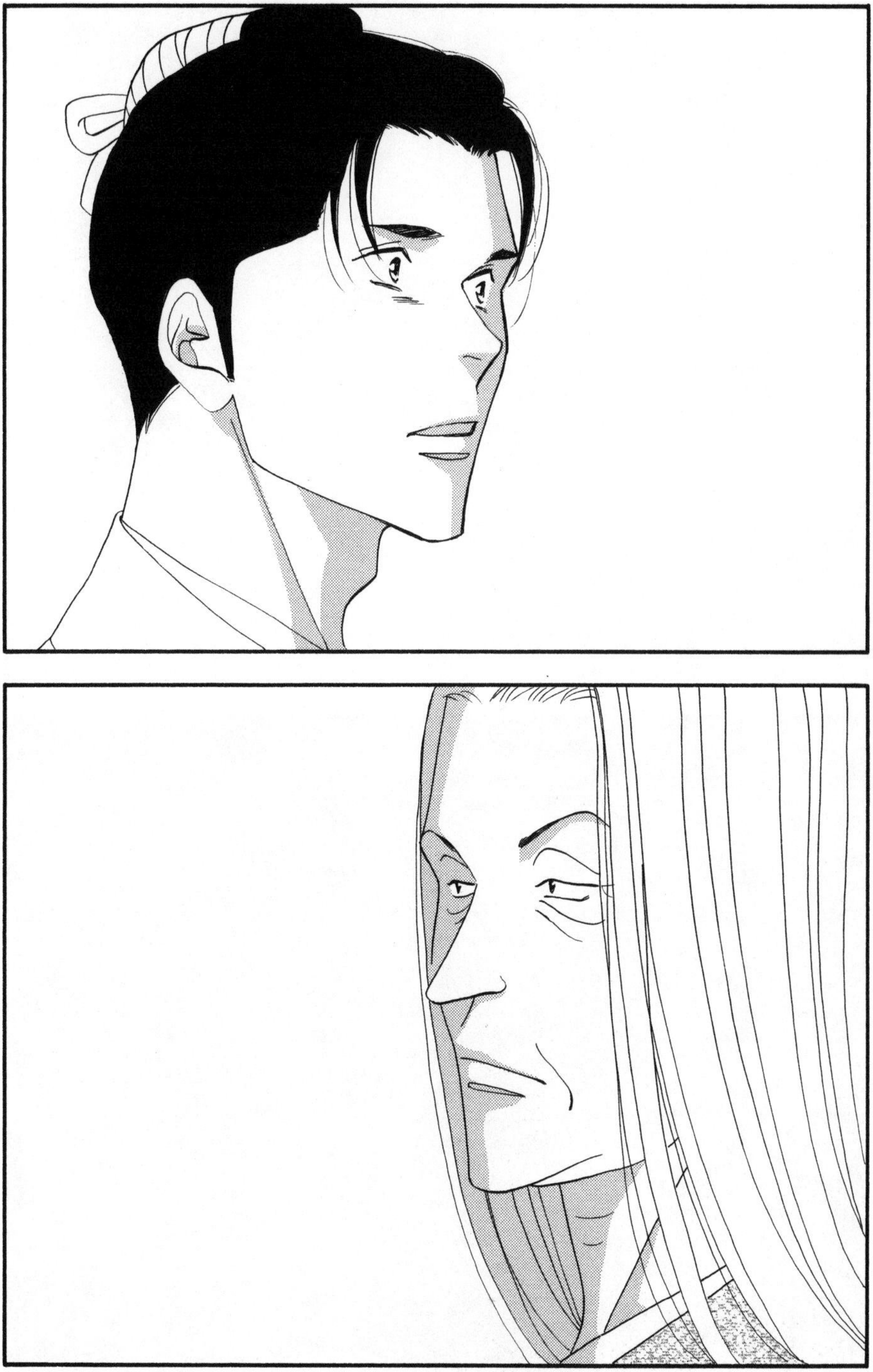

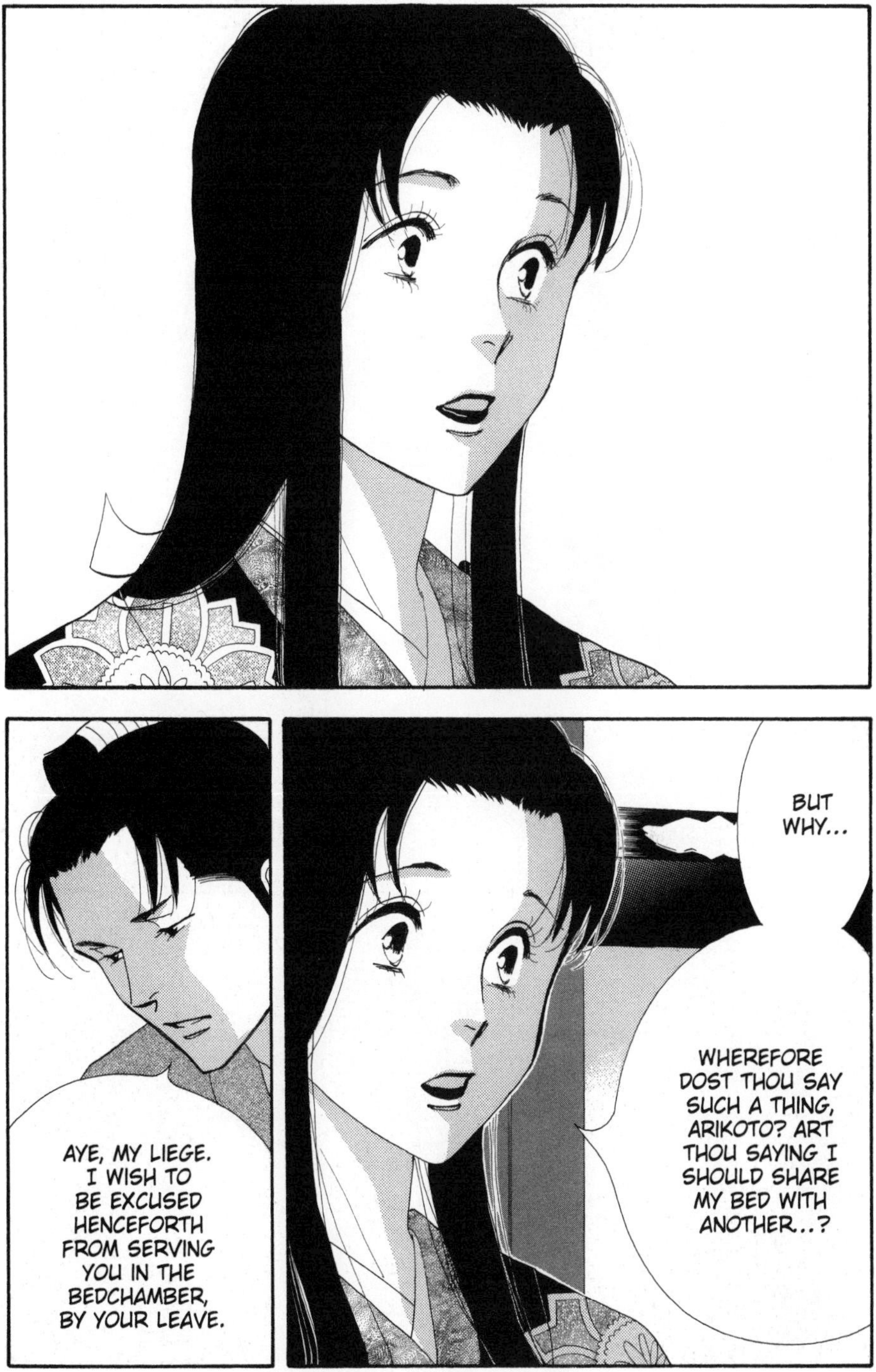
BUT WHY...
WHEREFORE DOST THOU SAY SUCH A THING, ARIKOTO? ART THOU SAYING I SHOULD SHARE MY BED WITH ANOTHER...?
AYE, MY LIEGE. I WISH TO BE EXCUSED HENCEFORTH FROM SERVING YOU IN THE BEDCHAMBER, BY YOUR LEAVE.

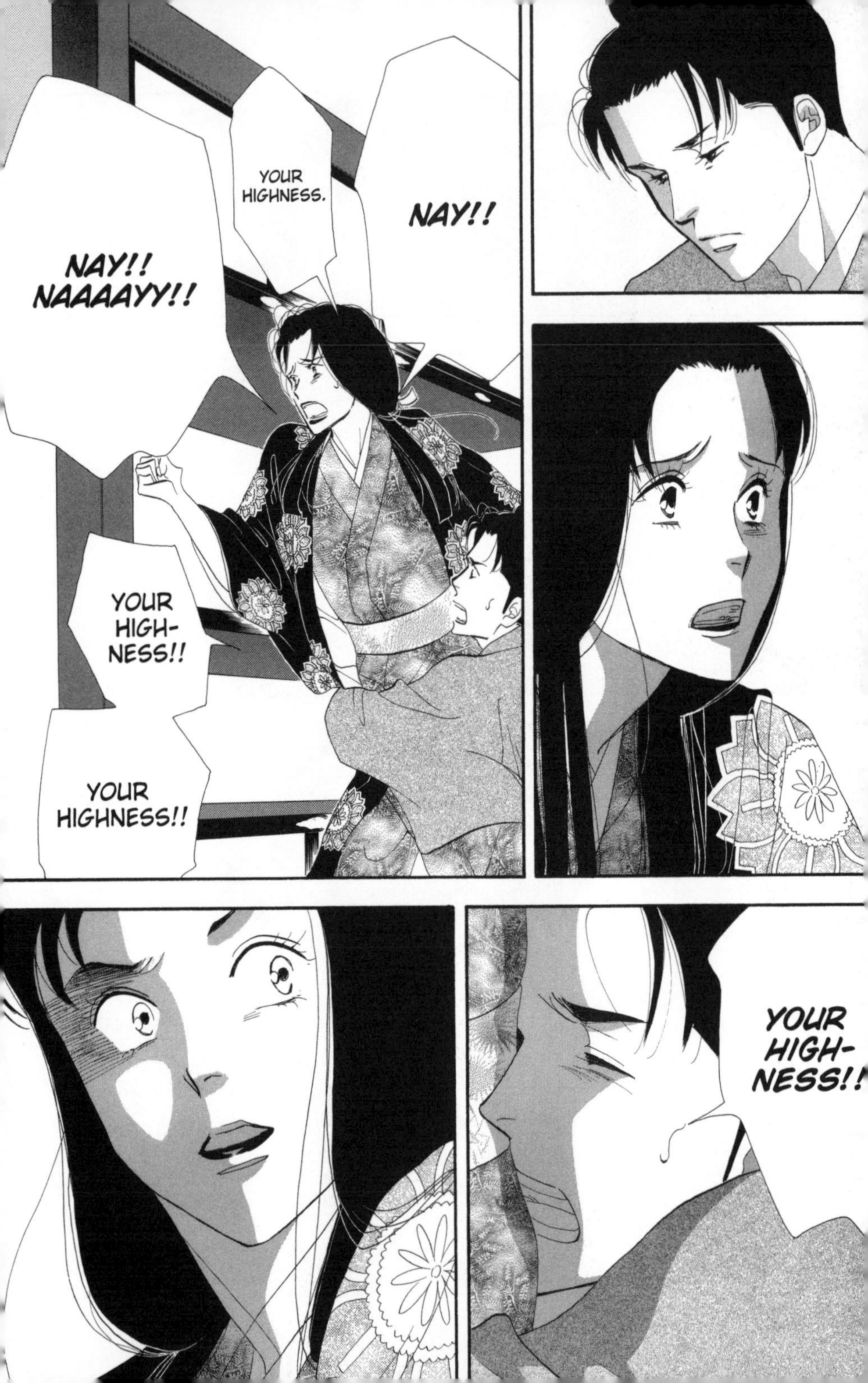
NAY!!
YOUR HIGHNESS.
NAY!! NAAAAYY!!
YOUR HIGH-NESS!!
YOUR HIGHNESS!!
YOUR HIGH-NESS!!

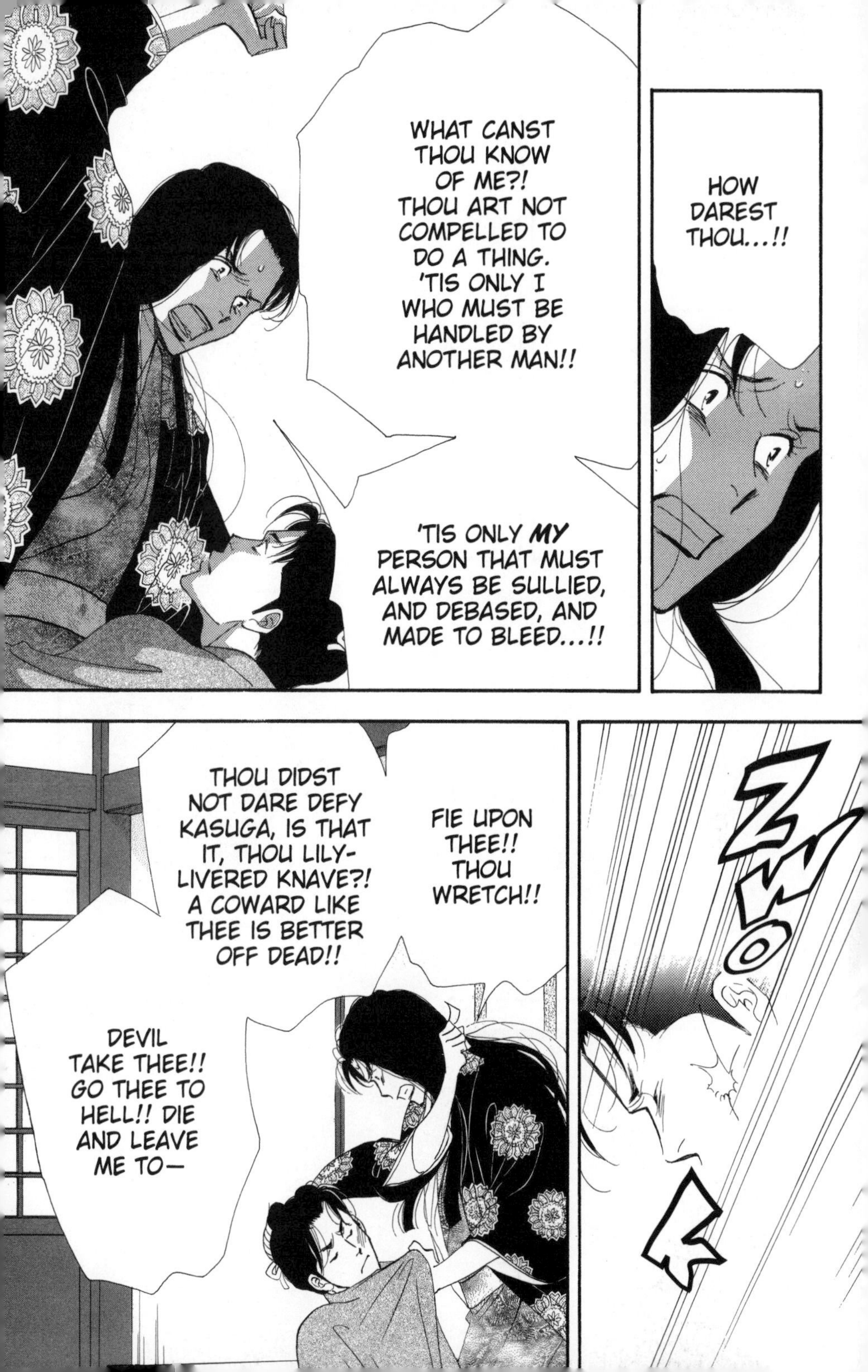
HOW DARESTTHOU...!!
WHAT CANST THOU KNOW OF ME?! THOU ART NOT COMPELLED TO DO A THING. 'TIS ONLY I WHO MUST BE HANDLED BY ANOTHER MAN!!
'TIS ONLY *MY* PERSON THAT MUST ALWAYS BE SULLIED, AND DEBASED, AND MADE TO BLEED...!!
ZWOK
FIE UPON THEE!! THOU WRETCH!!
THOU DIDST NOT DARE DEFY KASUGA, IS THAT IT, THOU LILY-LIVERED KNAVE?! A COWARD LIKE THEE IS BETTER OFF DEAD!!
DEVIL TAKE THEE!! GO THEE TO HELL!! DIE AND LEAVE ME TO—

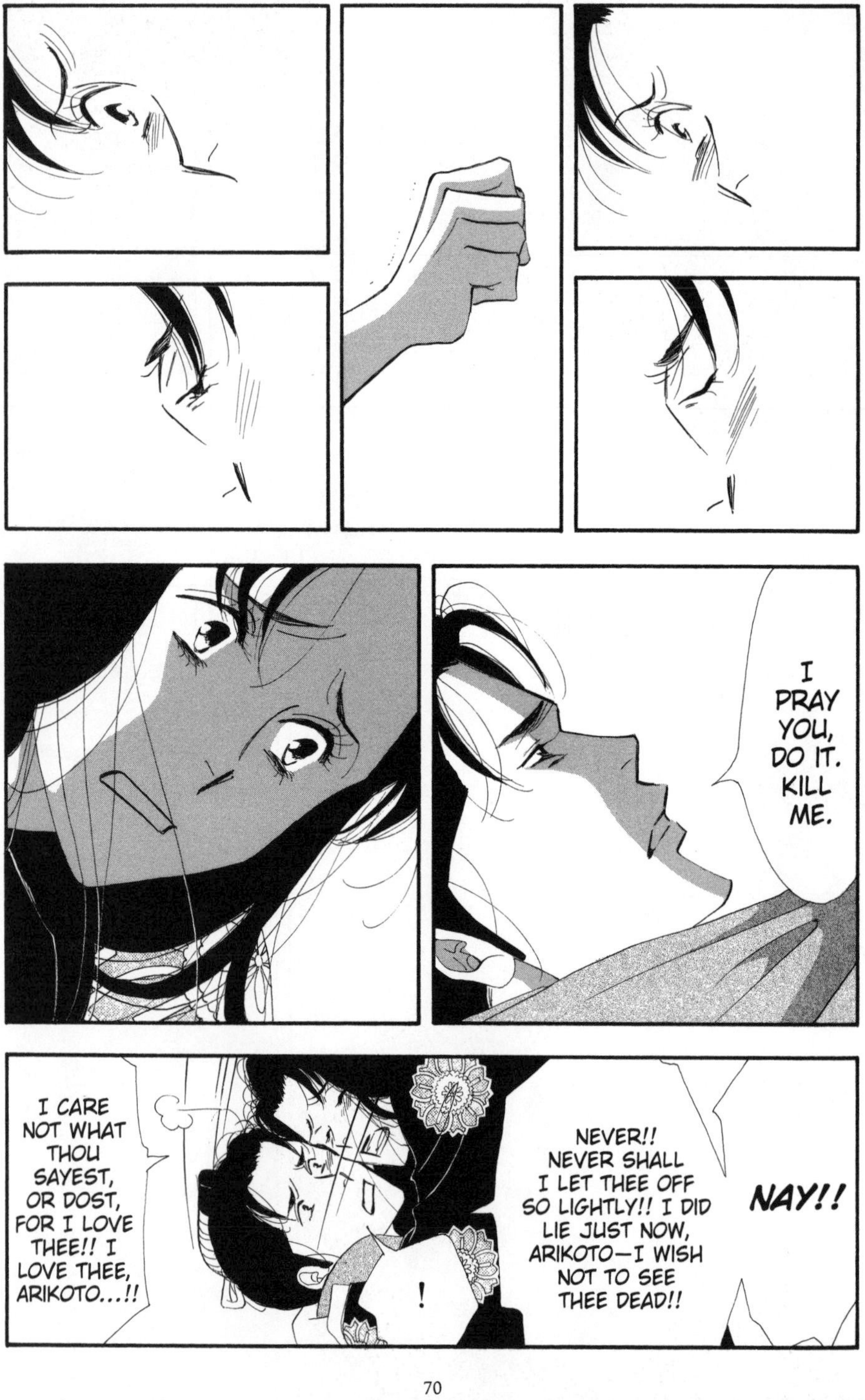
I PRAY YOU, DO IT. KILL ME.
NAY!!
NEVER!! NEVER SHALL I LET THEE OFF SO LIGHTLY!! I DID LIE JUST NOW, ARIKOTO—I WISH NOT TO SEE THEE DEAD!!
!
I CARE NOT WHAT THOU SAYEST, OR DOST, FOR I LOVE THEE!! I LOVE THEE, ARIKOTO...!!

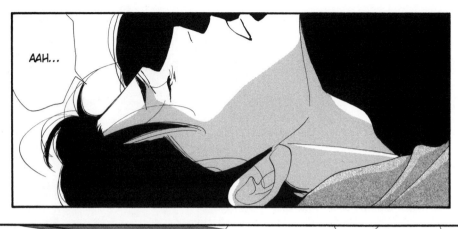

AAH...

AND I YOU, MY LIEGE...

OH, I AM TRULY HEARTLESS! NO MATTER HOW MUCH SUFFERING YOU MUST ENDURE, I WISH YOU TO ENDURE IT AND LIVE!

IF I AM TOLD THAT CONTINUING THE REIGN OF THE TOKUGAWA BE YOUR ONLY WAY FORWARD, THEN I HAVE NO CHOICE BUT TO COMPLY...!!

ARIKOTO!

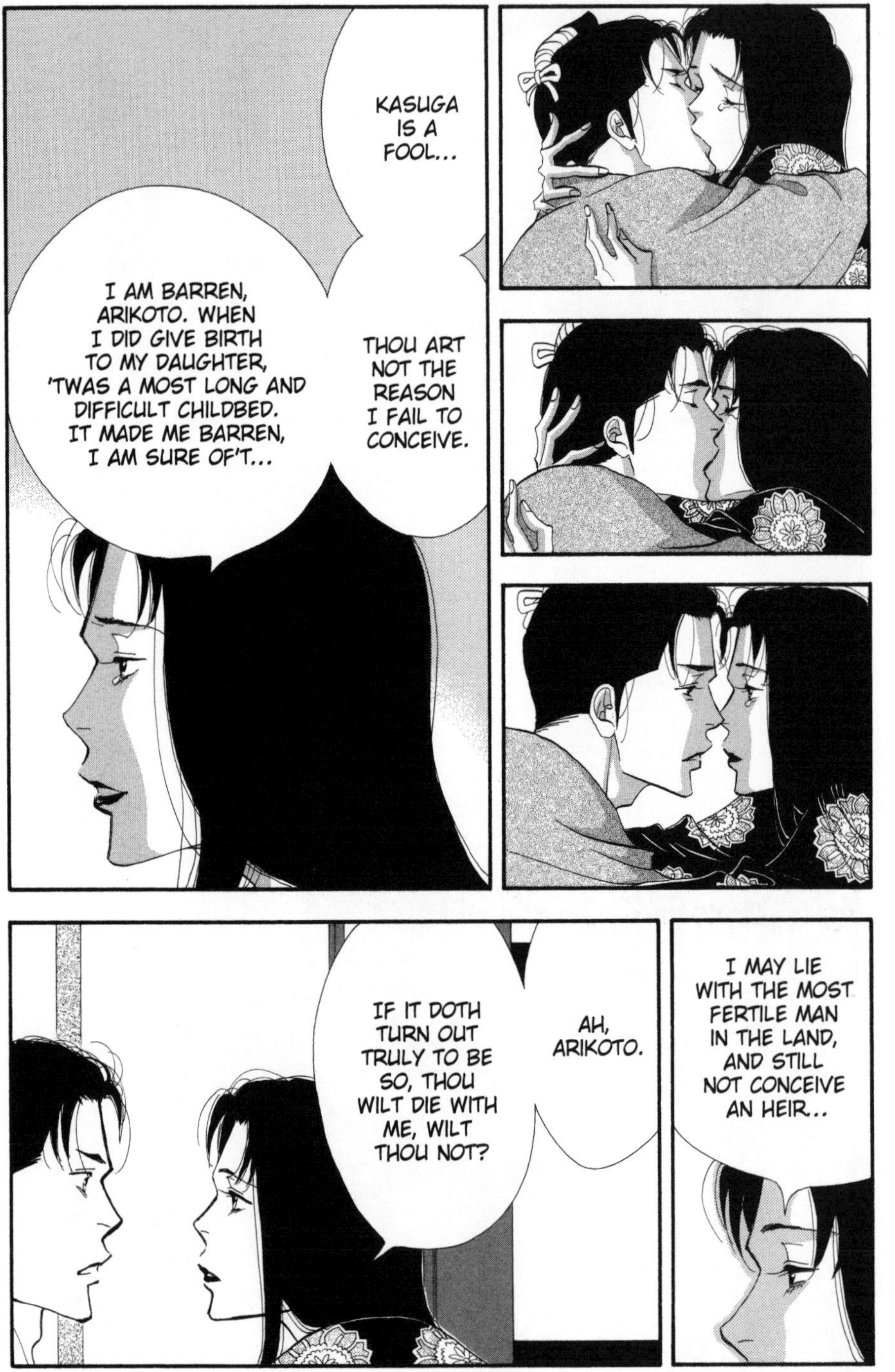
KASUGA IS A FOOL...
THOU ART NOT THE REASON I FAIL TO CONCEIVE.
I AM BARREN, ARIKOTO. WHEN I DID GIVE BIRTH TO MY DAUGHTER, 'TWAS A MOST LONG AND DIFFICULT CHILDBED. IT MADE ME BARREN, I AM SURE OF'T...
I MAY LIE WITH THE MOST FERTILE MAN IN THE LAND, AND STILL NOT CONCEIVE AN HEIR...
AH, ARIKOTO.
IF IT DOTH TURN OUT TRULY TO BE SO, THOU WILT DIE WITH ME, WILT THOU NOT?

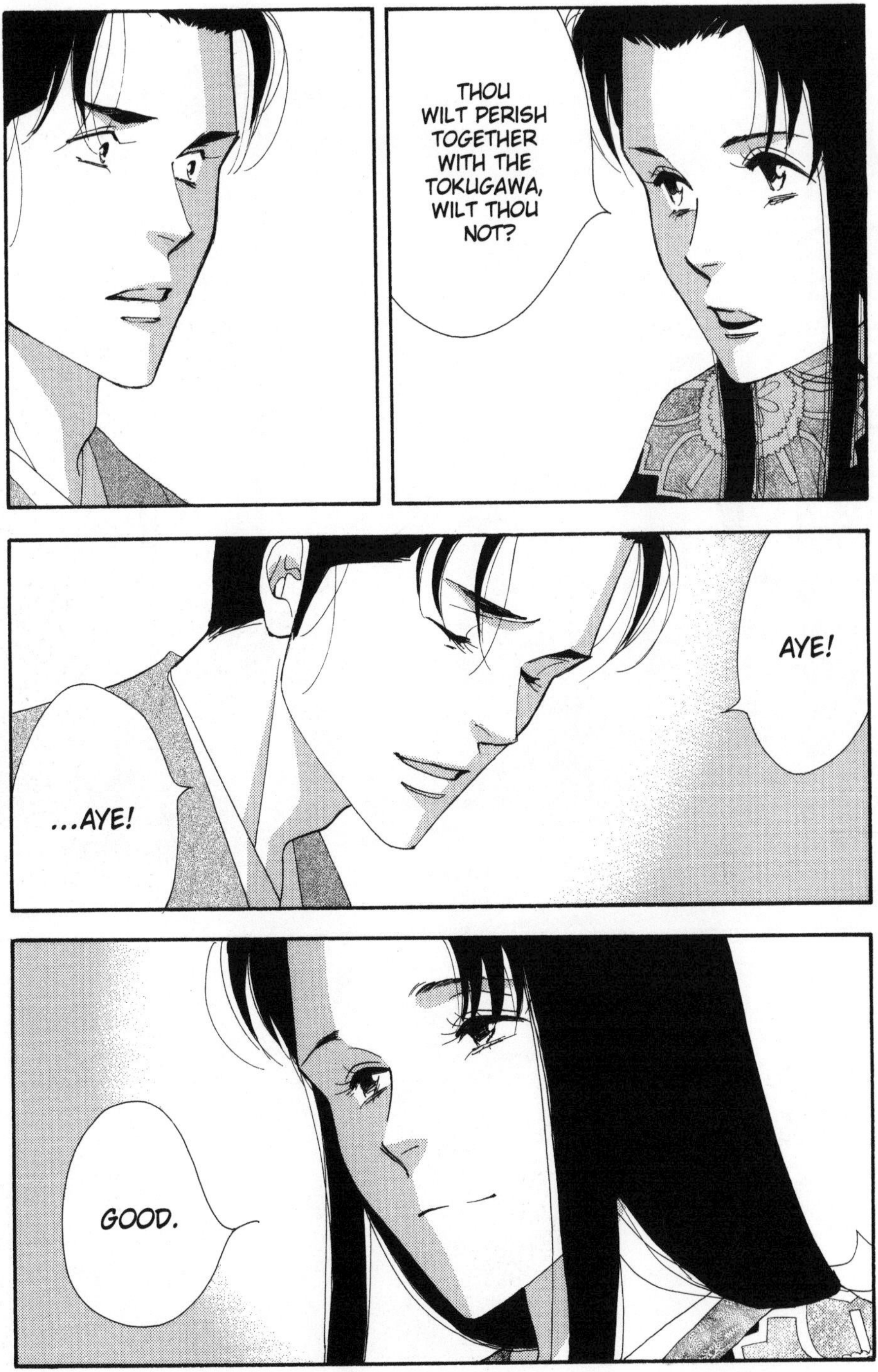
THOU WILT PERISH TOGETHER WITH THE TOKUGAWA, WILT THOU NOT?
AYE!
...AYE!
GOOD.

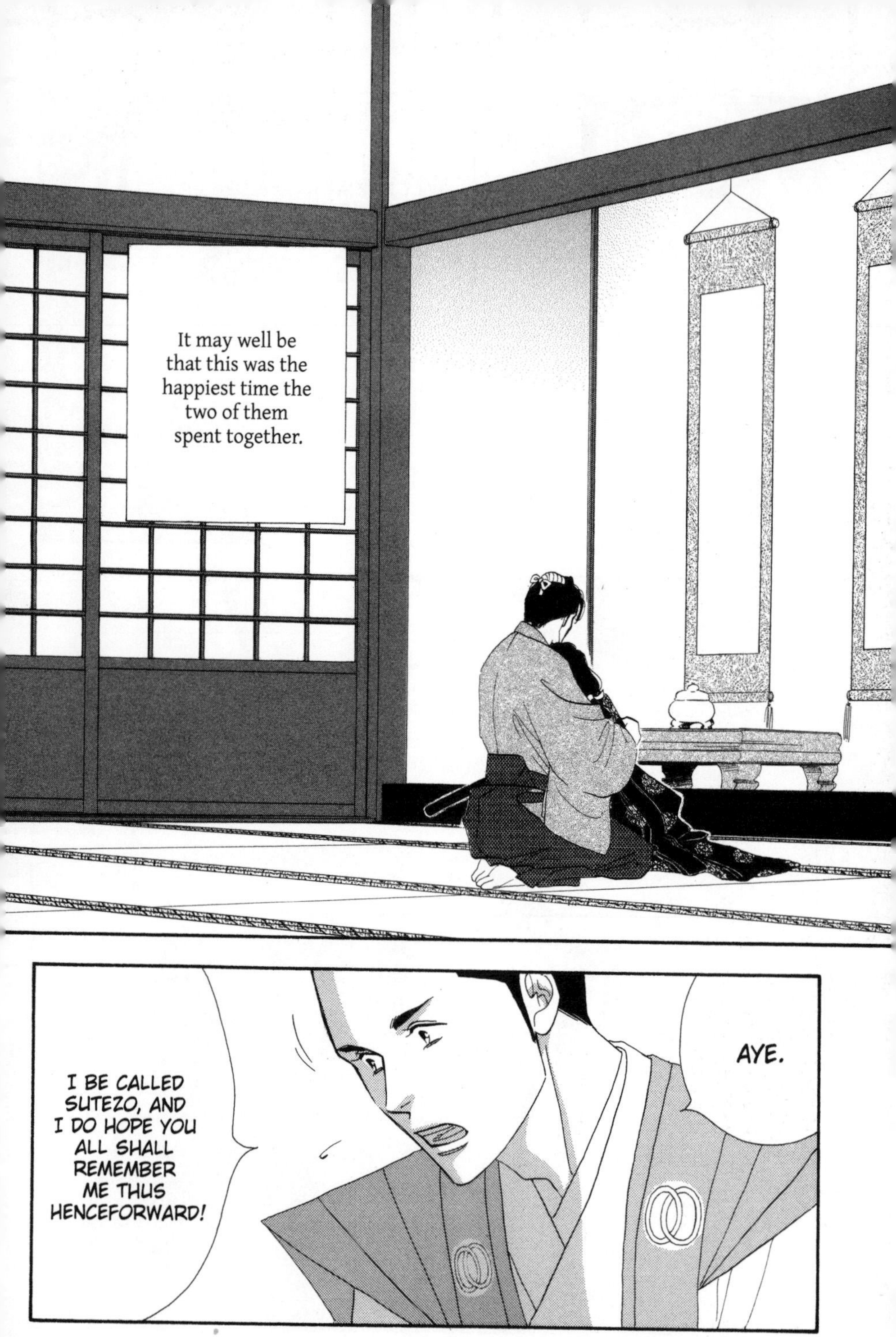
It may well be that this was the happiest time the two of them spent together.
AYE.
I BE CALLED SUTEZO, AND I DO HOPE YOU ALL SHALL REMEMBER ME THUS HENCEFORWARD!

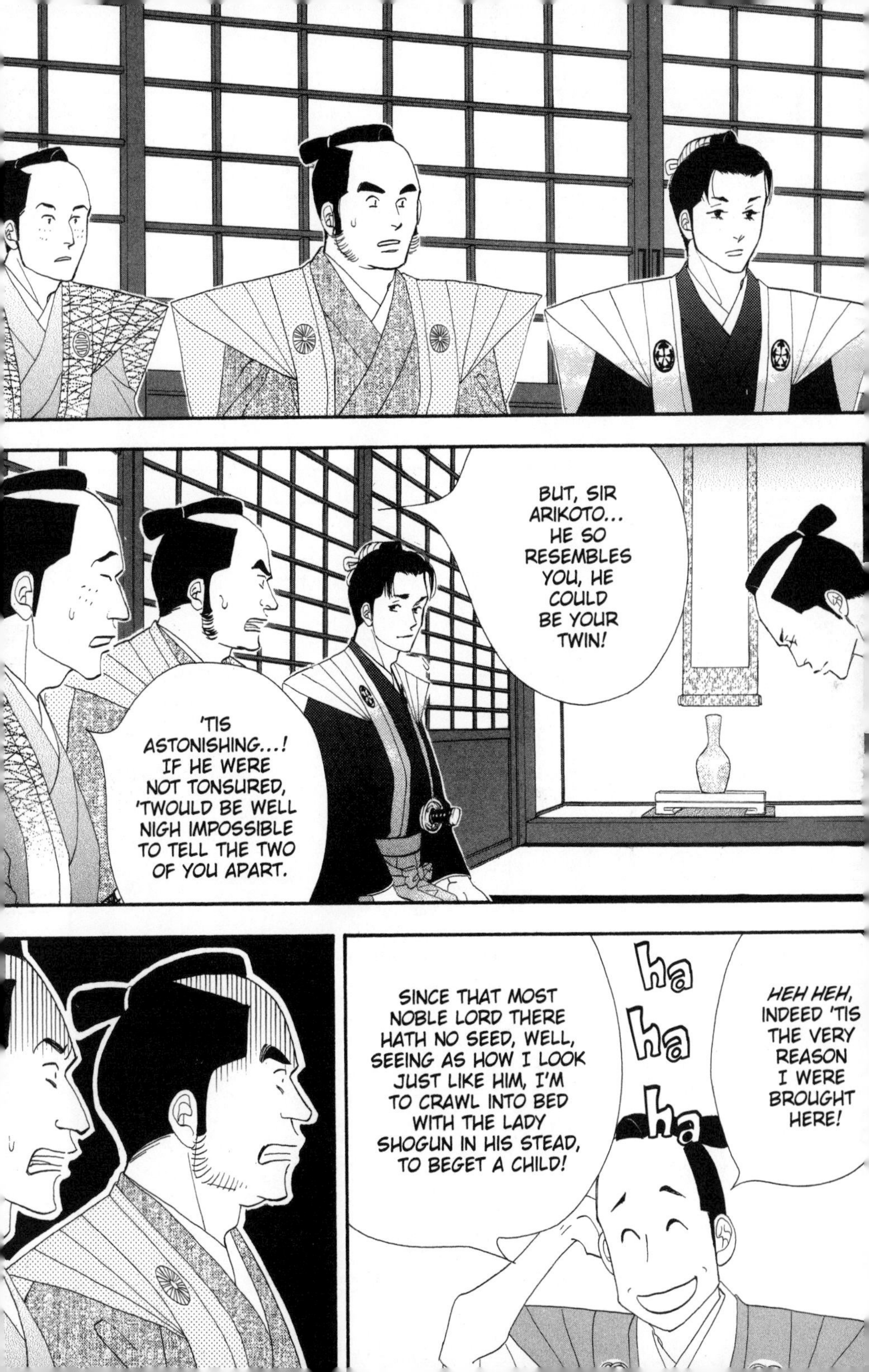
BUT, SIR ARIKOTO... HE SO RESEMBLES YOU, HE COULD BE YOUR TWIN!
'TIS ASTONISHING...! IF HE WERE NOT TONSURED, 'TWOULD BE WELL NIGH IMPOSSIBLE TO TELL THE TWO OF YOU APART.
HEH HEH, INDEED 'TIS THE VERY REASON I WERE BROUGHT HERE!
ha ha ha
SINCE THAT MOST NOBLE LORD THERE HATH NO SEED, WELL, SEEING AS HOW I LOOK JUST LIKE HIM, I'M TO CRAWL INTO BED WITH THE LADY SHOGUN IN HIS STEAD, TO BEGET A CHILD!

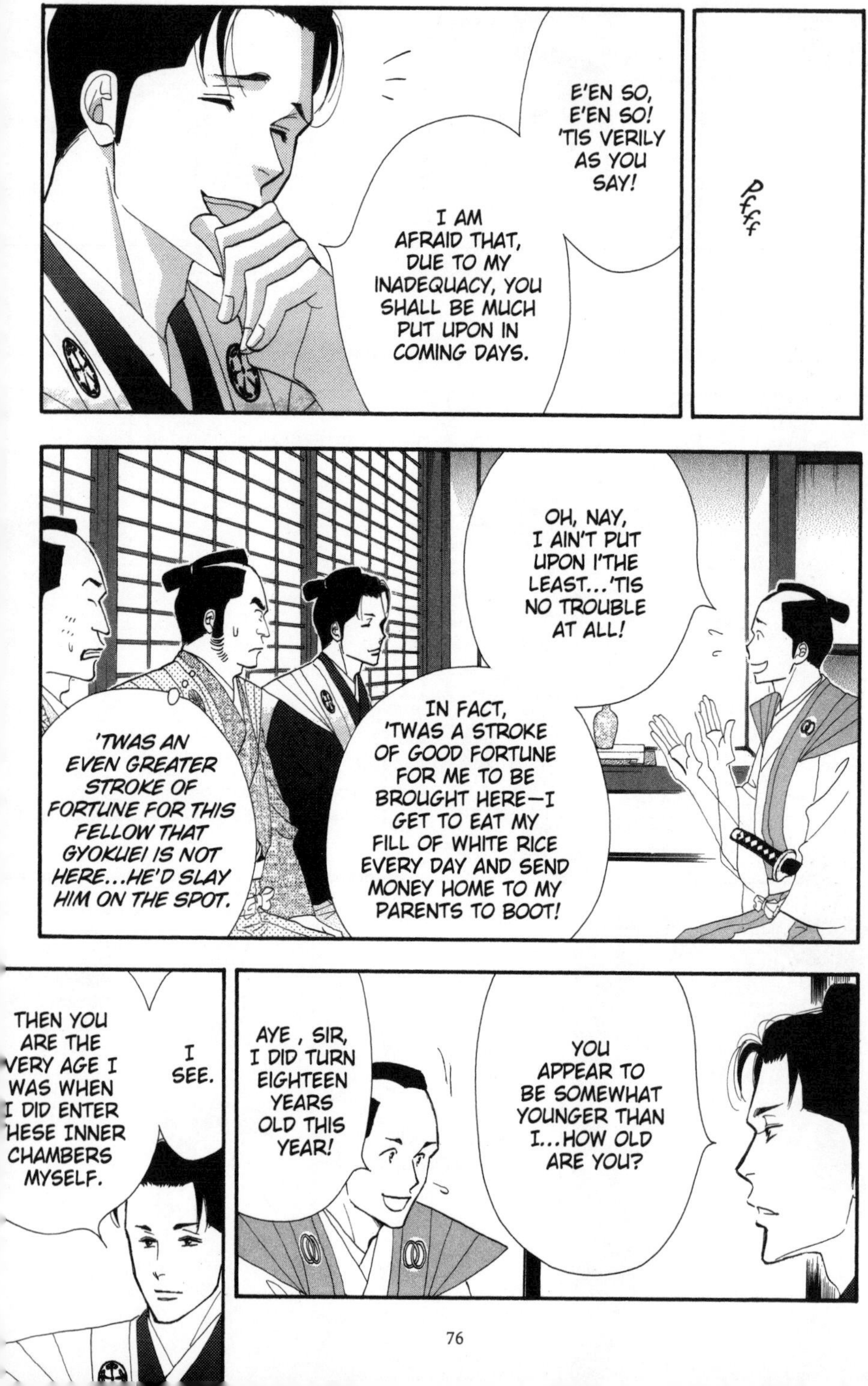
Pfff
E'EN SO, E'EN SO! 'TIS VERILY AS YOU SAY!
I AM AFRAID THAT, DUE TO MY INADEQUACY, YOU SHALL BE MUCH PUT UPON IN COMING DAYS.
OH, NAY, I AIN'T PUT UPON I'THE LEAST...'TIS NO TROUBLE AT ALL!
IN FACT, 'TWAS A STROKE OF GOOD FORTUNE FOR ME TO BE BROUGHT HERE—I GET TO EAT MY FILL OF WHITE RICE EVERY DAY AND SEND MONEY HOME TO MY PARENTS TO BOOT!
'TWAS AN EVEN GREATER STROKE OF FORTUNE FOR THIS FELLOW THAT GYOKUEI IS NOT HERE...HE'D SLAY HIM ON THE SPOT.
YOU APPEAR TO BE SOMEWHAT YOUNGER THAN I...HOW OLD ARE YOU?
AYE , SIR, I DID TURN EIGHTEEN YEARS OLD THIS YEAR!
I SEE.
THEN YOU ARE THE VERY AGE I WAS WHEN I DID ENTER HESE INNER CHAMBERS MYSELF.

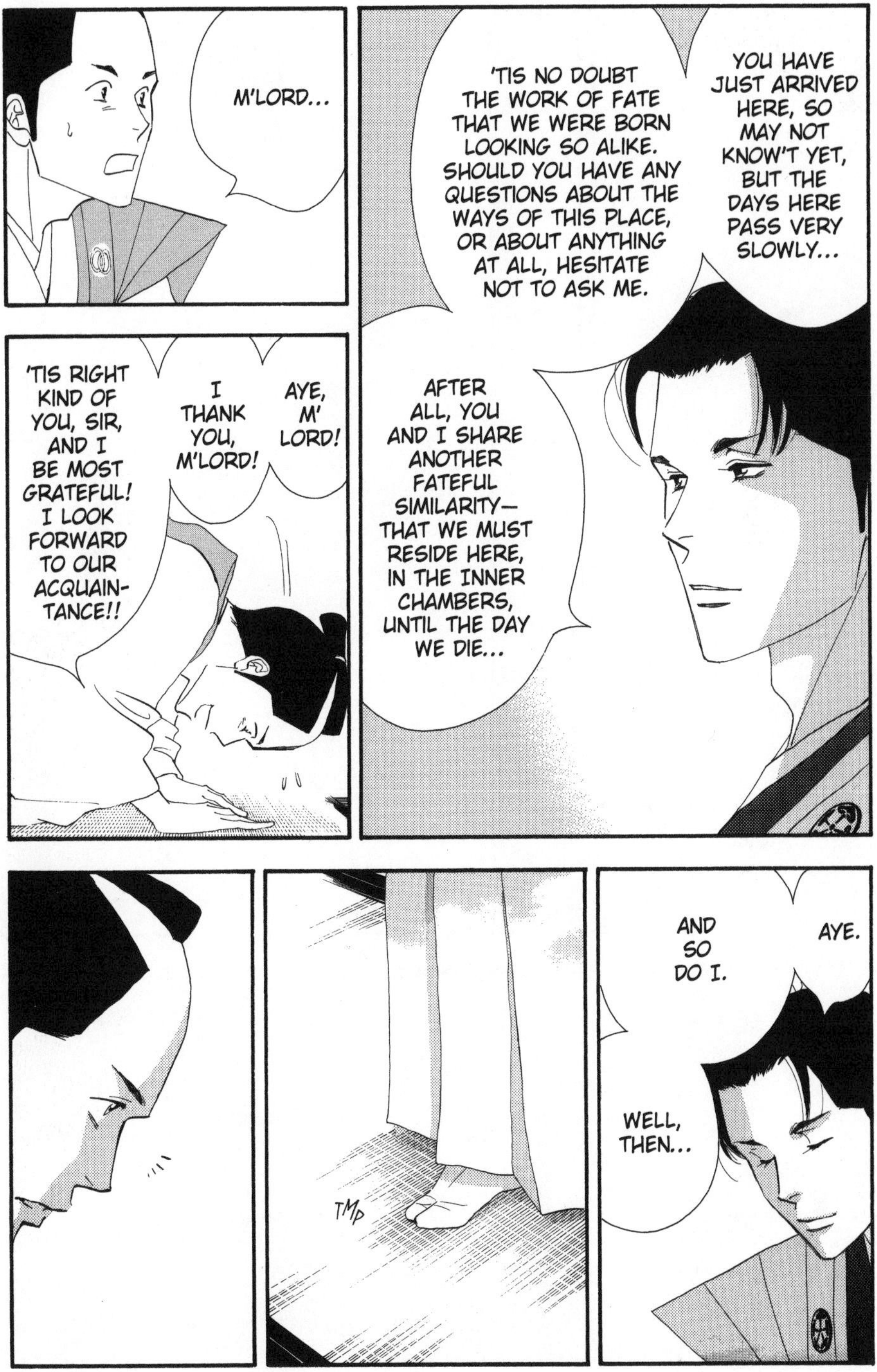
YOU HAVE JUST ARRIVED HERE, SO MAY NOT KNOW'T YET, BUT THE DAYS HERE PASS VERY SLOWLY...
'TIS NO DOUBT THE WORK OF FATE THAT WE WERE BORN LOOKING SO ALIKE. SHOULD YOU HAVE ANY QUESTIONS ABOUT THE WAYS OF THIS PLACE, OR ABOUT ANYTHING AT ALL, HESITATE NOT TO ASK ME.
AFTER ALL, YOU AND I SHARE ANOTHER FATEFUL SIMILARITY— THAT WE MUST RESIDE HERE, IN THE INNER CHAMBERS, UNTIL THE DAY WE DIE...
M'LORD...
AYE, M' LORD!
I THANK YOU, M'LORD!
'TIS RIGHT KIND OF YOU, SIR, AND I BE MOST GRATEFUL! I LOOK FORWARD TO OUR ACQUAIN- TANCE!!
AYE.
AND SO DO I.
WELL, THEN...
TMP

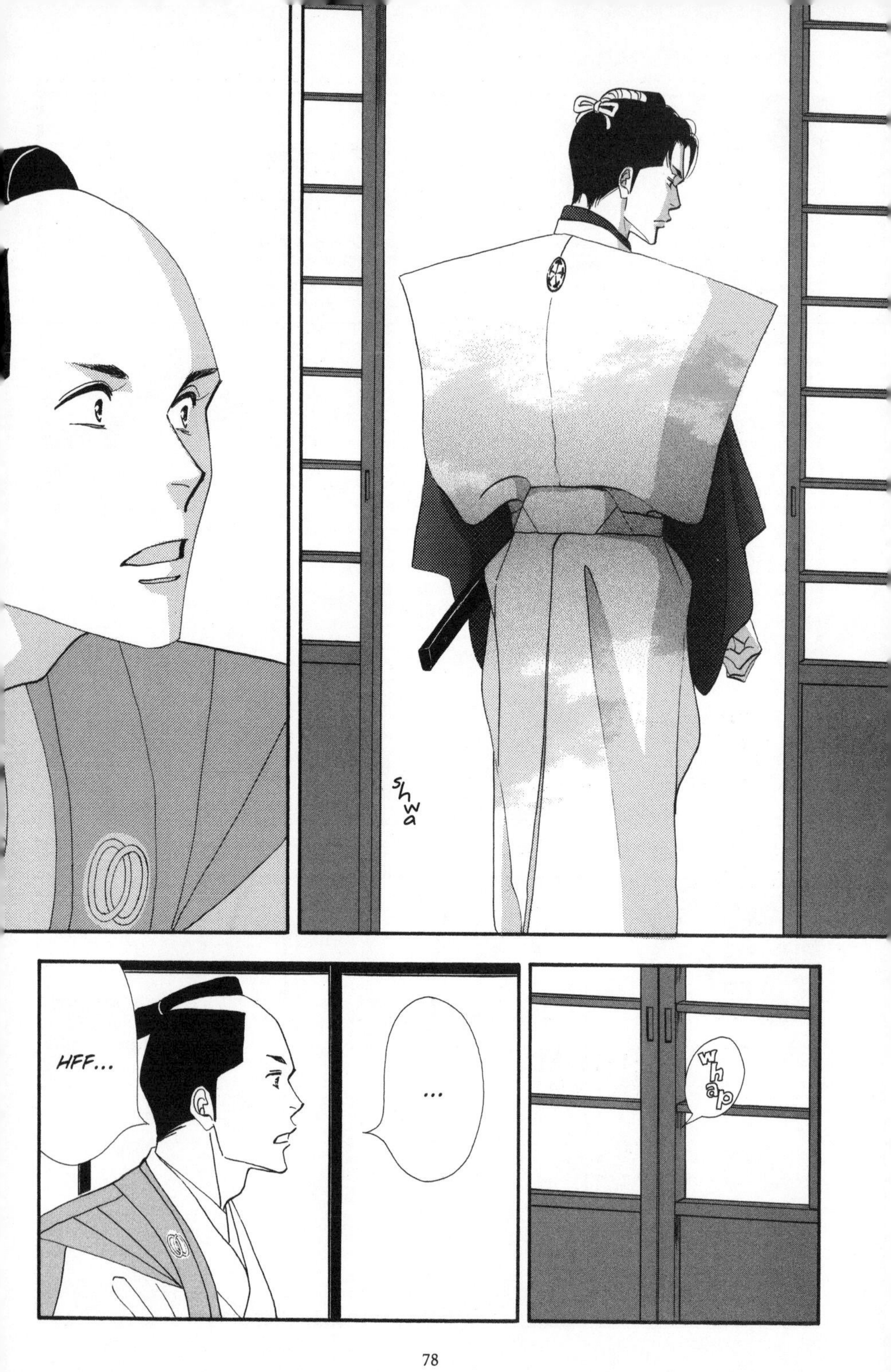
shwa
whap
...
HFF...

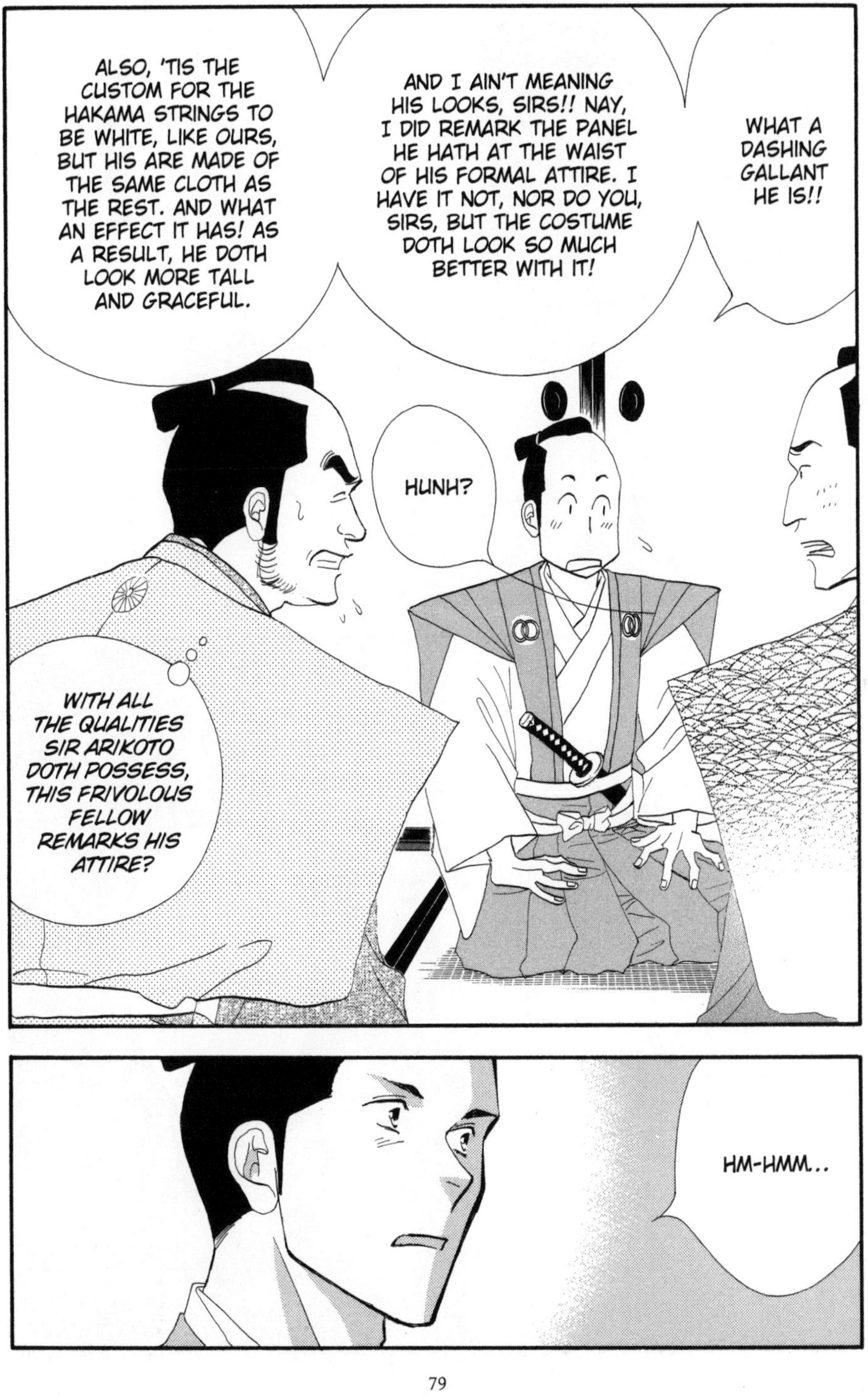
WHAT A DASHING GALLANT HE IS!!
AND I AIN'T MEANING HIS LOOKS, SIRS!! NAY, I DID REMARK THE PANEL HE HATH AT THE WAIST OF HIS FORMAL ATTIRE. I HAVE IT NOT, NOR DO YOU, SIRS, BUT THE COSTUME DOTH LOOK SO MUCH BETTER WITH IT!
ALSO, 'TIS THE CUSTOM FOR THE HAKAMA STRINGS TO BE WHITE, LIKE OURS, BUT HIS ARE MADE OF THE SAME CLOTH AS THE REST. AND WHAT AN EFFECT IT HAS! AS A RESULT, HE DOTH LOOK MORE TALL AND GRACEFUL.
HUNH?
WITH ALL THE QUALITIES SIR ARIKOTO DOTH POSSESS, THIS FRIVOLOUS FELLOW REMARKS HIS ATTIRE?
HM-HMM..

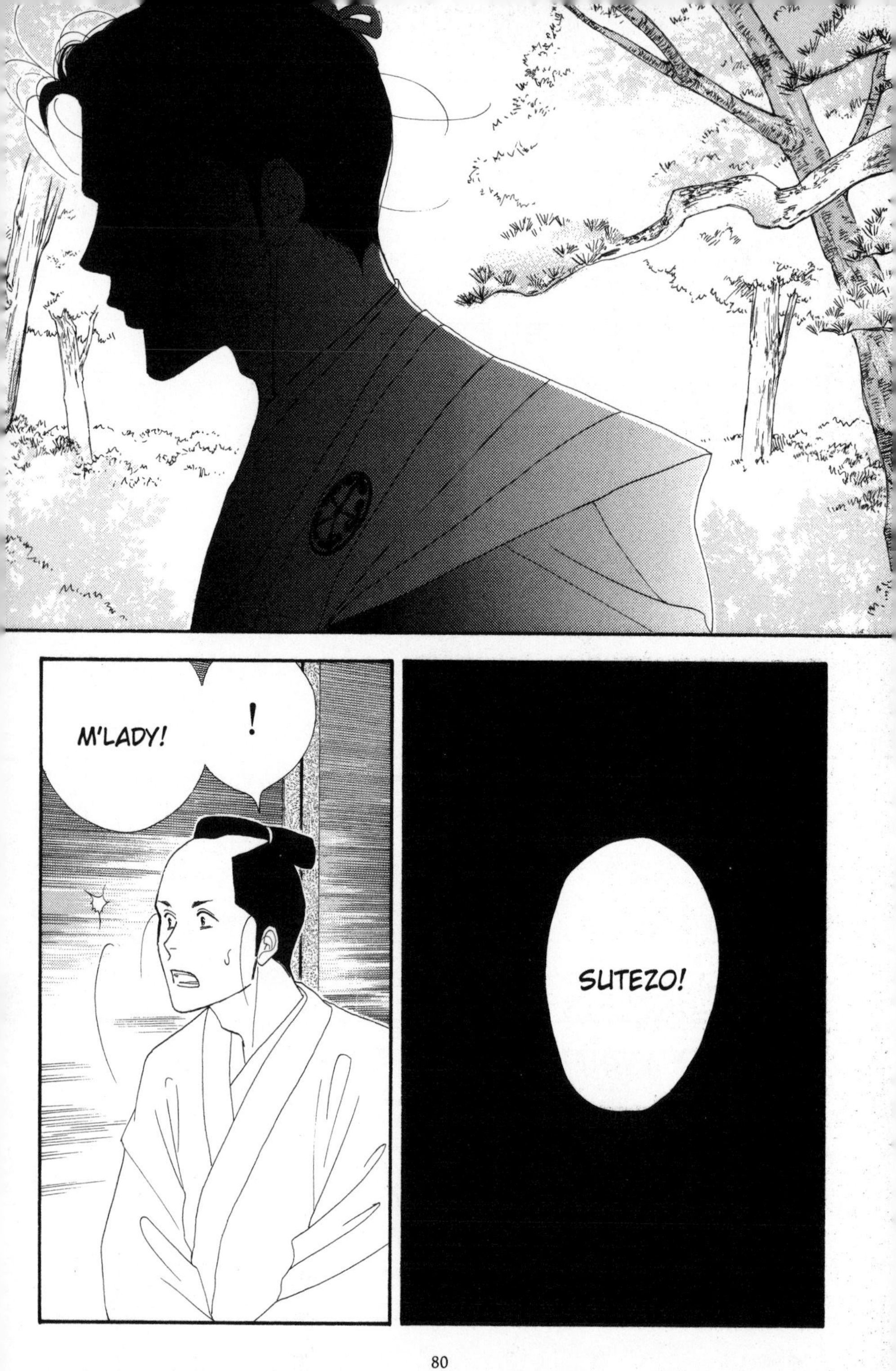
SUTEZO!
!
M'LADY!

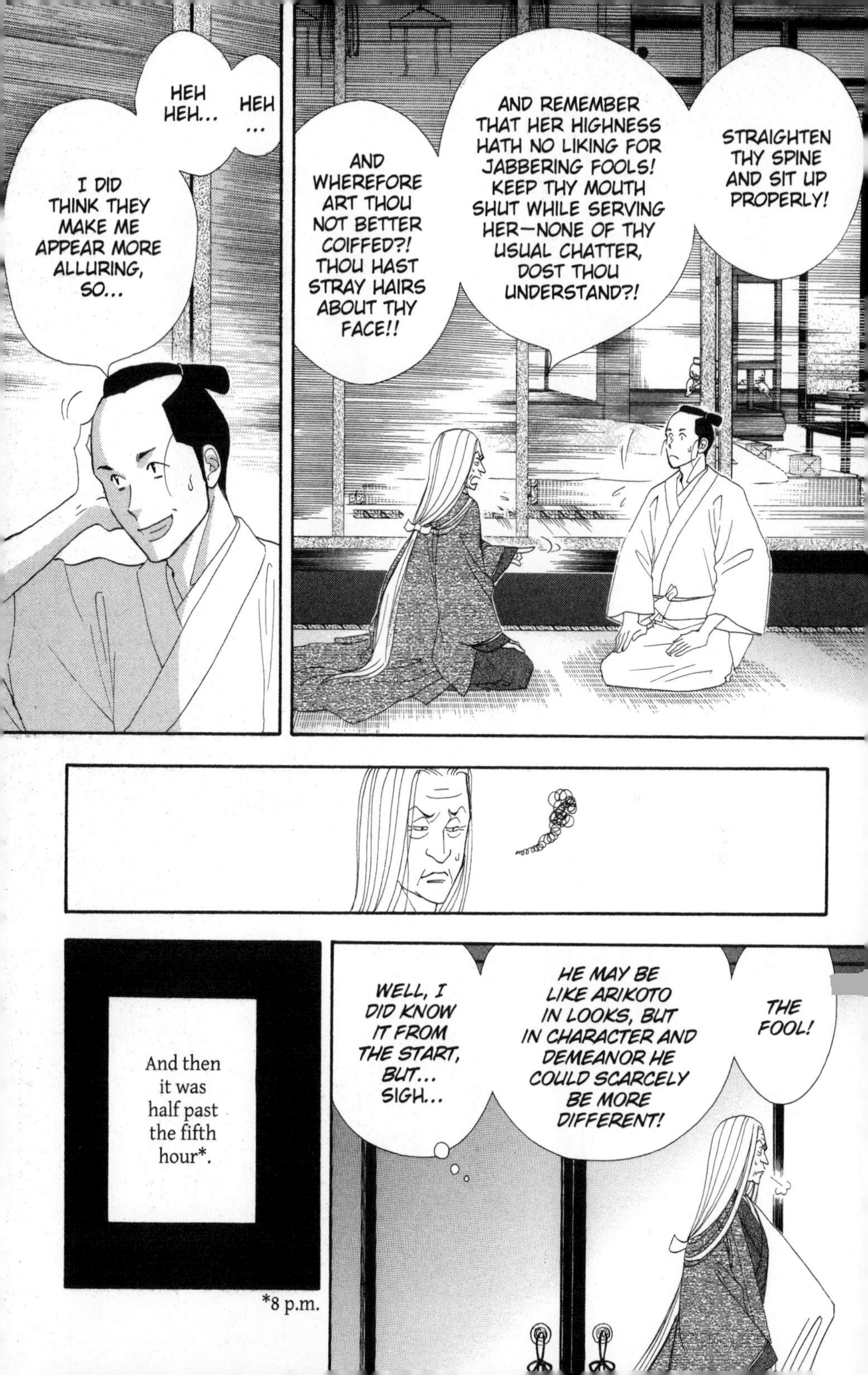
STRAIGHTEN THY SPINE AND SIT UP PROPERLY!
AND REMEMBER THAT HER HIGHNESS HATH NO LIKING FOR JABBERING FOOLS! KEEP THY MOUTH SHUT WHILE SERVING HER—NONE OF THY USUAL CHATTER, DOST THOU UNDERSTAND?!
AND WHEREFORE ART THOU NOT BETTER COIFFED?! THOU HAST STRAY HAIRS ABOUT THY FACE!!
HEH HEH... HEH...
I DID THINK THEY MAKE ME APPEAR MORE ALLURING, SO...
THE FOOL!
HE MAY BE LIKE ARIKOTO IN LOOKS, BUT IN CHARACTER AND DEMEANOR HE COULD SCARCELY BE MORE DIFFERENT!
WELL, I DID KNOW IT FROM THE START, BUT... SIGH...
And then it was half past the fifth hour*.

*8 p.m.

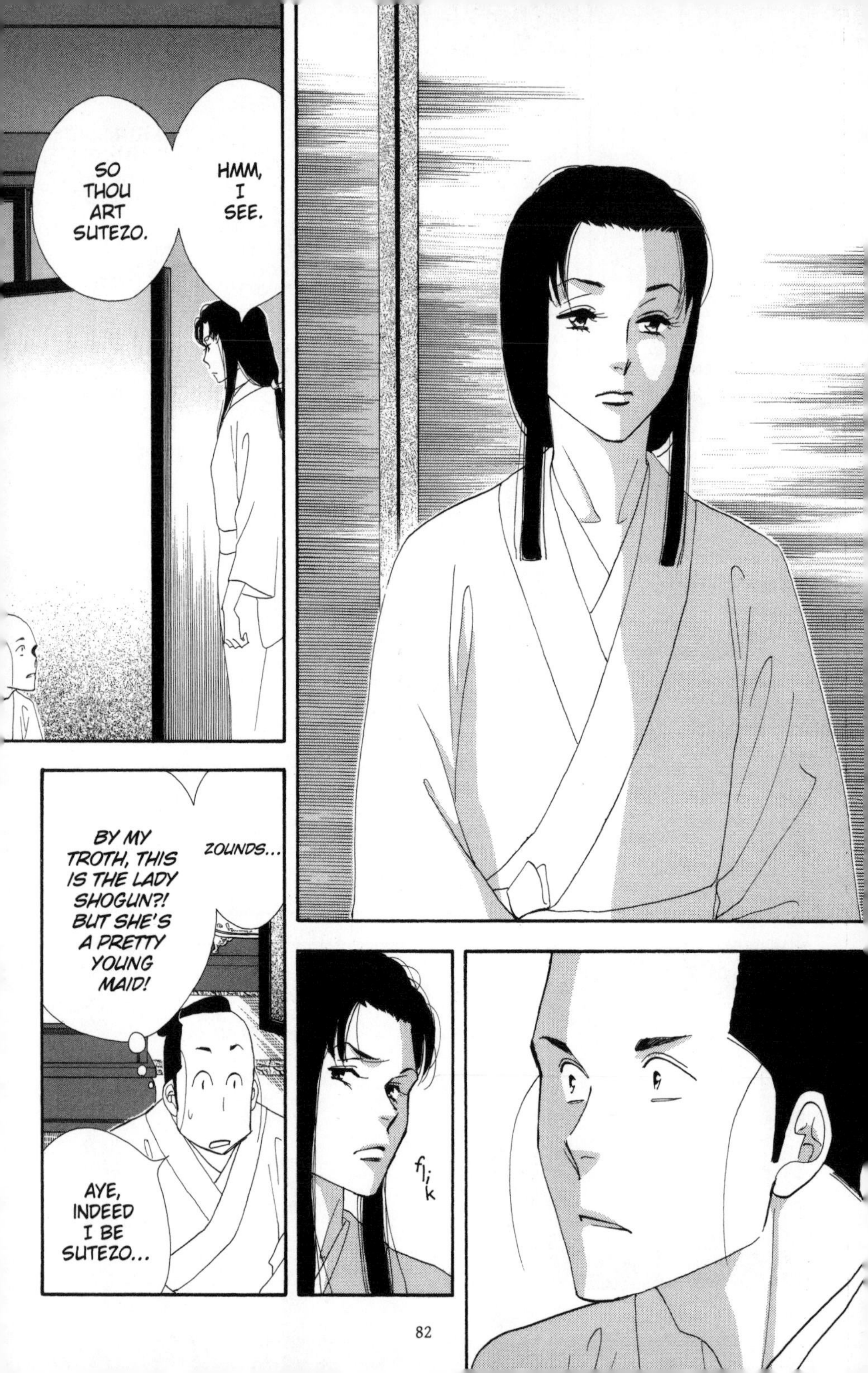
HMM, I SEE.
SO THOU ART SUTEZO.
ZOUNDS...
BY MY TROTH, THIS IS THE LADY SHOGUN?! BUT SHE'S A PRETTY YOUNG MAID!
AYE, INDEED I BE SUTEZO...
flik

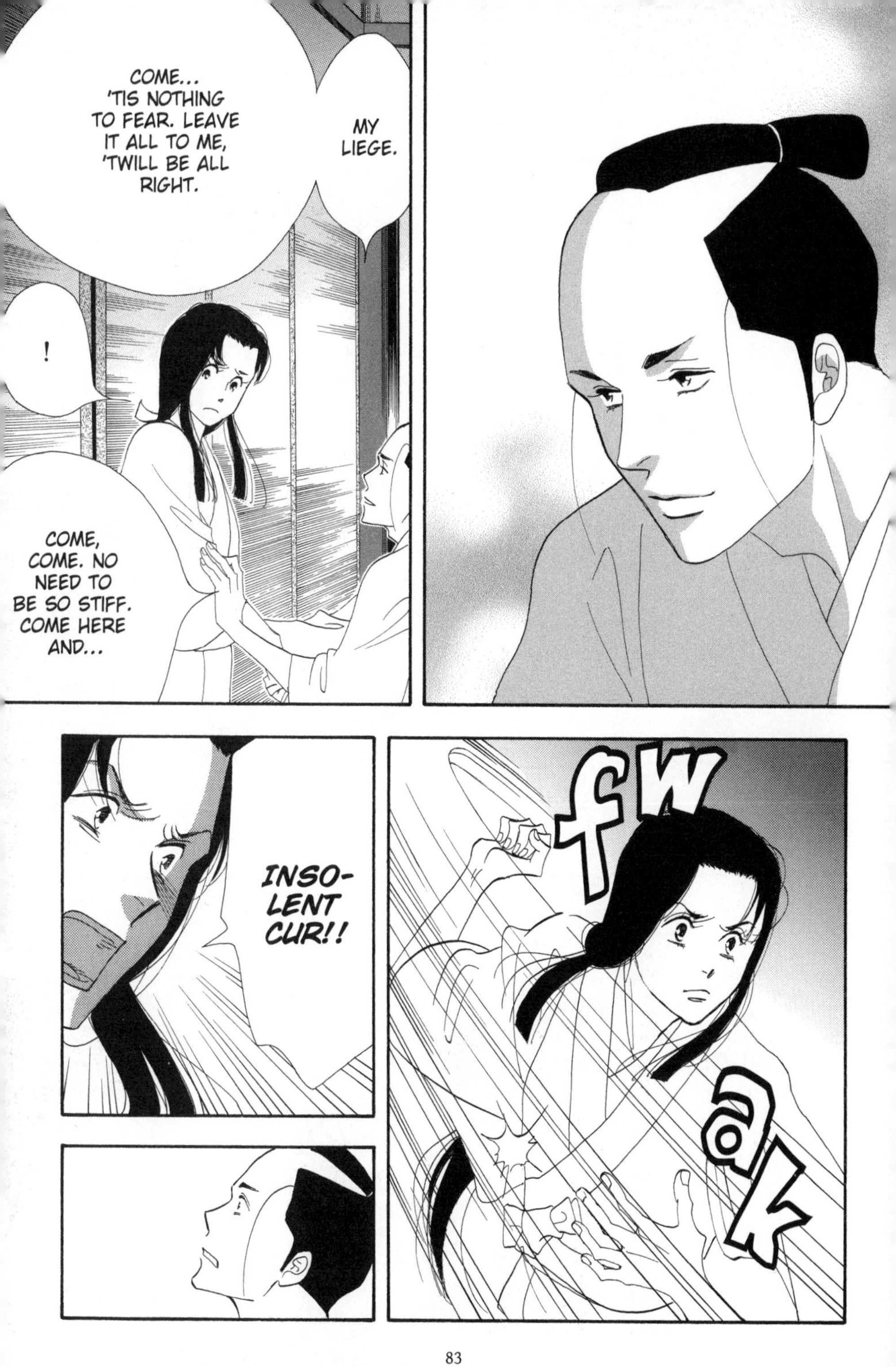
MY LIEGE.
COME... 'TIS NOTHING TO FEAR. LEAVE IT ALL TO ME, 'TWILL BE ALL RIGHT.
!
COME, COME. NO NEED TO BE SO STIFF. COME HERE AND...
fw
ak
INSO-LENT CUR!!

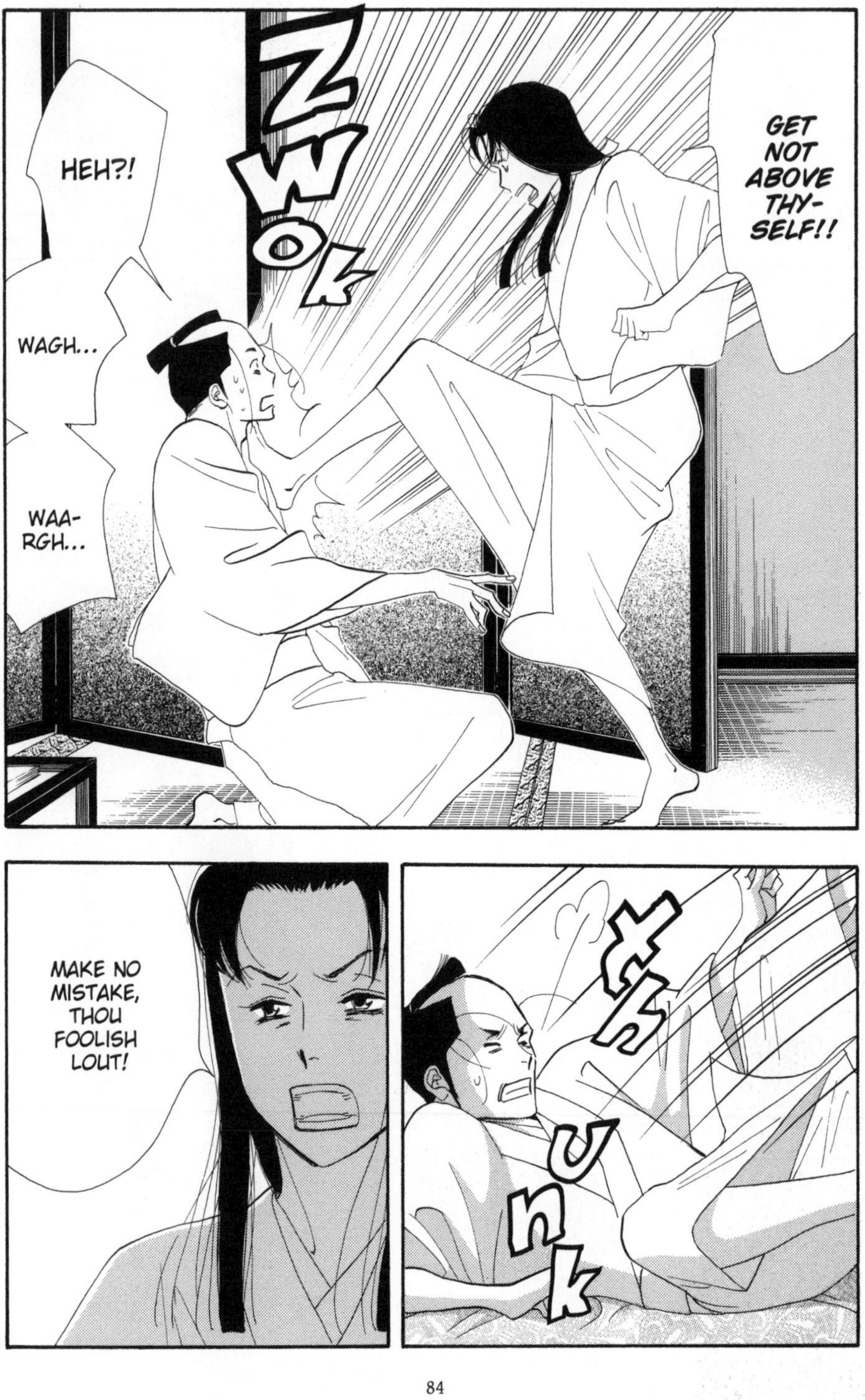
GET NOT ABOVE THY-SELF!!
ZWOK
HEH?!
WAGH...
WAA-RGH...
THUNK
MAKE NO MISTAKE, THOU FOOLISH LOUT!

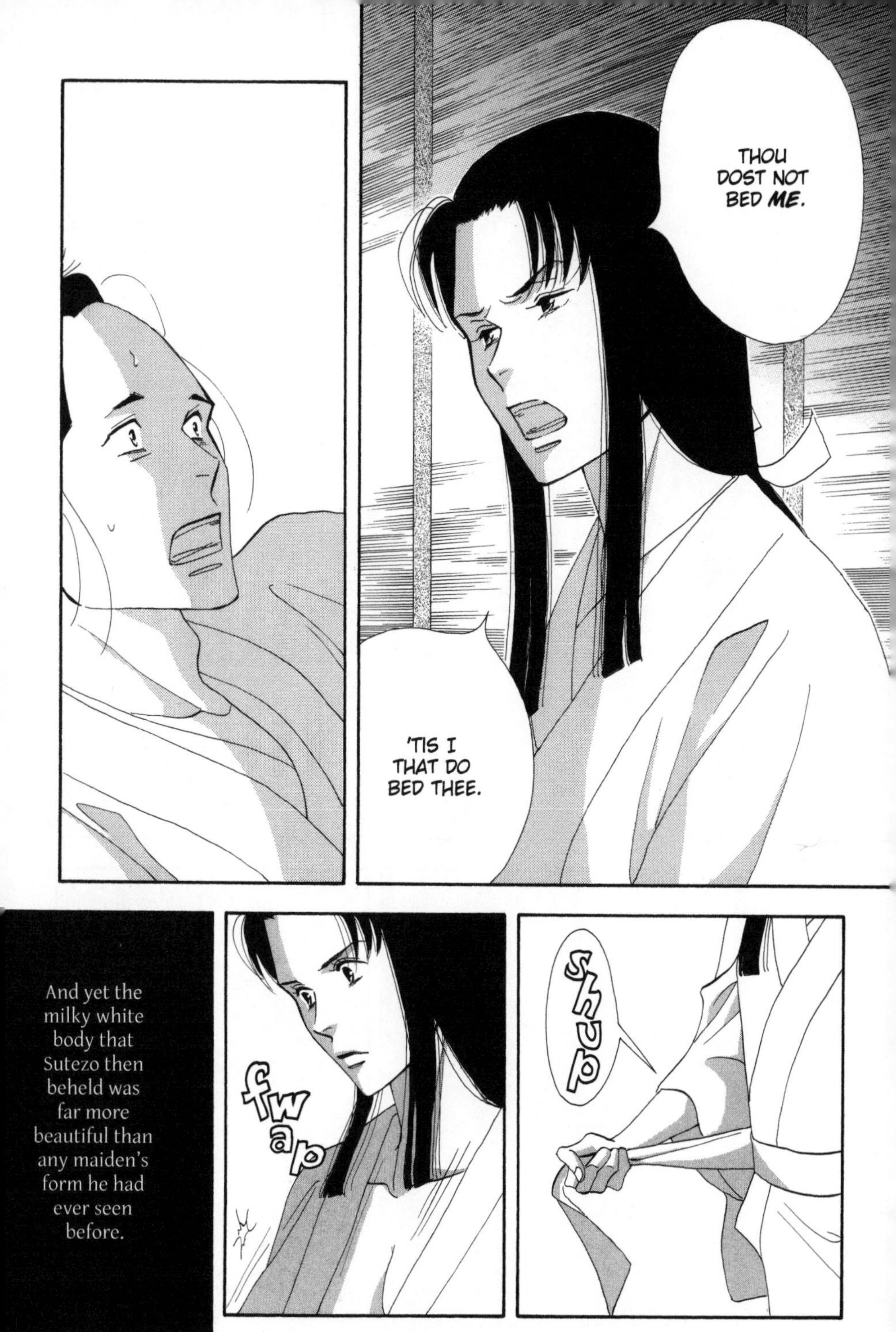
THOU DOST NOT BED ME.
'TIS I THAT DO BED THEE.
shup
fwap
And yet the milky white body that Sutezo then beheld was far more beautiful than any maiden's form he had ever seen before.

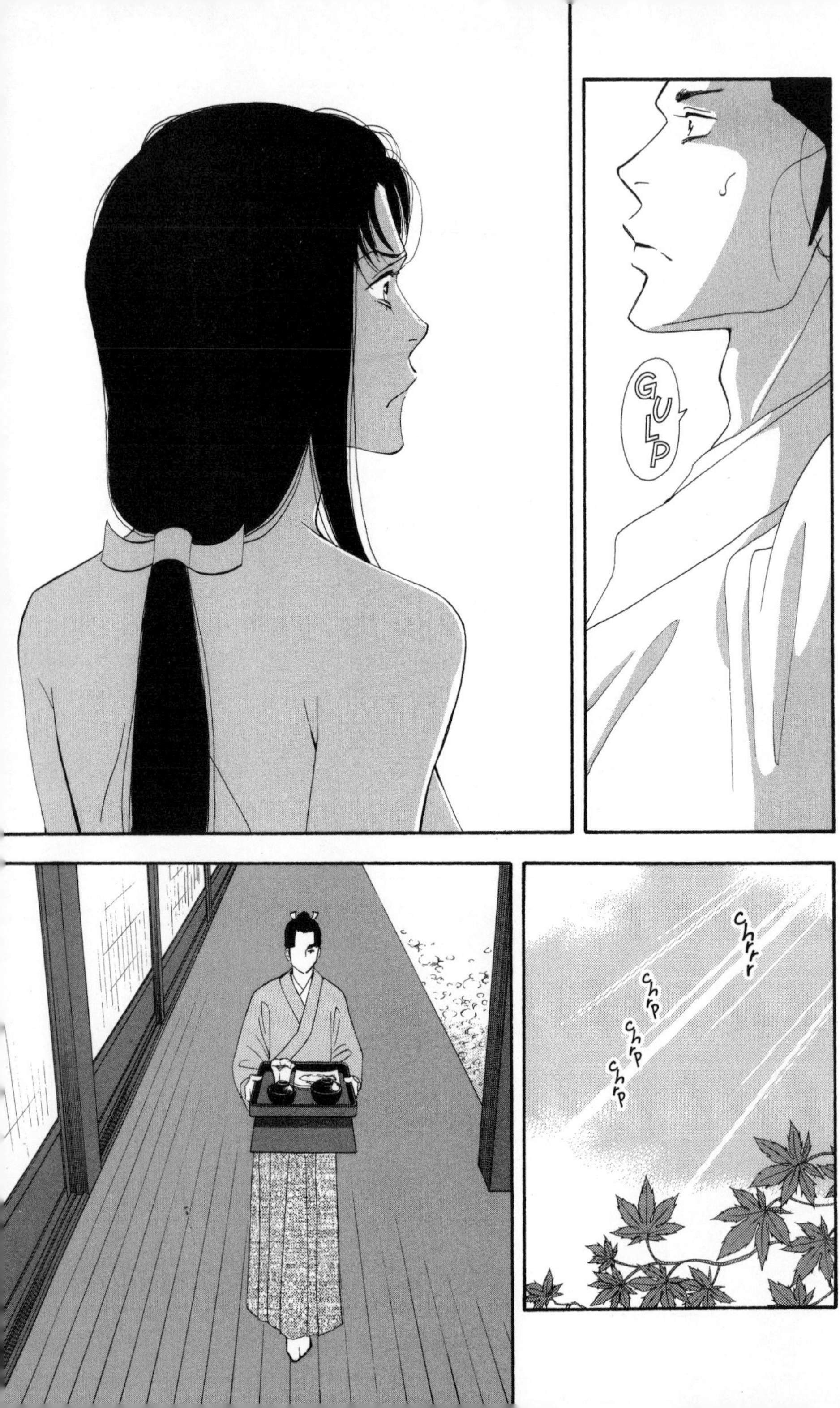
GULP
chrrr
chrp
chrp
chrp

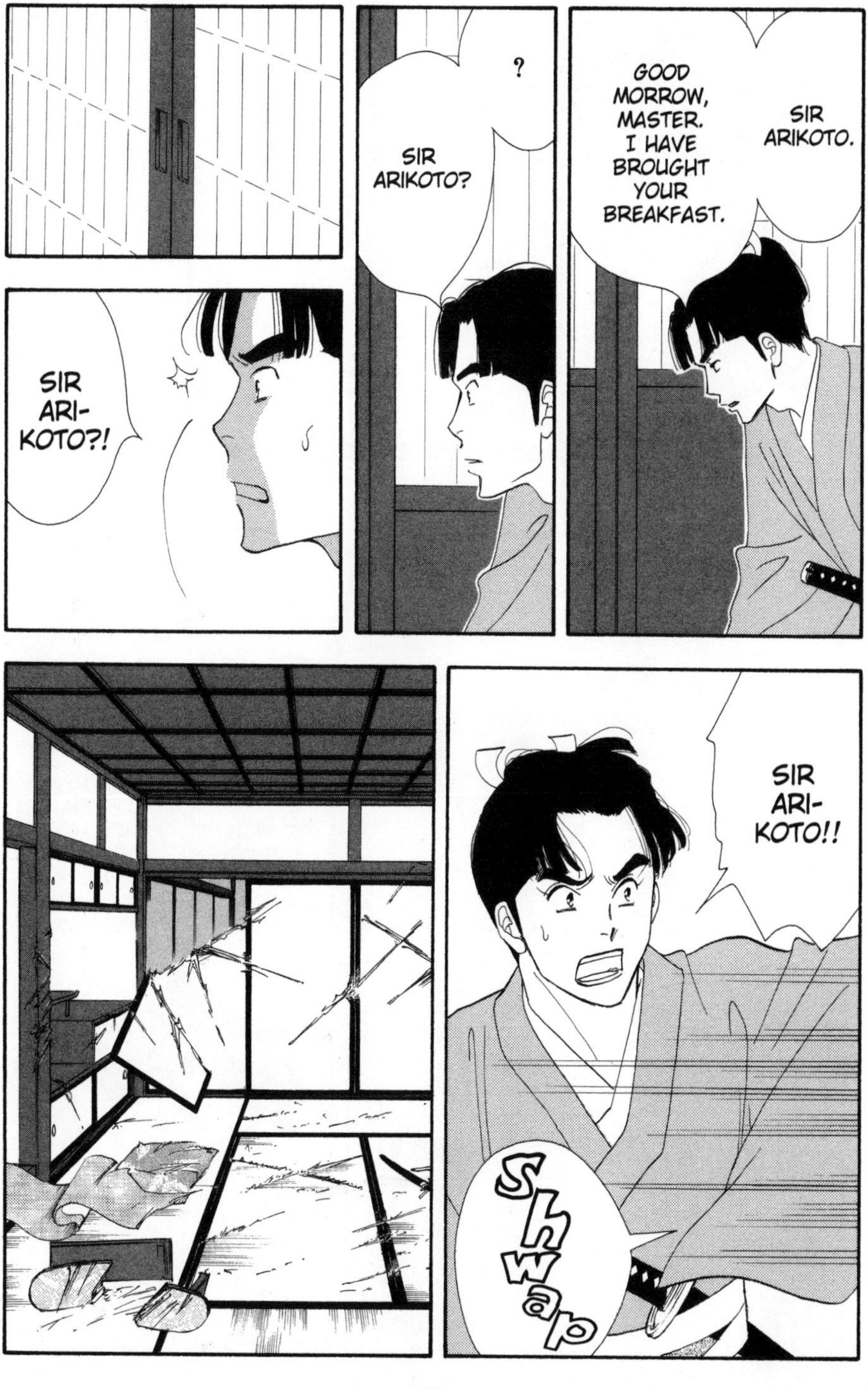
SIR ARIKOTO.
GOOD MORROW, MASTER. I HAVE BROUGHT YOUR BREAKFAST.
?
SIR ARIKOTO?
SIR ARI-KOTO?!
SIR ARI-KOTO!!
Shwap

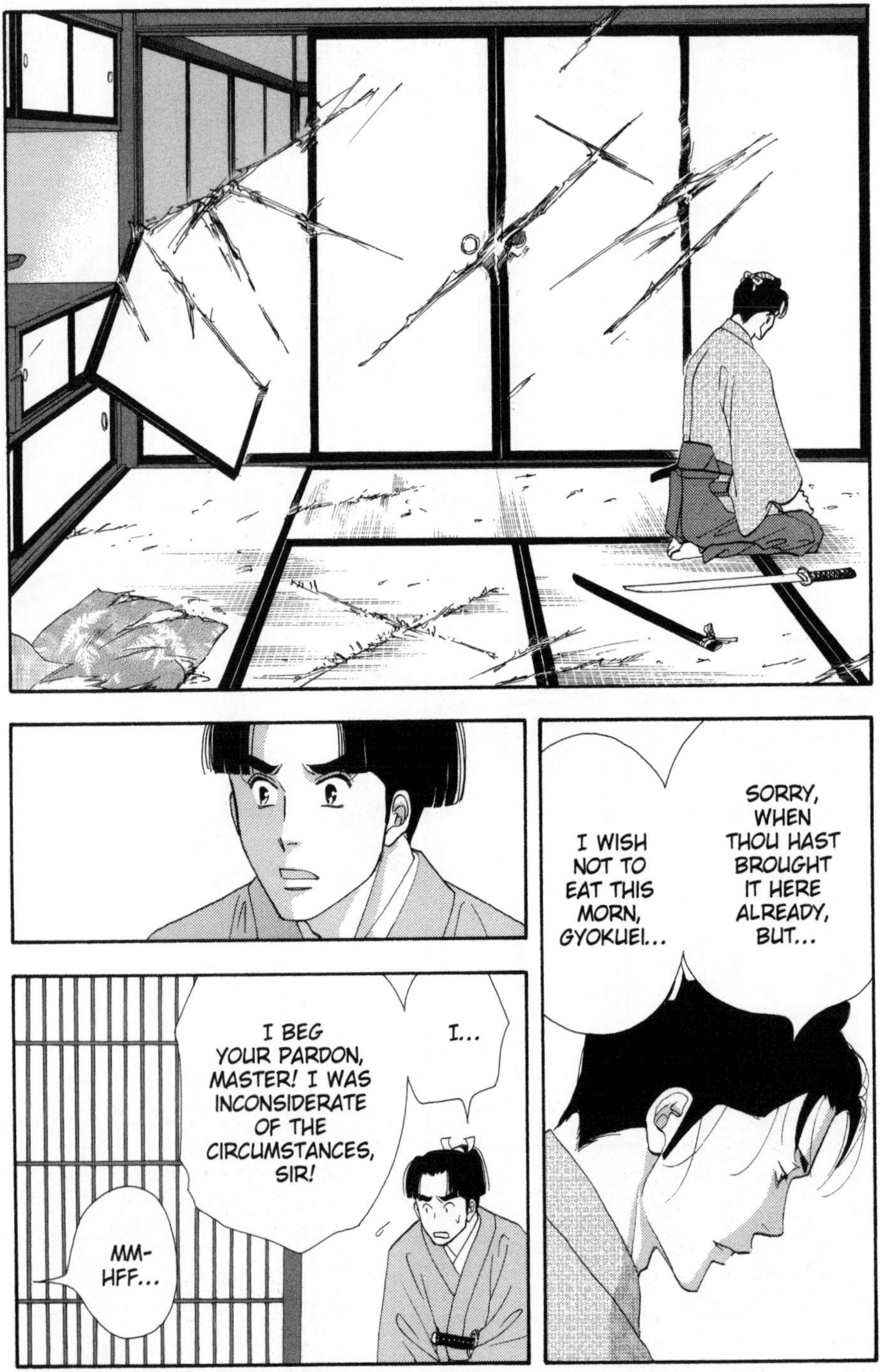
SORRY, WHEN THOU HAST BROUGHT IT HERE ALREADY, BUT...
I WISH NOT TO EAT THIS MORN, GYOKUEI...
I...
I BEG YOUR PARDON, MASTER! I WAS INCONSIDERATE OF THE CIRCUMSTANCES, SIR!
MM-HFF...

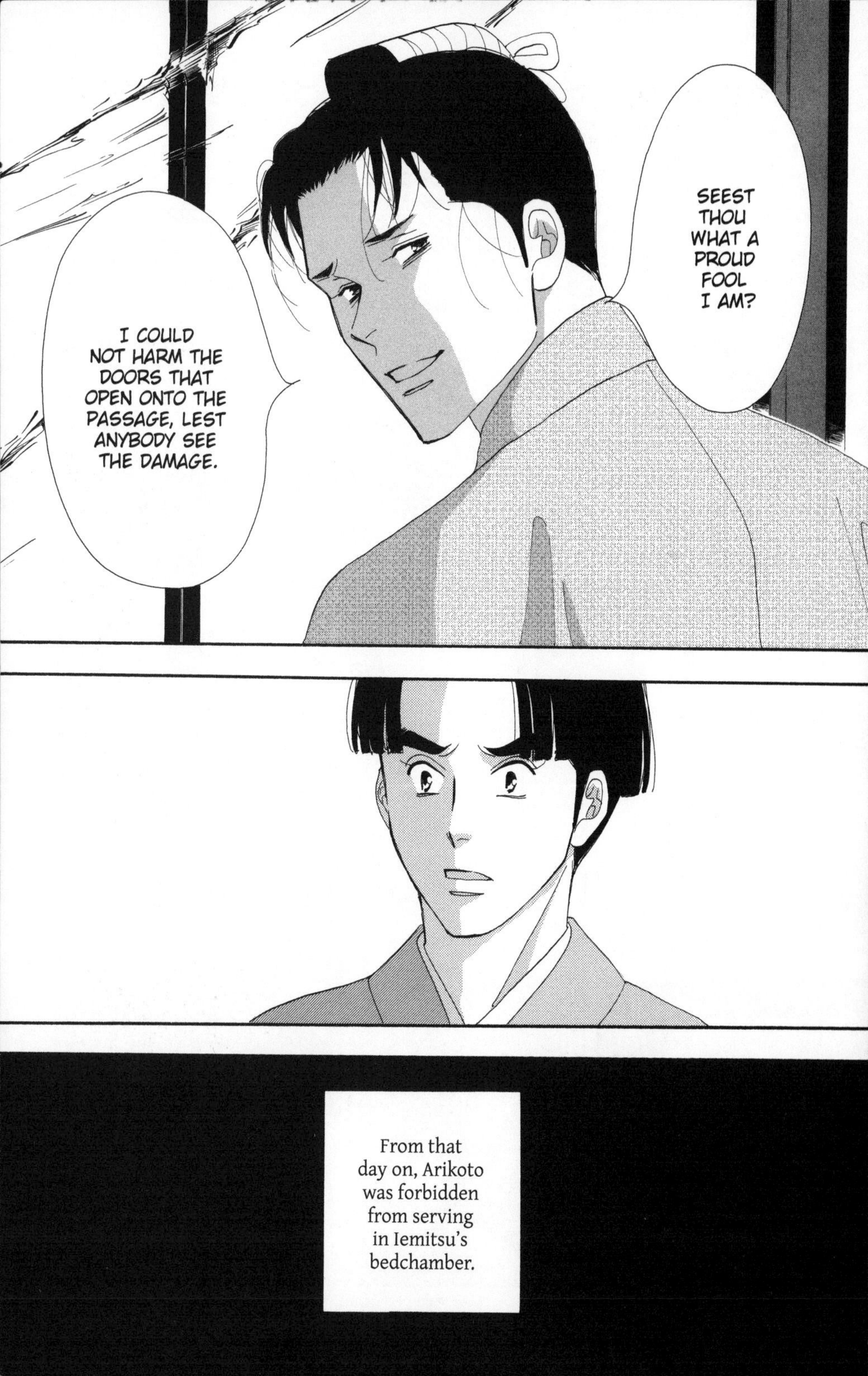
SEEST THOU WHAT A PROUD FOOL I AM?
I COULD NOT HARM THE DOORS THAT OPEN ONTO THE PASSAGE, LEST ANYBODY SEE THE DAMAGE.
From that day on, Arikoto was forbidden from serving in Iemitsu's bedchamber.

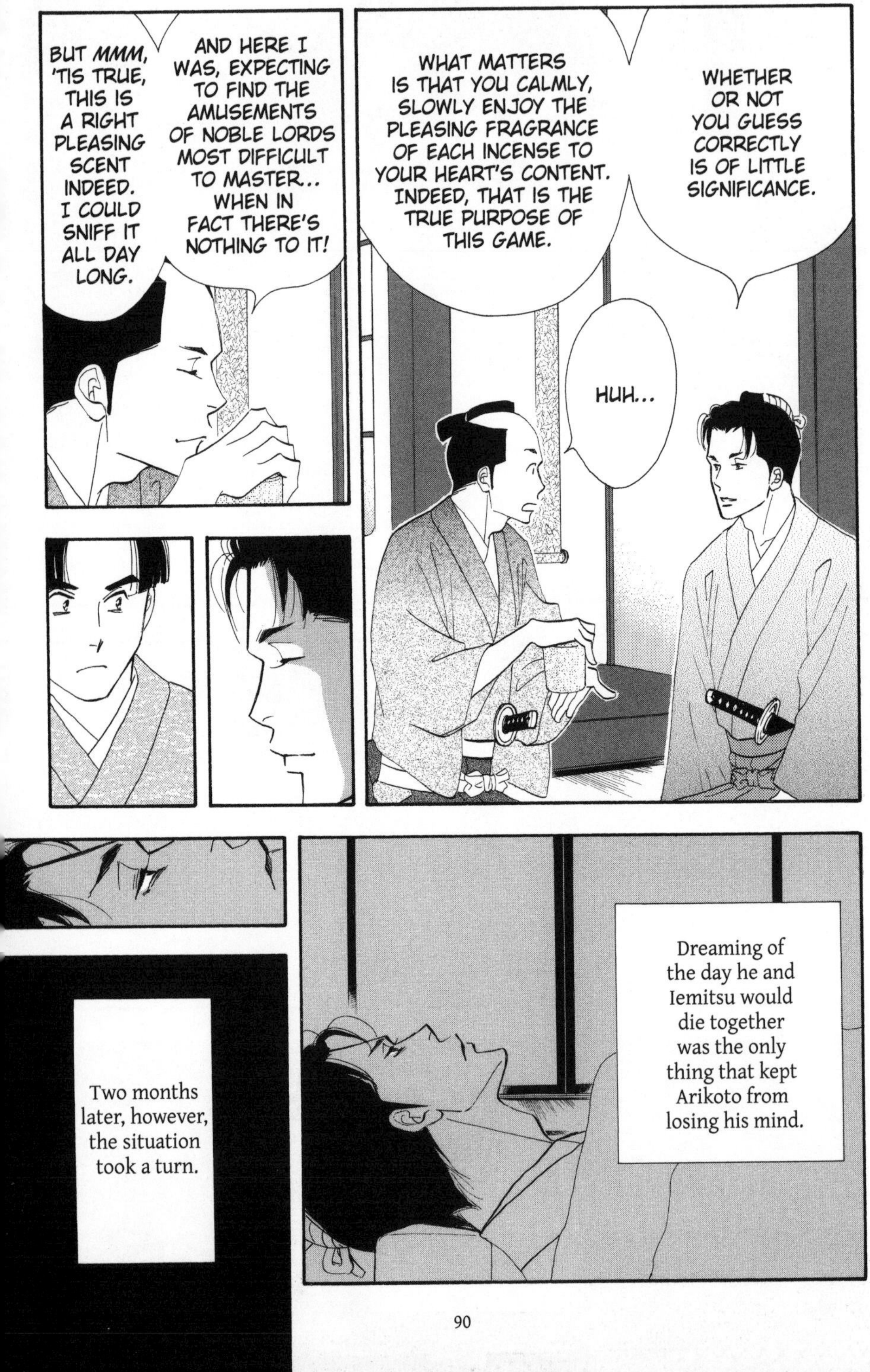
WHETHER OR NOT YOU GUESS CORRECTLY IS OF LITTLE SIGNIFICANCE.
WHAT MATTERS IS THAT YOU CALMLY, SLOWLY ENJOY THE PLEASING FRAGRANCE OF EACH INCENSE TO YOUR HEART'S CONTENT. INDEED, THAT IS THE TRUE PURPOSE OF THIS GAME.
HUH...
AND HERE I WAS, EXPECTING TO FIND THE AMUSEMENTS OF NOBLE LORDS MOST DIFFICULT TO MASTER... WHEN IN FACT THERE'S NOTHING TO IT!
BUT *MMM*, 'TIS TRUE, THIS IS A RIGHT PLEASING SCENT INDEED. I COULD SNIFF IT ALL DAY LONG.
Dreaming of the day he and Iemitsu would die together was the only thing that kept Arikoto from losing his mind.
Two months later, however, the situation took a turn.

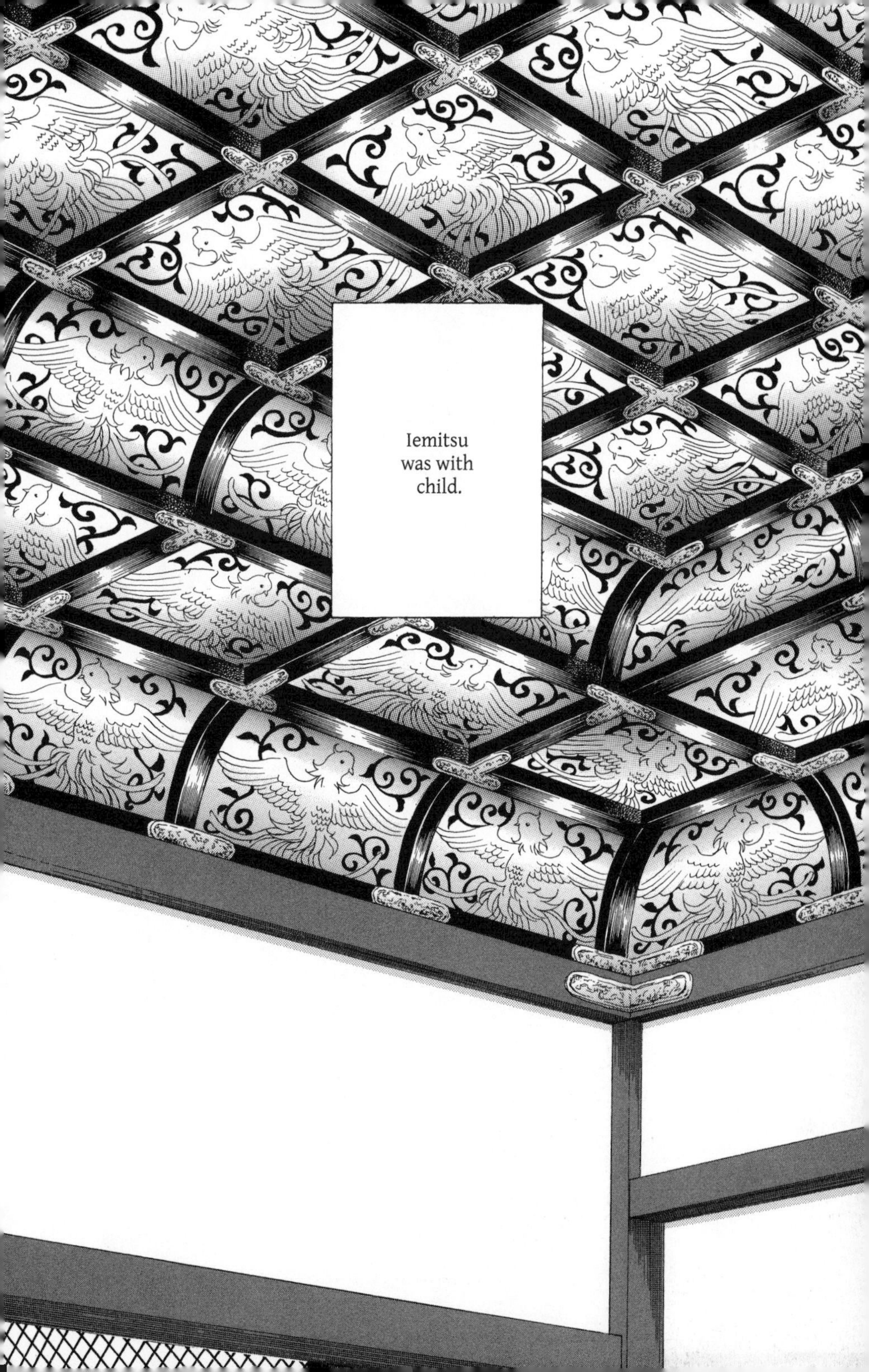
Iemitsu was with child.

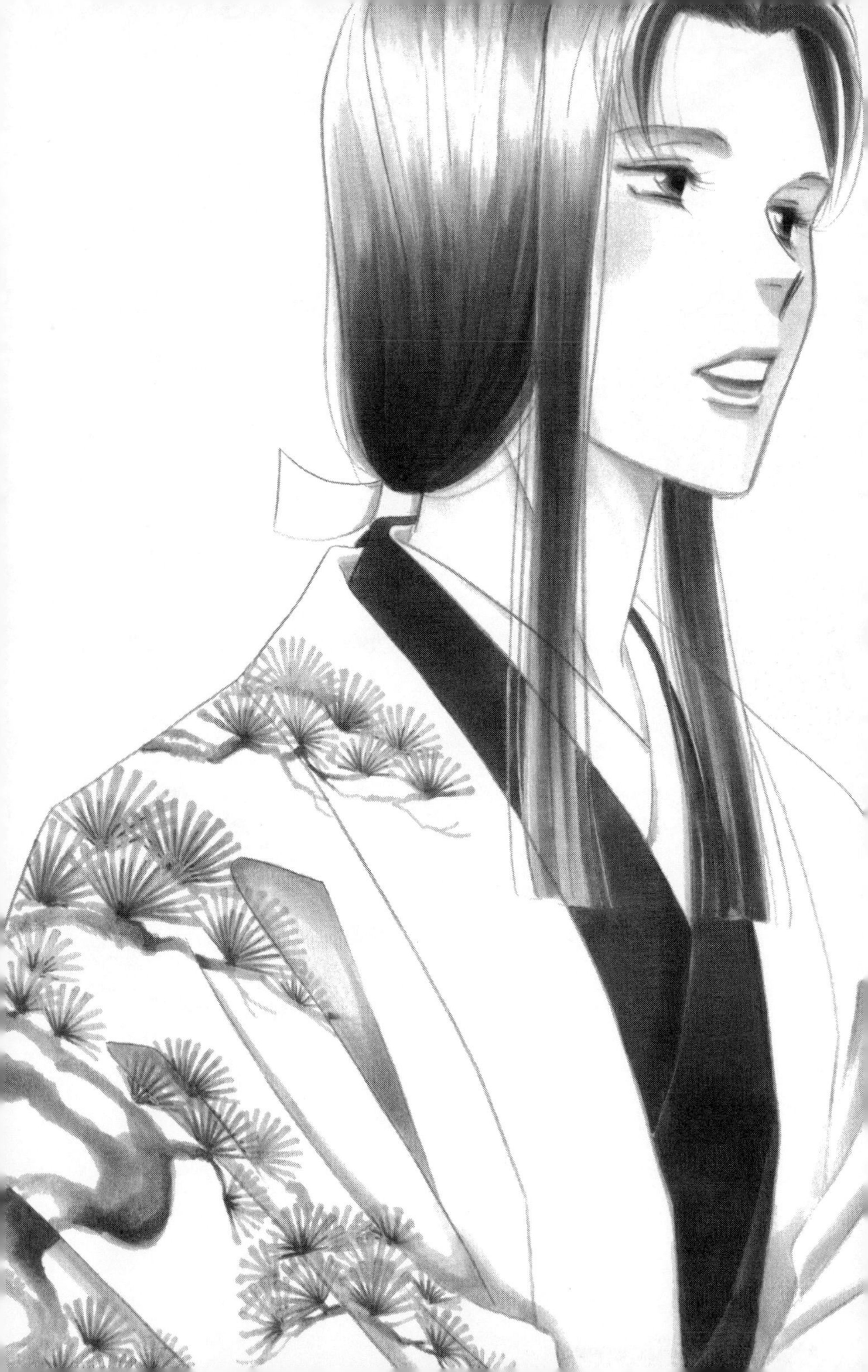

Ōoku

● THE INNER CHAMBERS

Ōoku

⬦ THE INNER CHAMBERS

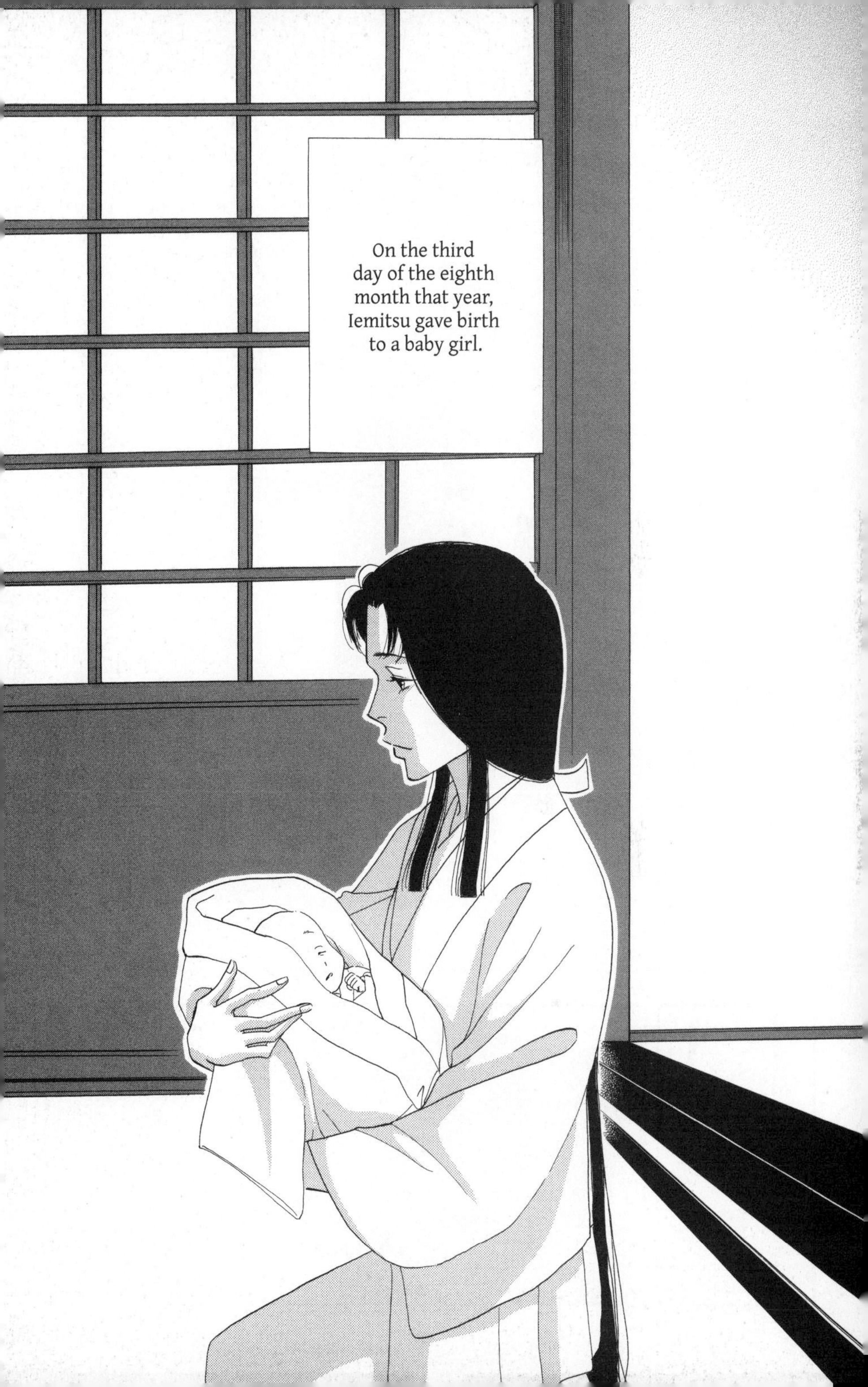
On the third day of the eighth month that year, Iemitsu gave birth to a baby girl.

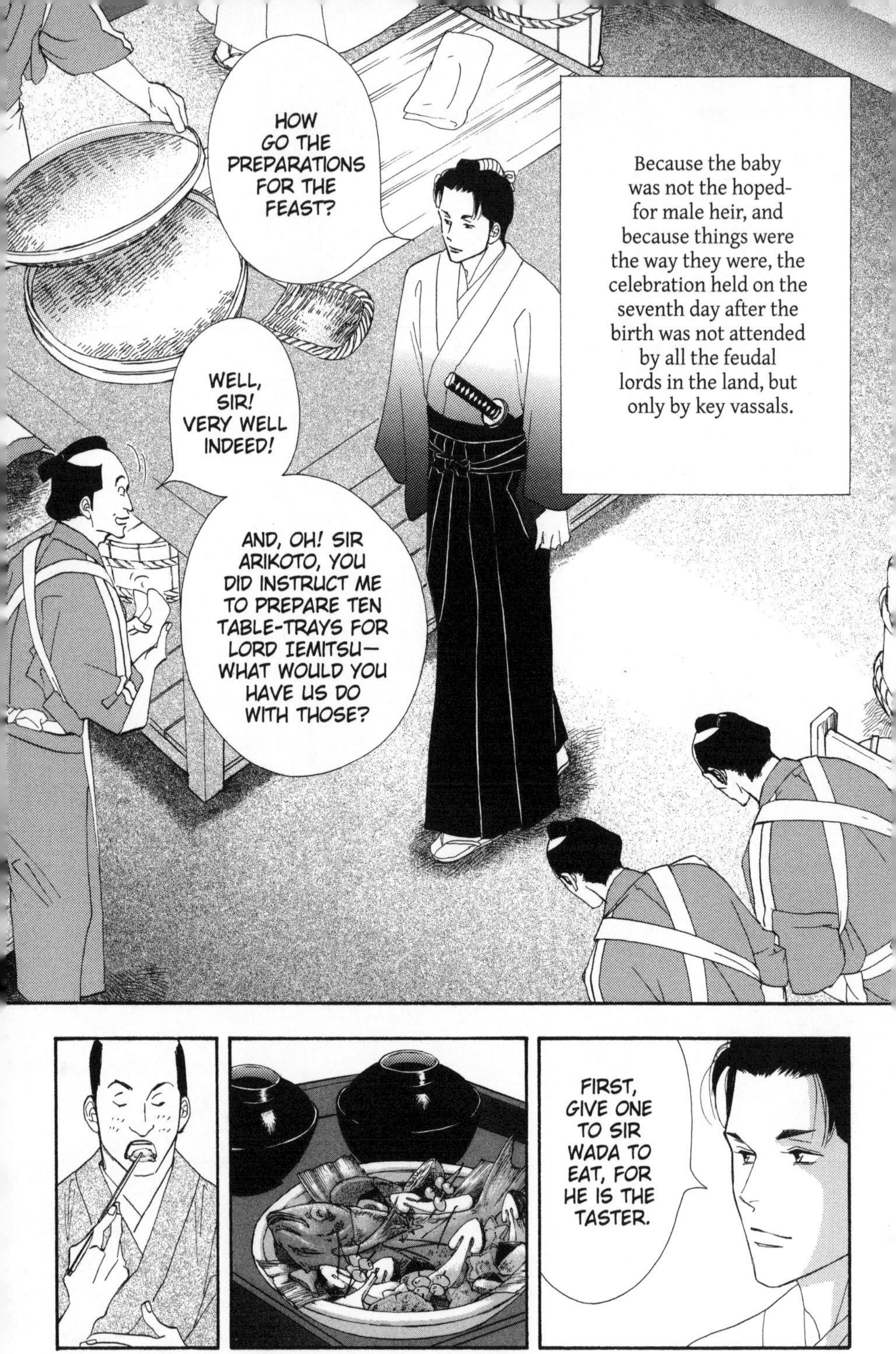
Because the baby was not the hoped-for male heir, and because things were the way they were, the celebration held on the seventh day after the birth was not attended by all the feudal lords in the land, but only by key vassals.
HOW GO THE PREPARATIONS FOR THE FEAST?
WELL, SIR! VERY WELL INDEED!
AND, OH! SIR ARIKOTO, YOU DID INSTRUCT ME TO PREPARE TEN TABLE-TRAYS FOR LORD IEMITSU—WHAT WOULD YOU HAVE US DO WITH THOSE?
FIRST, GIVE ONE TO SIR WADA TO EAT, FOR HE IS THE TASTER.

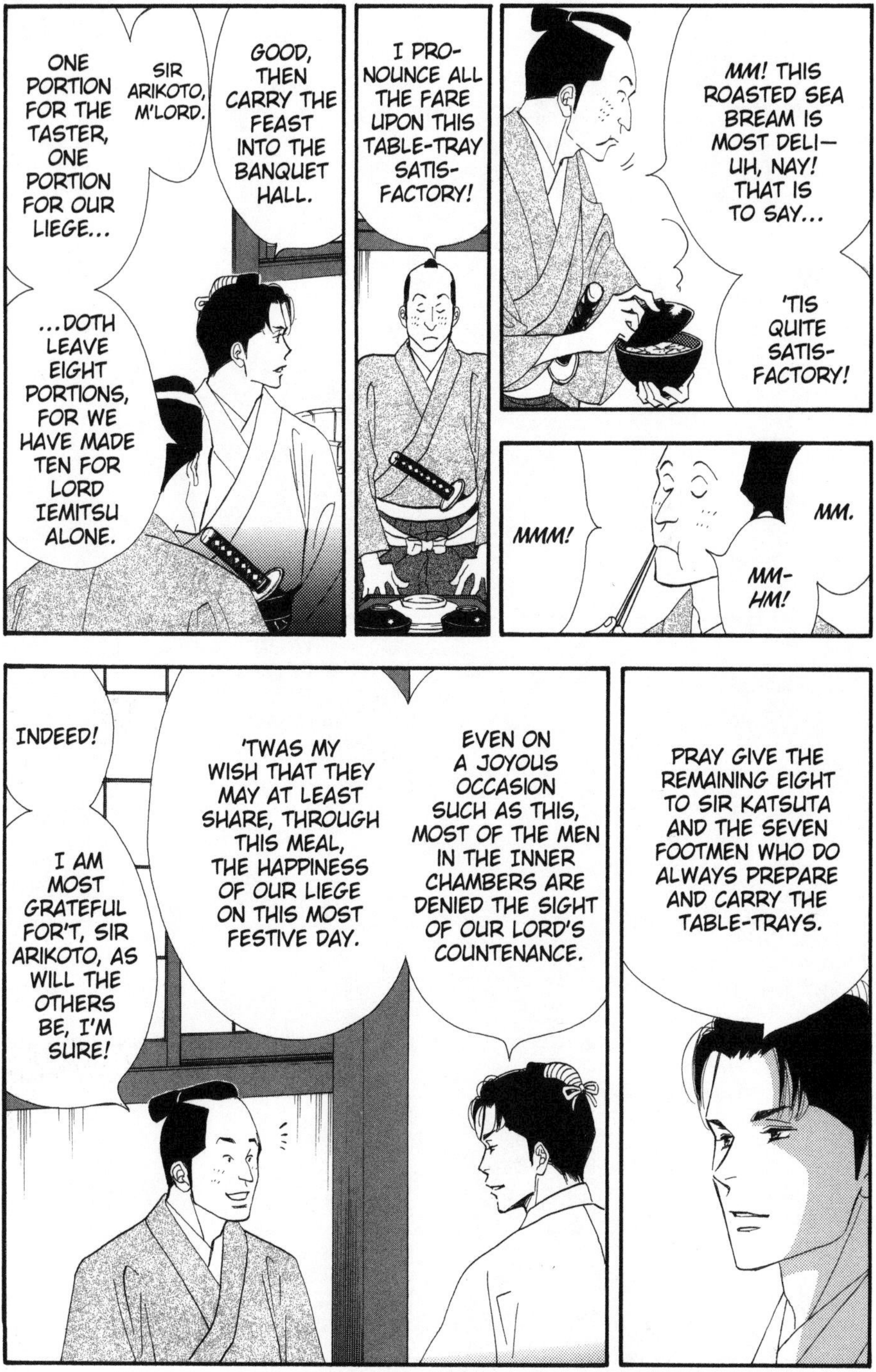
MM! THIS ROASTED SEA BREAM IS MOST DELI— UH, NAY! THAT IS TO SAY...
'TIS QUITE SATIS-FACTORY!
MM.
MM-HM!
MMM!
I PRO-NOUNCE ALL THE FARE UPON THIS TABLE-TRAY SATIS-FACTORY!
GOOD, THEN CARRY THE FEAST INTO THE BANQUET HALL.
SIR ARIKOTO, M'LORD.
ONE PORTION FOR THE TASTER, ONE PORTION FOR OUR LIEGE...
...DOTH LEAVE EIGHT PORTIONS, FOR WE HAVE MADE TEN FOR LORD IEMITSU ALONE.
PRAY GIVE THE REMAINING EIGHT TO SIR KATSUTA AND THE SEVEN FOOTMEN WHO DO ALWAYS PREPARE AND CARRY THE TABLE-TRAYS.
EVEN ON A JOYOUS OCCASION SUCH AS THIS, MOST OF THE MEN IN THE INNER CHAMBERS ARE DENIED THE SIGHT OF OUR LORD'S COUNTENANCE.
'TWAS MY WISH THAT THEY MAY AT LEAST SHARE, THROUGH THIS MEAL, THE HAPPINESS OF OUR LIEGE ON THIS MOST FESTIVE DAY.
INDEED!
I AM MOST GRATEFUL FOR'T, SIR ARIKOTO, AS WILL THE OTHERS BE, I'M SURE!

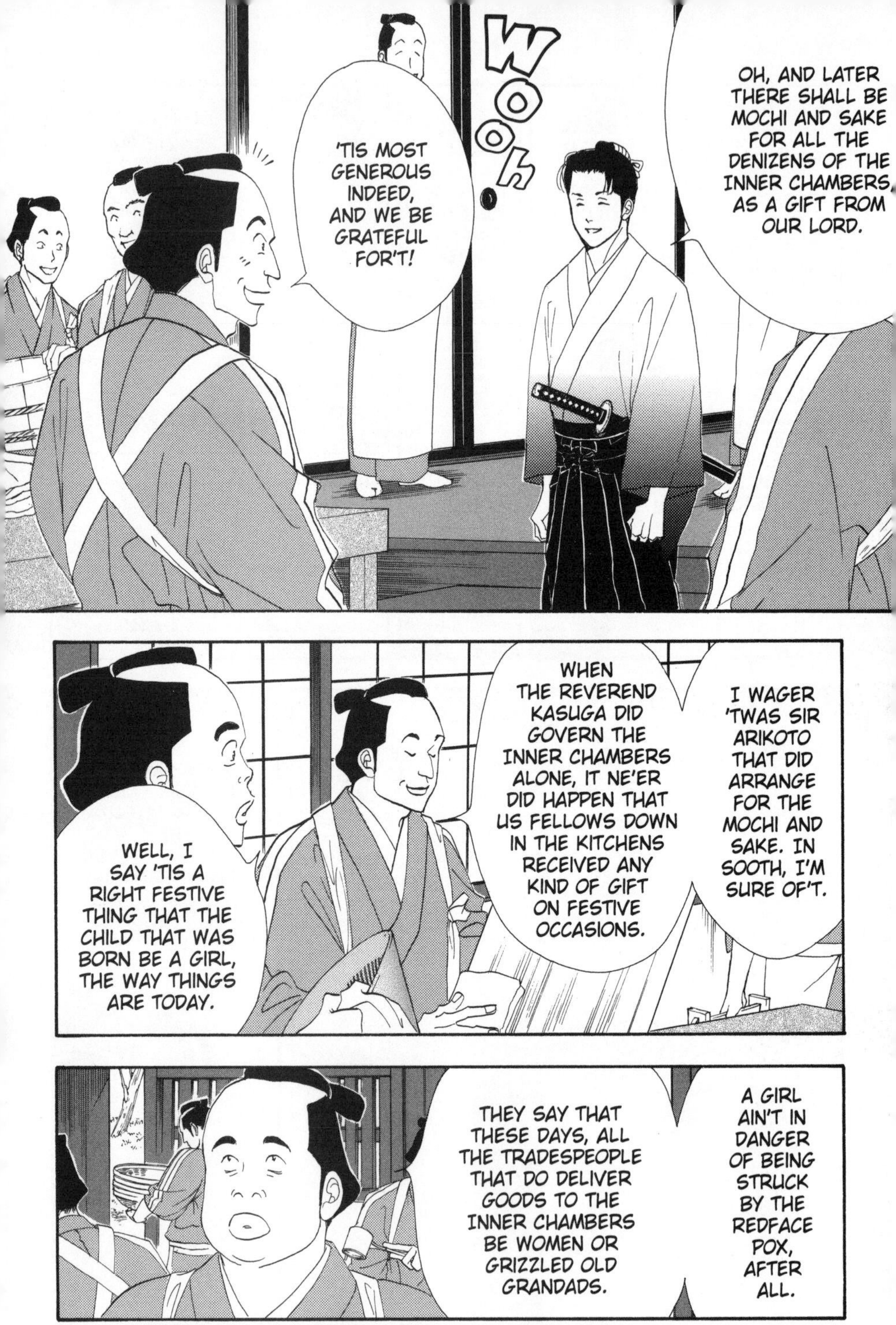
OH, AND LATER THERE SHALL BE MOCHI AND SAKE FOR ALL THE DENIZENS OF THE INNER CHAMBERS, AS A GIFT FROM OUR LORD.
Wooh!
'TIS MOST GENEROUS INDEED, AND WE BE GRATEFUL FOR'T!
I WAGER 'TWAS SIR ARIKOTO THAT DID ARRANGE FOR THE MOCHI AND SAKE. IN SOOTH, I'M SURE OF'T.
WHEN THE REVEREND KASUGA DID GOVERN THE INNER CHAMBERS ALONE, IT NE'ER DID HAPPEN THAT US FELLOWS DOWN IN THE KITCHENS RECEIVED ANY KIND OF GIFT ON FESTIVE OCCASIONS.
WELL, I SAY 'TIS A RIGHT FESTIVE THING THAT THE CHILD THAT WAS BORN BE A GIRL, THE WAY THINGS ARE TODAY.
A GIRL AIN'T IN DANGER OF BEING STRUCK BY THE REDFACE POX, AFTER ALL.
THEY SAY THAT THESE DAYS, ALL THE TRADESPEOPLE THAT DO DELIVER GOODS TO THE INNER CHAMBERS BE WOMEN OR GRIZZLED OLD GRANDADS.

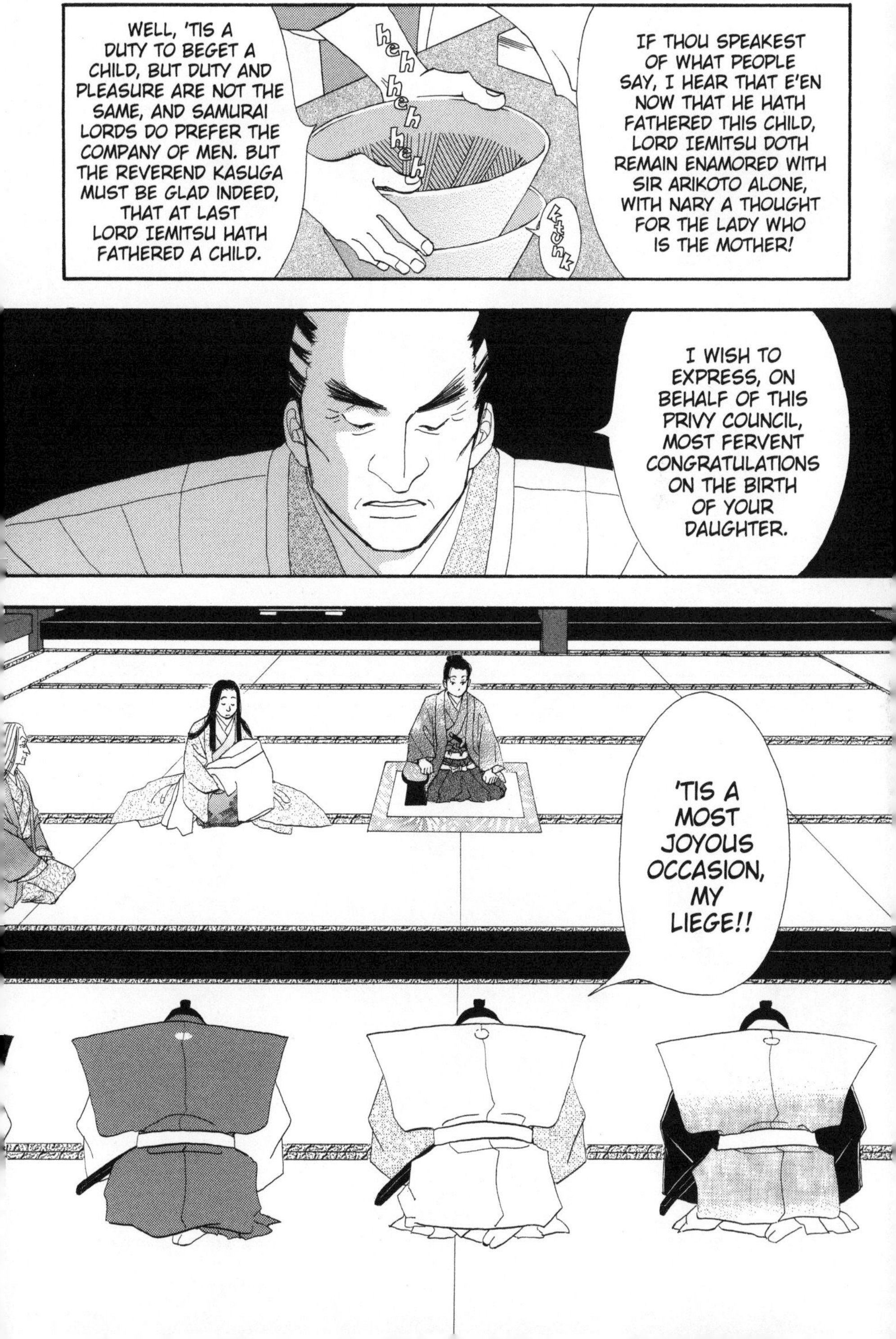
IF THOU SPEAKEST OF WHAT PEOPLE SAY, I HEAR THAT E'EN NOW THAT HE HATH FATHERED THIS CHILD, LORD IEMITSU DOTH REMAIN ENAMORED WITH SIR ARIKOTO ALONE, WITH NARY A THOUGHT FOR THE LADY WHO IS THE MOTHER!
ktunk
heh heh heh heh
WELL, 'TIS A DUTY TO BEGET A CHILD, BUT DUTY AND PLEASURE ARE NOT THE SAME, AND SAMURAI LORDS DO PREFER THE COMPANY OF MEN. BUT THE REVEREND KASUGA MUST BE GLAD INDEED, THAT AT LAST LORD IEMITSU HATH FATHERED A CHILD.
I WISH TO EXPRESS, ON BEHALF OF THIS PRIVY COUNCIL, MOST FERVENT CONGRATULATIONS ON THE BIRTH OF YOUR DAUGHTER.
'TIS A MOST JOYOUS OCCASION, MY LIEGE!!

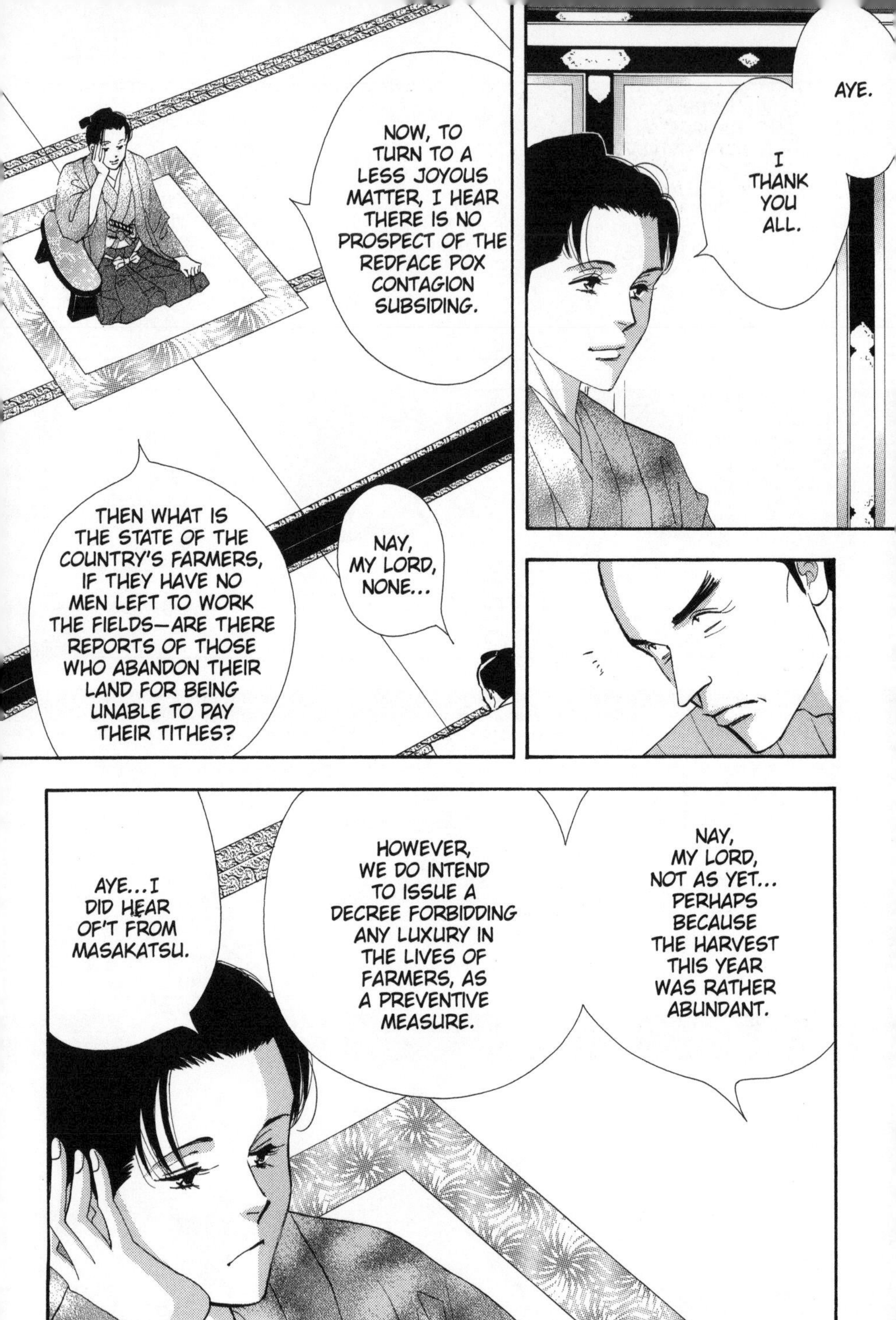
AYE.
I THANK YOU ALL.
NOW, TO TURN TO A LESS JOYOUS MATTER, I HEAR THERE IS NO PROSPECT OF THE REDFACE POX CONTAGION SUBSIDING.
NAY, MY LORD, NONE...
THEN WHAT IS THE STATE OF THE COUNTRY'S FARMERS, IF THEY HAVE NO MEN LEFT TO WORK THE FIELDS—ARE THERE REPORTS OF THOSE WHO ABANDON THEIR LAND FOR BEING UNABLE TO PAY THEIR TITHES?
NAY, MY LORD, NOT AS YET... PERHAPS BECAUSE THE HARVEST THIS YEAR WAS RATHER ABUNDANT.
HOWEVER, WE DO INTEND TO ISSUE A DECREE FORBIDDING ANY LUXURY IN THE LIVES OF FARMERS, AS A PREVENTIVE MEASURE.
AYE...I DID HEAR OF'T FROM MASAKATSU.

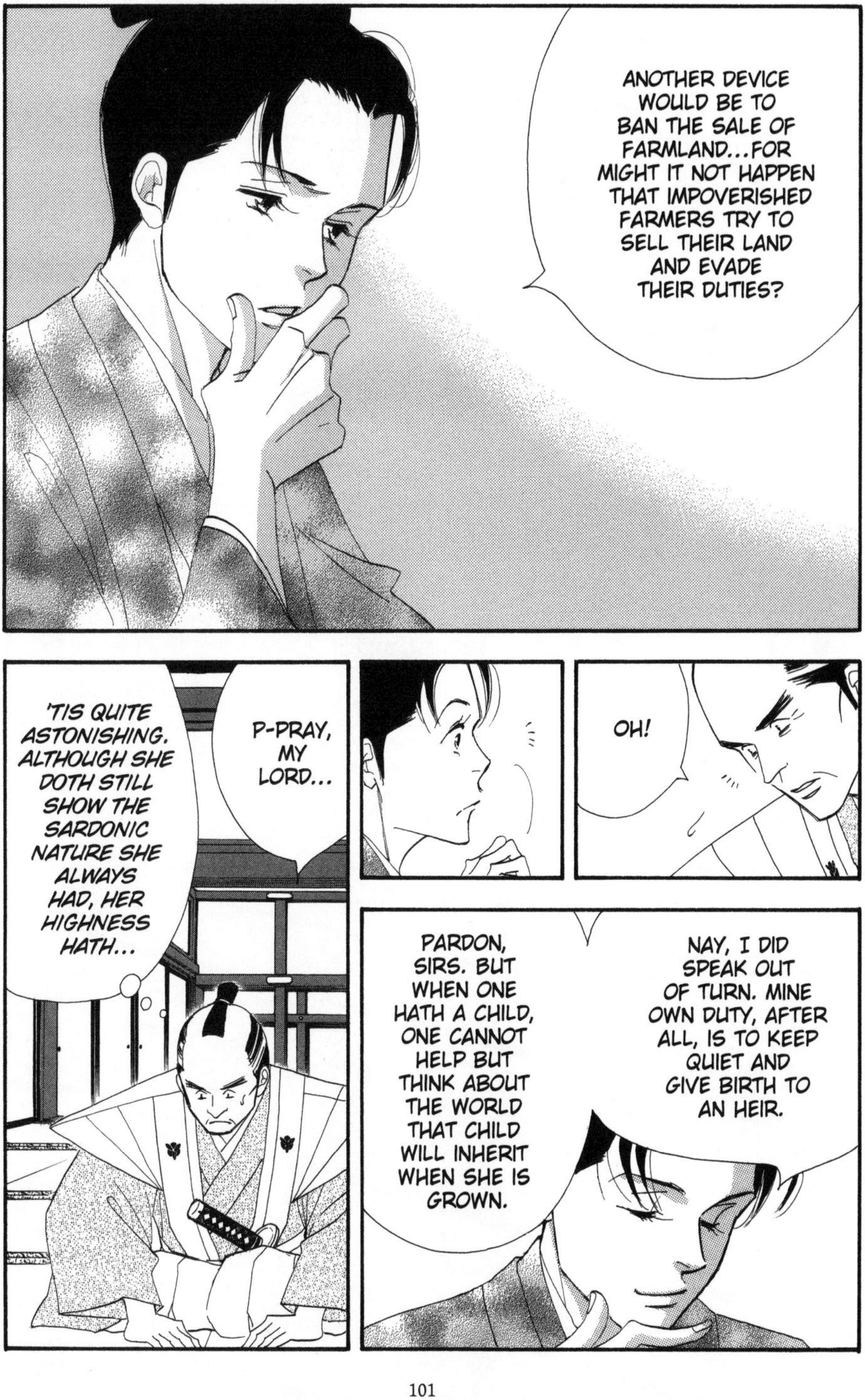
ANOTHER DEVICE WOULD BE TO BAN THE SALE OF FARMLAND...FOR MIGHT IT NOT HAPPEN THAT IMPOVERISHED FARMERS TRY TO SELL THEIR LAND AND EVADE THEIR DUTIES?
OH!
PARDON, SIRS. BUT WHEN ONE HATH A CHILD, ONE CANNOT HELP BUT THINK ABOUT THE WORLD THAT CHILD WILL INHERIT WHEN SHE IS GROWN.
NAY, I DID SPEAK OUT OF TURN. MINE OWN DUTY, AFTER ALL, IS TO KEEP QUIET AND GIVE BIRTH TO AN HEIR.
P-PRAY, MY LORD...
'TIS QUITE ASTONISHING. ALTHOUGH SHE DOTH STILL SHOW THE SARDONIC NATURE SHE ALWAYS HAD, HER HIGHNESS HATH...

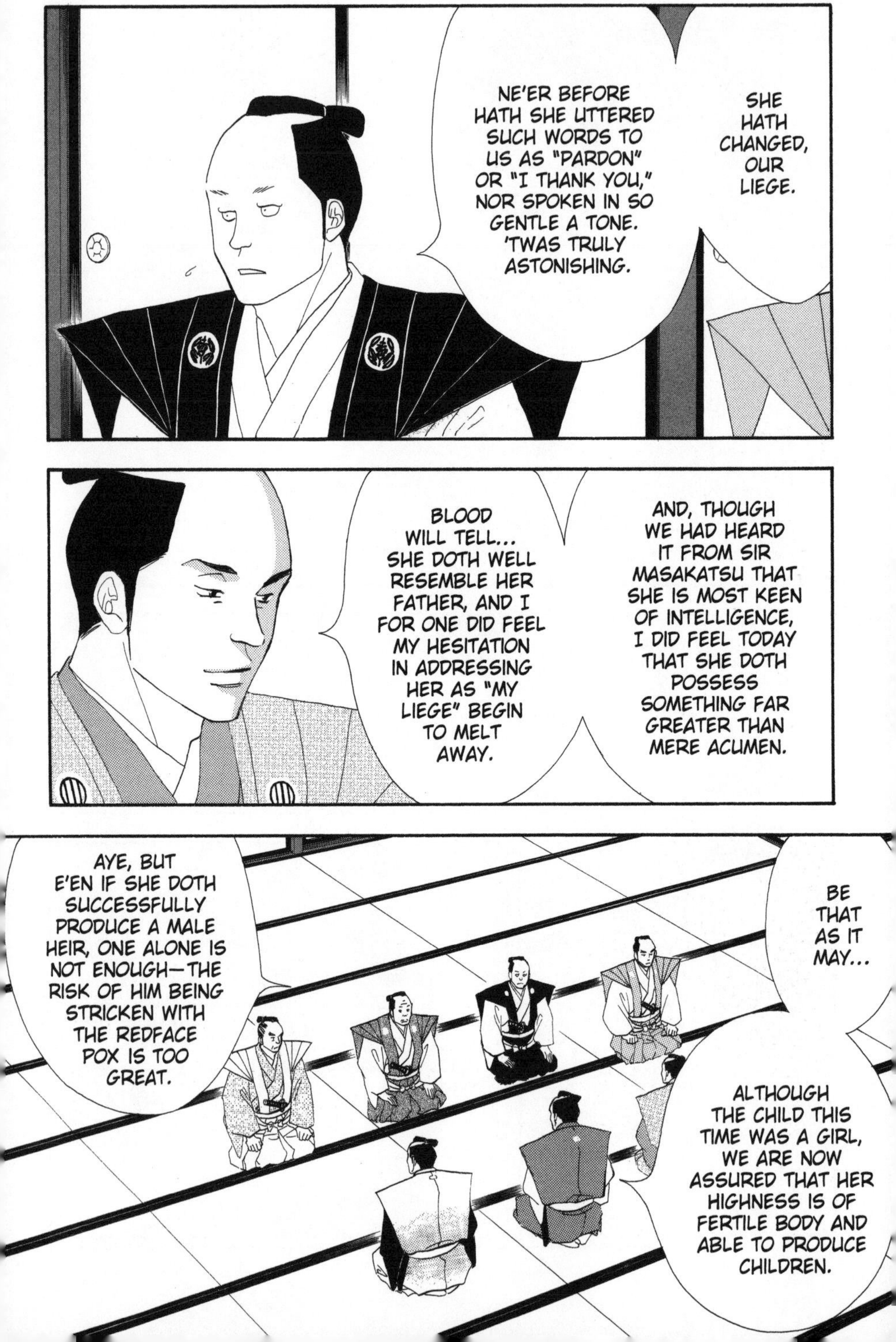
SHE HATH CHANGED, OUR LIEGE.
NE'ER BEFORE HATH SHE UTTERED SUCH WORDS TO US AS "PARDON" OR "I THANK YOU," NOR SPOKEN IN SO GENTLE A TONE. 'TWAS TRULY ASTONISHING.
AND, THOUGH WE HAD HEARD IT FROM SIR MASAKATSU THAT SHE IS MOST KEEN OF INTELLIGENCE, I DID FEEL TODAY THAT SHE DOTH POSSESS SOMETHING FAR GREATER THAN MERE ACUMEN.
BLOOD WILL TELL... SHE DOTH WELL RESEMBLE HER FATHER, AND I FOR ONE DID FEEL MY HESITATION IN ADDRESSING HER AS "MY LIEGE" BEGIN TO MELT AWAY.
BE THAT AS IT MAY...
ALTHOUGH THE CHILD THIS TIME WAS A GIRL, WE ARE NOW ASSURED THAT HER HIGHNESS IS OF FERTILE BODY AND ABLE TO PRODUCE CHILDREN.
AYE, BUT E'EN IF SHE DOTH SUCCESSFULLY PRODUCE A MALE HEIR, ONE ALONE IS NOT ENOUGH—THE RISK OF HIM BEING STRICKEN WITH THE REDFACE POX IS TOO GREAT.

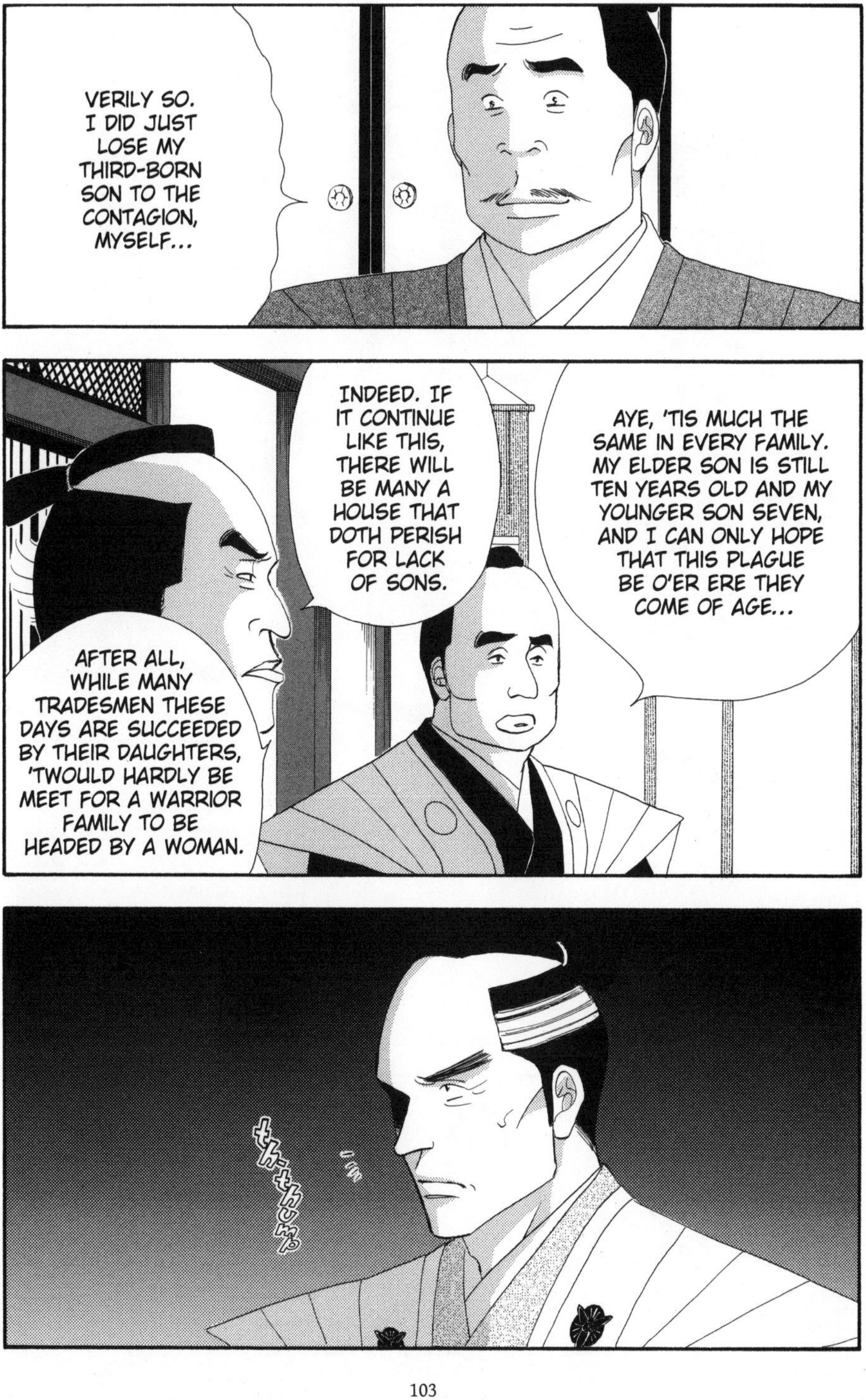
VERILY SO. I DID JUST LOSE MY THIRD-BORN SON TO THE CONTAGION, MYSELF...
AYE, 'TIS MUCH THE SAME IN EVERY FAMILY. MY ELDER SON IS STILL TEN YEARS OLD AND MY YOUNGER SON SEVEN, AND I CAN ONLY HOPE THAT THIS PLAGUE BE O'ER ERE THEY COME OF AGE...
INDEED. IF IT CONTINUE LIKE THIS, THERE WILL BE MANY A HOUSE THAT DOTH PERISH FOR LACK OF SONS.
AFTER ALL, WHILE MANY TRADESMEN THESE DAYS ARE SUCCEEDED BY THEIR DAUGHTERS, 'TWOULD HARDLY BE MEET FOR A WARRIOR FAMILY TO BE HEADED BY A WOMAN.
th-thump

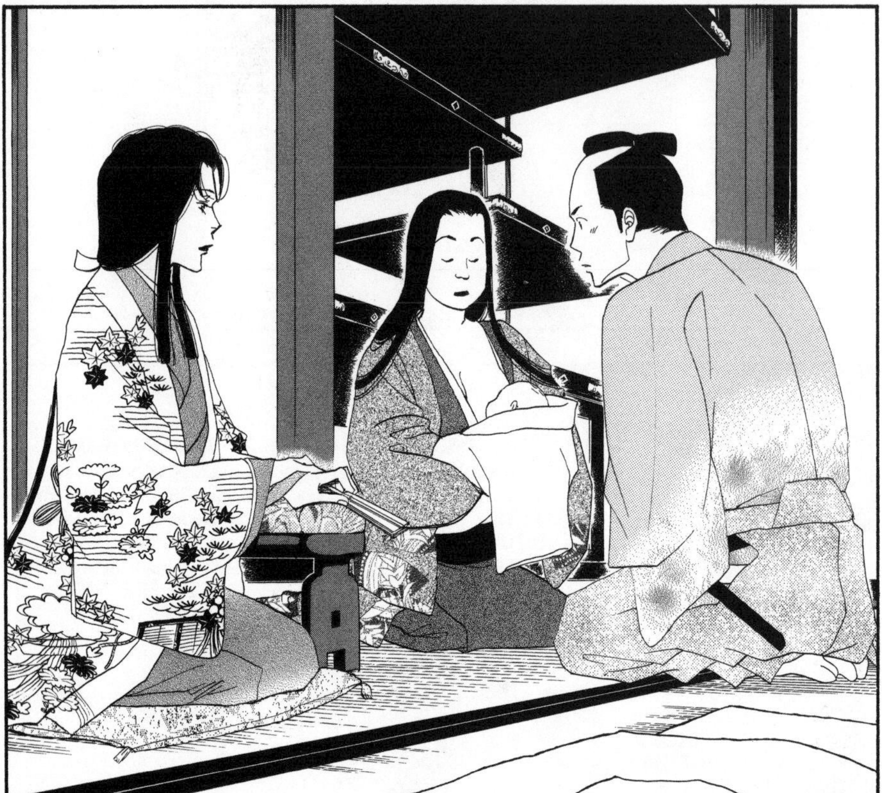

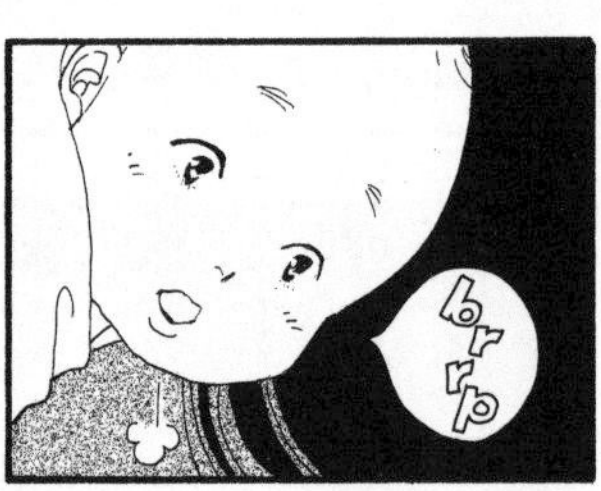
brrp

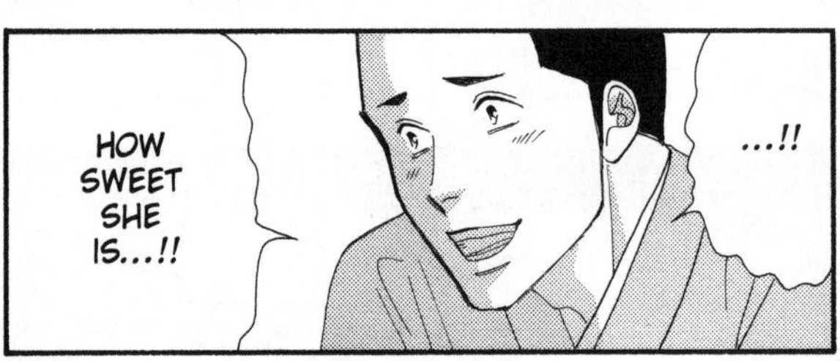
...!!
HOW SWEET SHE IS...!!

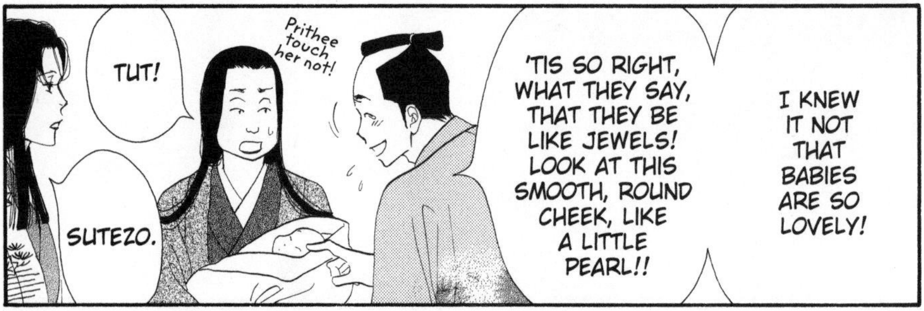
I KNEW IT NOT THAT BABIES ARE SO LOVELY!
'TIS SO RIGHT, WHAT THEY SAY, THAT THEY BE LIKE JEWELS! LOOK AT THIS SMOOTH, ROUND CHEEK, LIKE A LITTLE PEARL!!
Prithee touch her not!
TUT!
SUTEZO.

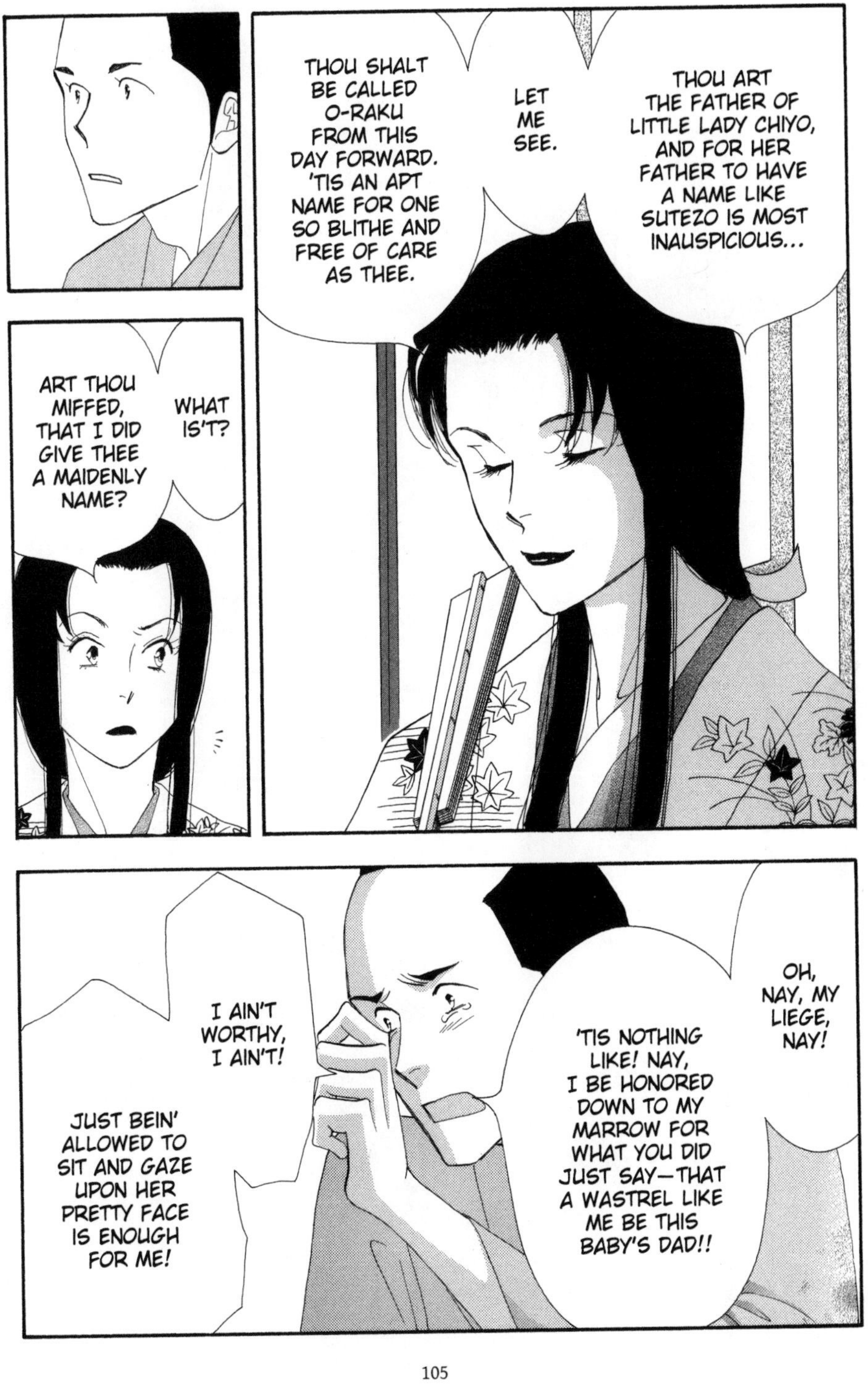
THOU ART THE FATHER OF LITTLE LADY CHIYO, AND FOR HER FATHER TO HAVE A NAME LIKE SUTEZO IS MOST INAUSPICIOUS...
LET ME SEE.
THOU SHALT BE CALLED O-RAKU FROM THIS DAY FORWARD. 'TIS AN APT NAME FOR ONE SO BLITHE AND FREE OF CARE AS THEE.
WHAT IS'T?
ART THOU MIFFED, THAT I DID GIVE THEE A MAIDENLY NAME?
OH, NAY, MY LIEGE, NAY!
'TIS NOTHING LIKE! NAY, I BE HONORED DOWN TO MY MARROW FOR WHAT YOU DID JUST SAY—THAT A WASTREL LIKE ME BE THIS BABY'S DAD!!
I AIN'T WORTHY, I AIN'T!
JUST BEIN' ALLOWED TO SIT AND GAZE UPON HER PRETTY FACE IS ENOUGH FOR ME!

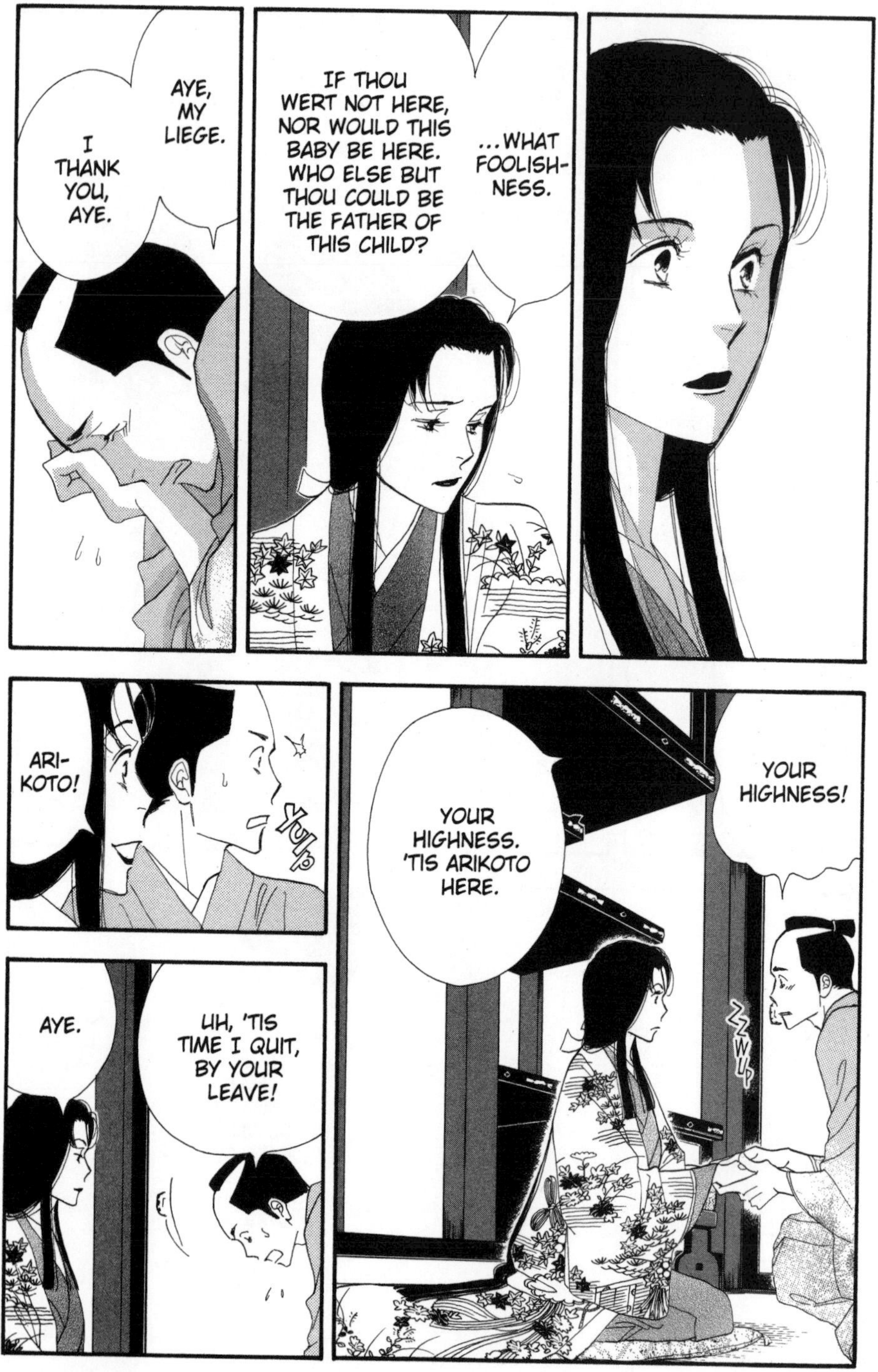
...WHAT FOOLISHNESS.
IF THOU WERT NOT HERE, NOR WOULD THIS BABY BE HERE. WHO ELSE BUT THOU COULD BE THE FATHER OF THIS CHILD?
AYE, MY LIEGE.
I THANK YOU, AYE.
YOUR HIGHNESS!
YOUR HIGHNESS. 'TIS ARIKOTO HERE.
ZZWUP
ARI-KOTO!
YUP
UH, 'TIS TIME I QUIT, BY YOUR LEAVE!
AYE.

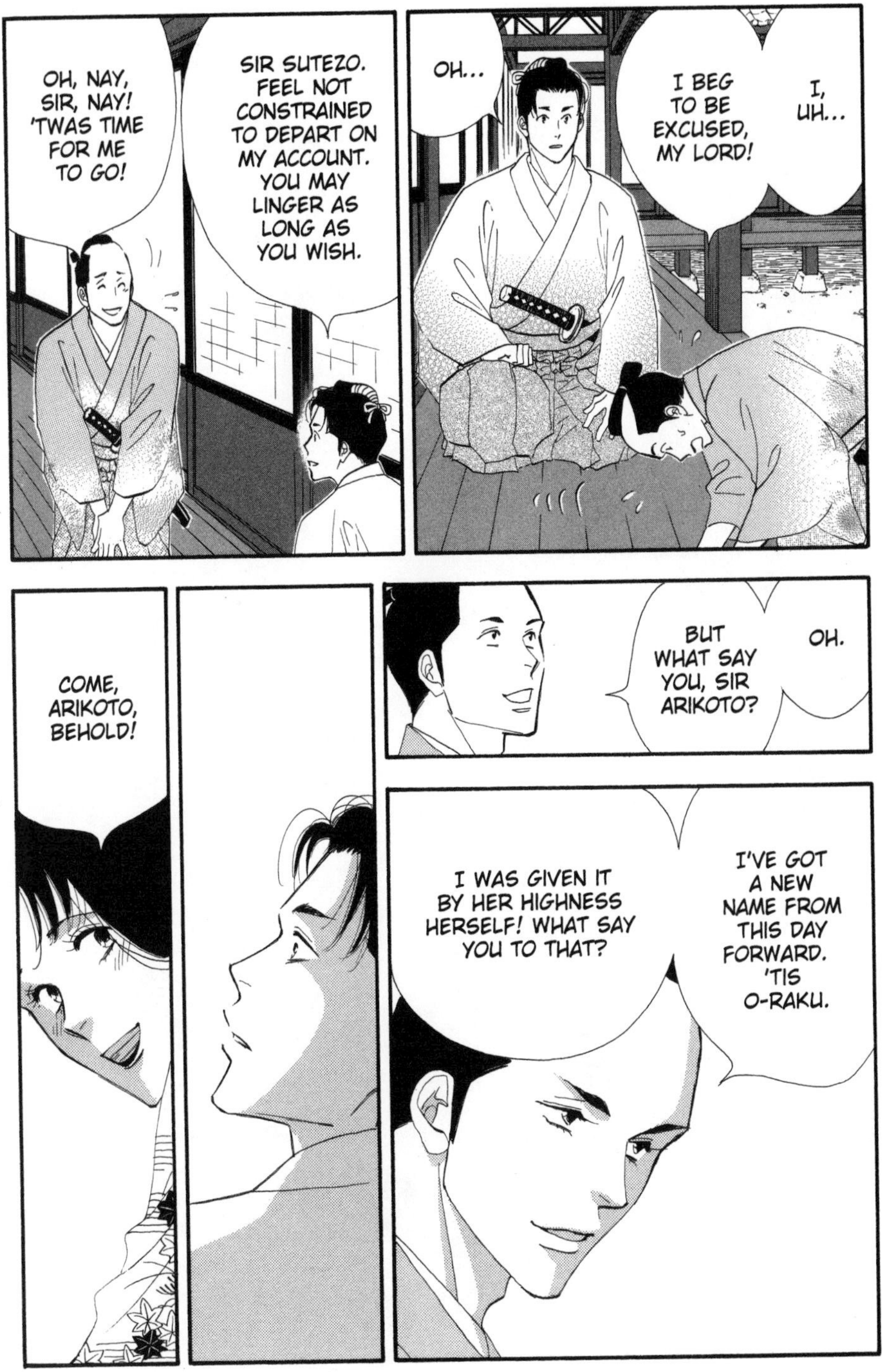
I, UH...
I BEG TO BE EXCUSED, MY LORD!
OH...
SIR SUTEZO. FEEL NOT CONSTRAINED TO DEPART ON MY ACCOUNT. YOU MAY LINGER AS LONG AS YOU WISH.
OH, NAY, SIR, NAY! 'TWAS TIME FOR ME TO GO!
OH.
BUT WHAT SAY YOU, SIR ARIKOTO?
I'VE GOT A NEW NAME FROM THIS DAY FORWARD. 'TIS O-RAKU.
I WAS GIVEN IT BY HER HIGHNESS HERSELF! WHAT SAY YOU TO THAT?
COME, ARIKOTO, BEHOLD!

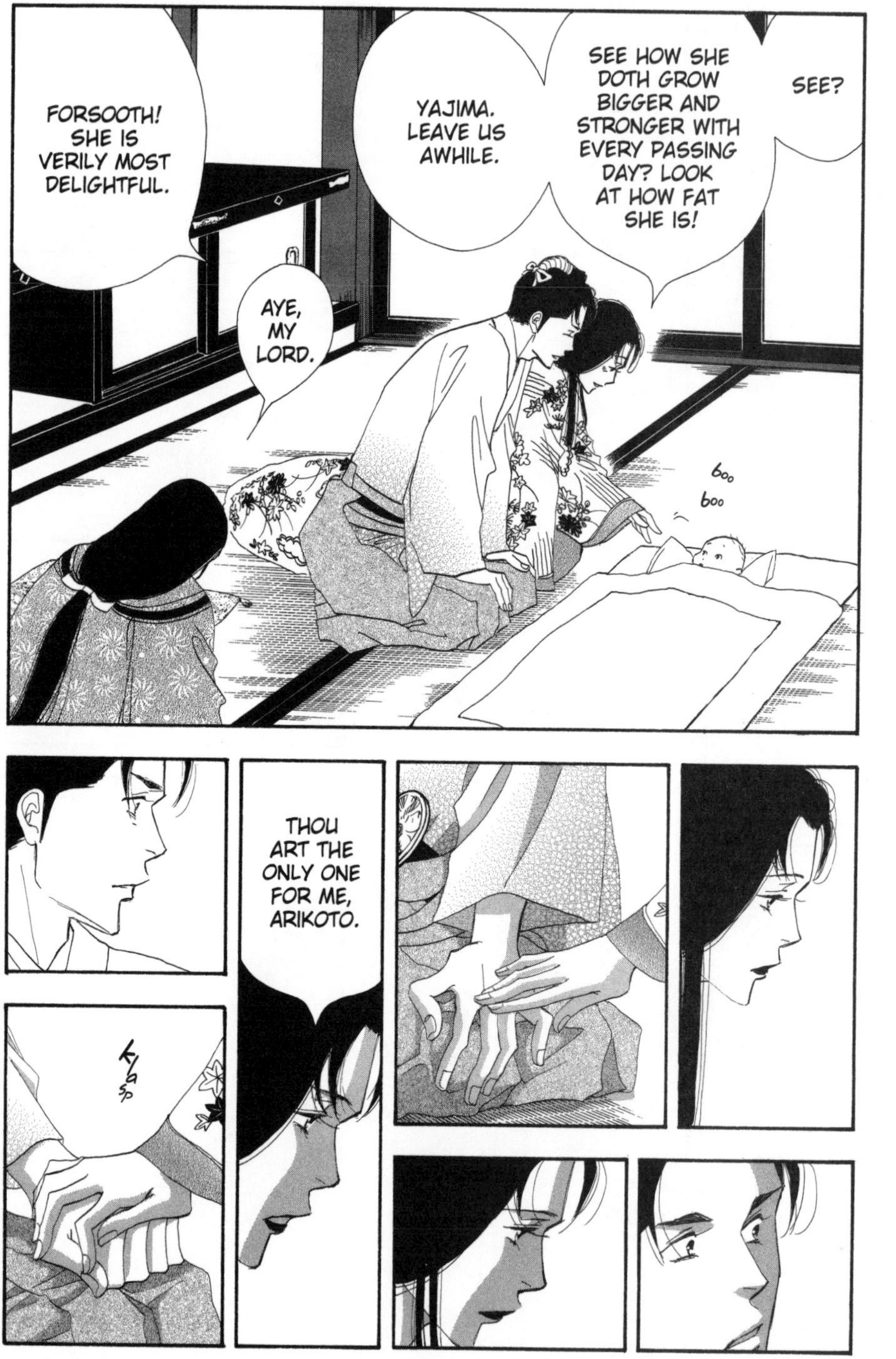
SEE?
SEE HOW SHE DOTH GROW BIGGER AND STRONGER WITH EVERY PASSING DAY? LOOK AT HOW FAT SHE IS!
YAJIMA. LEAVE US AWHILE.
FORSOOTH! SHE IS VERILY MOST DELIGHTFUL.
AYE, MY LORD.
boo boo
THOU ART THE ONLY ONE FOR ME, ARIKOTO.
klasp

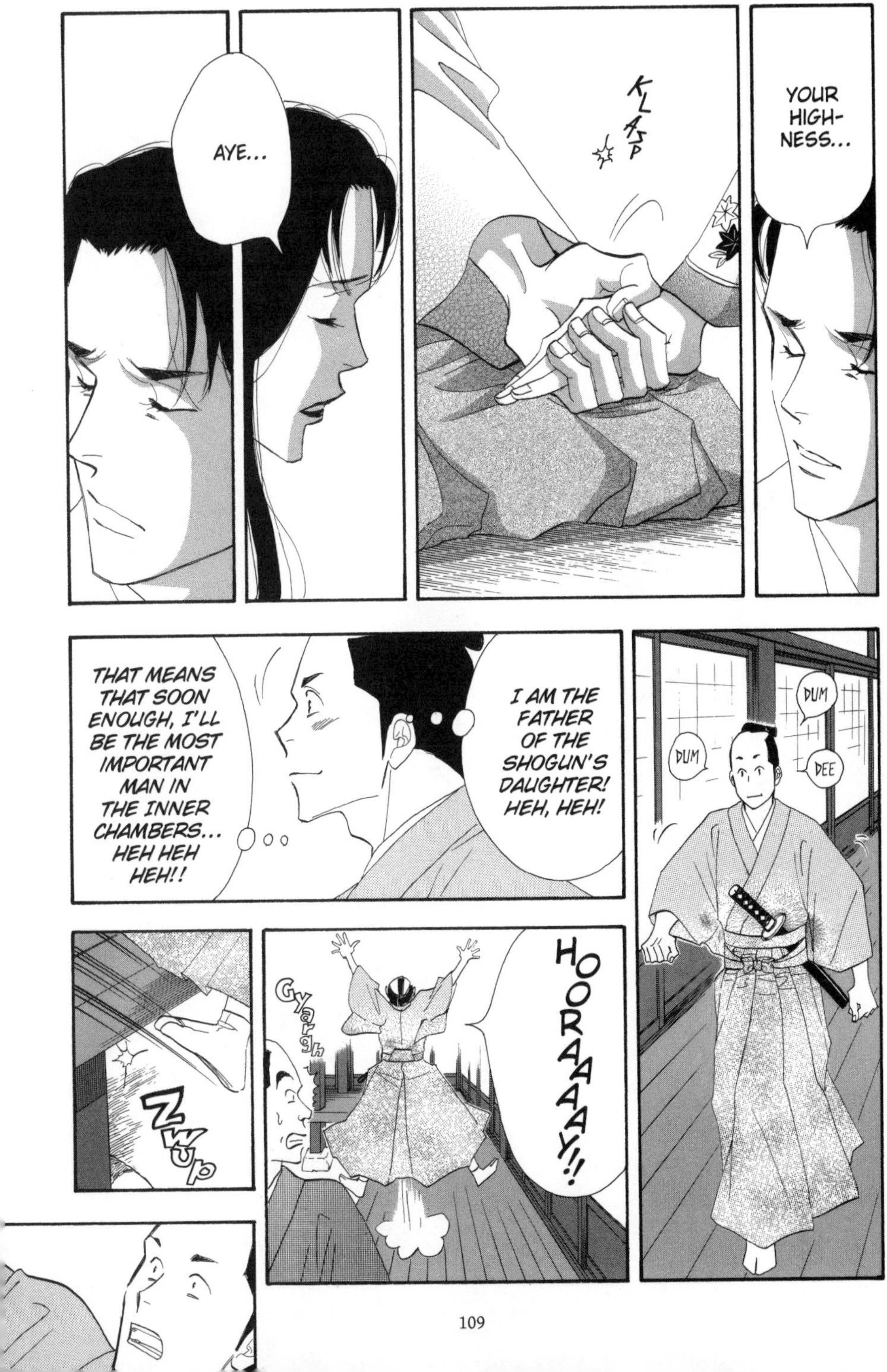
YOUR HIGHNESS...
KLASP
AYE...
DUM
DEE
DUM
I AM THE FATHER OF THE SHOGUN'S DAUGHTER! HEH, HEH!
THAT MEANS THAT SOON ENOUGH, I'LL BE THE MOST IMPORTANT MAN IN THE INNER CHAMBERS... HEH HEH HEH!!
HOORAAAAY!!
Gyargh
Zwup

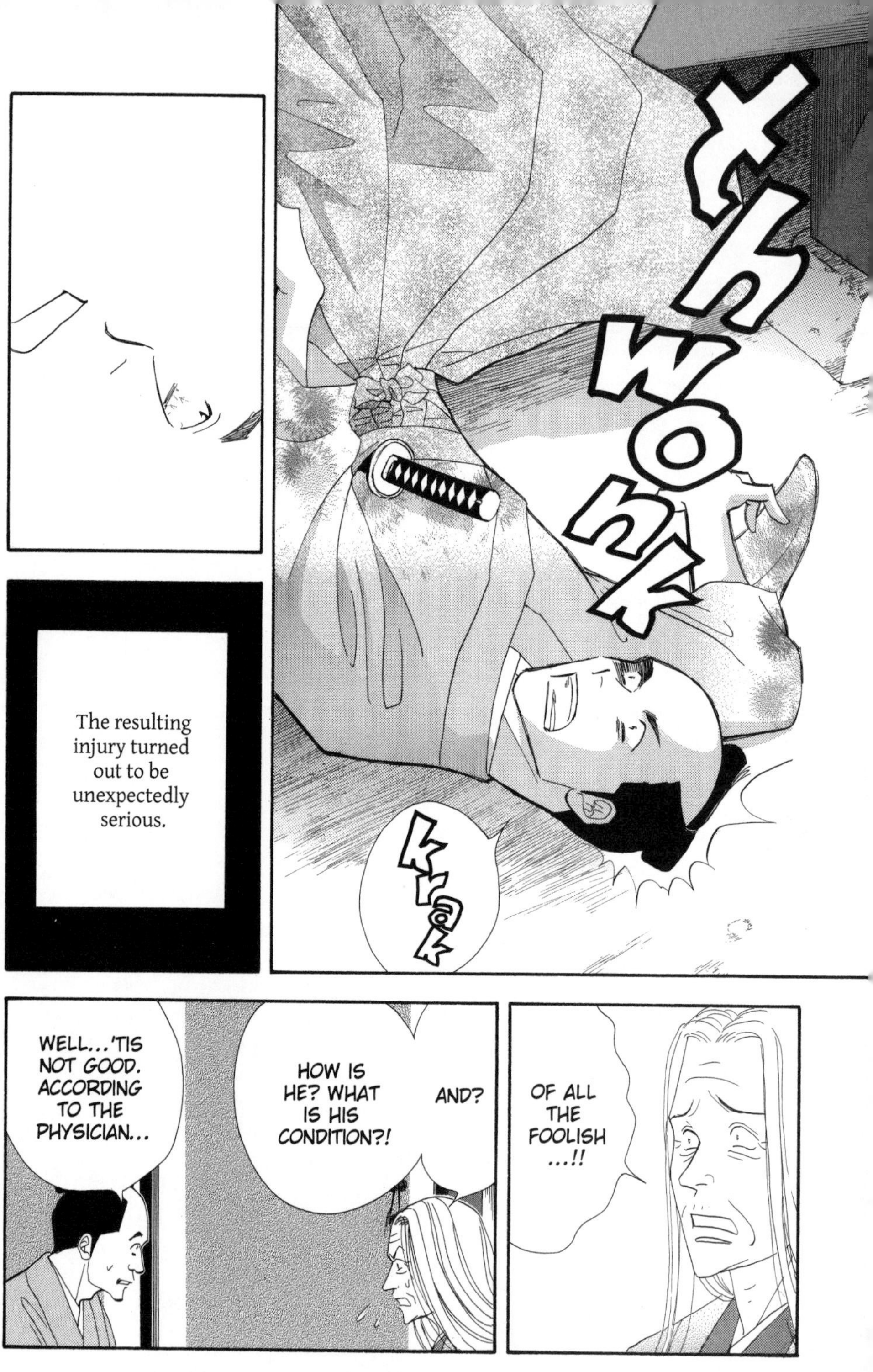
thwonk
krak
The resulting injury turned out to be unexpectedly serious.
OF ALL THE FOOLISH ...!!
HOW IS HE? WHAT IS HIS CONDITION?!
WELL...'TIS NOT GOOD. ACCORDING TO THE PHYSICIAN...
AND?

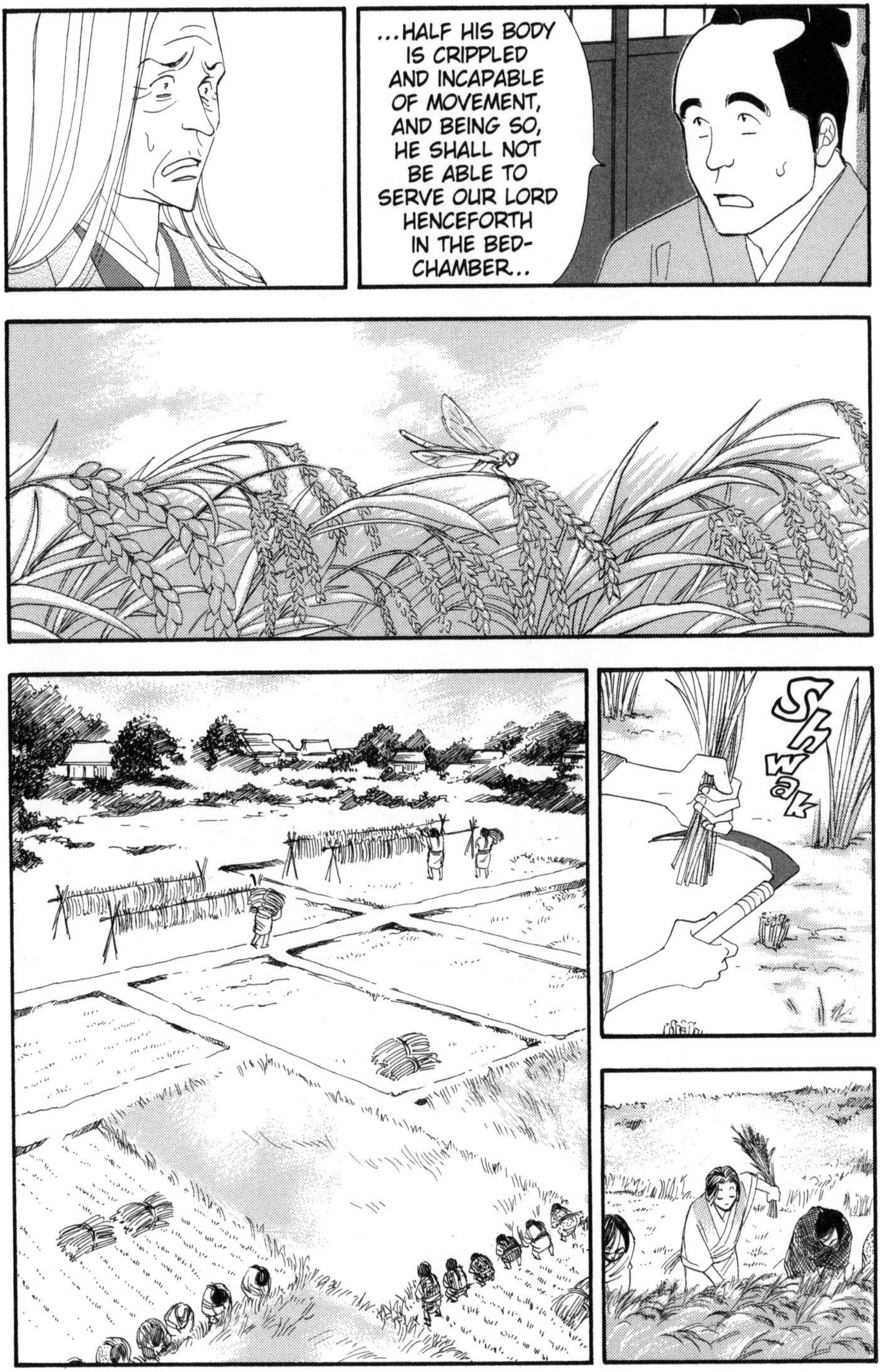
...HALF HIS BODY IS CRIPPLED AND INCAPABLE OF MOVEMENT, AND BEING SO, HE SHALL NOT BE ABLE TO SERVE OUR LORD HENCEFORTH IN THE BED-CHAMBER...
Shwak

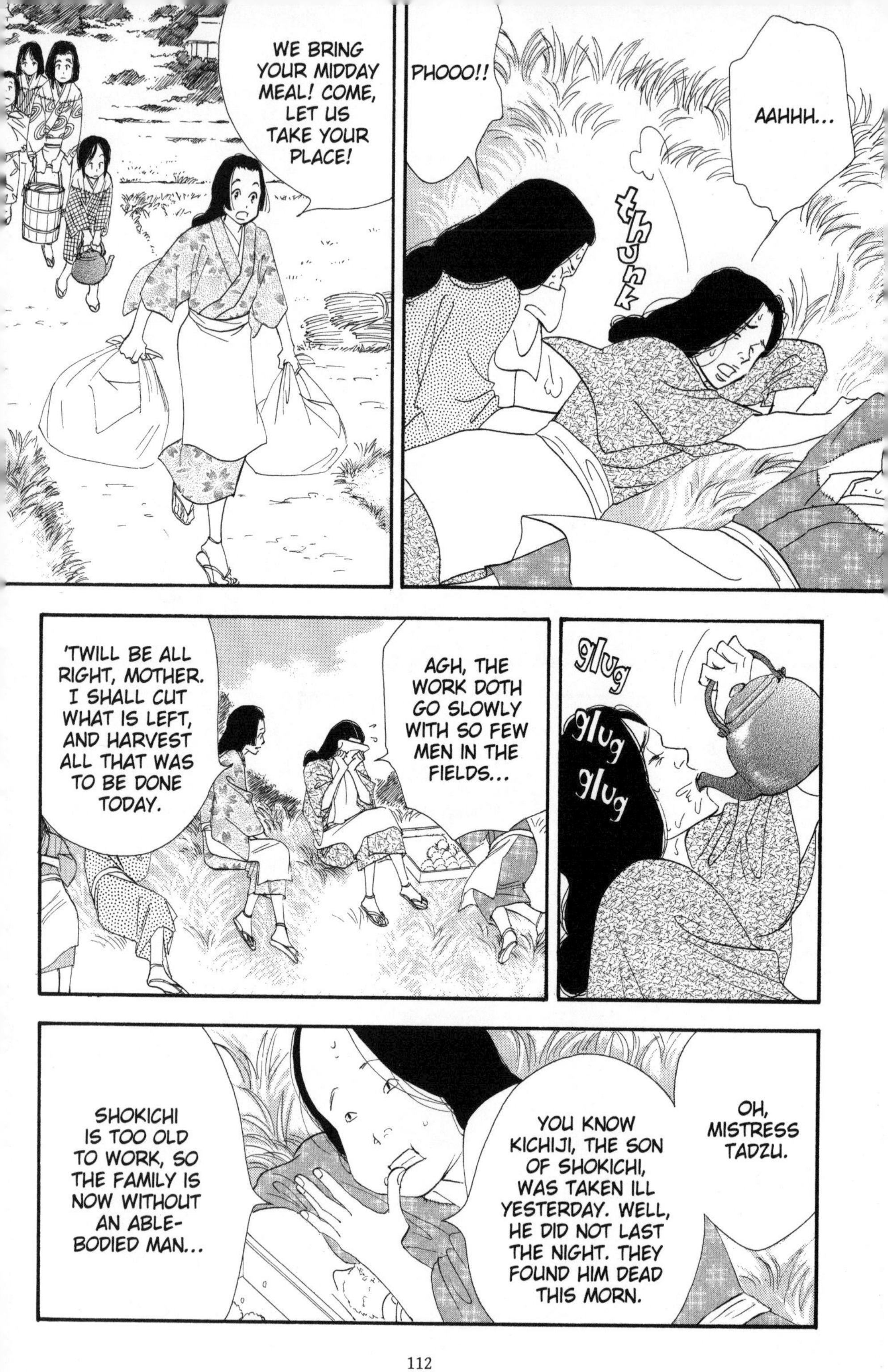
AAHHH...
thhunk
PHOOO!!
WE BRING YOUR MIDDAY MEAL! COME, LET US TAKE YOUR PLACE!
glug
glug
glug
AGH, THE WORK DOTH GO SLOWLY WITH SO FEW MEN IN THE FIELDS...
'TWILL BE ALL RIGHT, MOTHER. I SHALL CUT WHAT IS LEFT, AND HARVEST ALL THAT WAS TO BE DONE TODAY.
OH, MISTRESS TADZU.
YOU KNOW KICHIJI, THE SON OF SHOKICHI, WAS TAKEN ILL YESTERDAY. WELL, HE DID NOT LAST THE NIGHT. THEY FOUND HIM DEAD THIS MORN.
SHOKICHI IS TOO OLD TO WORK, SO THE FAMILY IS NOW WITHOUT AN ABLE-BODIED MAN...

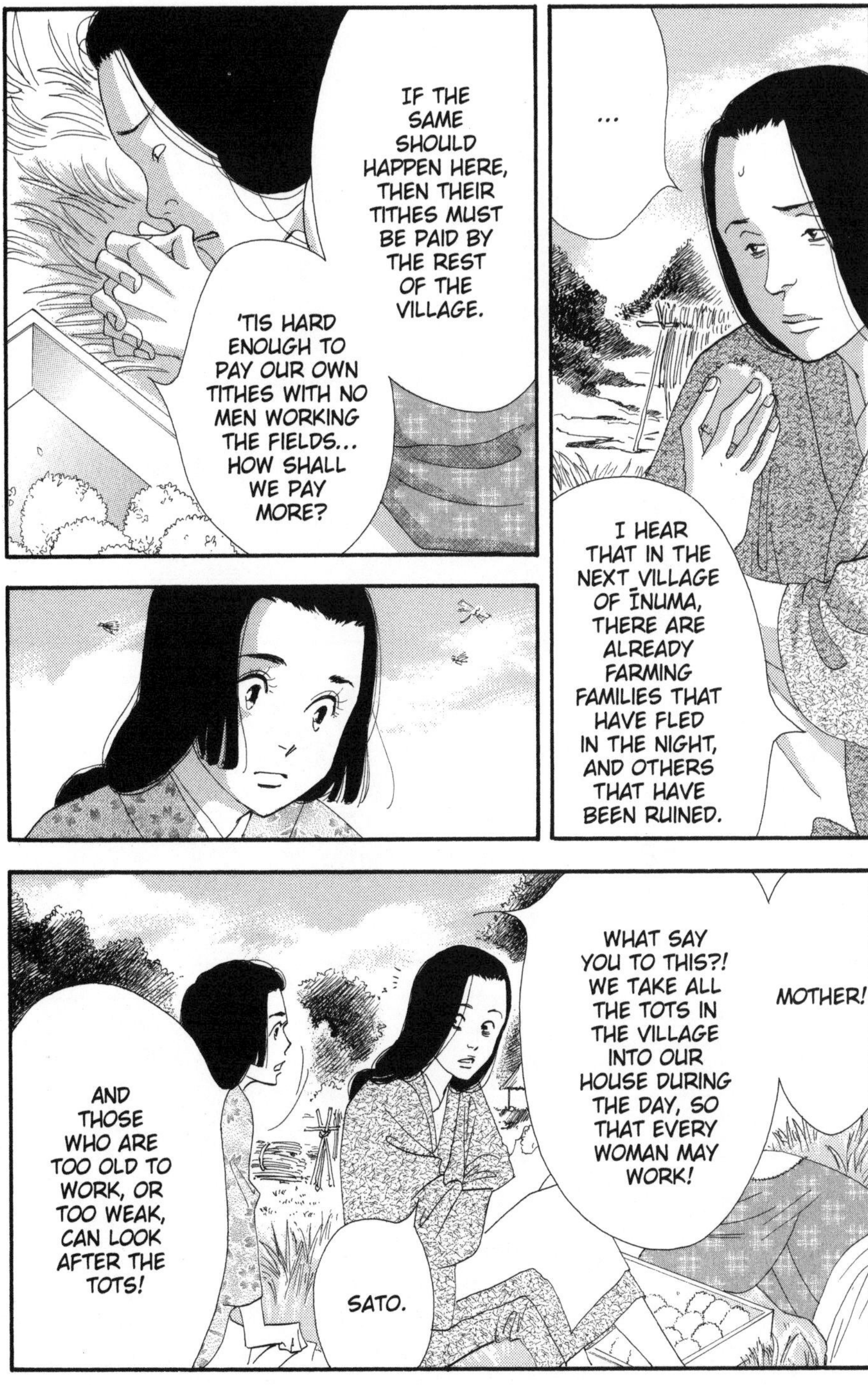
...
I HEAR THAT IN THE NEXT VILLAGE OF INUMA, THERE ARE ALREADY FARMING FAMILIES THAT HAVE FLED IN THE NIGHT, AND OTHERS THAT HAVE BEEN RUINED.
IF THE SAME SHOULD HAPPEN HERE, THEN THEIR TITHES MUST BE PAID BY THE REST OF THE VILLAGE.
'TIS HARD ENOUGH TO PAY OUR OWN TITHES WITH NO MEN WORKING THE FIELDS... HOW SHALL WE PAY MORE?
MOTHER!
WHAT SAY YOU TO THIS?! WE TAKE ALL THE TOTS IN THE VILLAGE INTO OUR HOUSE DURING THE DAY, SO THAT EVERY WOMAN MAY WORK!
AND THOSE WHO ARE TOO OLD TO WORK, OR TOO WEAK, CAN LOOK AFTER THE TOTS!
SATO.

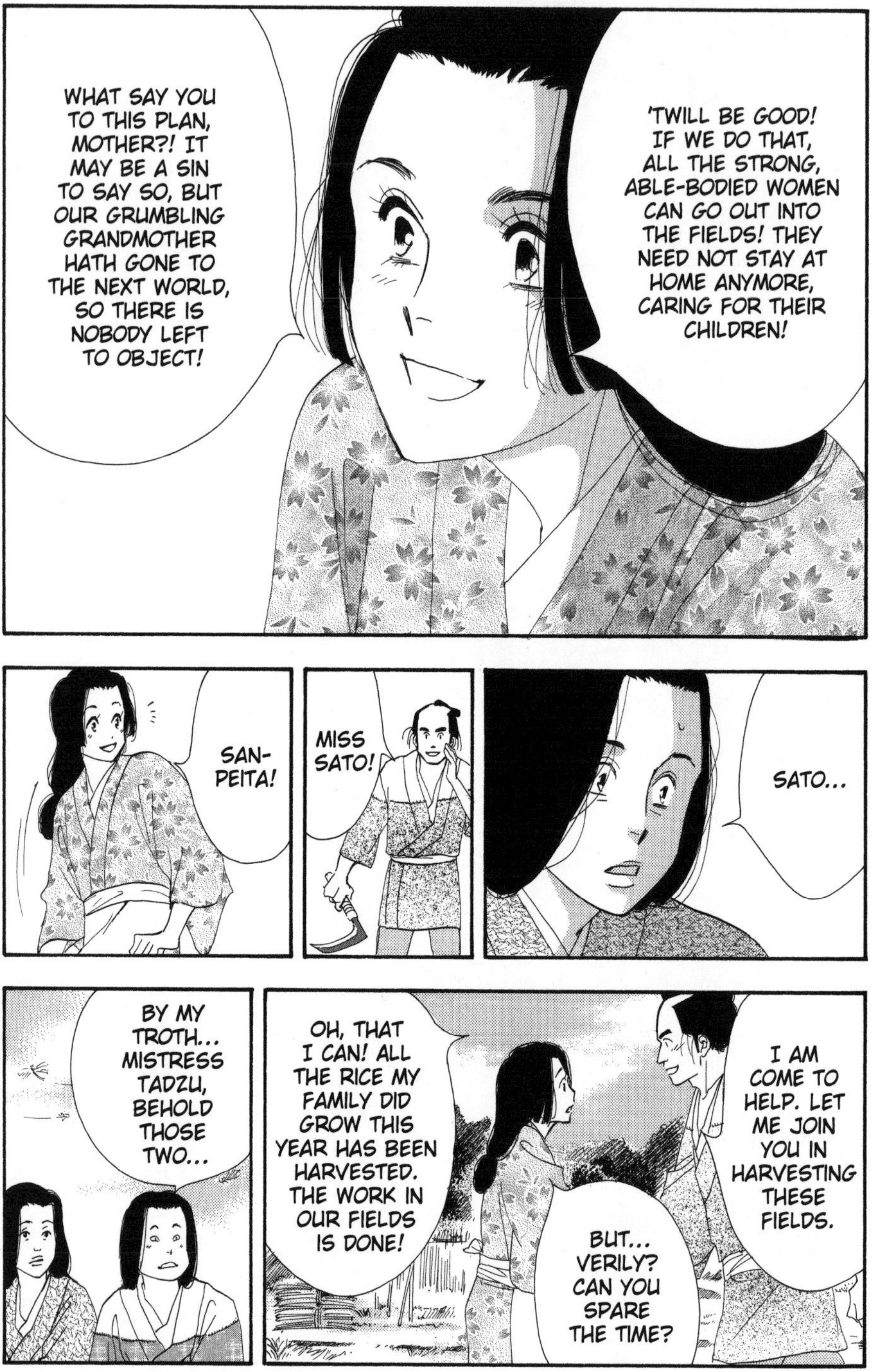
'TWILL BE GOOD! IF WE DO THAT, ALL THE STRONG, ABLE-BODIED WOMEN CAN GO OUT INTO THE FIELDS! THEY NEED NOT STAY AT HOME ANYMORE, CARING FOR THEIR CHILDREN!
WHAT SAY YOU TO THIS PLAN, MOTHER?! IT MAY BE A SIN TO SAY SO, BUT OUR GRUMBLING GRANDMOTHER HATH GONE TO THE NEXT WORLD, SO THERE IS NOBODY LEFT TO OBJECT!
SATO...
MISS SATO!
SAN-PEITA!
I AM COME TO HELP. LET ME JOIN YOU IN HARVESTING THESE FIELDS.
BUT... VERILY? CAN YOU SPARE THE TIME?
OH, THAT I CAN! ALL THE RICE MY FAMILY DID GROW THIS YEAR HAS BEEN HARVESTED. THE WORK IN OUR FIELDS IS DONE!
BY MY TROTH... MISTRESS TADZU, BEHOLD THOSE TWO...

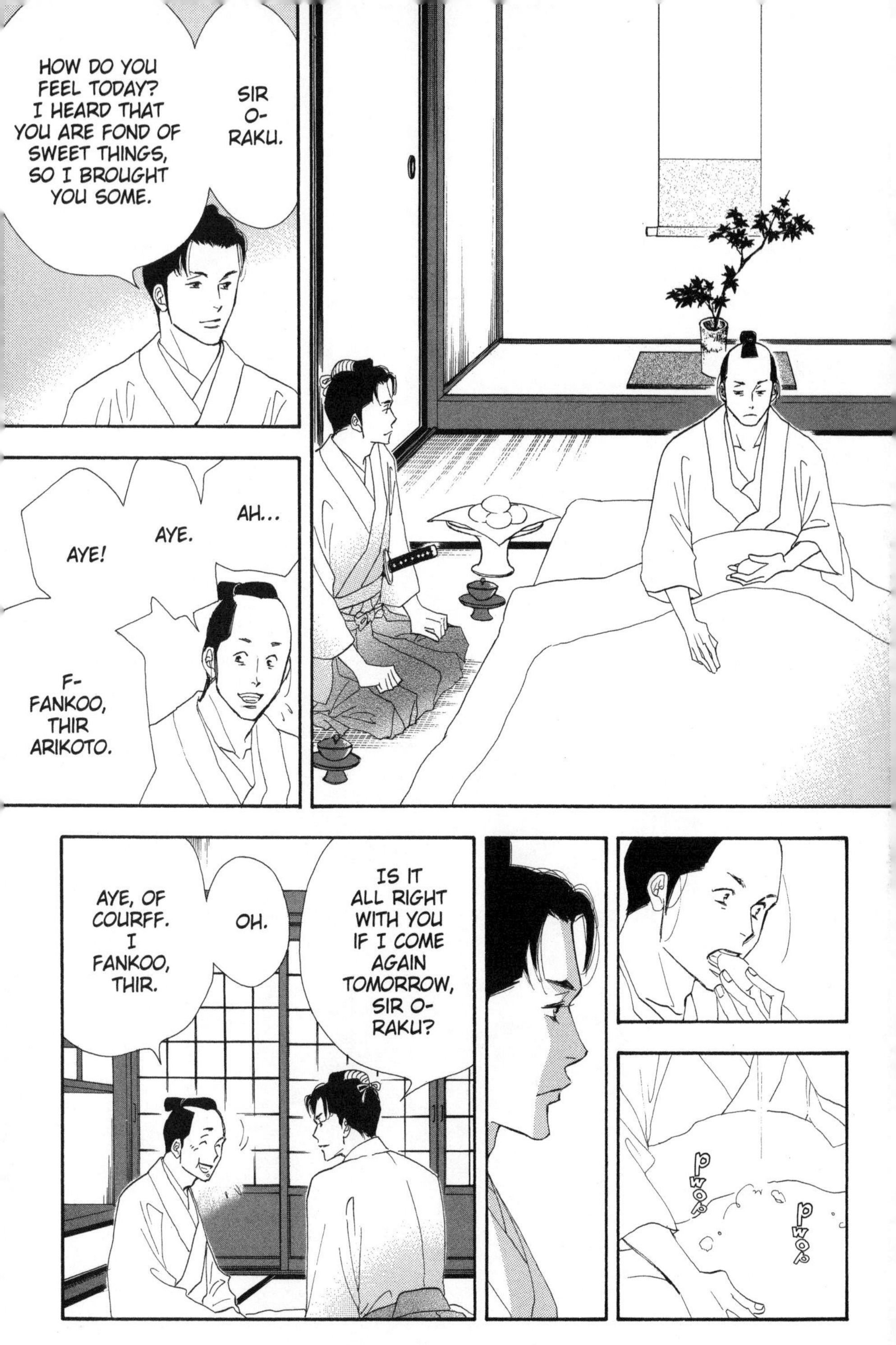
SIR O-RAKU.
HOW DO YOU FEEL TODAY? I HEARD THAT YOU ARE FOND OF SWEET THINGS, SO I BROUGHT YOU SOME.
AH...
AYE.
AYE!
F-FANKOO, THIR ARIKOTO.
pwop
pwop
IS IT ALL RIGHT WITH YOU IF I COME AGAIN TOMORROW, SIR O-RAKU?
OH.
AYE, OF COURFF. I FANKOO, THIR.

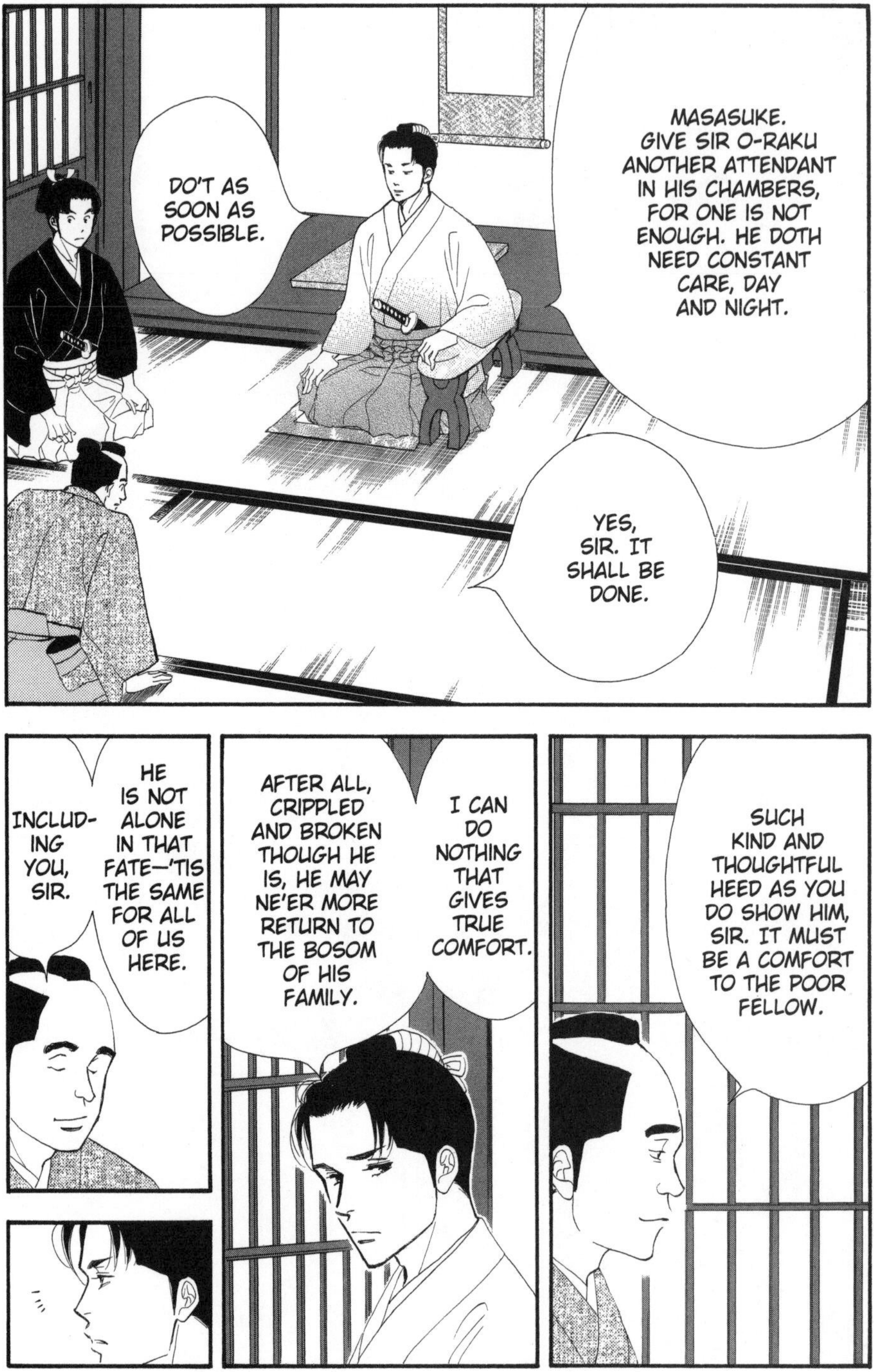
MASASUKE. GIVE SIR O-RAKU ANOTHER ATTENDANT IN HIS CHAMBERS, FOR ONE IS NOT ENOUGH. HE DOTH NEED CONSTANT CARE, DAY AND NIGHT.
DO'T AS SOON AS POSSIBLE.
YES, SIR. IT SHALL BE DONE.
SUCH KIND AND THOUGHTFUL HEED AS YOU DO SHOW HIM, SIR. IT MUST BE A COMFORT TO THE POOR FELLOW.
I CAN DO NOTHING THAT GIVES TRUE COMFORT.
AFTER ALL, CRIPPLED AND BROKEN THOUGH HE IS, HE MAY NE'ER MORE RETURN TO THE BOSOM OF HIS FAMILY.
HE IS NOT ALONE IN THAT FATE—'TIS THE SAME FOR ALL OF US HERE.
INCLUD-ING YOU, SIR.

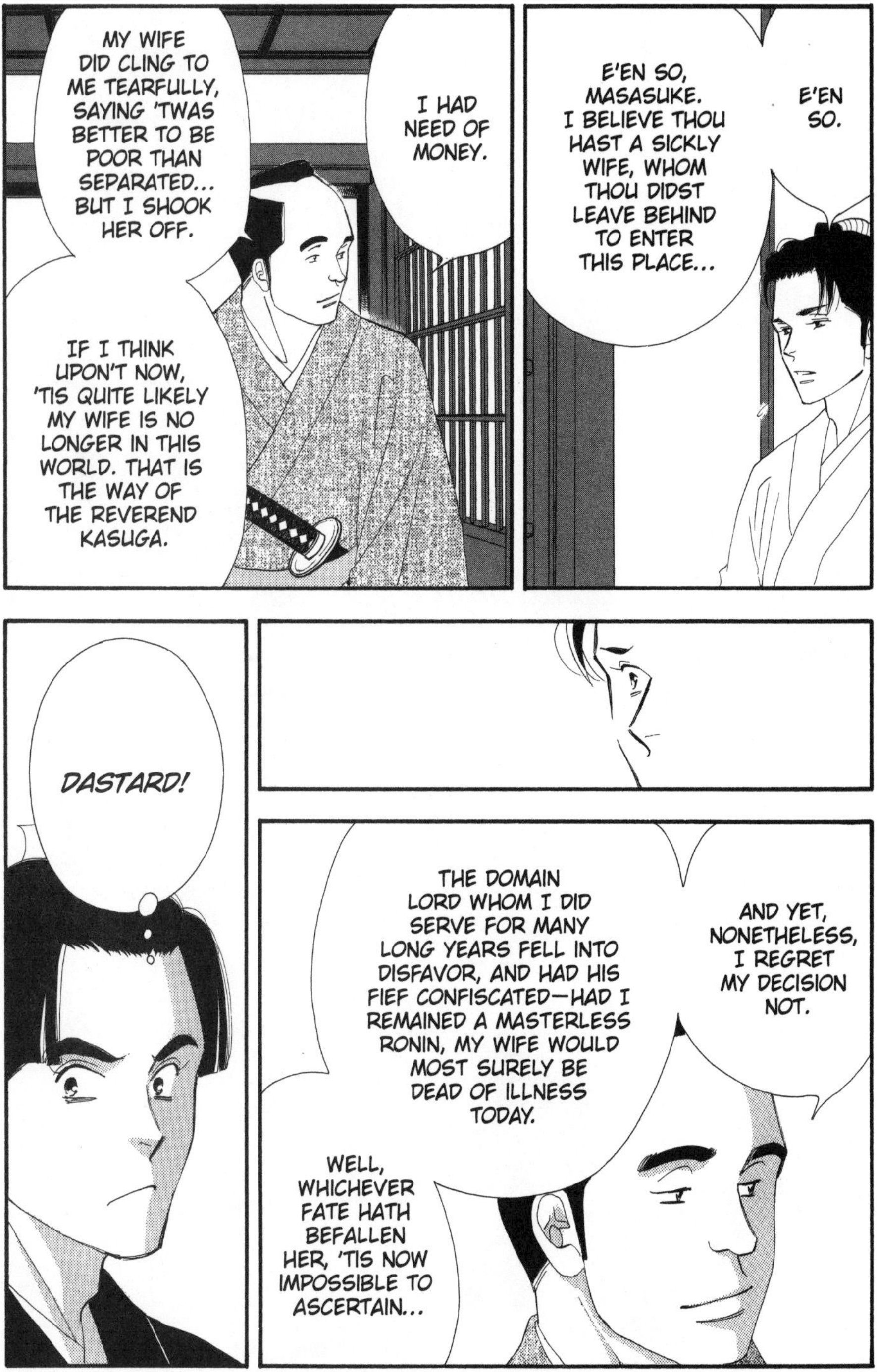
E'EN SO.
E'EN SO, MASASUKE. I BELIEVE THOU HAST A SICKLY WIFE, WHOM THOU DIDST LEAVE BEHIND TO ENTER THIS PLACE...
I HAD NEED OF MONEY.
MY WIFE DID CLING TO ME TEARFULLY, SAYING 'TWAS BETTER TO BE POOR THAN SEPARATED... BUT I SHOOK HER OFF.
IF I THINK UPON'T NOW, 'TIS QUITE LIKELY MY WIFE IS NO LONGER IN THIS WORLD. THAT IS THE WAY OF THE REVEREND KASUGA.
AND YET, NONETHELESS, I REGRET MY DECISION NOT.
THE DOMAIN LORD WHOM I DID SERVE FOR MANY LONG YEARS FELL INTO DISFAVOR, AND HAD HIS FIEF CONFISCATED—HAD I REMAINED A MASTERLESS RONIN, MY WIFE WOULD MOST SURELY BE DEAD OF ILLNESS TODAY.
WELL, WHICHEVER FATE HATH BEFALLEN HER, 'TIS NOW IMPOSSIBLE TO ASCERTAIN...
DASTARD!

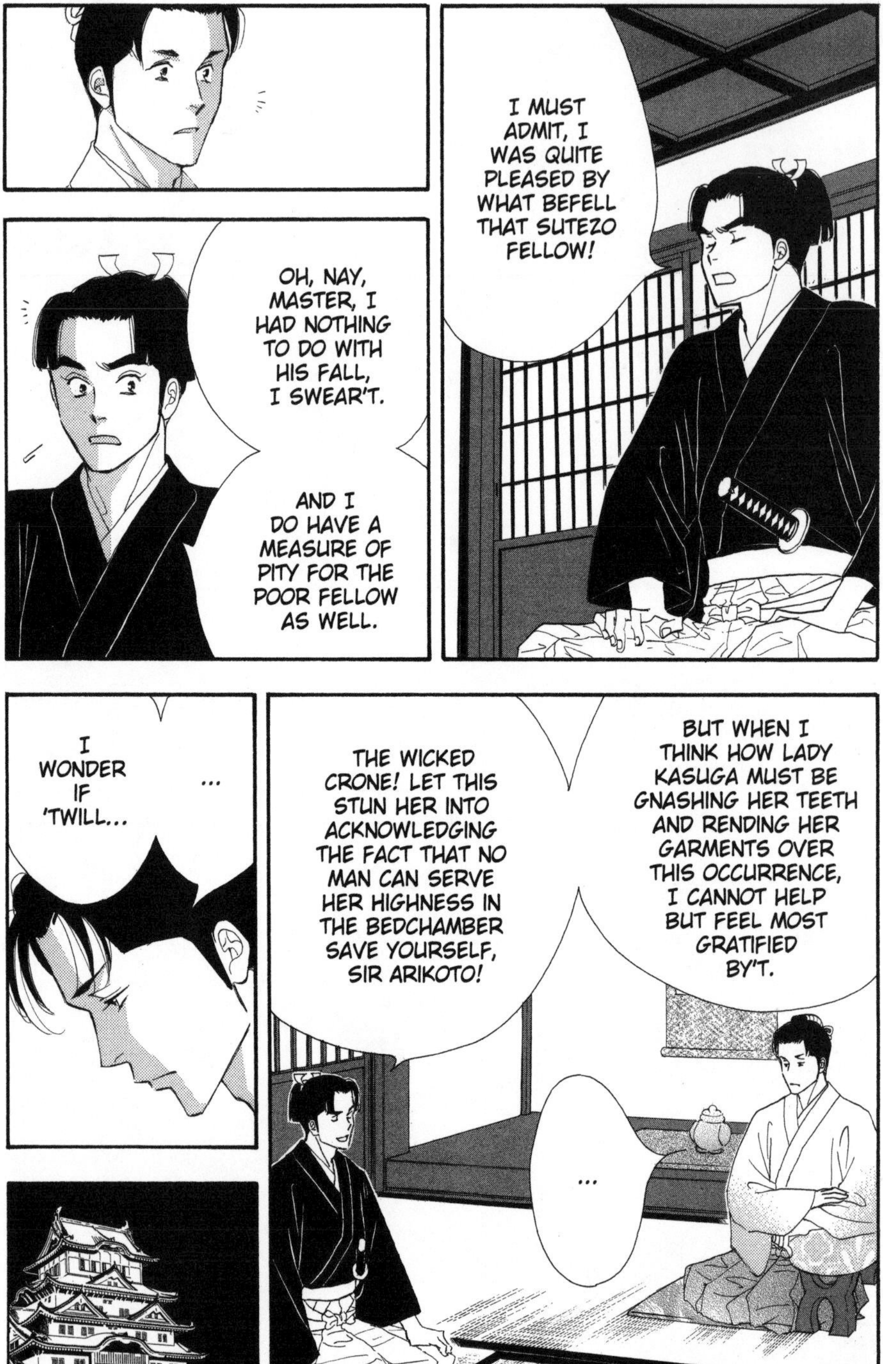
I MUST ADMIT, I WAS QUITE PLEASED BY WHAT BEFELL THAT SUTEZO FELLOW!
OH, NAY, MASTER, I HAD NOTHING TO DO WITH HIS FALL, I SWEAR'T.
AND I DO HAVE A MEASURE OF PITY FOR THE POOR FELLOW AS WELL.
BUT WHEN I THINK HOW LADY KASUGA MUST BE GNASHING HER TEETH AND RENDING HER GARMENTS OVER THIS OCCURRENCE, I CANNOT HELP BUT FEEL MOST GRATIFIED BY'T.
THE WICKED CRONE! LET THIS STUN HER INTO ACKNOWLEDGING THE FACT THAT NO MAN CAN SERVE HER HIGHNESS IN THE BEDCHAMBER SAVE YOURSELF, SIR ARIKOTO!
...
...
I WONDER IF 'TWILL...

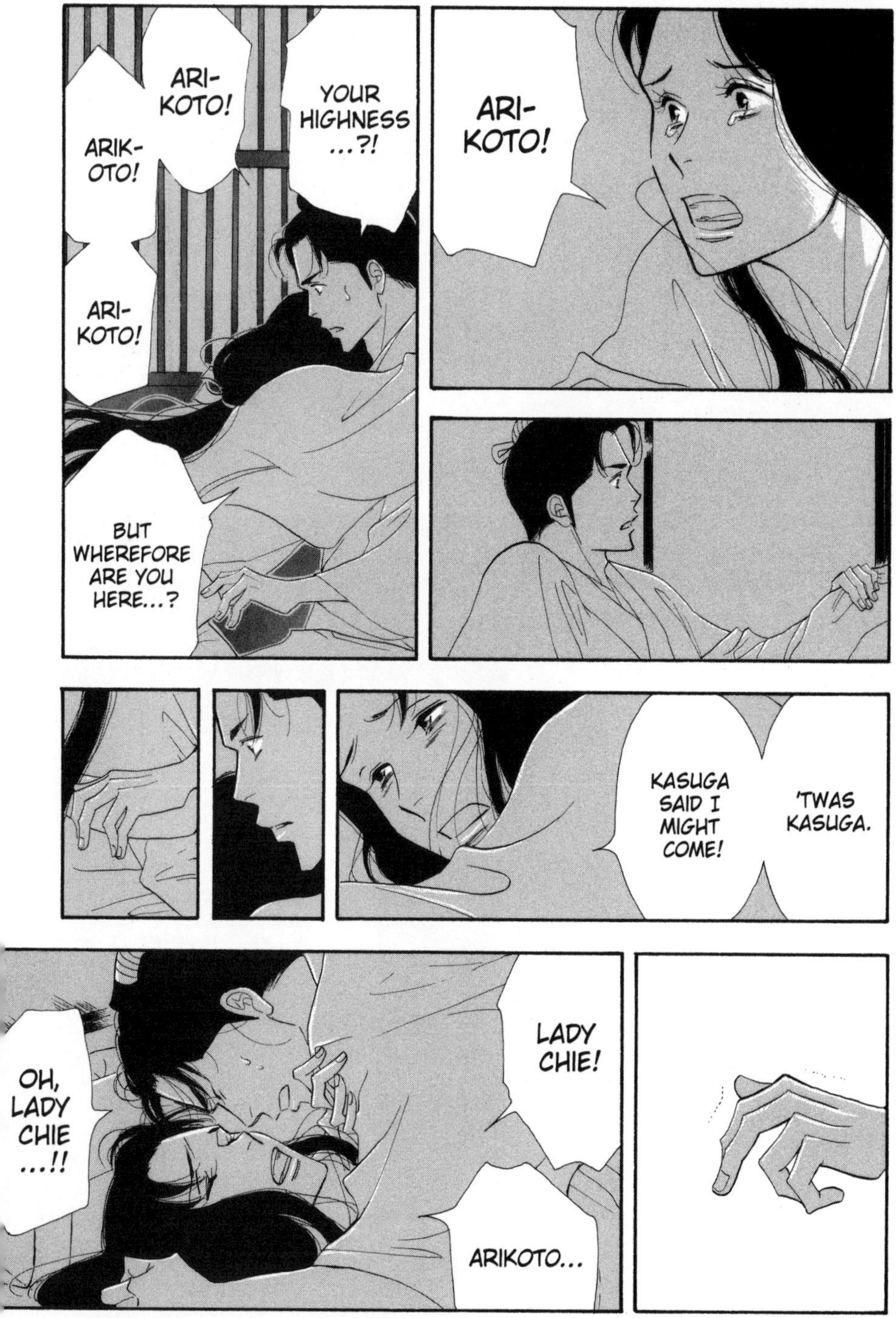
ARI-KOTO!
YOUR HIGHNESS ...?!
ARI-KOTO!
ARIK-OTO!
ARI-KOTO!
BUT WHEREFORE ARE YOU HERE...?
'TWAS KASUGA.
KASUGA SAID I MIGHT COME!
LADY CHIE!
ARIKOTO...
OH, LADY CHIE ...!!

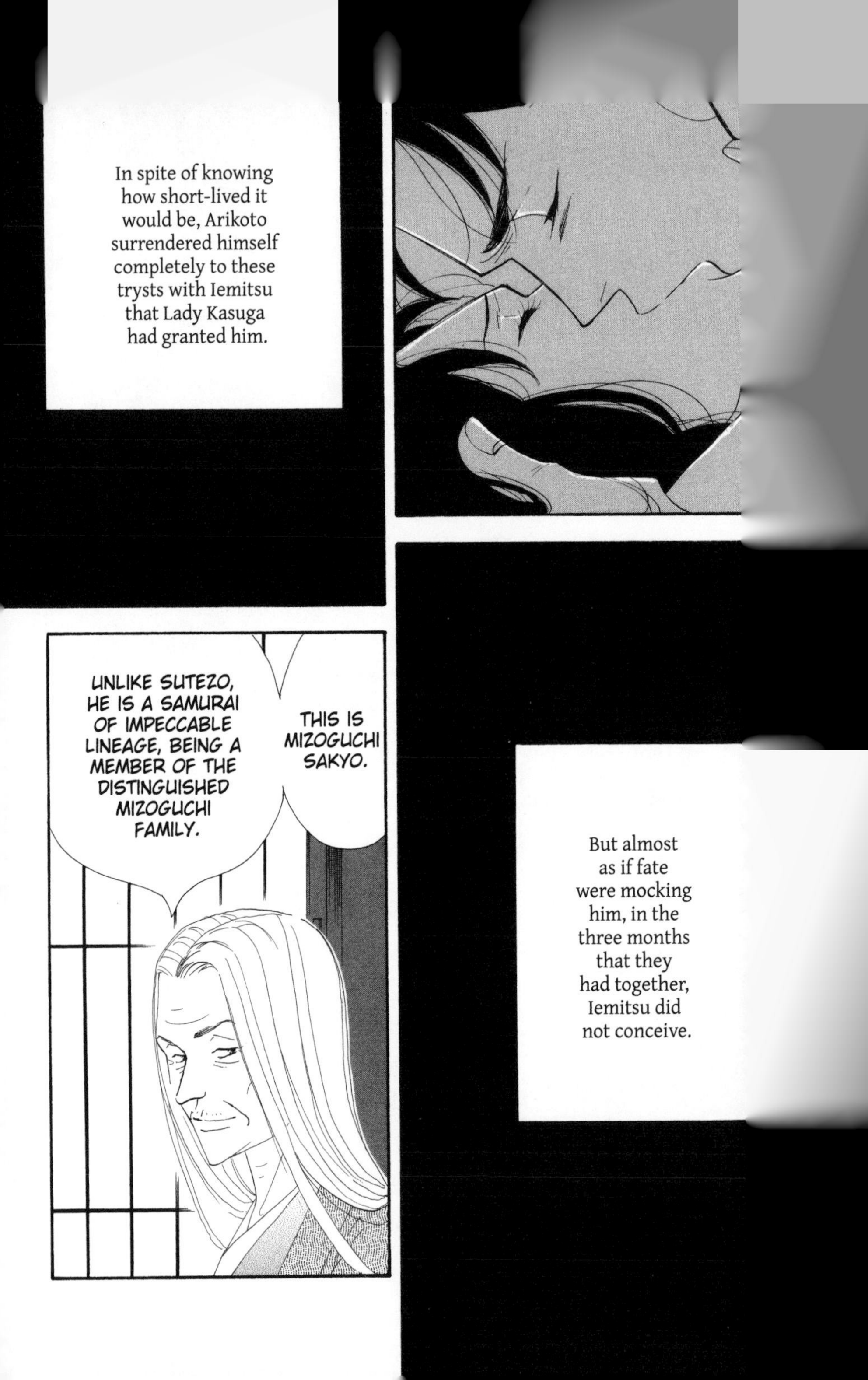
In spite of knowing how short-lived it would be, Arikoto surrendered himself completely to these trysts with Iemitsu that Lady Kasuga had granted him.
But almost as if fate were mocking him, in the three months that they had together, Iemitsu did not conceive.
THIS IS MIZOGUCHI SAKYO.
UNLIKE SUTEZO, HE IS A SAMURAI OF IMPECCABLE LINEAGE, BEING A MEMBER OF THE DISTINGUISHED MIZOGUCHI FAMILY.

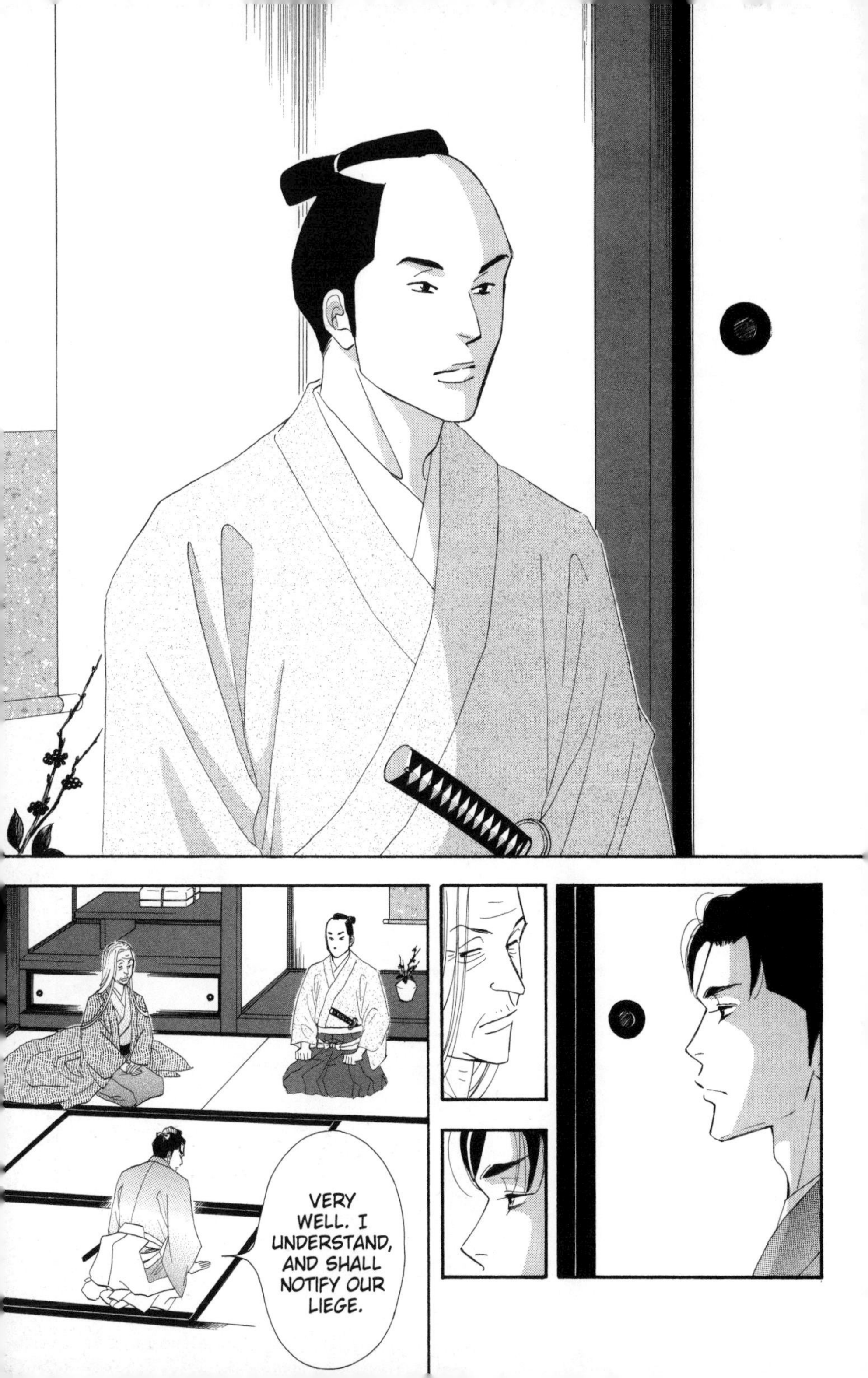
VERY WELL. I UNDERSTAND, AND SHALL NOTIFY OUR LIEGE.

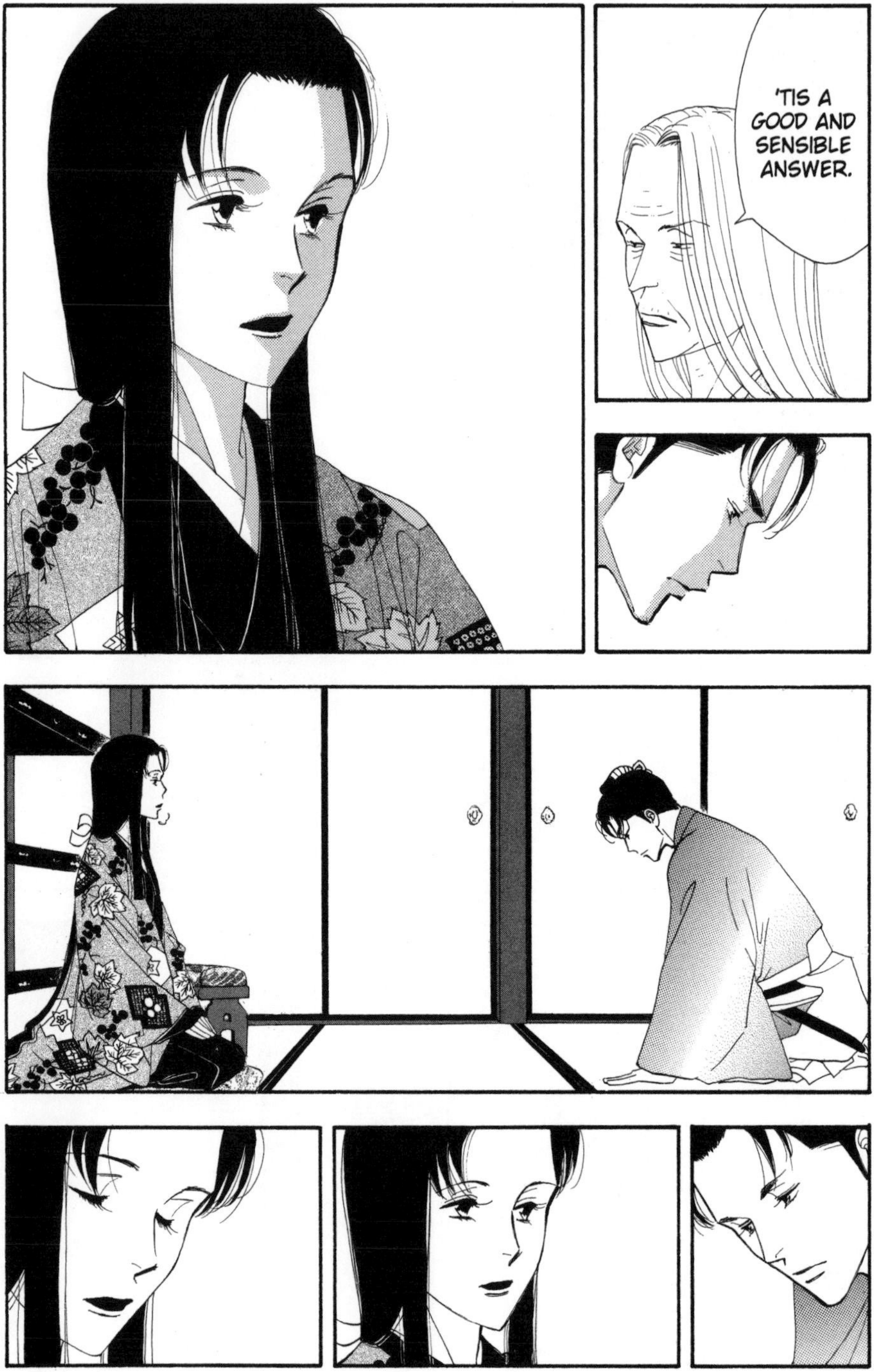
'TIS A GOOD AND SENSIBLE ANSWER.

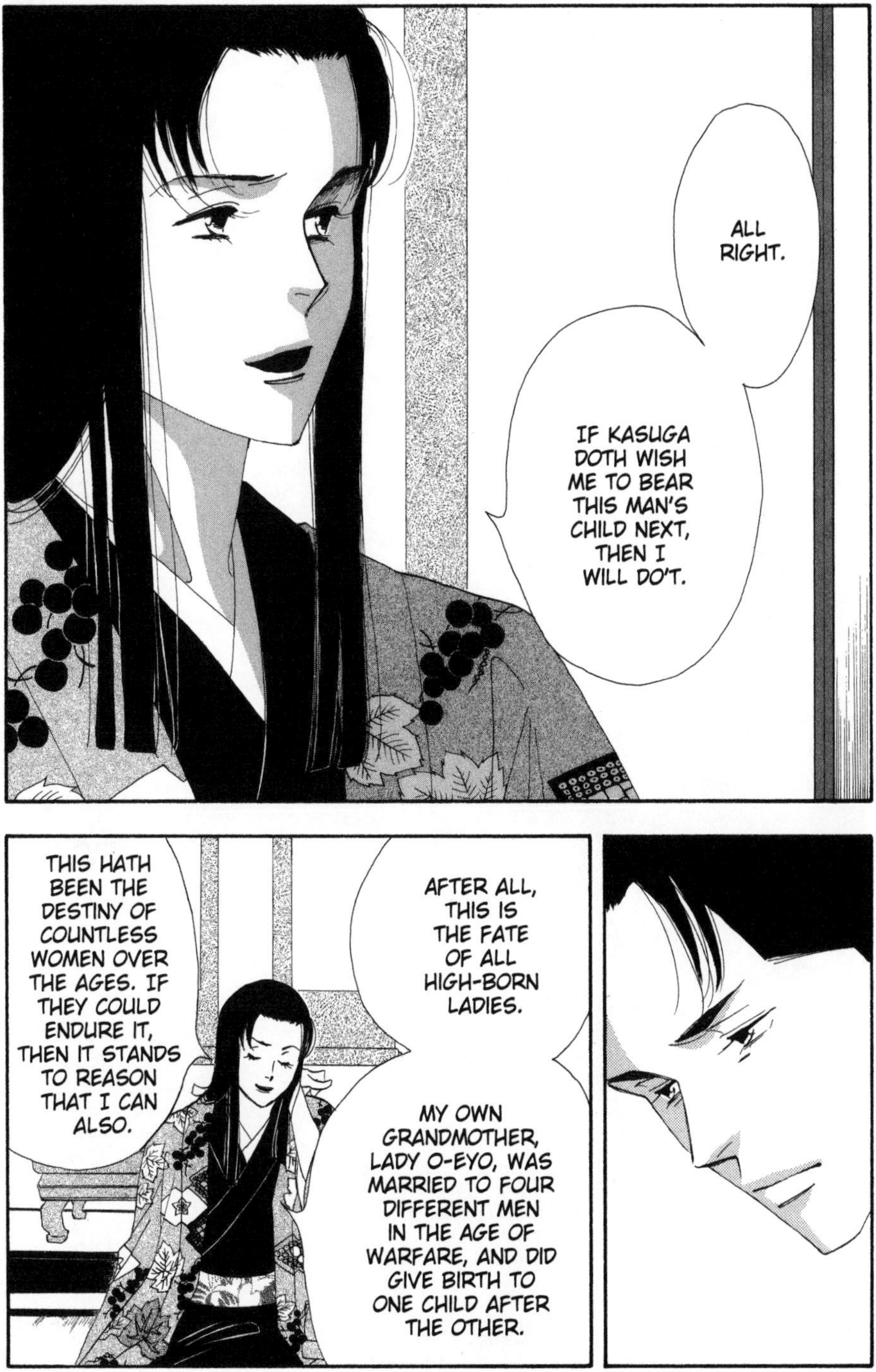
ALL RIGHT.
IF KASUGA DOTH WISH ME TO BEAR THIS MAN'S CHILD NEXT, THEN I WILL DO'T.
AFTER ALL, THIS IS THE FATE OF ALL HIGH-BORN LADIES.
THIS HATH BEEN THE DESTINY OF COUNTLESS WOMEN OVER THE AGES. IF THEY COULD ENDURE IT, THEN IT STANDS TO REASON THAT I CAN ALSO.
MY OWN GRANDMOTHER, LADY O-EYO, WAS MARRIED TO FOUR DIFFERENT MEN IN THE AGE OF WARFARE, AND DID GIVE BIRTH TO ONE CHILD AFTER THE OTHER.

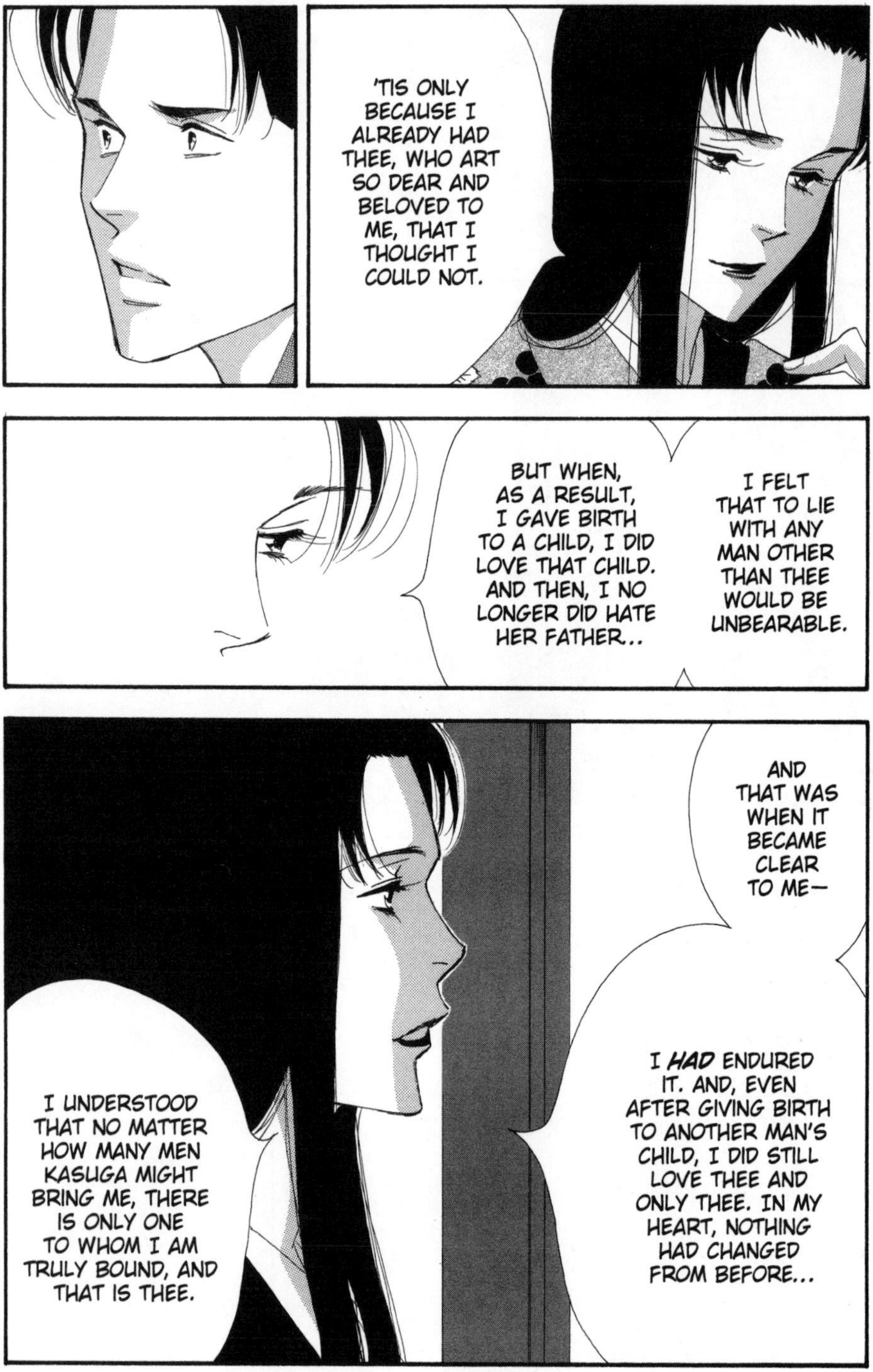
'TIS ONLY BECAUSE I ALREADY HAD THEE, WHO ART SO DEAR AND BELOVED TO ME, THAT I THOUGHT I COULD NOT.
I FELT THAT TO LIE WITH ANY MAN OTHER THAN THEE WOULD BE UNBEARABLE.
BUT WHEN, AS A RESULT, I GAVE BIRTH TO A CHILD, I DID LOVE THAT CHILD. AND THEN, I NO LONGER DID HATE HER FATHER...
AND THAT WAS WHEN IT BECAME CLEAR TO ME—
I *HAD* ENDURED IT. AND, EVEN AFTER GIVING BIRTH TO ANOTHER MAN'S CHILD, I DID STILL LOVE THEE AND ONLY THEE. IN MY HEART, NOTHING HAD CHANGED FROM BEFORE...
I UNDERSTOOD THAT NO MATTER HOW MANY MEN KASUGA MIGHT BRING ME, THERE IS ONLY ONE TO WHOM I AM TRULY BOUND, AND THAT IS THEE.

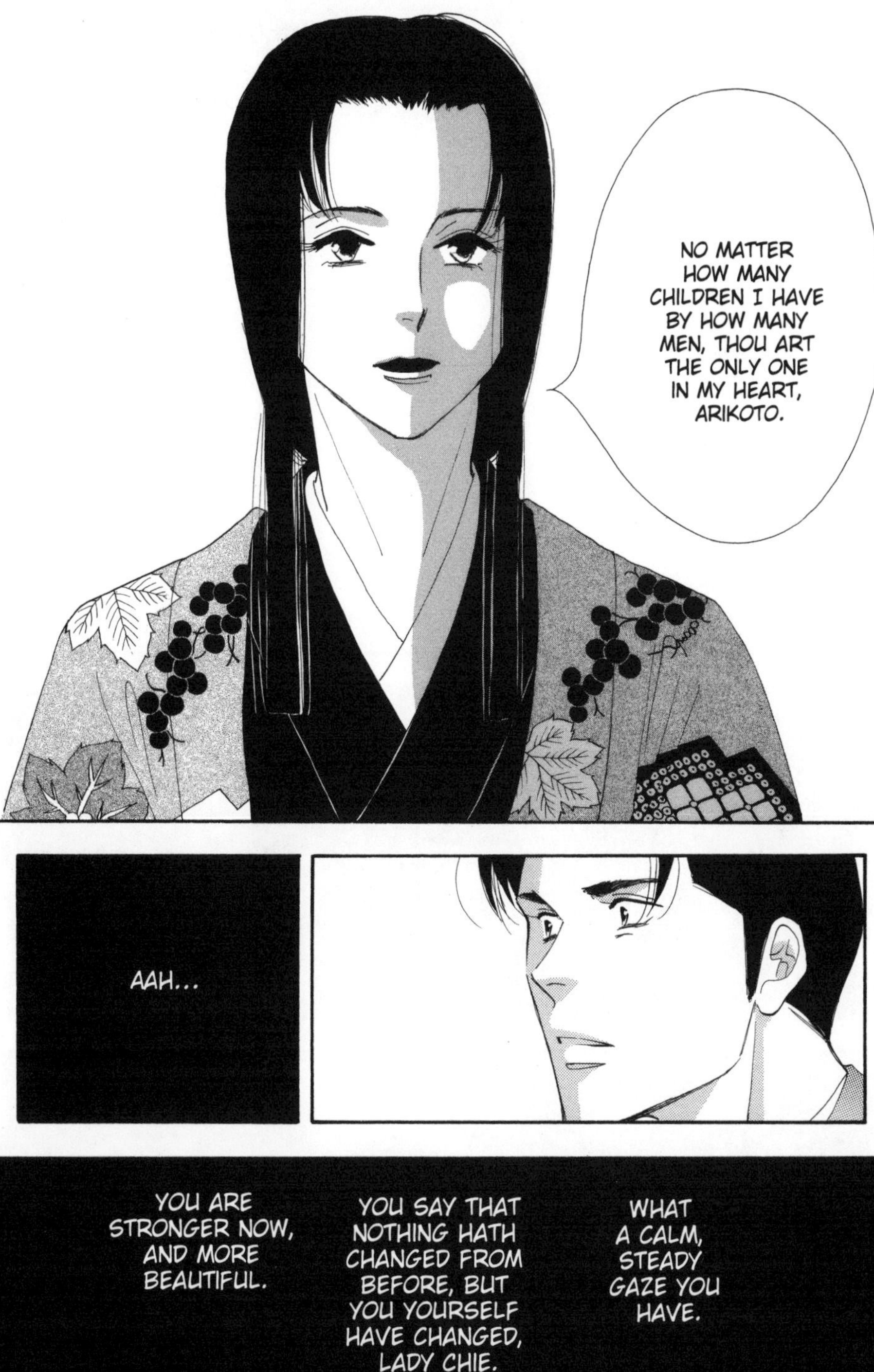
NO MATTER HOW MANY CHILDREN I HAVE BY HOW MANY MEN, THOU ART THE ONLY ONE IN MY HEART, ARIKOTO.
AAH...
WHAT A CALM, STEADY GAZE YOU HAVE.
YOU SAY THAT NOTHING HATH CHANGED FROM BEFORE, BUT YOU YOURSELF HAVE CHANGED, LADY CHIE.
YOU ARE STRONGER NOW, AND MORE BEAUTIFUL.

'TIS
BECAUSE
YOU HAVE
BECOME
A MOTHER.

ALAS,
MOTHERHOOD
IS SOMETHING
I WAS UNABLE
TO GIVE YOU.

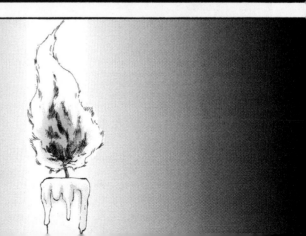

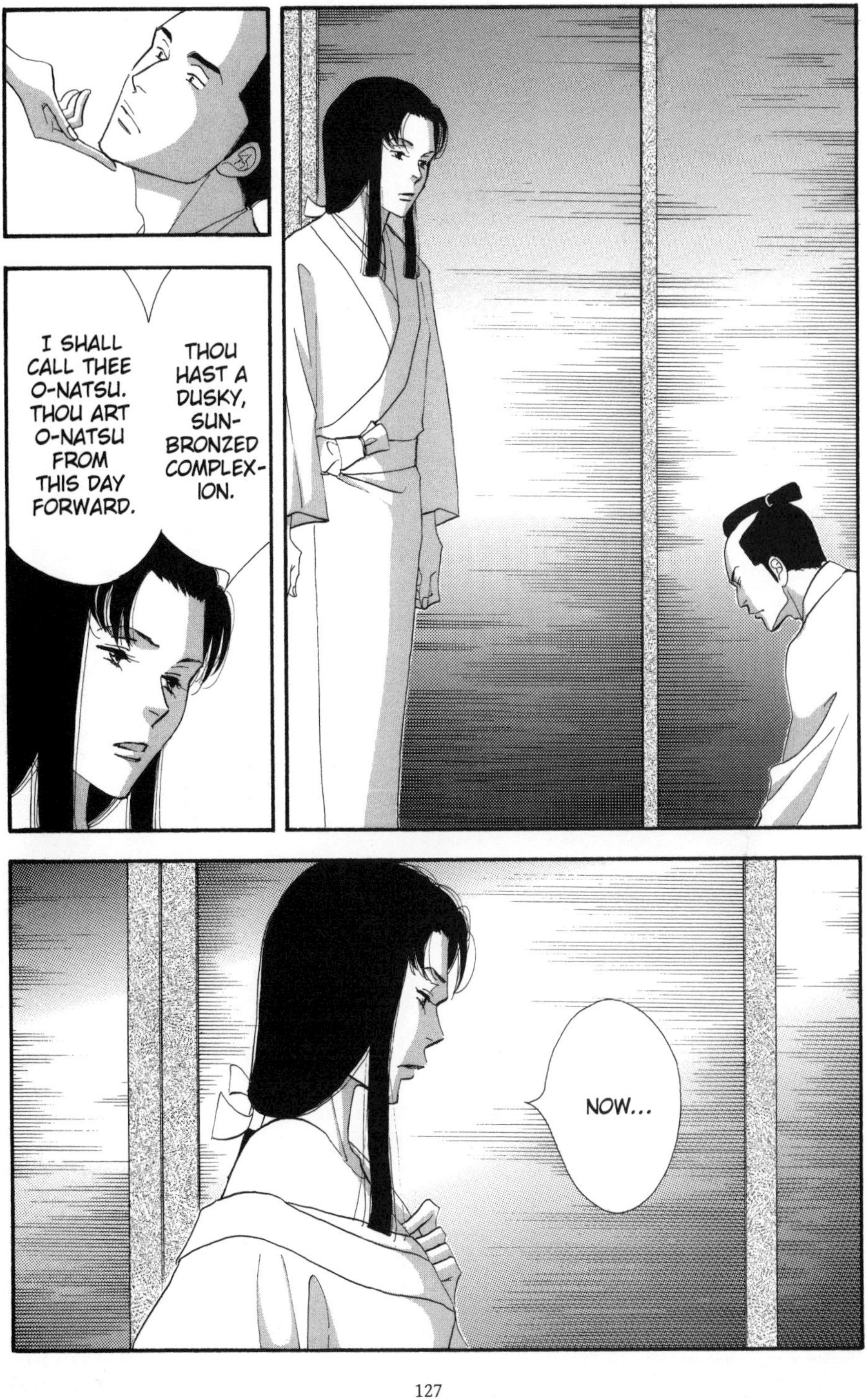
THOU HAST A DUSKY, SUN-BRONZED COMPLEXION.
I SHALL CALL THEE O-NATSU. THOU ART O-NATSU FROM THIS DAY FORWARD.
NOW...

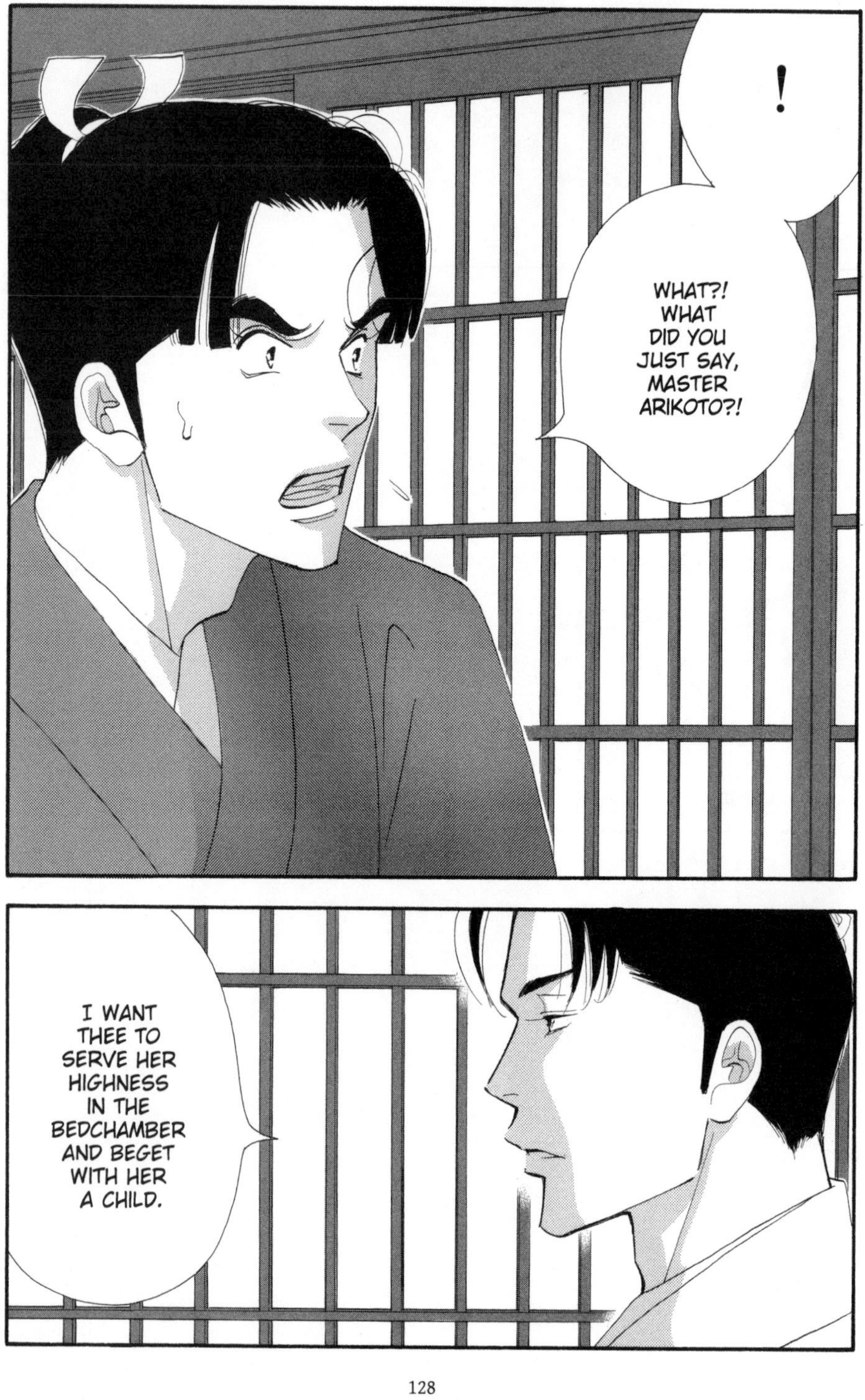
!
WHAT?! WHAT DID YOU JUST SAY, MASTER ARIKOTO?!
I WANT THEE TO SERVE HER HIGHNESS IN THE BEDCHAMBER AND BEGET WITH HER A CHILD.

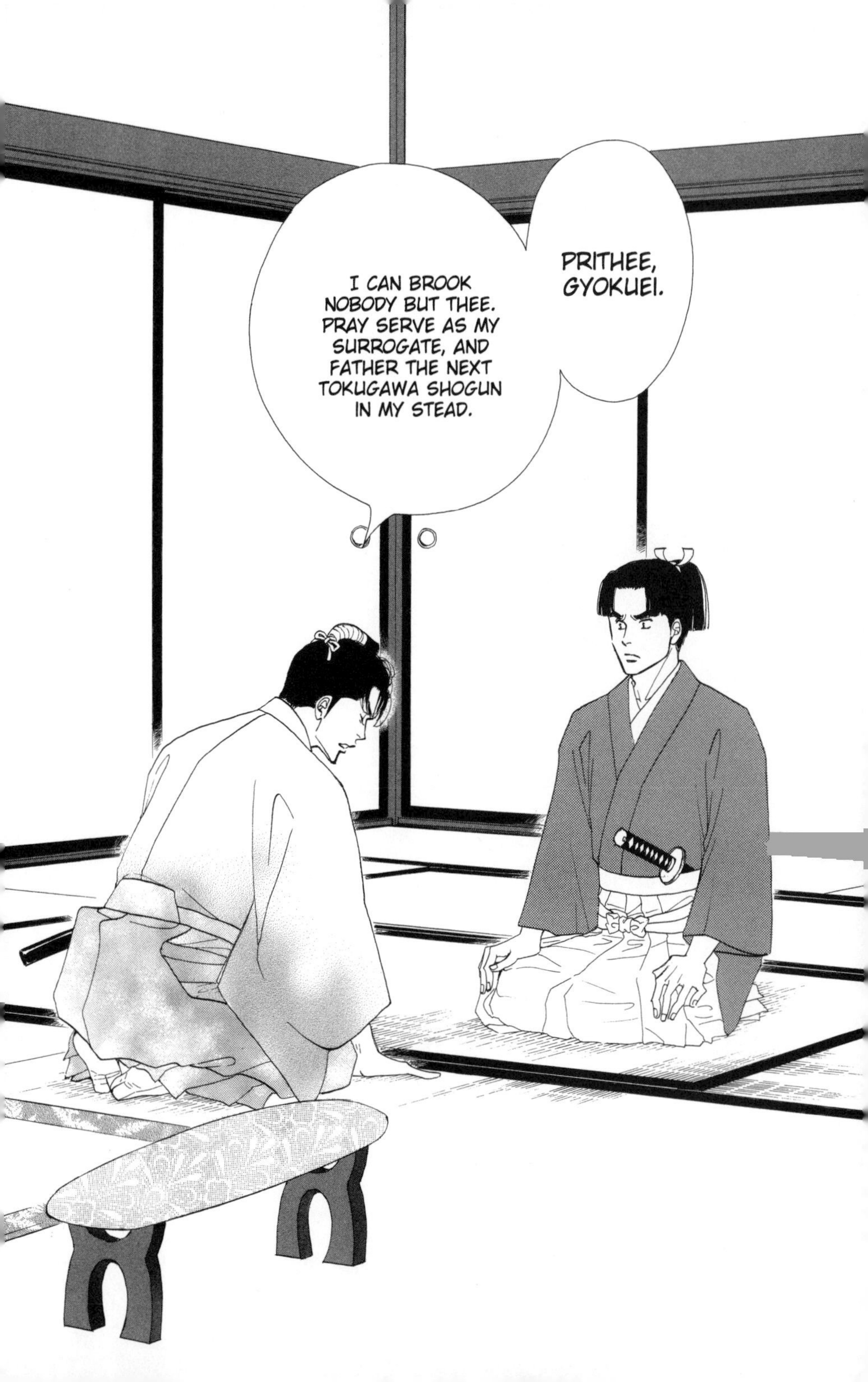
PRITHEE, GYOKUEI.
I CAN BROOK NOBODY BUT THEE. PRAY SERVE AS MY SURROGATE, AND FATHER THE NEXT TOKUGAWA SHOGUN IN MY STEAD.

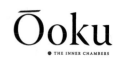

Ōoku

THE INNER CHAMBERS

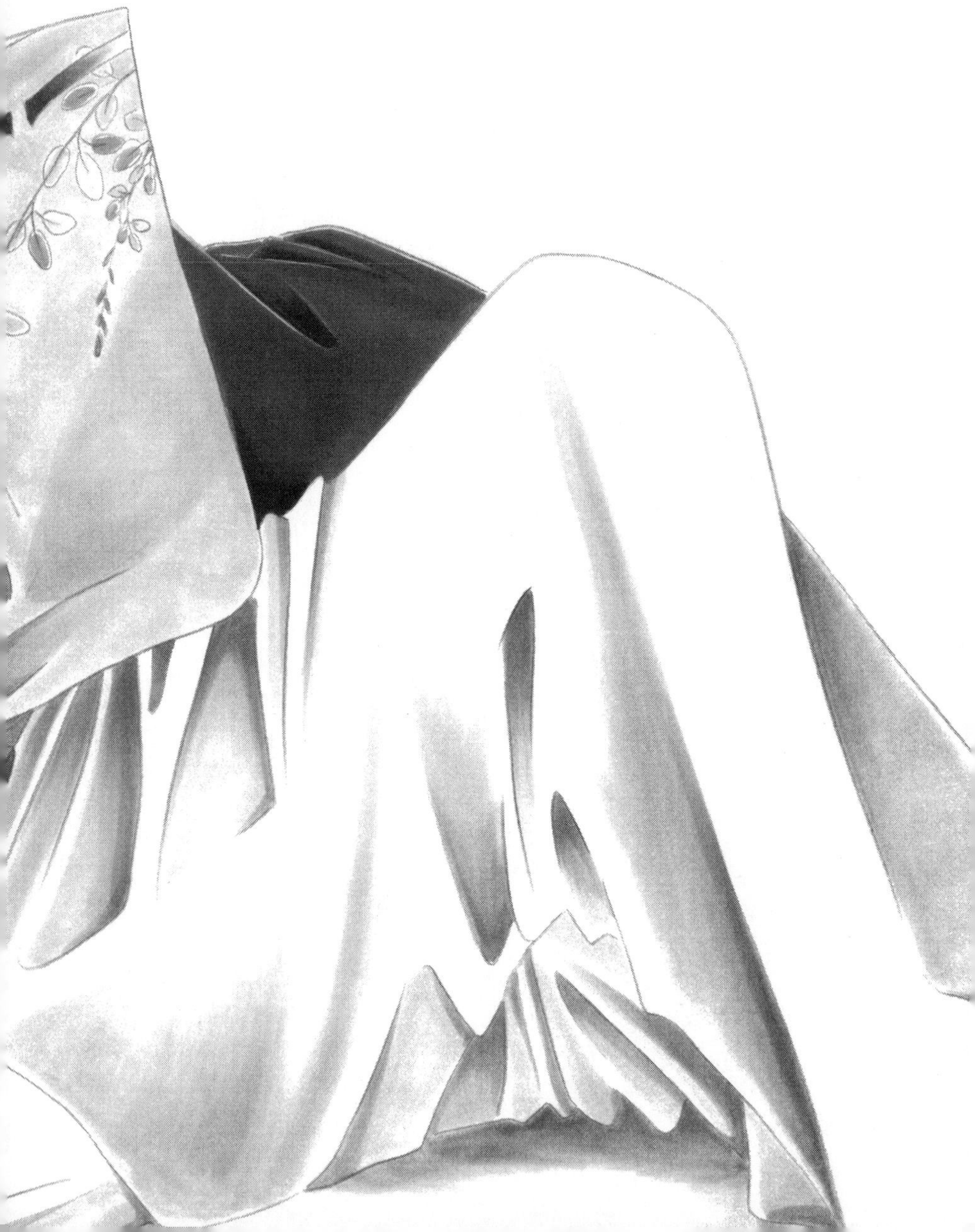

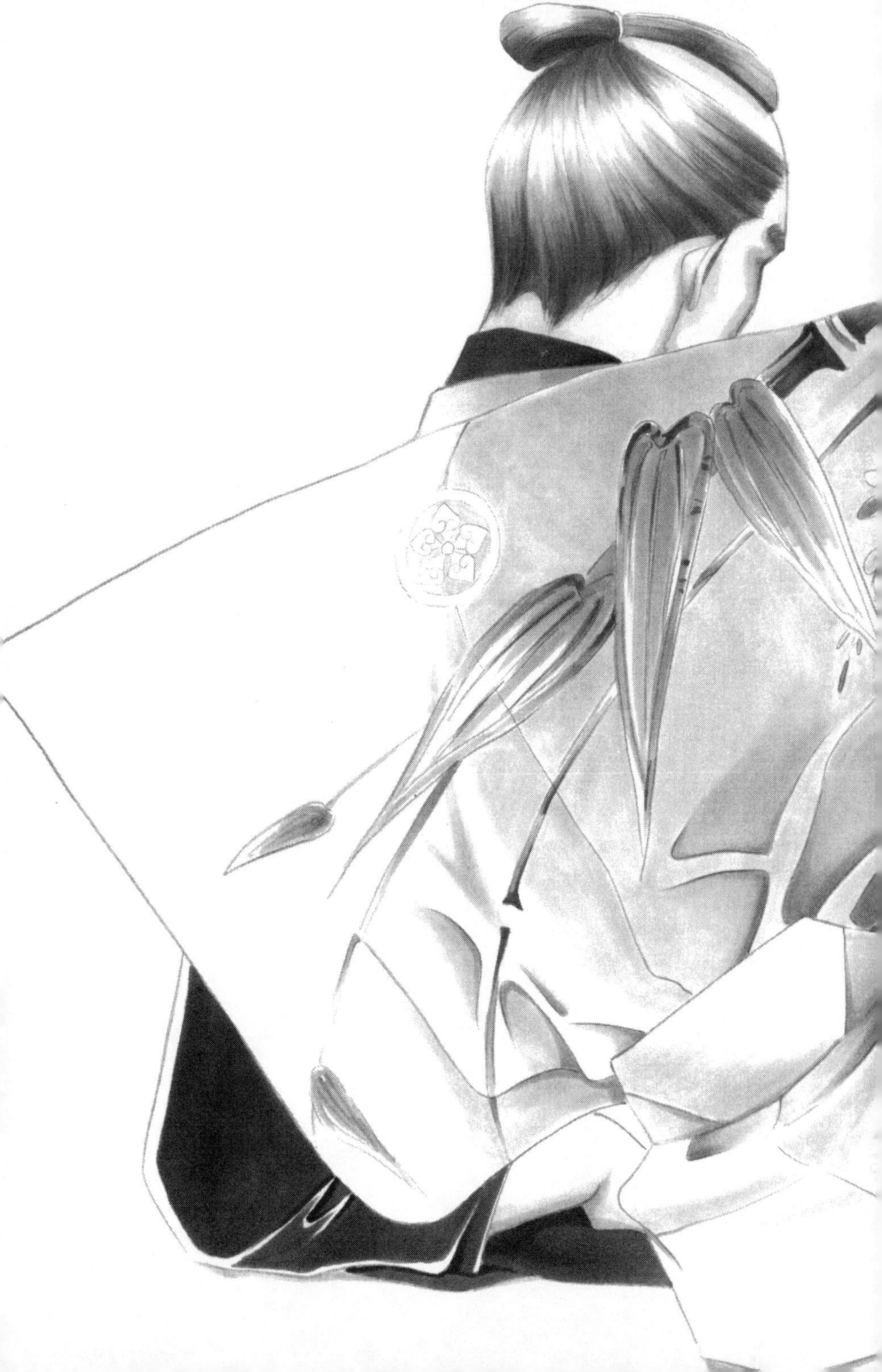

Ōoku
THE INNER CHAMBERS

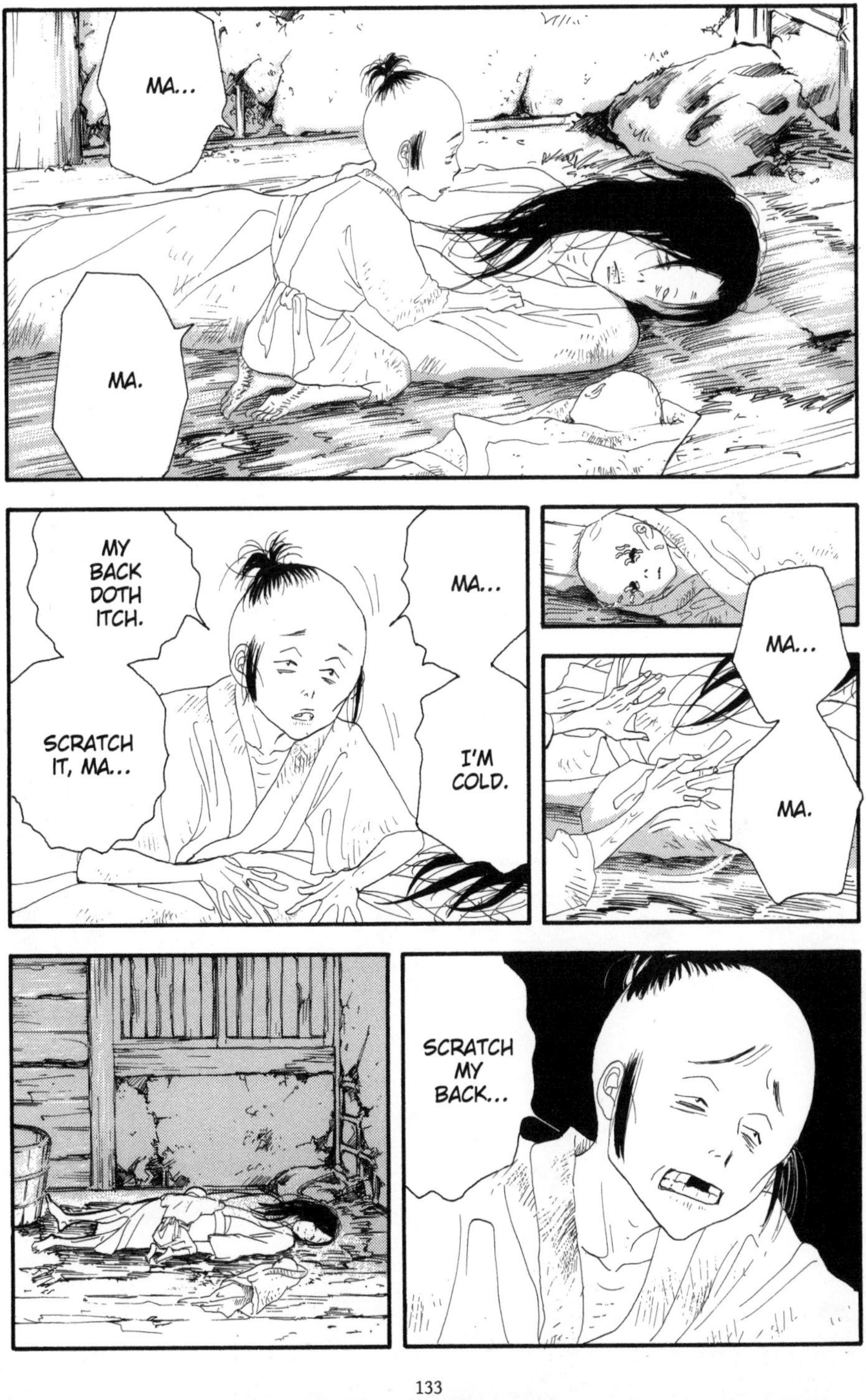
MA...
MA.
MA...
MA.
MA...
I'M COLD.
MY BACK DOTH ITCH.
SCRATCH IT, MA...
SCRATCH MY BACK...

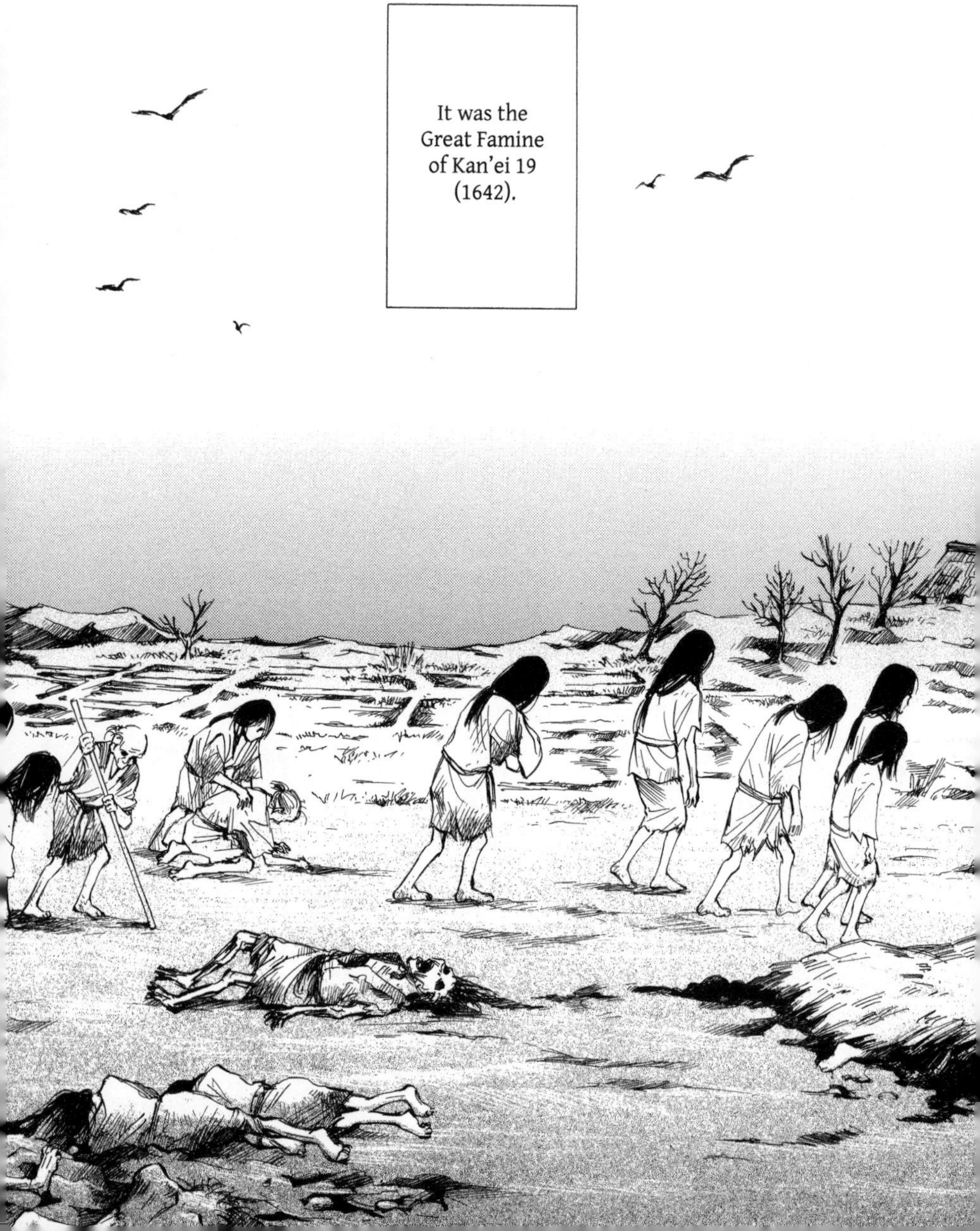
It was the Great Famine of Kan'ei 19 (1642).

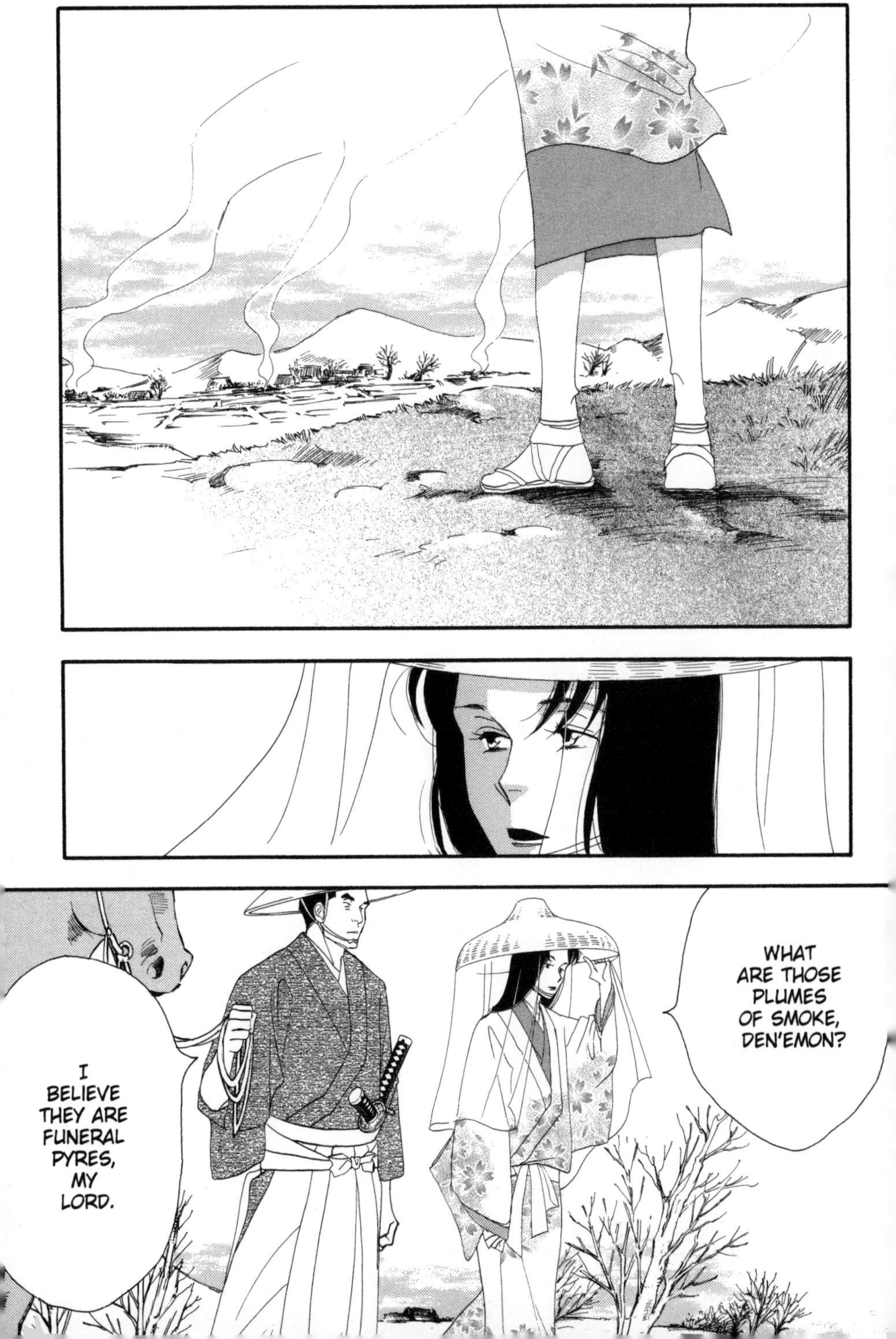
WHAT ARE THOSE PLUMES OF SMOKE, DEN'EMON?
I BELIEVE THEY ARE FUNERAL PYRES, MY LORD.

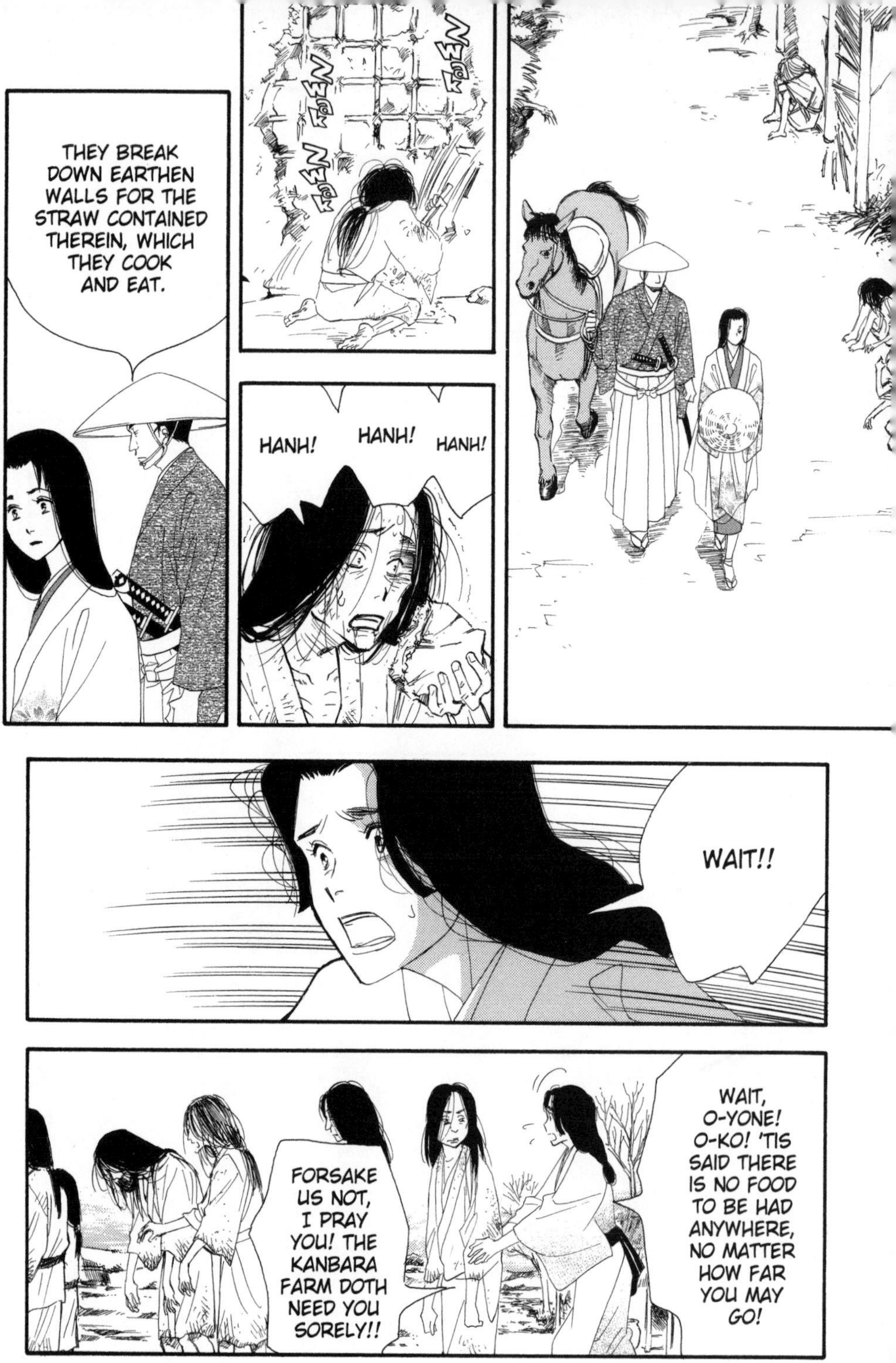
HANH! HANH! HANH!
THEY BREAK DOWN EARTHEN WALLS FOR THE STRAW CONTAINED THEREIN, WHICH THEY COOK AND EAT.
WAIT!!
WAIT, O-YONE! O-KO! 'TIS SAID THERE IS NO FOOD TO BE HAD ANYWHERE, NO MATTER HOW FAR YOU MAY GO!
FORSAKE US NOT, I PRAY YOU! THE KANBARA FARM DOTH NEED YOU SORELY!!

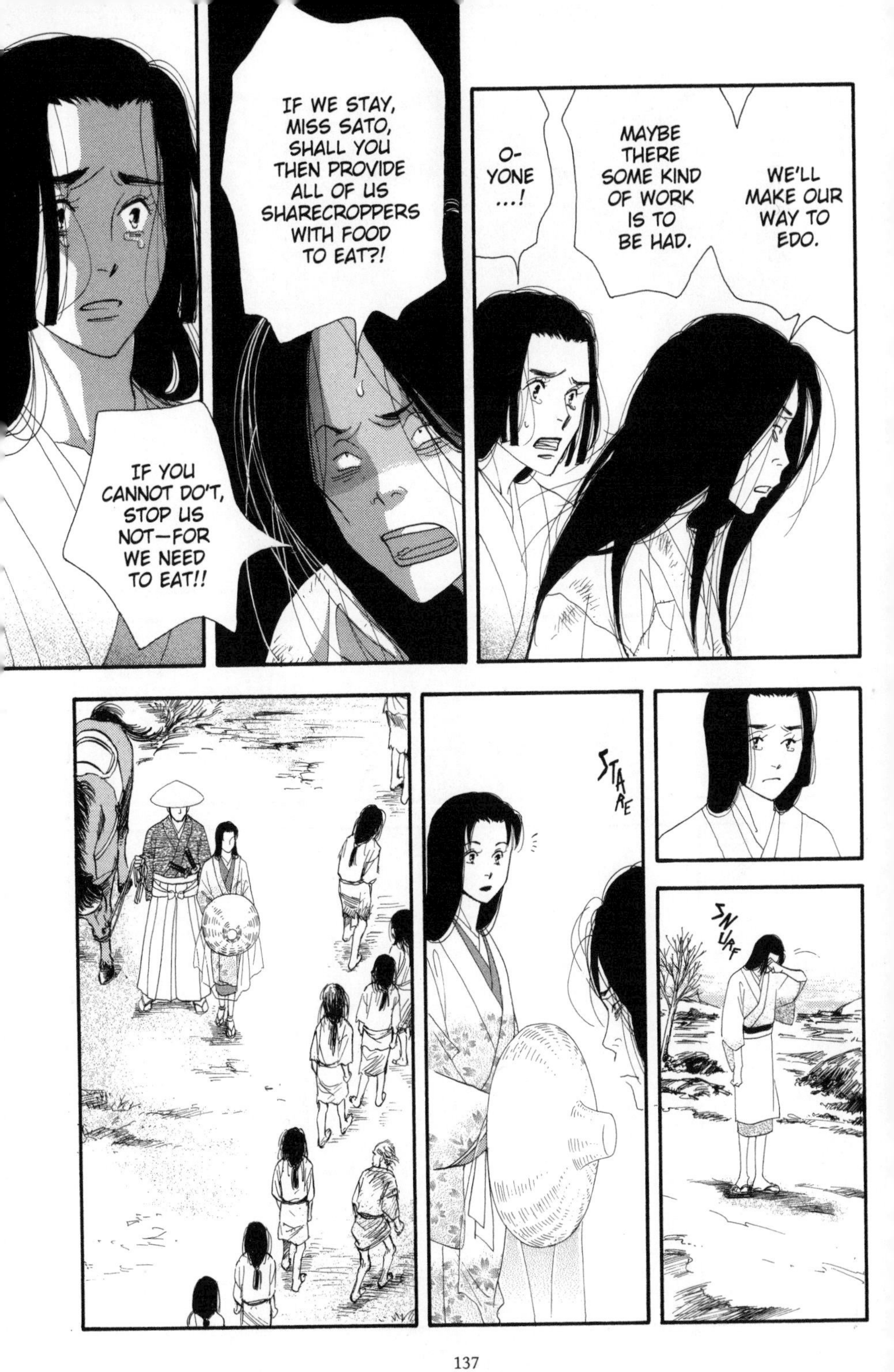
WE'LL MAKE OUR WAY TO EDO.
MAYBE THERE SOME KIND OF WORK IS TO BE HAD.
O-YONE...!
IF WE STAY, MISS SATO, SHALL YOU THEN PROVIDE ALL OF US SHARECROPPERS WITH FOOD TO EAT?!
IF YOU CANNOT DO'T, STOP US NOT—FOR WE NEED TO EAT!!
SNURF
STARE

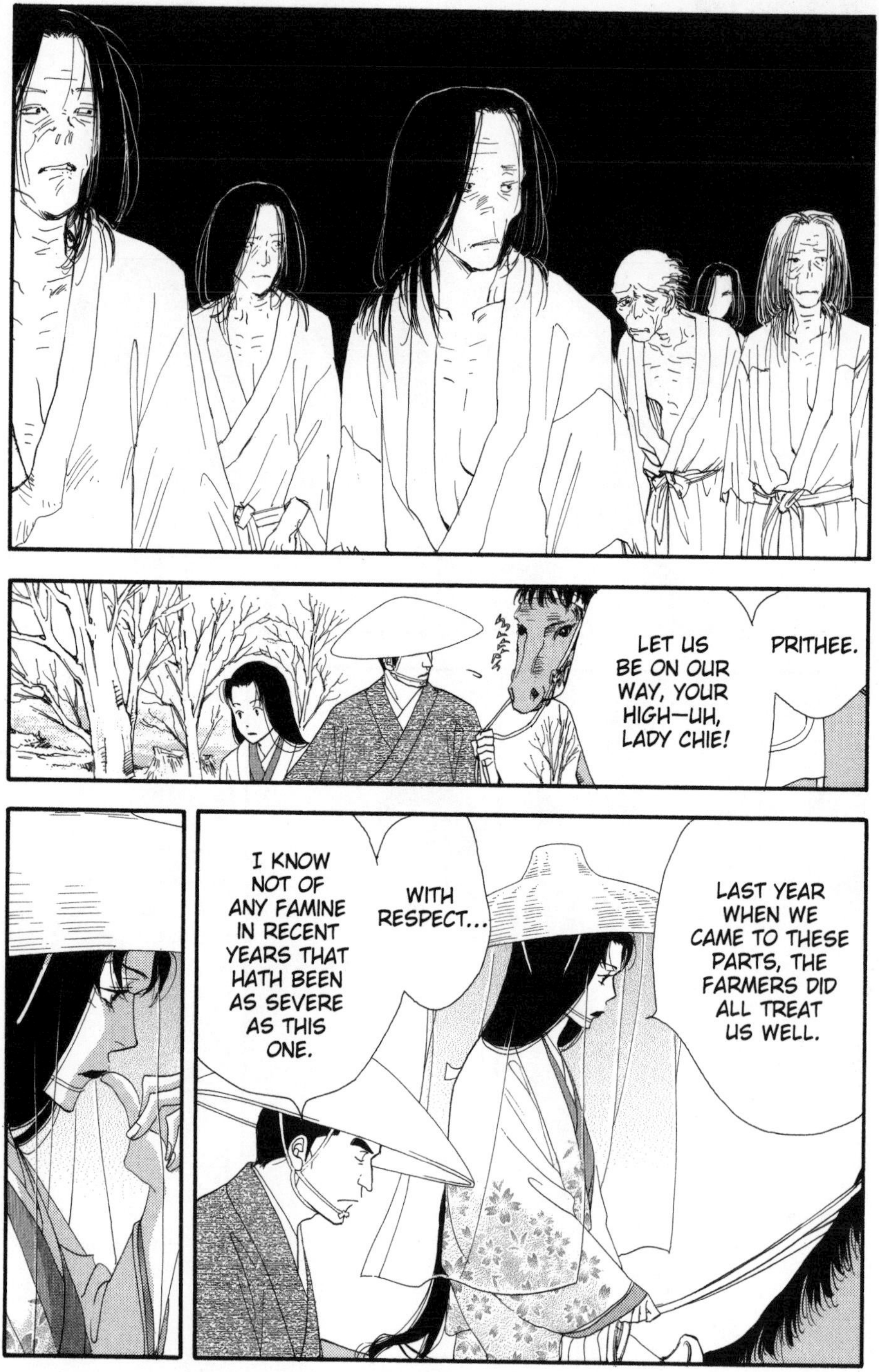
PRITHEE.
LET US BE ON OUR WAY, YOUR HIGH—UH, LADY CHIE!
LAST YEAR WHEN WE CAME TO THESE PARTS, THE FARMERS DID ALL TREAT US WELL.
WITH RESPECT...
I KNOW NOT OF ANY FAMINE IN RECENT YEARS THAT HATH BEEN AS SEVERE AS THIS ONE.

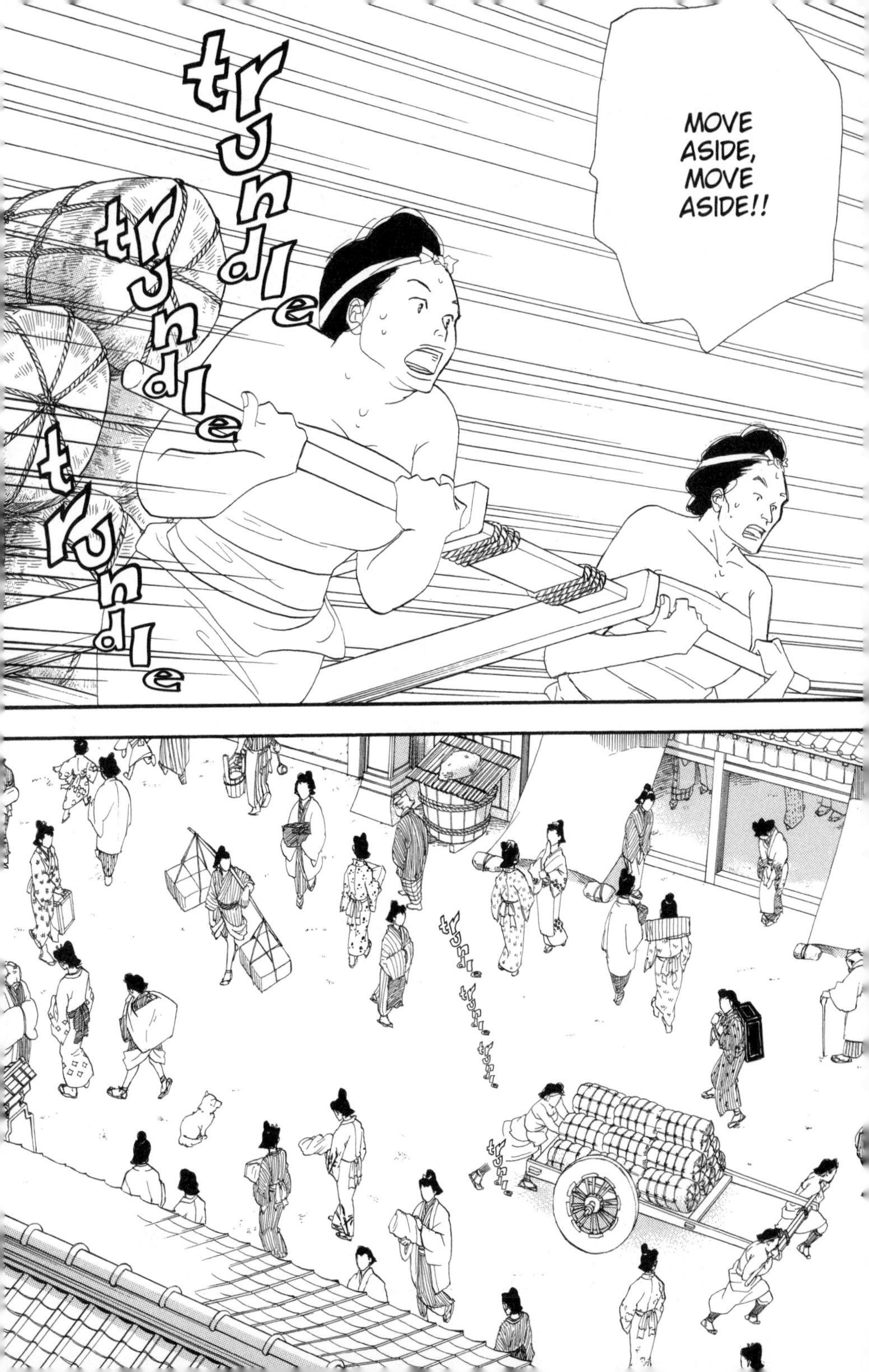
MOVE ASIDE, MOVE ASIDE!!
trundle
trundle
trundle
trundle
trundle
trundle
trundle

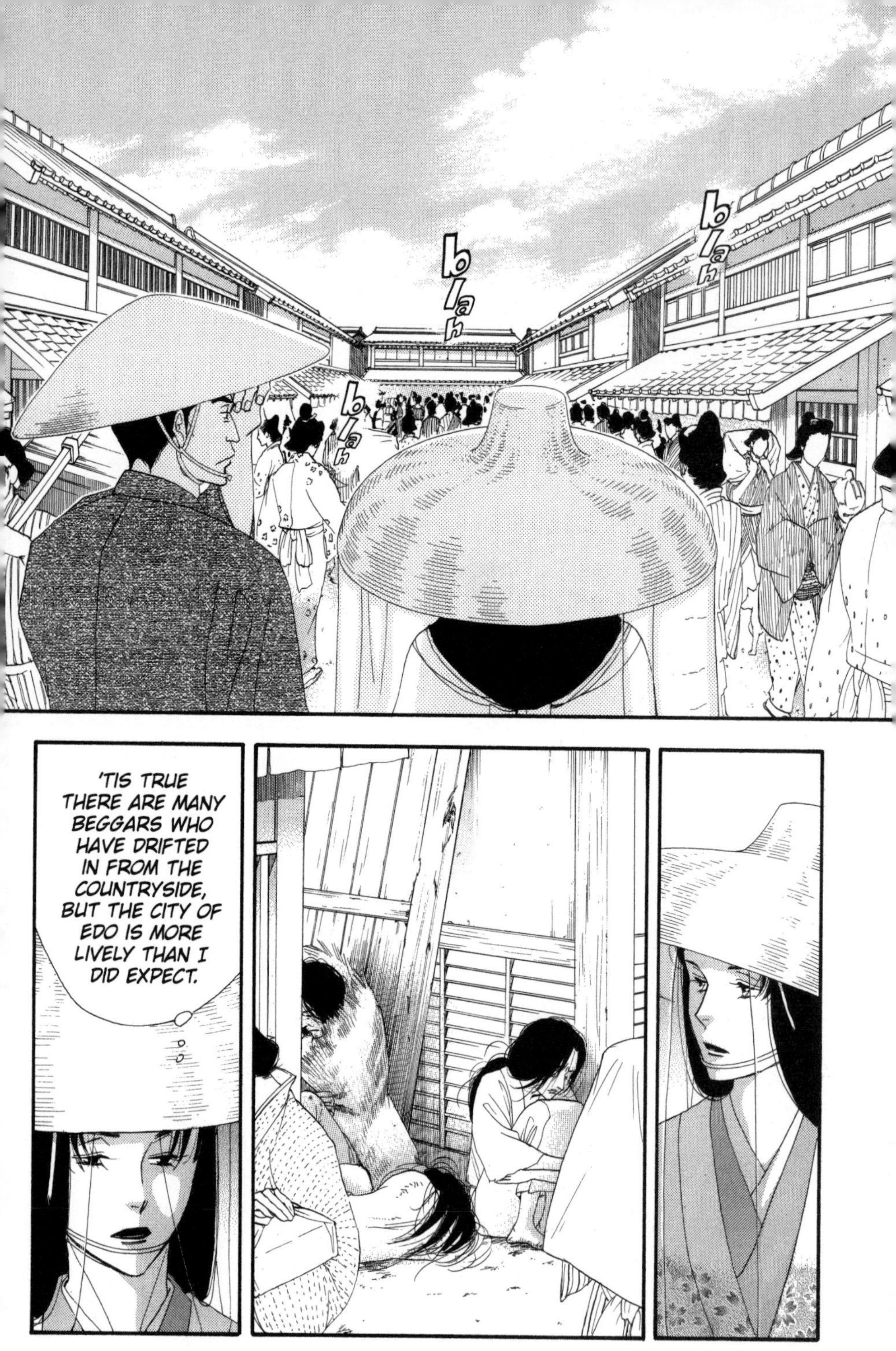
blah
blah
blah
'TIS TRUE THERE ARE MANY BEGGARS WHO HAVE DRIFTED IN FROM THE COUNTRYSIDE, BUT THE CITY OF EDO IS MORE LIVELY THAN I DID EXPECT.

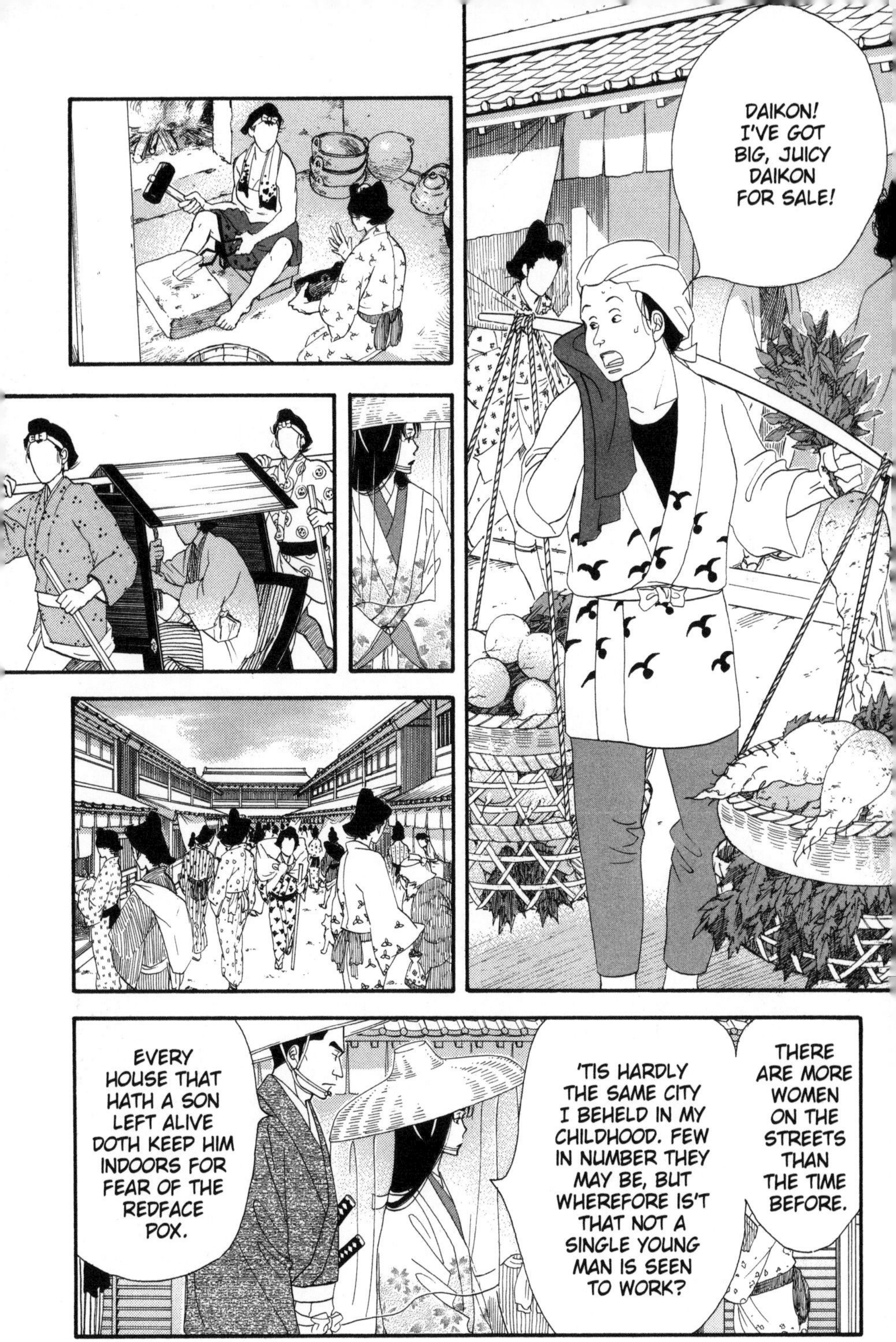
DAIKON! I'VE GOT BIG, JUICY DAIKON FOR SALE!
THERE ARE MORE WOMEN ON THE STREETS THAN THE TIME BEFORE.
'TIS HARDLY THE SAME CITY I BEHELD IN MY CHILDHOOD. FEW IN NUMBER THEY MAY BE, BUT WHEREFORE IS'T THAT NOT A SINGLE YOUNG MAN IS SEEN TO WORK?
EVERY HOUSE THAT HATH A SON LEFT ALIVE DOTH KEEP HIM INDOORS FOR FEAR OF THE REDFACE POX.

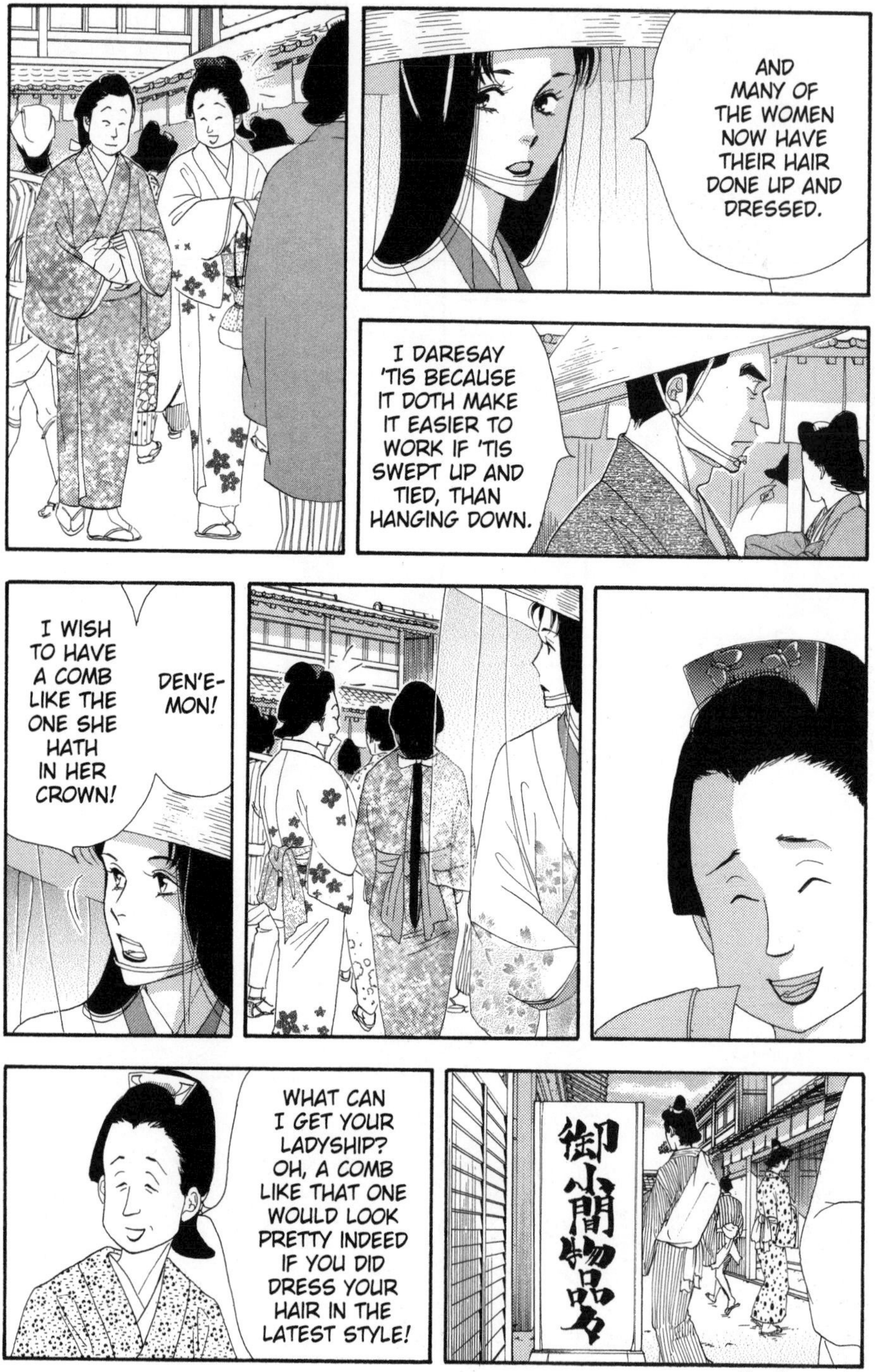
AND MANY OF THE WOMEN NOW HAVE THEIR HAIR DONE UP AND DRESSED.
I DARESAY 'TIS BECAUSE IT DOTH MAKE IT EASIER TO WORK IF 'TIS SWEPT UP AND TIED, THAN HANGING DOWN.
DEN'E-MON!
I WISH TO HAVE A COMB LIKE THE ONE SHE HATH IN HER CROWN!
WHAT CAN I GET YOUR LADYSHIP? OH, A COMB LIKE THAT ONE WOULD LOOK PRETTY INDEED IF YOU DID DRESS YOUR HAIR IN THE LATEST STYLE!

Sign=Ornaments

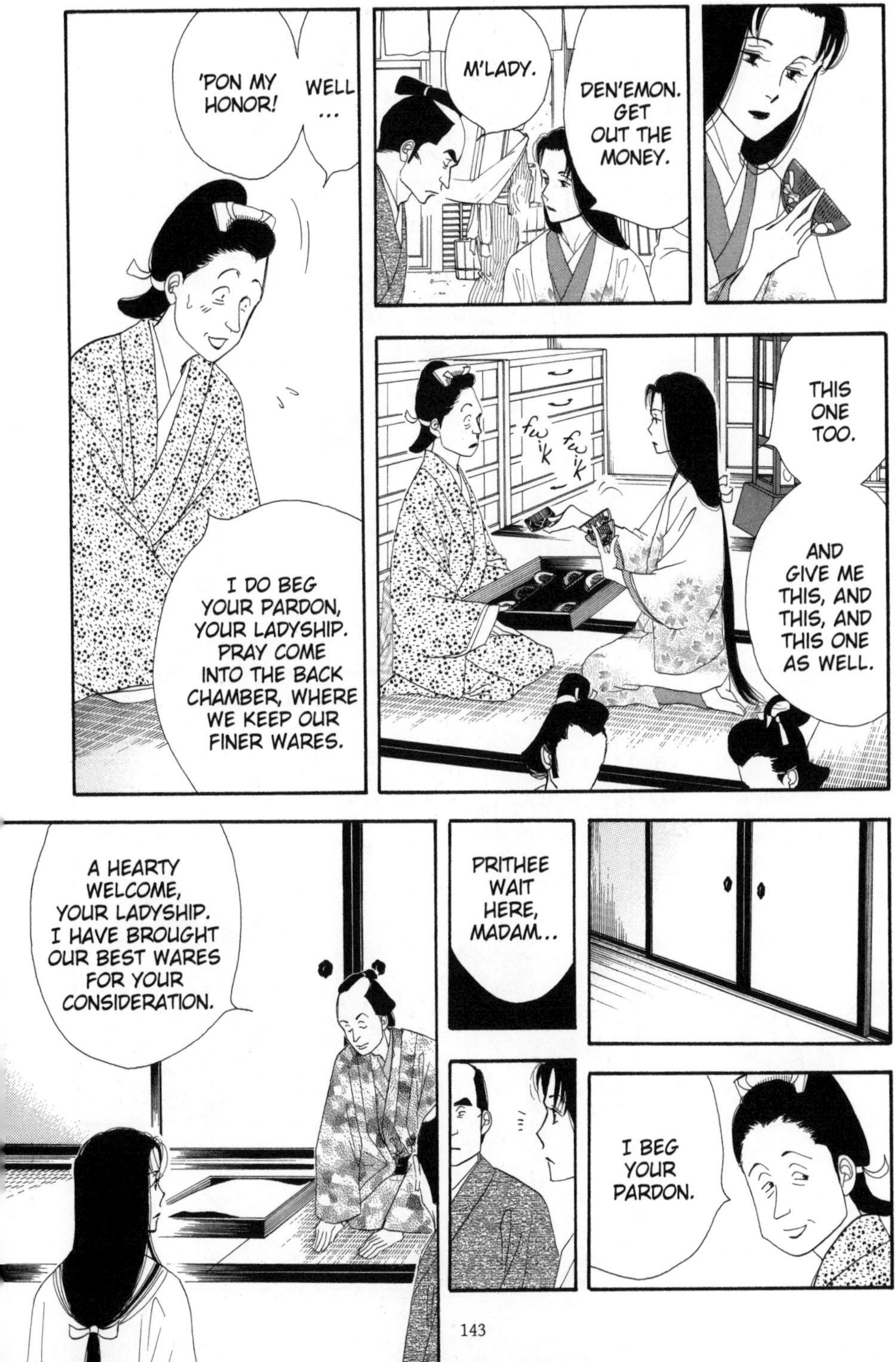
DEN'EMON. GET OUT THE MONEY.
M'LADY.
THIS ONE TOO.
AND GIVE ME THIS, AND THIS, AND THIS ONE AS WELL.
WELL ...
'PON MY HONOR!
I DO BEG YOUR PARDON, YOUR LADYSHIP. PRAY COME INTO THE BACK CHAMBER, WHERE WE KEEP OUR FINER WARES.
PRITHEE WAIT HERE, MADAM...
I BEG YOUR PARDON.
A HEARTY WELCOME, YOUR LADYSHIP. I HAVE BROUGHT OUR BEST WARES FOR YOUR CONSIDERATION.

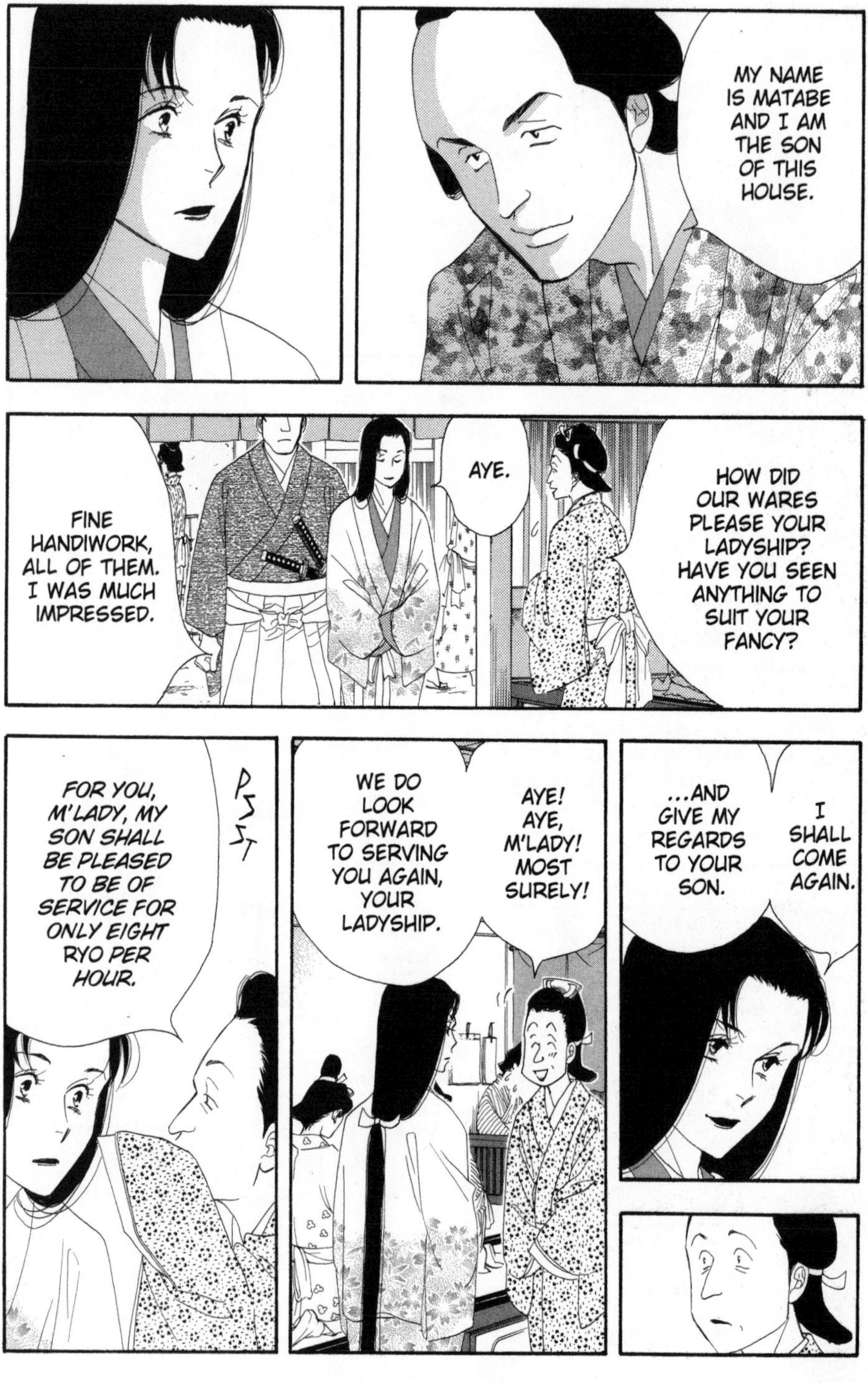
MY NAME IS MATABE AND I AM THE SON OF THIS HOUSE.
HOW DID OUR WARES PLEASE YOUR LADYSHIP? HAVE YOU SEEN ANYTHING TO SUIT YOUR FANCY?
AYE.
FINE HANDIWORK, ALL OF THEM. I WAS MUCH IMPRESSED.
I SHALL COME AGAIN.
...AND GIVE MY REGARDS TO YOUR SON.
AYE! AYE, M'LADY! MOST SURELY!
WE DO LOOK FORWARD TO SERVING YOU AGAIN, YOUR LADYSHIP.
PSST
FOR YOU, M'LADY, MY SON SHALL BE PLEASED TO BE OF SERVICE FOR ONLY EIGHT RYO PER HOUR.

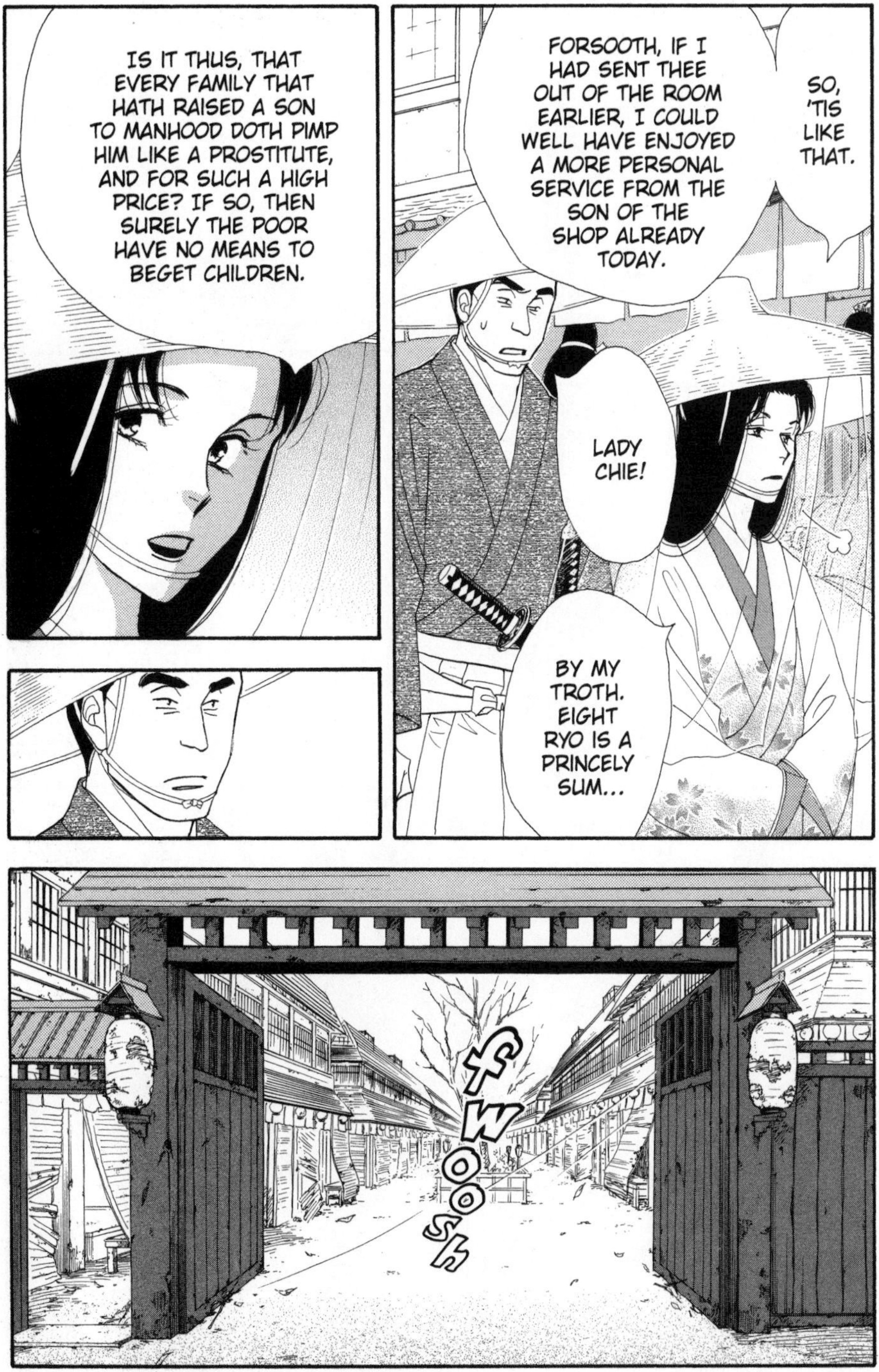
SO, 'TIS LIKE THAT.
FORSOOTH, IF I HAD SENT THEE OUT OF THE ROOM EARLIER, I COULD WELL HAVE ENJOYED A MORE PERSONAL SERVICE FROM THE SON OF THE SHOP ALREADY TODAY.
LADY CHIE!
BY MY TROTH. EIGHT RYO IS A PRINCELY SUM...
IS IT THUS, THAT EVERY FAMILY THAT HATH RAISED A SON TO MANHOOD DOTH PIMP HIM LIKE A PROSTITUTE, AND FOR SUCH A HIGH PRICE? IF SO, THEN SURELY THE POOR HAVE NO MEANS TO BEGET CHILDREN.
fwoosh

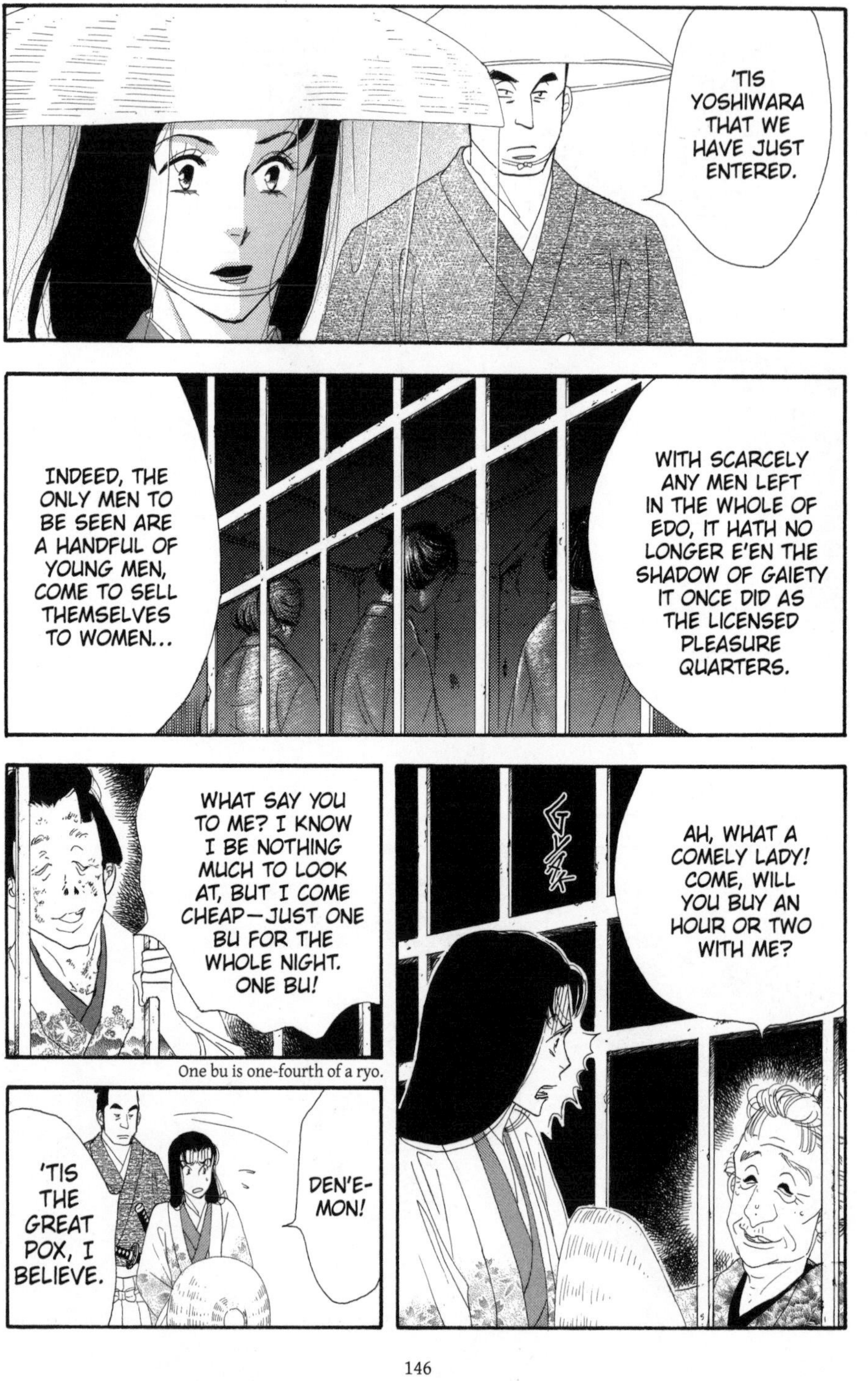
'TIS YOSHIWARA THAT WE HAVE JUST ENTERED.
WITH SCARCELY ANY MEN LEFT IN THE WHOLE OF EDO, IT HATH NO LONGER E'EN THE SHADOW OF GAIETY IT ONCE DID AS THE LICENSED PLEASURE QUARTERS.
INDEED, THE ONLY MEN TO BE SEEN ARE A HANDFUL OF YOUNG MEN, COME TO SELL THEMSELVES TO WOMEN...
AH, WHAT A COMELY LADY! COME, WILL YOU BUY AN HOUR OR TWO WITH ME?
GYAK
WHAT SAY YOU TO ME? I KNOW I BE NOTHING MUCH TO LOOK AT, BUT I COME CHEAP—JUST ONE BU FOR THE WHOLE NIGHT. ONE BU!
DEN'E-MON!
'TIS THE GREAT POX, I BELIEVE.
One bu is one-fourth of a ryo.

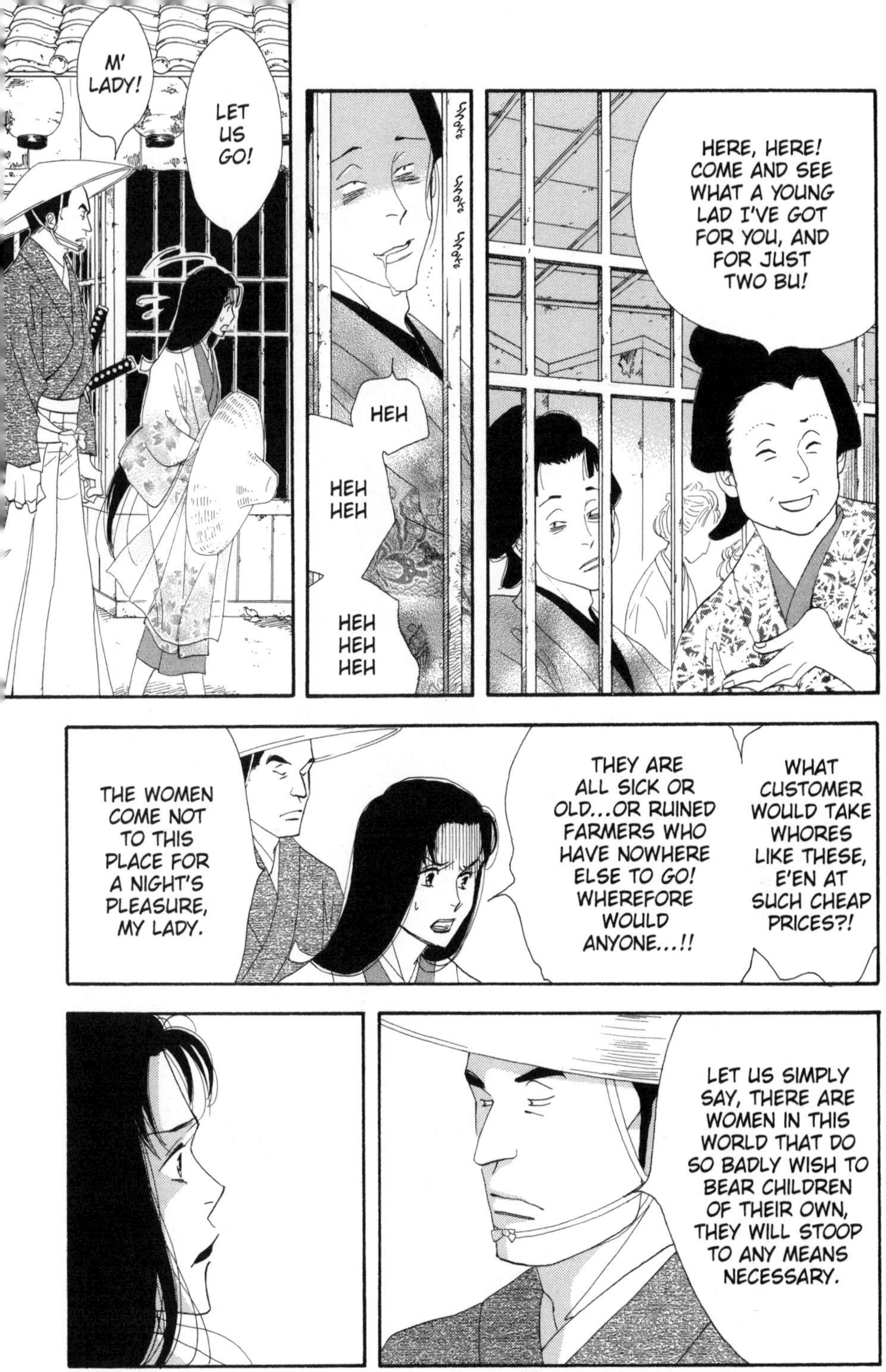
HERE, HERE! COME AND SEE WHAT A YOUNG LAD I'VE GOT FOR YOU, AND FOR JUST TWO BU!
Stroke
Stroke
Stroke
HEH
HEH HEH
HEH HEH HEH
LET US GO!
M' LADY!
WHAT CUSTOMER WOULD TAKE WHORES LIKE THESE, E'EN AT SUCH CHEAP PRICES?!
THEY ARE ALL SICK OR OLD...OR RUINED FARMERS WHO HAVE NOWHERE ELSE TO GO! WHEREFORE WOULD ANYONE...!!
THE WOMEN COME NOT TO THIS PLACE FOR A NIGHT'S PLEASURE, MY LADY.
LET US SIMPLY SAY, THERE ARE WOMEN IN THIS WORLD THAT DO SO BADLY WISH TO BEAR CHILDREN OF THEIR OWN, THEY WILL STOOP TO ANY MEANS NECESSARY.

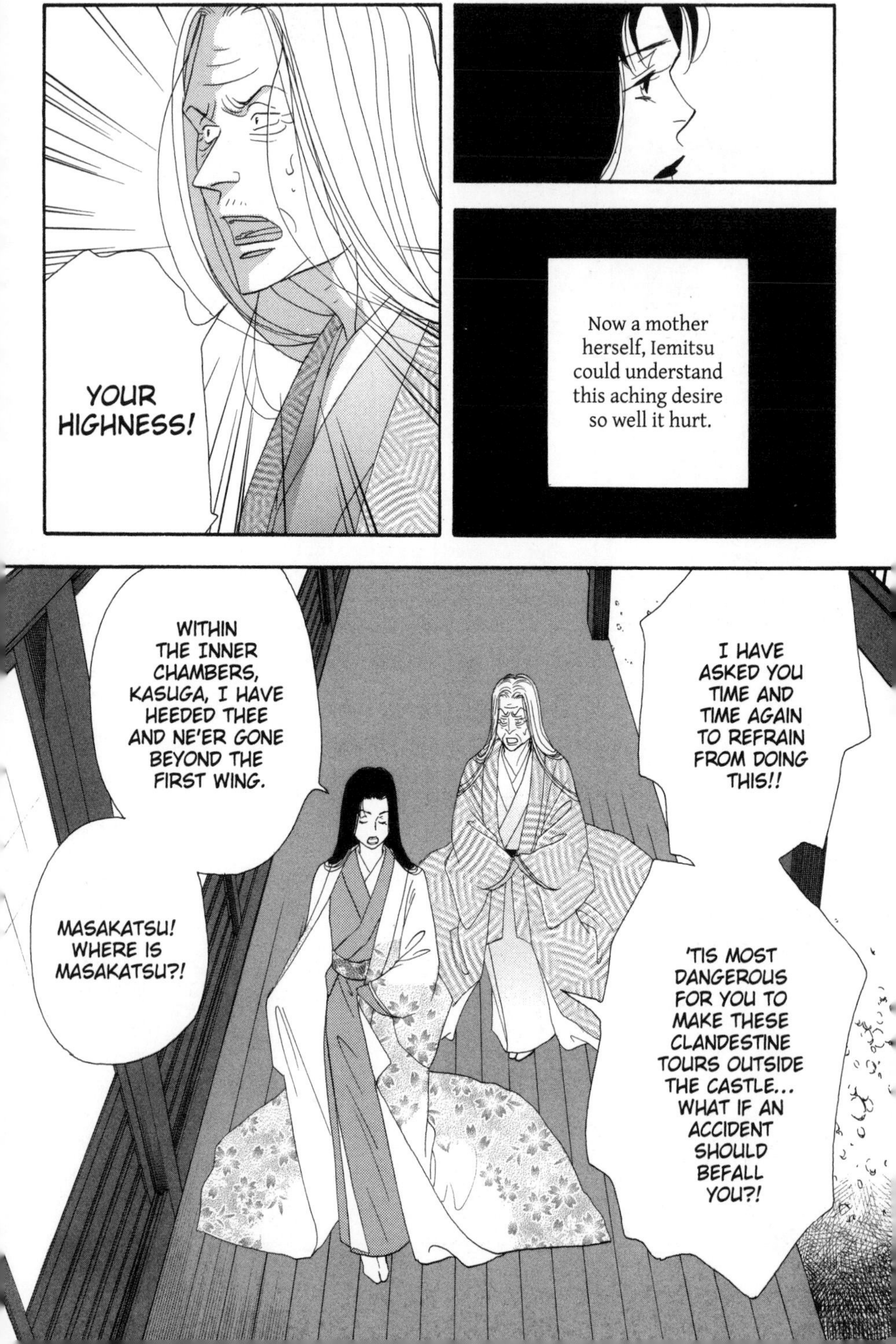
Now a mother herself, Iemitsu could understand this aching desire so well it hurt.
YOUR HIGHNESS!
I HAVE ASKED YOU TIME AND TIME AGAIN TO REFRAIN FROM DOING THIS!!
'TIS MOST DANGEROUS FOR YOU TO MAKE THESE CLANDESTINE TOURS OUTSIDE THE CASTLE... WHAT IF AN ACCIDENT SHOULD BEFALL YOU?!
WITHIN THE INNER CHAMBERS, KASUGA, I HAVE HEEDED THEE AND NE'ER GONE BEYOND THE FIRST WING.
MASAKATSU! WHERE IS MASAKATSU?!

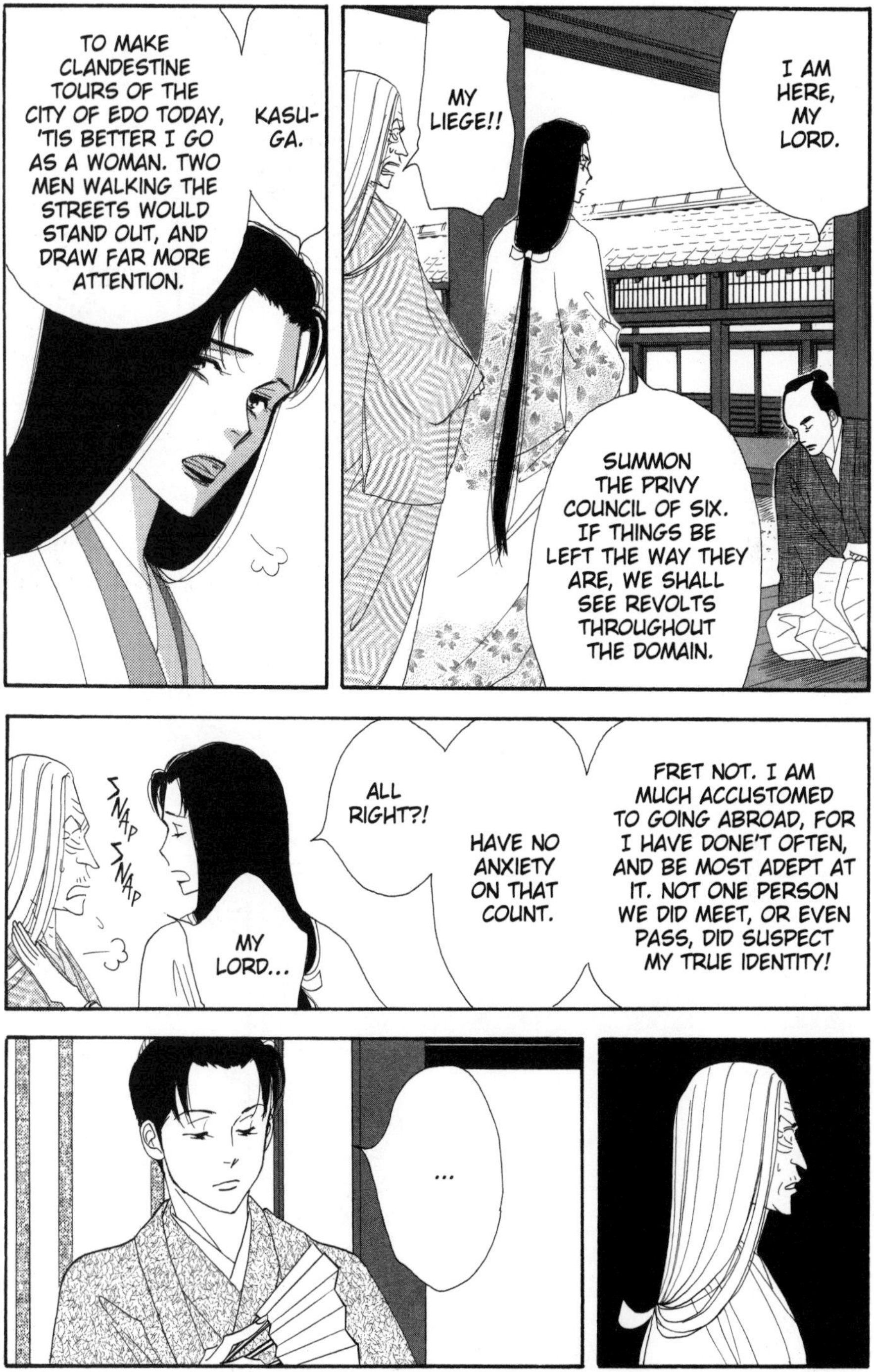
I AM HERE, MY LORD.
MY LIEGE!!
SUMMON THE PRIVY COUNCIL OF SIX. IF THINGS BE LEFT THE WAY THEY ARE, WE SHALL SEE REVOLTS THROUGHOUT THE DOMAIN.
KASU-GA.
TO MAKE CLANDESTINE TOURS OF THE CITY OF EDO TODAY, 'TIS BETTER I GO AS A WOMAN. TWO MEN WALKING THE STREETS WOULD STAND OUT, AND DRAW FAR MORE ATTENTION.
FRET NOT. I AM MUCH ACCUSTOMED TO GOING ABROAD, FOR I HAVE DONE'T OFTEN, AND BE MOST ADEPT AT IT. NOT ONE PERSON WE DID MEET, OR EVEN PASS, DID SUSPECT MY TRUE IDENTITY!
HAVE NO ANXIETY ON THAT COUNT.
ALL RIGHT?!
MY LORD...
SNAP SNAP
...

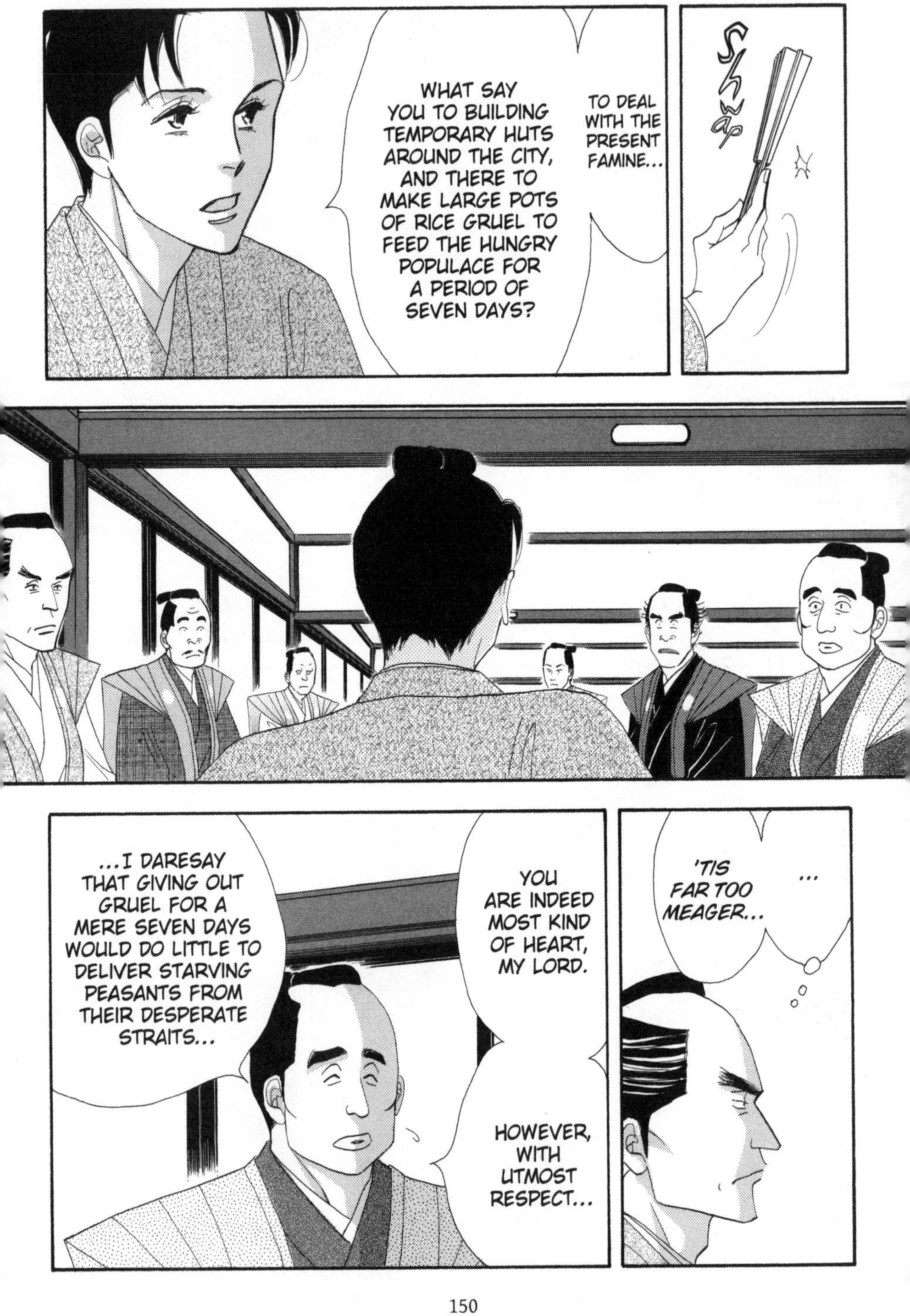
Shwap
TO DEAL WITH THE PRESENT FAMINE...
WHAT SAY YOU TO BUILDING TEMPORARY HUTS AROUND THE CITY, AND THERE TO MAKE LARGE POTS OF RICE GRUEL TO FEED THE HUNGRY POPULACE FOR A PERIOD OF SEVEN DAYS?
...
'TIS FAR TOO MEAGER...
YOU ARE INDEED MOST KIND OF HEART, MY LORD.
HOWEVER, WITH UTMOST RESPECT...
...I DARESAY THAT GIVING OUT GRUEL FOR A MERE SEVEN DAYS WOULD DO LITTLE TO DELIVER STARVING PEASANTS FROM THEIR DESPERATE STRAITS...

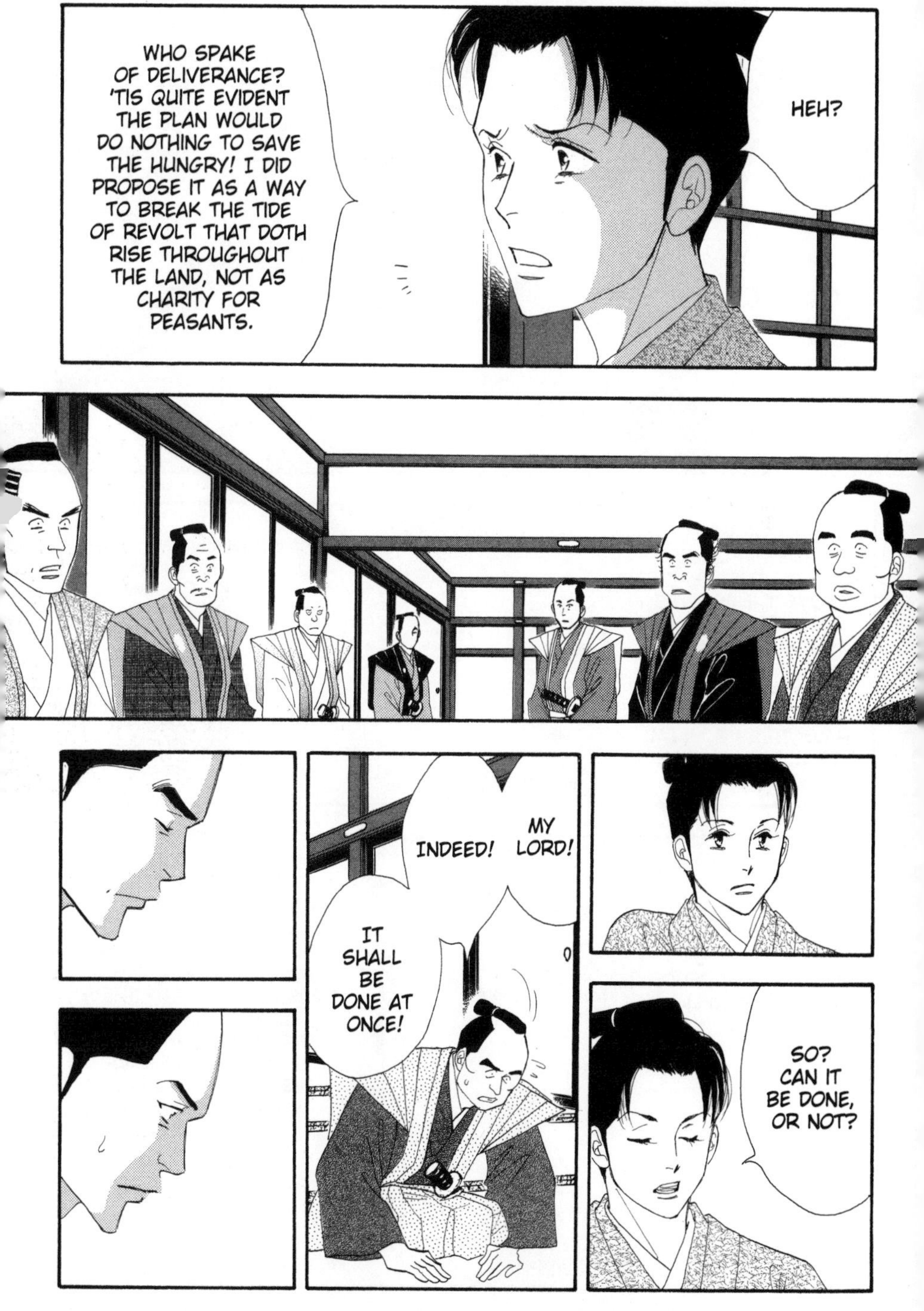
HEH?
WHO SPAKE OF DELIVERANCE? 'TIS QUITE EVIDENT THE PLAN WOULD DO NOTHING TO SAVE THE HUNGRY! I DID PROPOSE IT AS A WAY TO BREAK THE TIDE OF REVOLT THAT DOTH RISE THROUGHOUT THE LAND, NOT AS CHARITY FOR PEASANTS.
SO? CAN IT BE DONE, OR NOT?
MY LORD!
INDEED!
IT SHALL BE DONE AT ONCE!

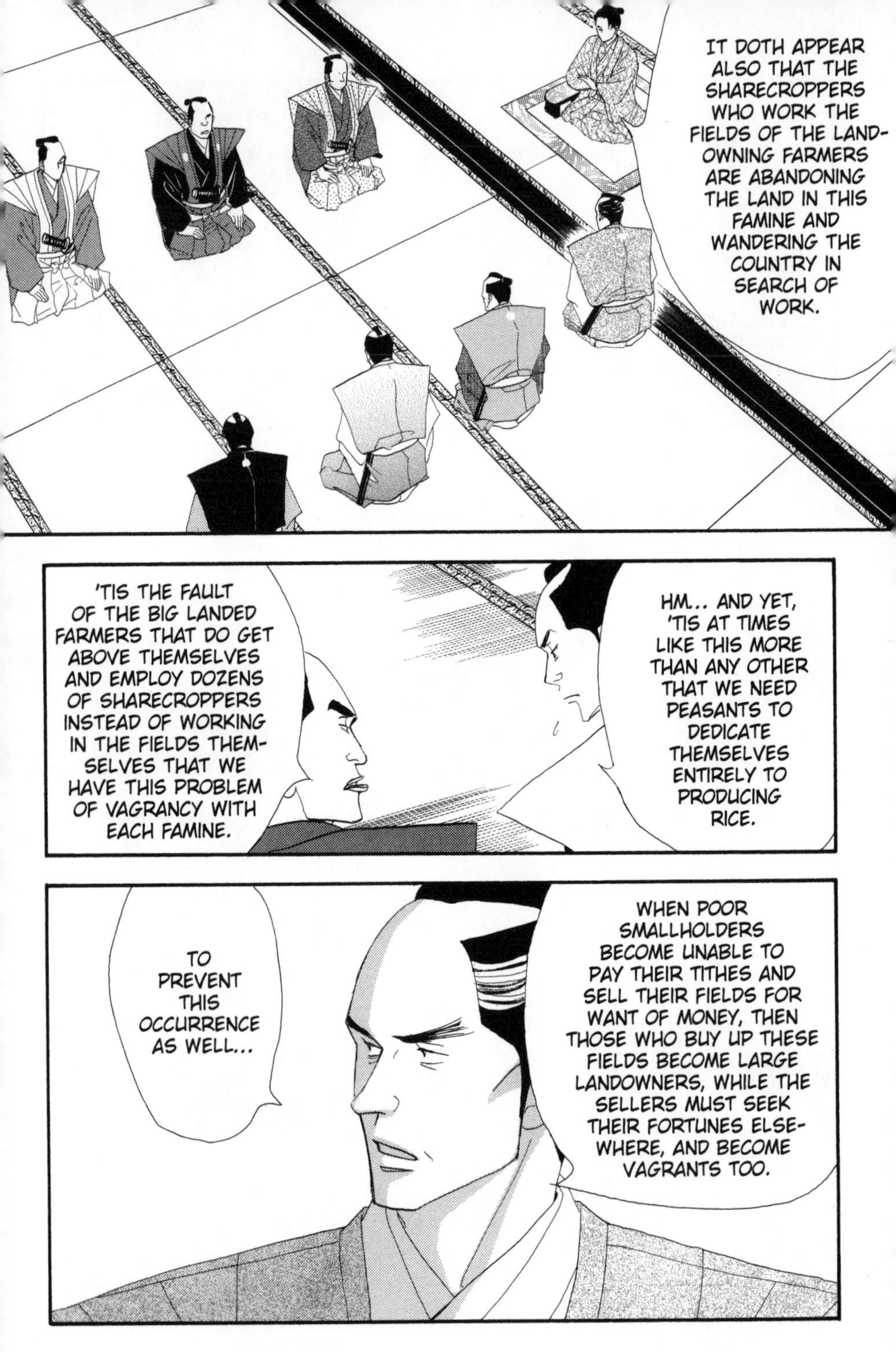
IT DOTH APPEAR ALSO THAT THE SHARECROPPERS WHO WORK THE FIELDS OF THE LAND-OWNING FARMERS ARE ABANDONING THE LAND IN THIS FAMINE AND WANDERING THE COUNTRY IN SEARCH OF WORK.
HM... AND YET, 'TIS AT TIMES LIKE THIS MORE THAN ANY OTHER THAT WE NEED PEASANTS TO DEDICATE THEMSELVES ENTIRELY TO PRODUCING RICE.
'TIS THE FAULT OF THE BIG LANDED FARMERS THAT DO GET ABOVE THEMSELVES AND EMPLOY DOZENS OF SHARECROPPERS INSTEAD OF WORKING IN THE FIELDS THEM-SELVES THAT WE HAVE THIS PROBLEM OF VAGRANCY WITH EACH FAMINE.
WHEN POOR SMALLHOLDERS BECOME UNABLE TO PAY THEIR TITHES AND SELL THEIR FIELDS FOR WANT OF MONEY, THEN THOSE WHO BUY UP THESE FIELDS BECOME LARGE LANDOWNERS, WHILE THE SELLERS MUST SEEK THEIR FORTUNES ELSE-WHERE, AND BECOME VAGRANTS TOO.
TO PREVENT THIS OCCURRENCE AS WELL...

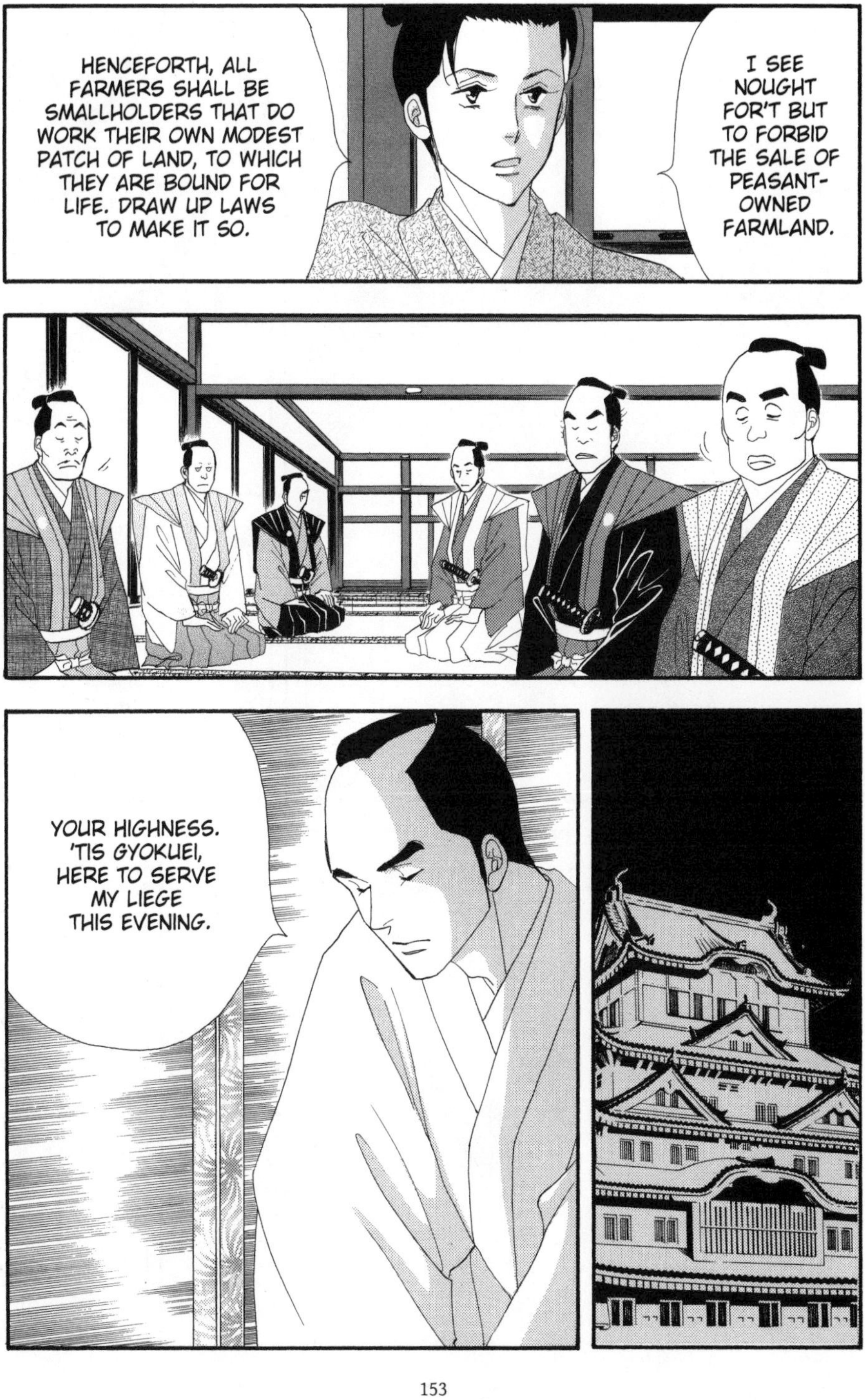
I SEE NOUGHT FOR'T BUT TO FORBID THE SALE OF PEASANT-OWNED FARMLAND.
HENCEFORTH, ALL FARMERS SHALL BE SMALLHOLDERS THAT DO WORK THEIR OWN MODEST PATCH OF LAND, TO WHICH THEY ARE BOUND FOR LIFE. DRAW UP LAWS TO MAKE IT SO.
YOUR HIGHNESS. 'TIS GYOKUEI, HERE TO SERVE MY LIEGE THIS EVENING.

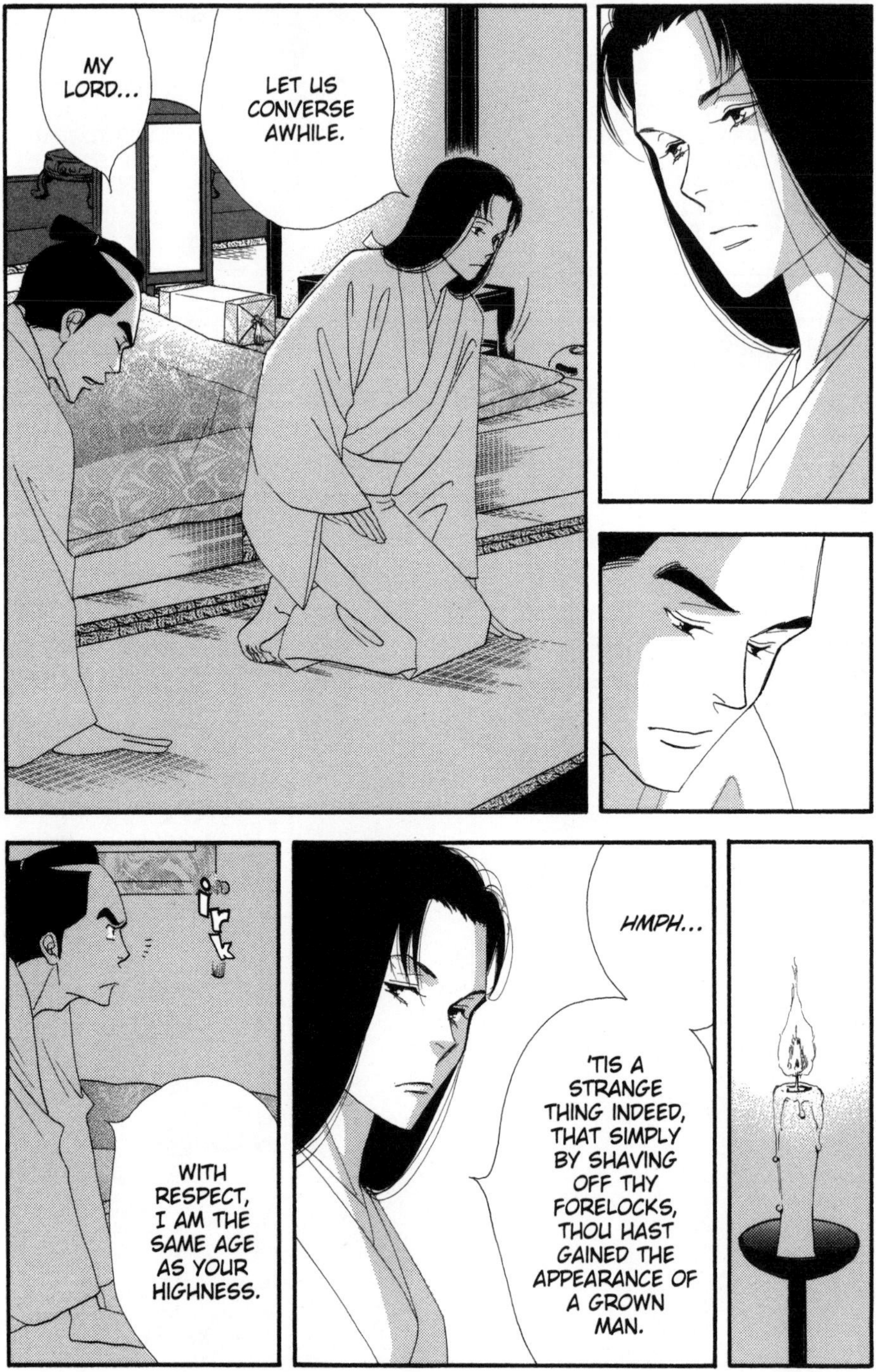
LET US CONVERSE AWHILE.
MY LORD...
HMPH...
'TIS A STRANGE THING INDEED, THAT SIMPLY BY SHAVING OFF THY FORELOCKS, THOU HAST GAINED THE APPEARANCE OF A GROWN MAN.
irk
WITH RESPECT, I AM THE SAME AGE AS YOUR HIGHNESS.

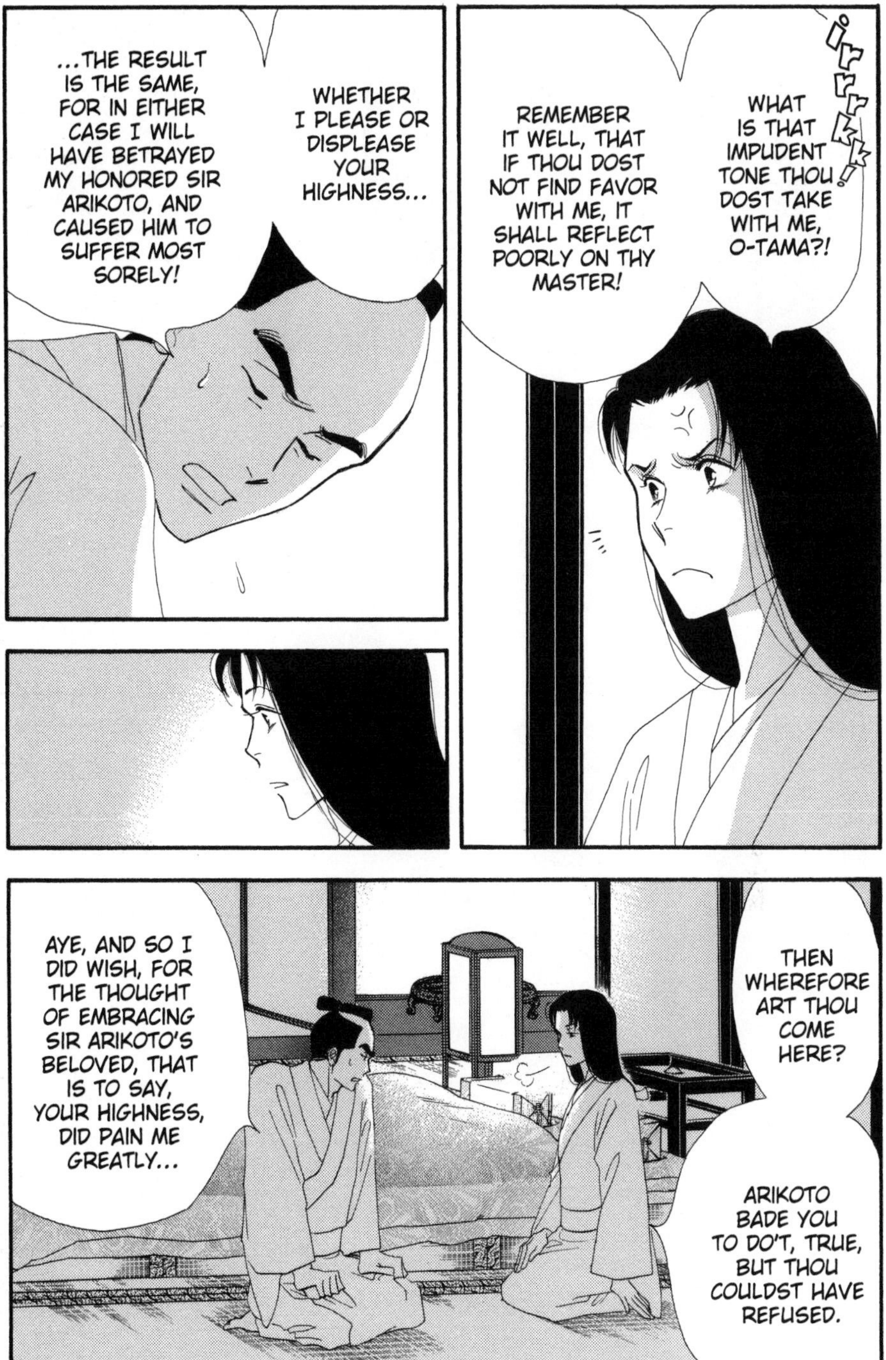
irrrkk!
WHAT IS THAT IMPUDENT TONE THOU DOST TAKE WITH ME, O-TAMA?!
REMEMBER IT WELL, THAT IF THOU DOST NOT FIND FAVOR WITH ME, IT SHALL REFLECT POORLY ON THY MASTER!
WHETHER I PLEASE OR DISPLEASE YOUR HIGHNESS...
...THE RESULT IS THE SAME, FOR IN EITHER CASE I WILL HAVE BETRAYED MY HONORED SIR ARIKOTO, AND CAUSED HIM TO SUFFER MOST SORELY!
THEN WHEREFORE ART THOU COME HERE?
ARIKOTO BADE YOU TO DO'T, TRUE, BUT THOU COULDST HAVE REFUSED.
AYE, AND SO I DID WISH, FOR THE THOUGHT OF EMBRACING SIR ARIKOTO'S BELOVED, THAT IS TO SAY, YOUR HIGHNESS, DID PAIN ME GREATLY...

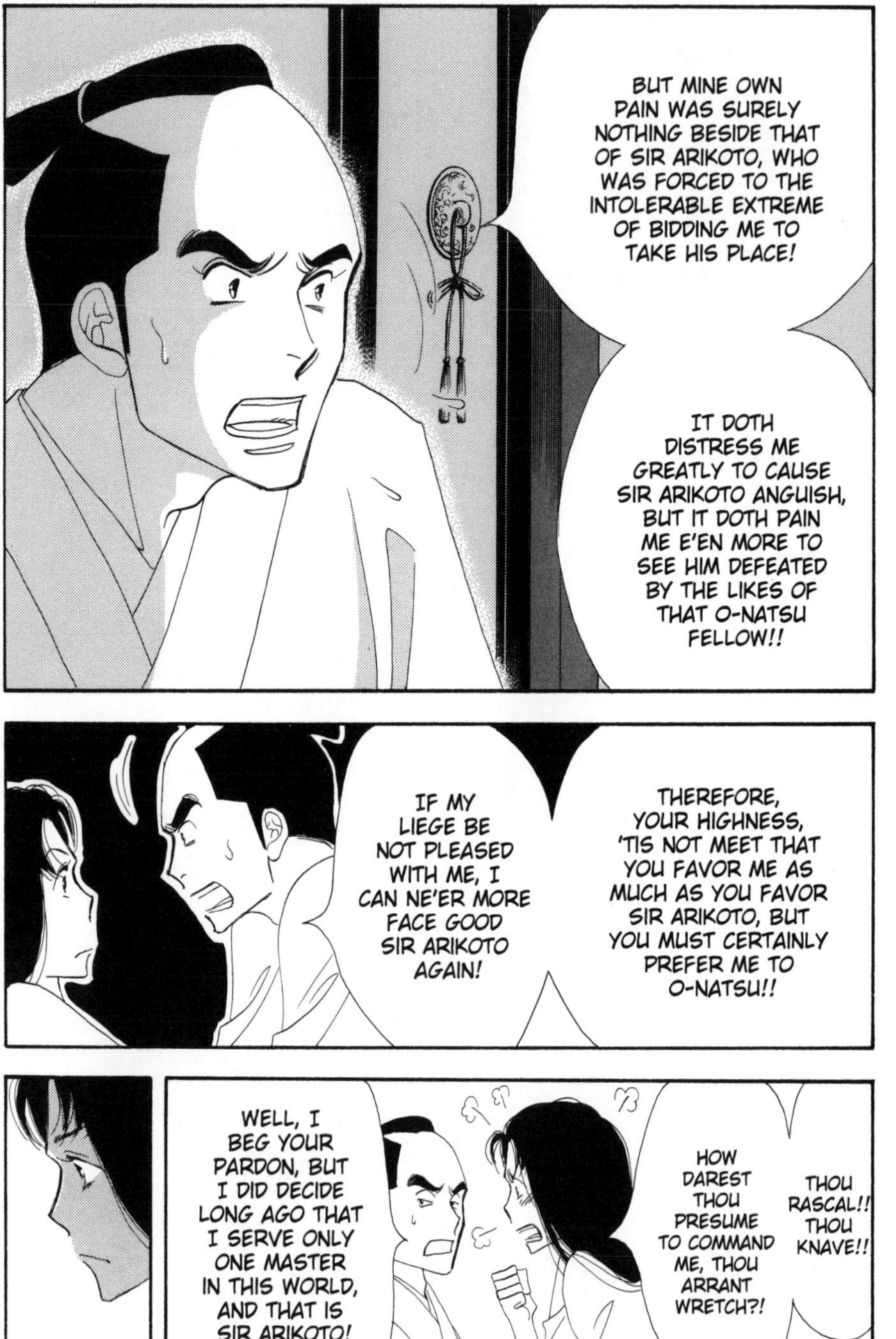
BUT MINE OWN PAIN WAS SURELY NOTHING BESIDE THAT OF SIR ARIKOTO, WHO WAS FORCED TO THE INTOLERABLE EXTREME OF BIDDING ME TO TAKE HIS PLACE!
IT DOTH DISTRESS ME GREATLY TO CAUSE SIR ARIKOTO ANGUISH, BUT IT DOTH PAIN ME E'EN MORE TO SEE HIM DEFEATED BY THE LIKES OF THAT O-NATSU FELLOW!!
THEREFORE, YOUR HIGHNESS, 'TIS NOT MEET THAT YOU FAVOR ME AS MUCH AS YOU FAVOR SIR ARIKOTO, BUT YOU MUST CERTAINLY PREFER ME TO O-NATSU!!
IF MY LIEGE BE NOT PLEASED WITH ME, I CAN NE'ER MORE FACE GOOD SIR ARIKOTO AGAIN!
THOU RASCAL!! THOU KNAVE!!
HOW DAREST THOU PRESUME TO COMMAND ME, THOU ARRANT WRETCH?!
WELL, I BEG YOUR PARDON, BUT I DID DECIDE LONG AGO THAT I SERVE ONLY ONE MASTER IN THIS WORLD, AND THAT IS SIR ARIKOTO!

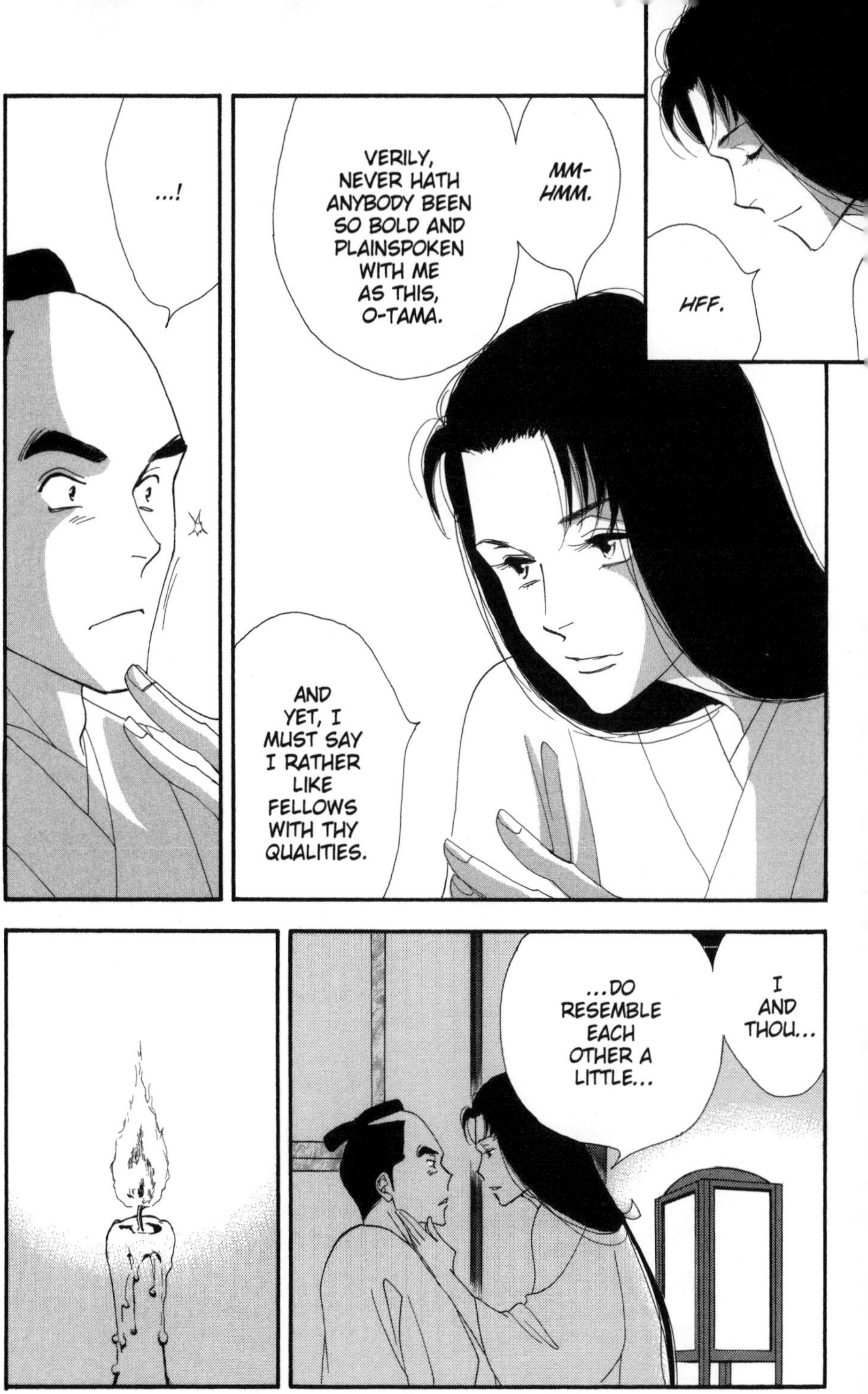
HFF.
MM-HMM.
VERILY, NEVER HATH ANYBODY BEEN SO BOLD AND PLAINSPOKEN WITH ME AS THIS, O-TAMA.
AND YET, I MUST SAY I RATHER LIKE FELLOWS WITH THY QUALITIES.
...!
I AND THOU...
...DO RESEMBLE EACH OTHER A LITTLE...

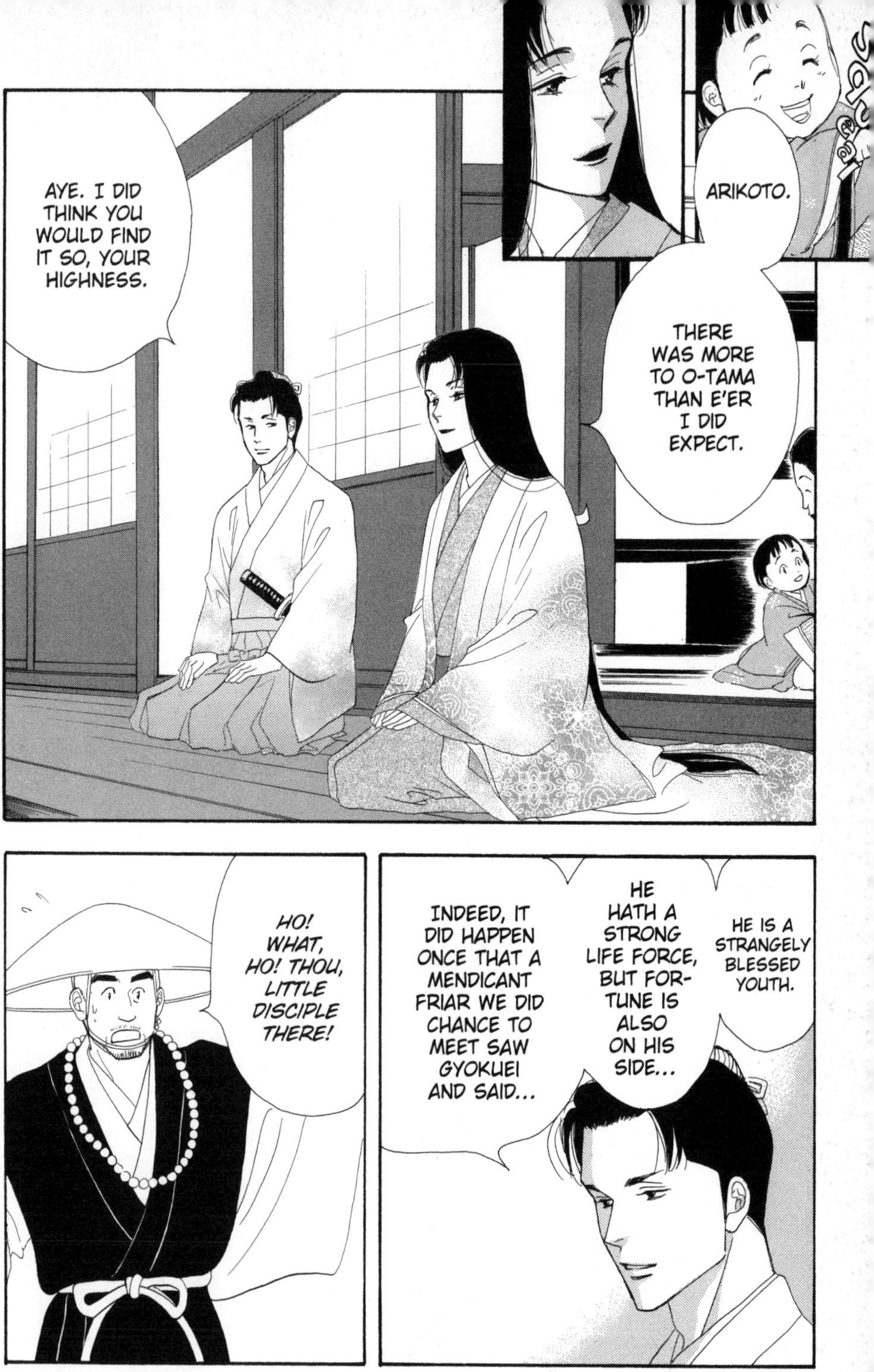
ARIKOTO.
THERE WAS MORE TO O-TAMA THAN E'ER I DID EXPECT.
AYE. I DID THINK YOU WOULD FIND IT SO, YOUR HIGHNESS.
HE IS A STRANGELY BLESSED YOUTH.
HE HATH A STRONG LIFE FORCE, BUT FOR-TUNE IS ALSO ON HIS SIDE...
INDEED, IT DID HAPPEN ONCE THAT A MENDICANT FRIAR WE DID CHANCE TO MEET SAW GYOKUEI AND SAID...
HO! WHAT, HO! THOU, LITTLE DISCIPLE THERE!

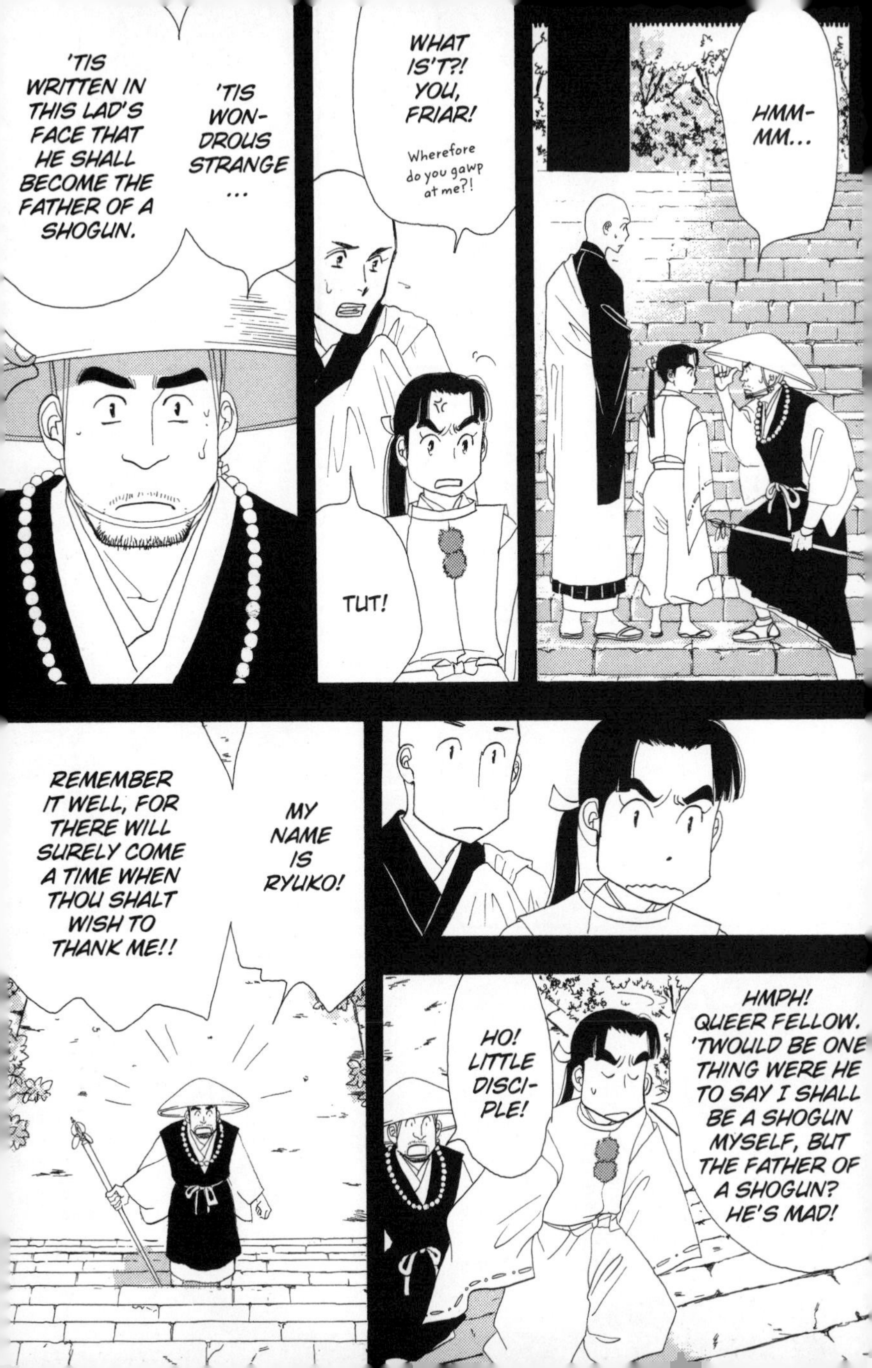
HMM-MM...
WHAT IS'T?! YOU, FRIAR!
Wherefore do you gawp at me?!
TUT!
'TIS WON-DROUS STRANGE...
'TIS WRITTEN IN THIS LAD'S FACE THAT HE SHALL BECOME THE FATHER OF A SHOGUN.
HMPH! QUEER FELLOW. 'TWOULD BE ONE THING WERE HE TO SAY I SHALL BE A SHOGUN MYSELF, BUT THE FATHER OF A SHOGUN? HE'S MAD!
HO! LITTLE DISCI-PLE!
MY NAME IS RYUKO!
REMEMBER IT WELL, FOR THERE WILL SURELY COME A TIME WHEN THOU SHALT WISH TO THANK ME!!

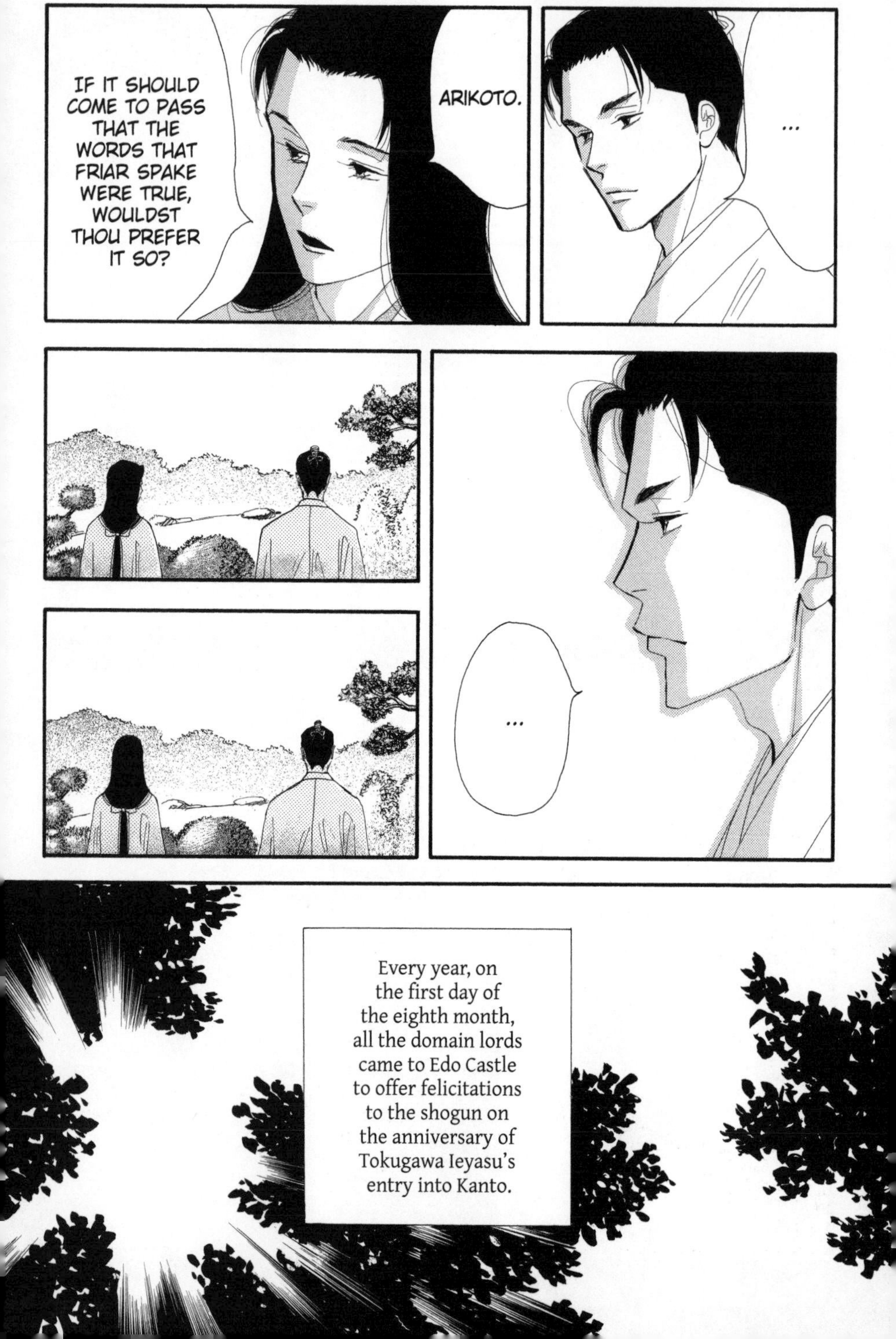
...
ARIKOTO.
IF IT SHOULD COME TO PASS THAT THE WORDS THAT FRIAR SPAKE WERE TRUE, WOULDST THOU PREFER IT SO?
...
Every year, on the first day of the eighth month, all the domain lords came to Edo Castle to offer felicitations to the shogun on the anniversary of Tokugawa Ieyasu's entry into Kanto.

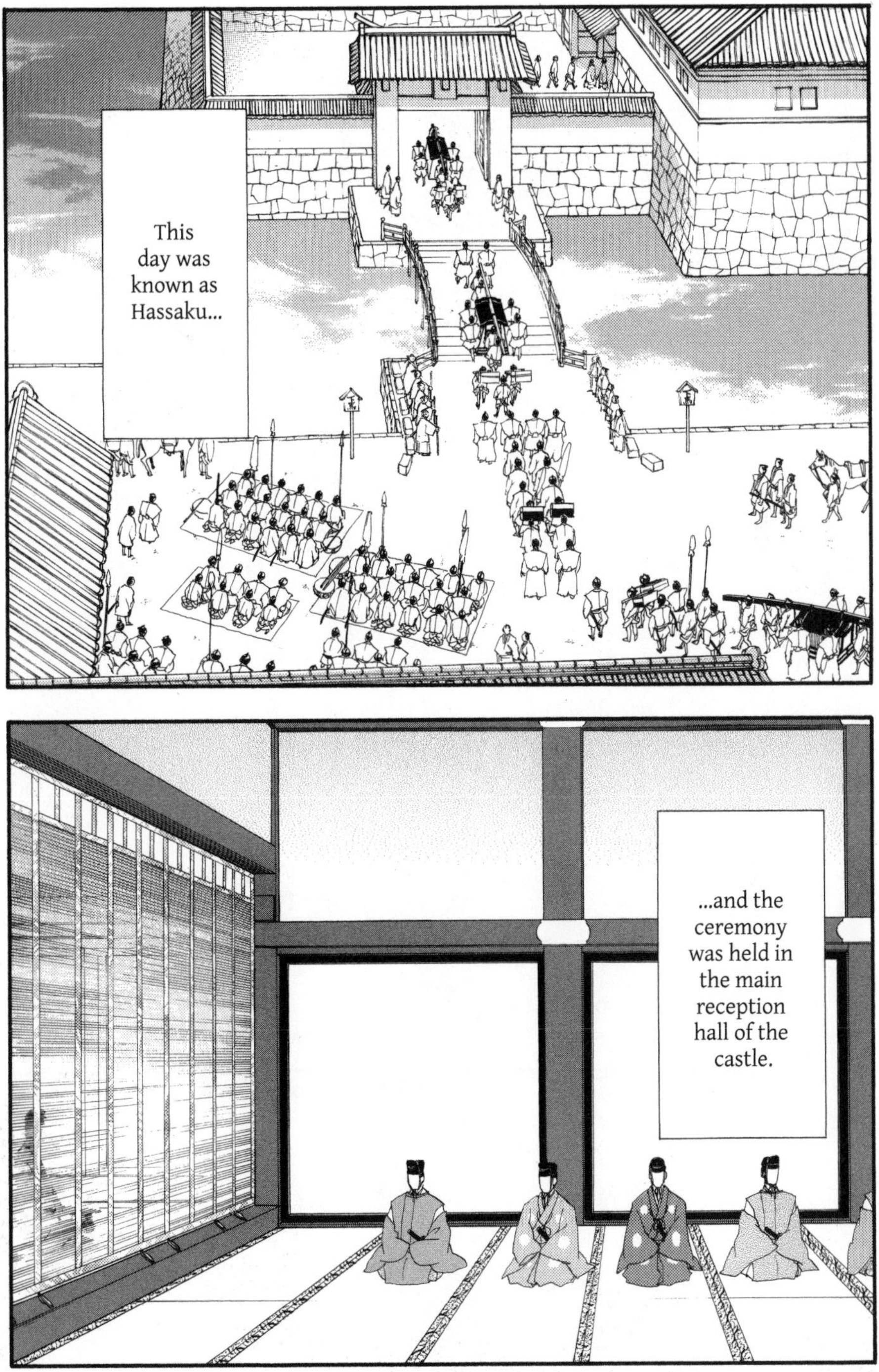
This day was known as Hassaku...
...and the ceremony was held in the main reception hall of the castle.

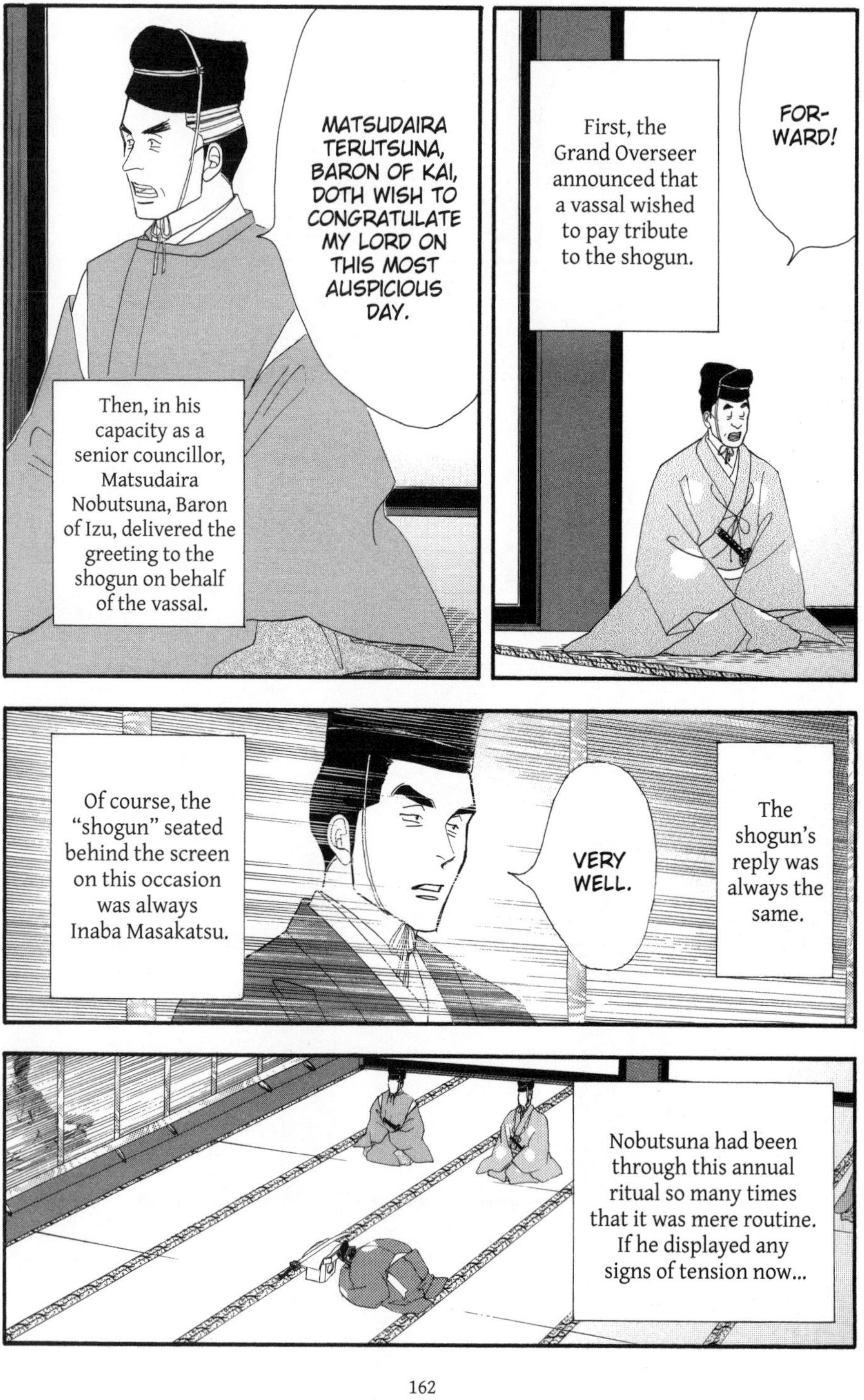
FOR-WARD!
First, the Grand Overseer announced that a vassal wished to pay tribute to the shogun.
MATSUDAIRA TERUTSUNA, BARON OF KAI, DOTH WISH TO CONGRATULATE MY LORD ON THIS MOST AUSPICIOUS DAY.
Then, in his capacity as a senior councillor, Matsudaira Nobutsuna, Baron of Izu, delivered the greeting to the shogun on behalf of the vassal.
The shogun's reply was always the same.
VERY WELL.
Of course, the "shogun" seated behind the screen on this occasion was always Inaba Masakatsu.
Nobutsuna had been through this annual ritual so many times that it was mere routine. If he displayed any signs of tension now...

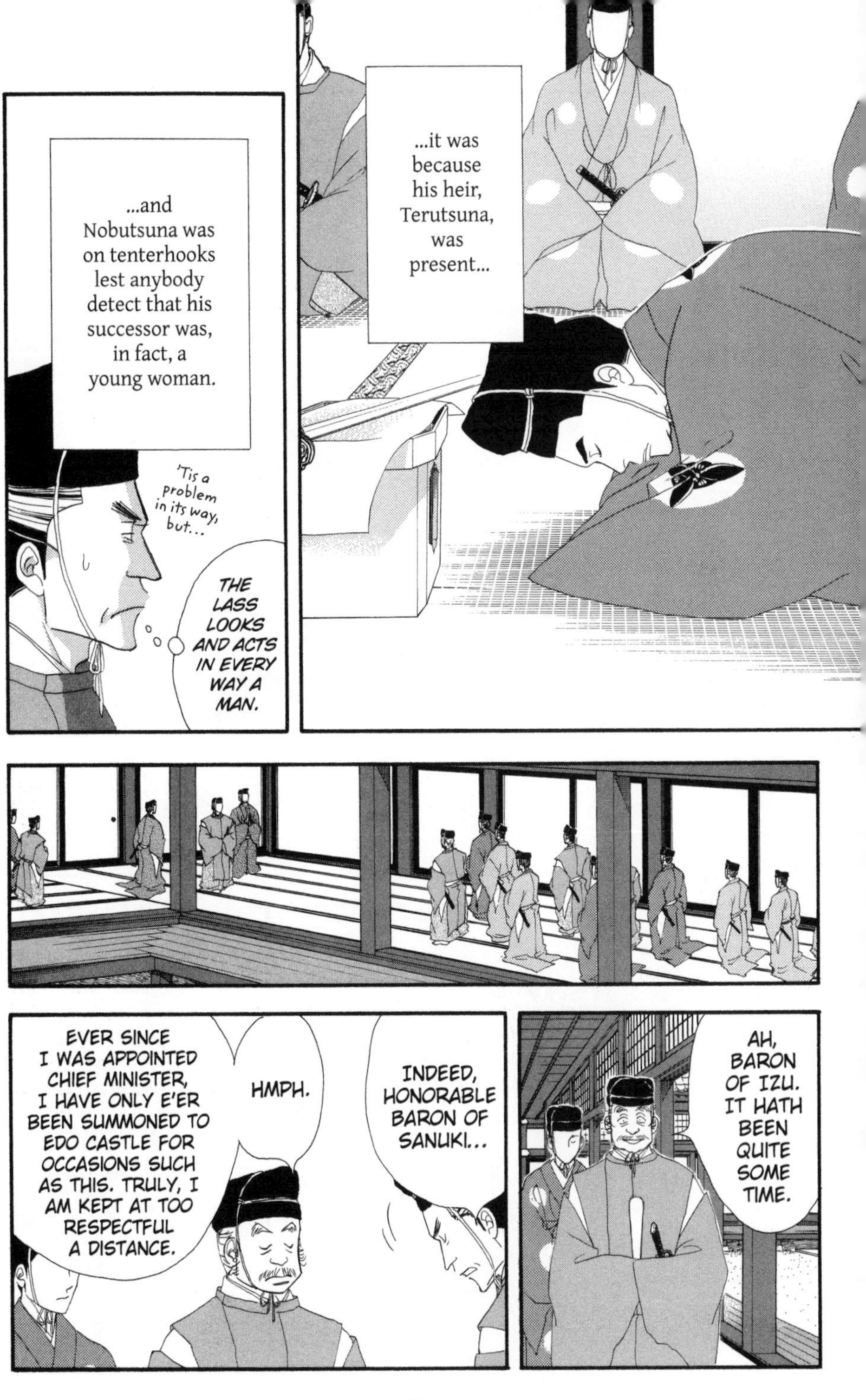
...it was because his heir, Terutsuna, was present...
...and Nobutsuna was on tenterhooks lest anybody detect that his successor was, in fact, a young woman.
'Tis a problem in its way, but...
THE LASS LOOKS AND ACTS IN EVERY WAY A MAN.
AH, BARON OF IZU. IT HATH BEEN QUITE SOME TIME.
INDEED, HONORABLE BARON OF SANUKI...
HMPH.
EVER SINCE I WAS APPOINTED CHIEF MINISTER, I HAVE ONLY E'ER BEEN SUMMONED TO EDO CASTLE FOR OCCASIONS SUCH AS THIS. TRULY, I AM KEPT AT TOO RESPECTFUL A DISTANCE.

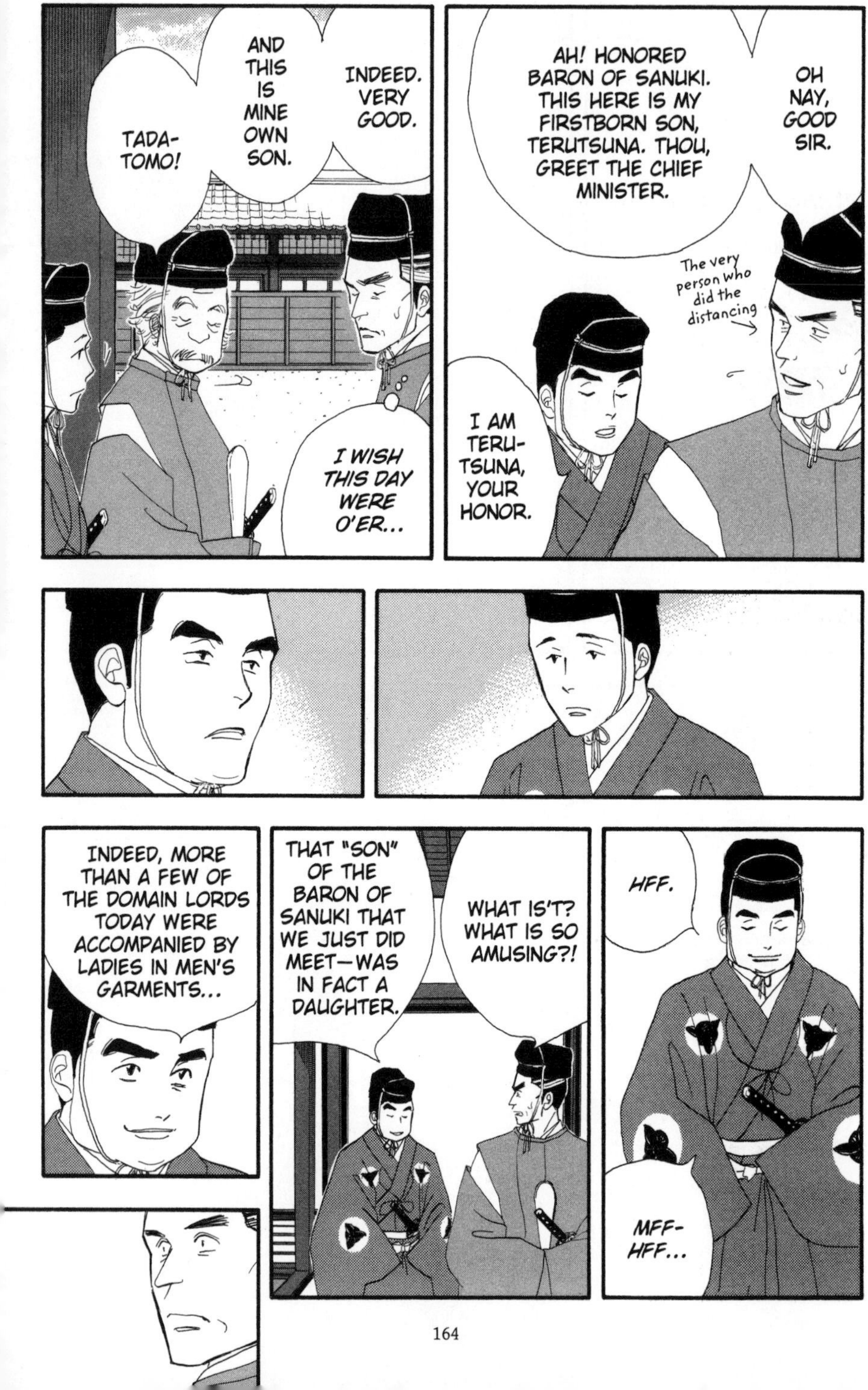
OH NAY, GOOD SIR.
AH! HONORED BARON OF SANUKI. THIS HERE IS MY FIRSTBORN SON, TERUTSUNA. THOU, GREET THE CHIEF MINISTER.
The very person who did the distancing
I AM TERU-TSUNA, YOUR HONOR.
INDEED. VERY GOOD.
AND THIS IS MINE OWN SON.
TADA-TOMO!
I WISH THIS DAY WERE O'ER...
HFF.
MFF-HFF...
WHAT IS'T? WHAT IS SO AMUSING?!
THAT "SON" OF THE BARON OF SANUKI THAT WE JUST DID MEET—WAS IN FACT A DAUGHTER.
INDEED, MORE THAN A FEW OF THE DOMAIN LORDS TODAY WERE ACCOMPANIED BY LADIES IN MEN'S GARMENTS...

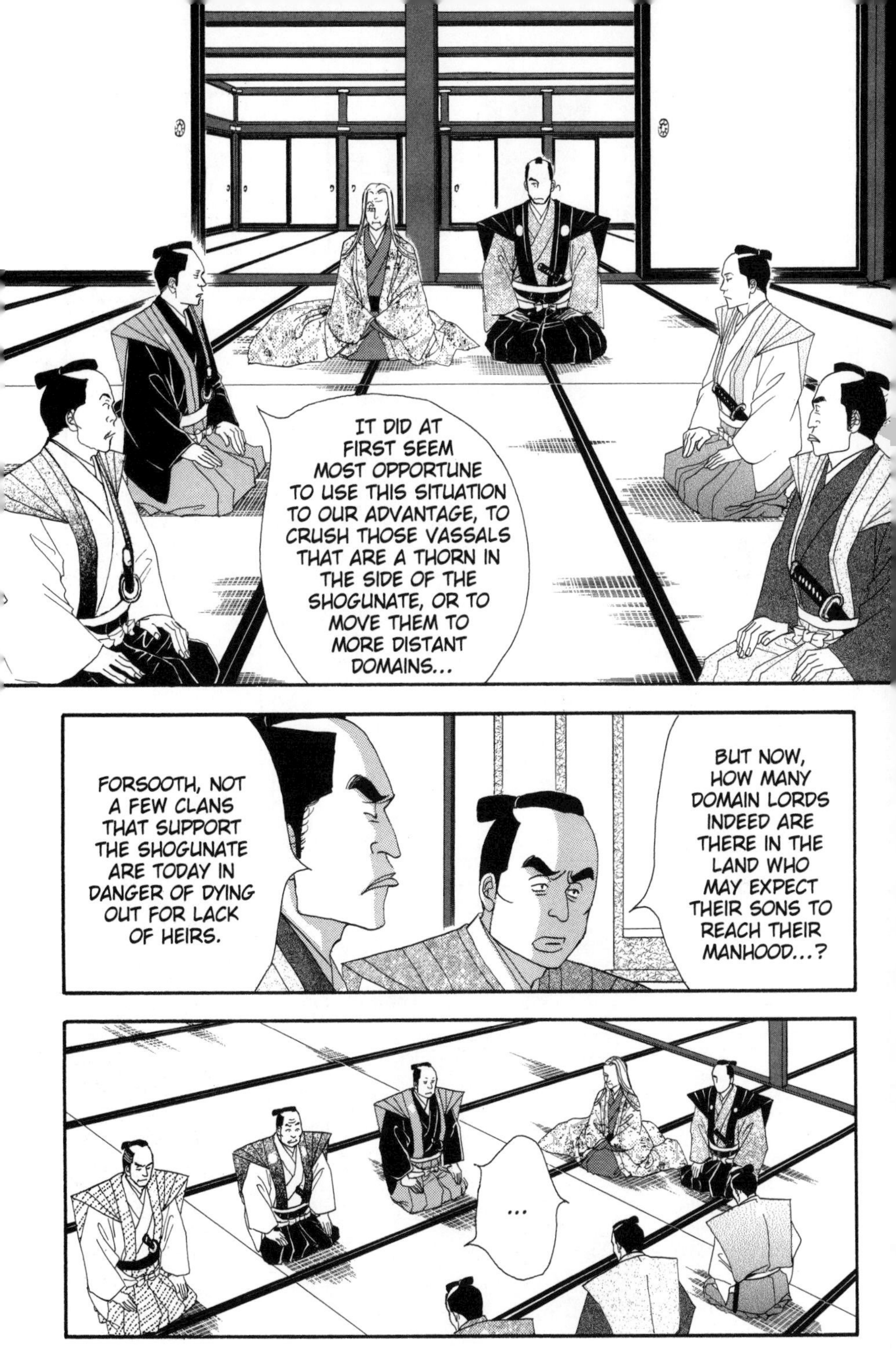
IT DID AT FIRST SEEM MOST OPPORTUNE TO USE THIS SITUATION TO OUR ADVANTAGE, TO CRUSH THOSE VASSALS THAT ARE A THORN IN THE SIDE OF THE SHOGUNATE, OR TO MOVE THEM TO MORE DISTANT DOMAINS...
BUT NOW, HOW MANY DOMAIN LORDS INDEED ARE THERE IN THE LAND WHO MAY EXPECT THEIR SONS TO REACH THEIR MANHOOD...?
FORSOOTH, NOT A FEW CLANS THAT SUPPORT THE SHOGUNATE ARE TODAY IN DANGER OF DYING OUT FOR LACK OF HEIRS.
...

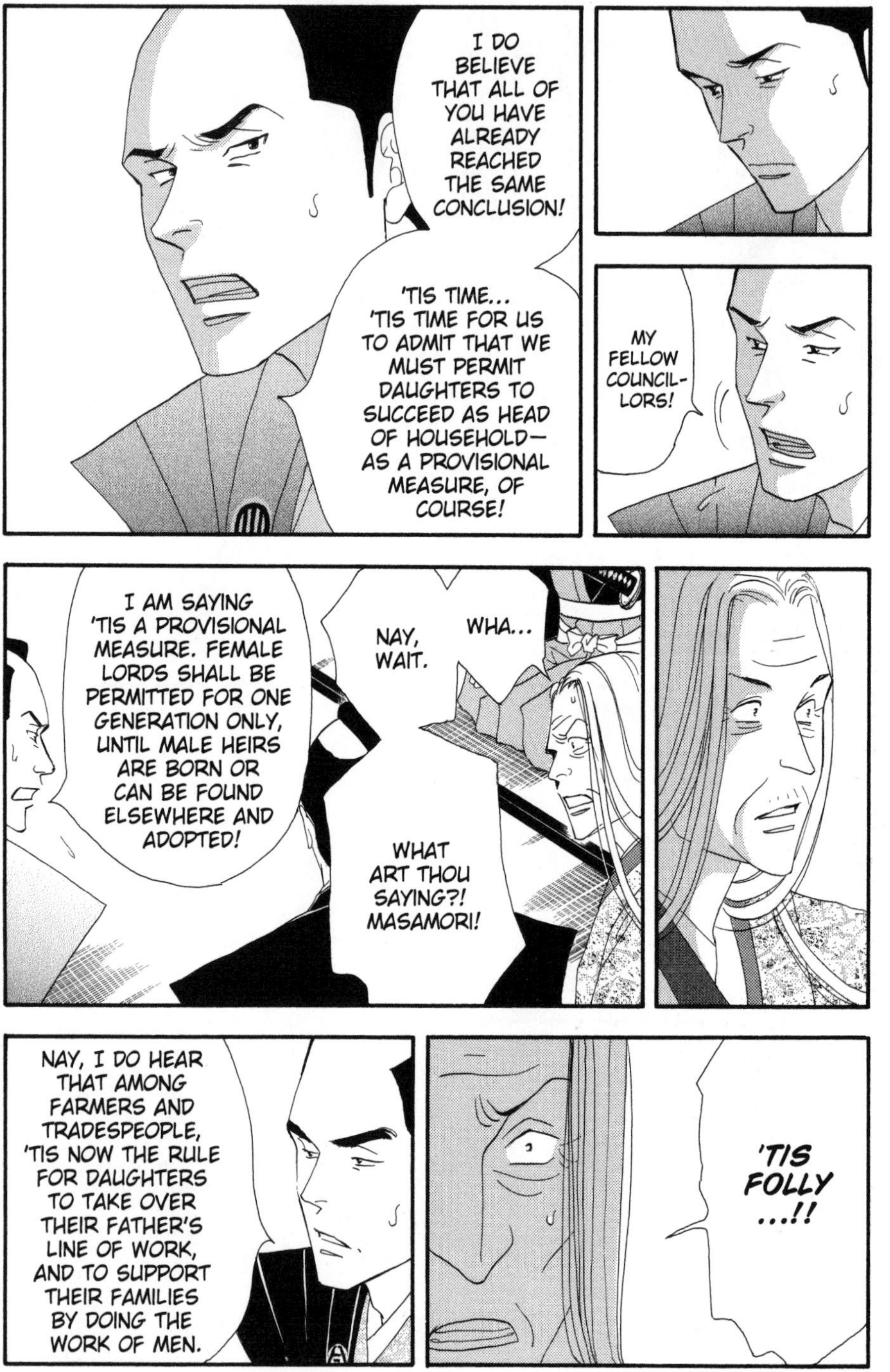
MY FELLOW COUNCIL-LORS!
I DO BELIEVE THAT ALL OF YOU HAVE ALREADY REACHED THE SAME CONCLUSION!
'TIS TIME... 'TIS TIME FOR US TO ADMIT THAT WE MUST PERMIT DAUGHTERS TO SUCCEED AS HEAD OF HOUSEHOLD—AS A PROVISIONAL MEASURE, OF COURSE!
WHA...
NAY, WAIT.
I AM SAYING 'TIS A PROVISIONAL MEASURE. FEMALE LORDS SHALL BE PERMITTED FOR ONE GENERATION ONLY, UNTIL MALE HEIRS ARE BORN OR CAN BE FOUND ELSEWHERE AND ADOPTED!
WHAT ART THOU SAYING?! MASAMORI!
'TIS FOLLY ...!!
NAY, I DO HEAR THAT AMONG FARMERS AND TRADESPEOPLE, 'TIS NOW THE RULE FOR DAUGHTERS TO TAKE OVER THEIR FATHER'S LINE OF WORK, AND TO SUPPORT THEIR FAMILIES BY DOING THE WORK OF MEN.

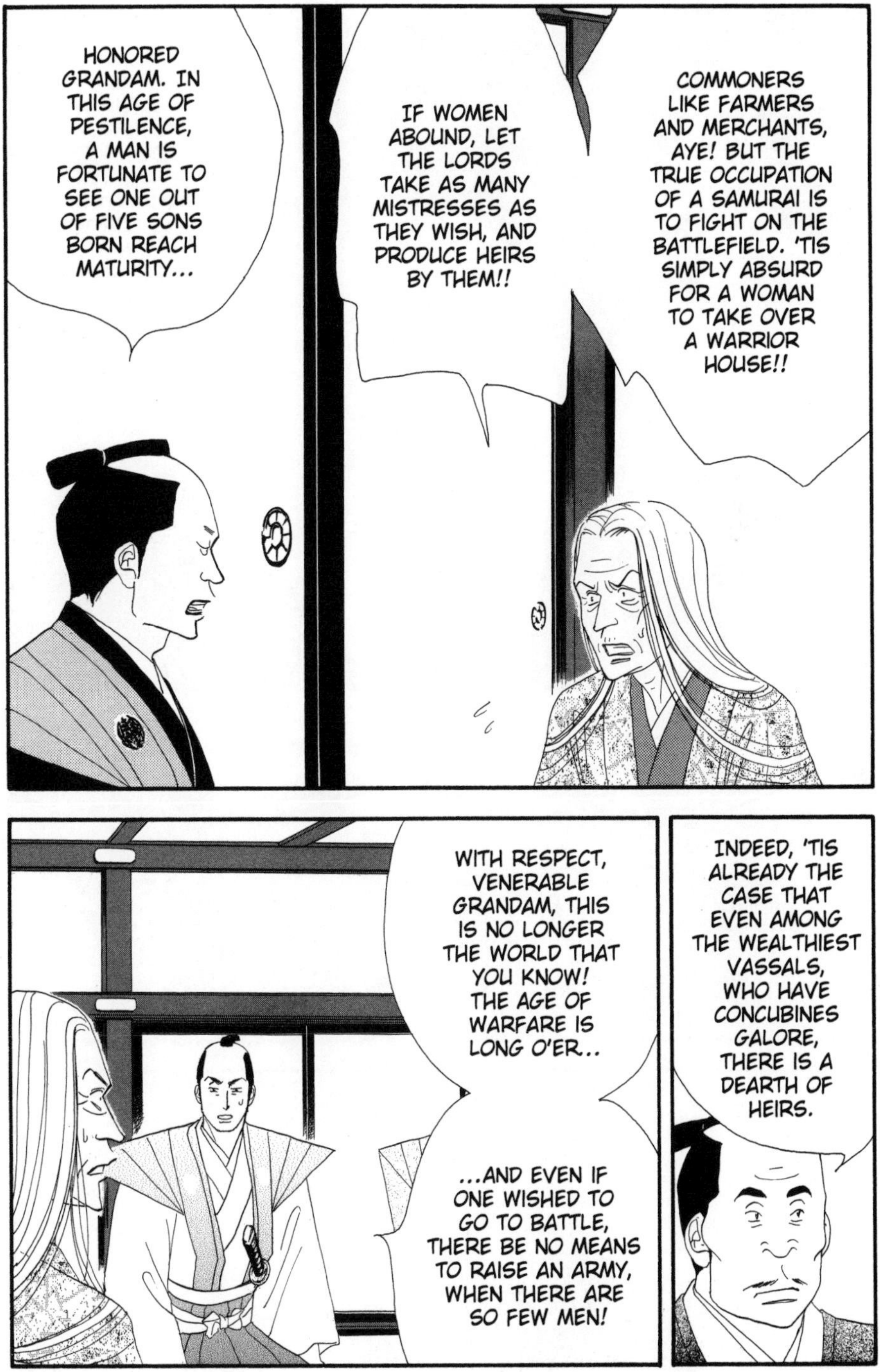
COMMONERS LIKE FARMERS AND MERCHANTS, AYE! BUT THE TRUE OCCUPATION OF A SAMURAI IS TO FIGHT ON THE BATTLEFIELD. 'TIS SIMPLY ABSURD FOR A WOMAN TO TAKE OVER A WARRIOR HOUSE!!
IF WOMEN ABOUND, LET THE LORDS TAKE AS MANY MISTRESSES AS THEY WISH, AND PRODUCE HEIRS BY THEM!!
HONORED GRANDAM. IN THIS AGE OF PESTILENCE, A MAN IS FORTUNATE TO SEE ONE OUT OF FIVE SONS BORN REACH MATURITY...
INDEED, 'TIS ALREADY THE CASE THAT EVEN AMONG THE WEALTHIEST VASSALS, WHO HAVE CONCUBINES GALORE, THERE IS A DEARTH OF HEIRS.
WITH RESPECT, VENERABLE GRANDAM, THIS IS NO LONGER THE WORLD THAT YOU KNOW! THE AGE OF WARFARE IS LONG O'ER...
...AND EVEN IF ONE WISHED TO GO TO BATTLE, THERE BE NO MEANS TO RAISE AN ARMY, WHEN THERE ARE SO FEW MEN!

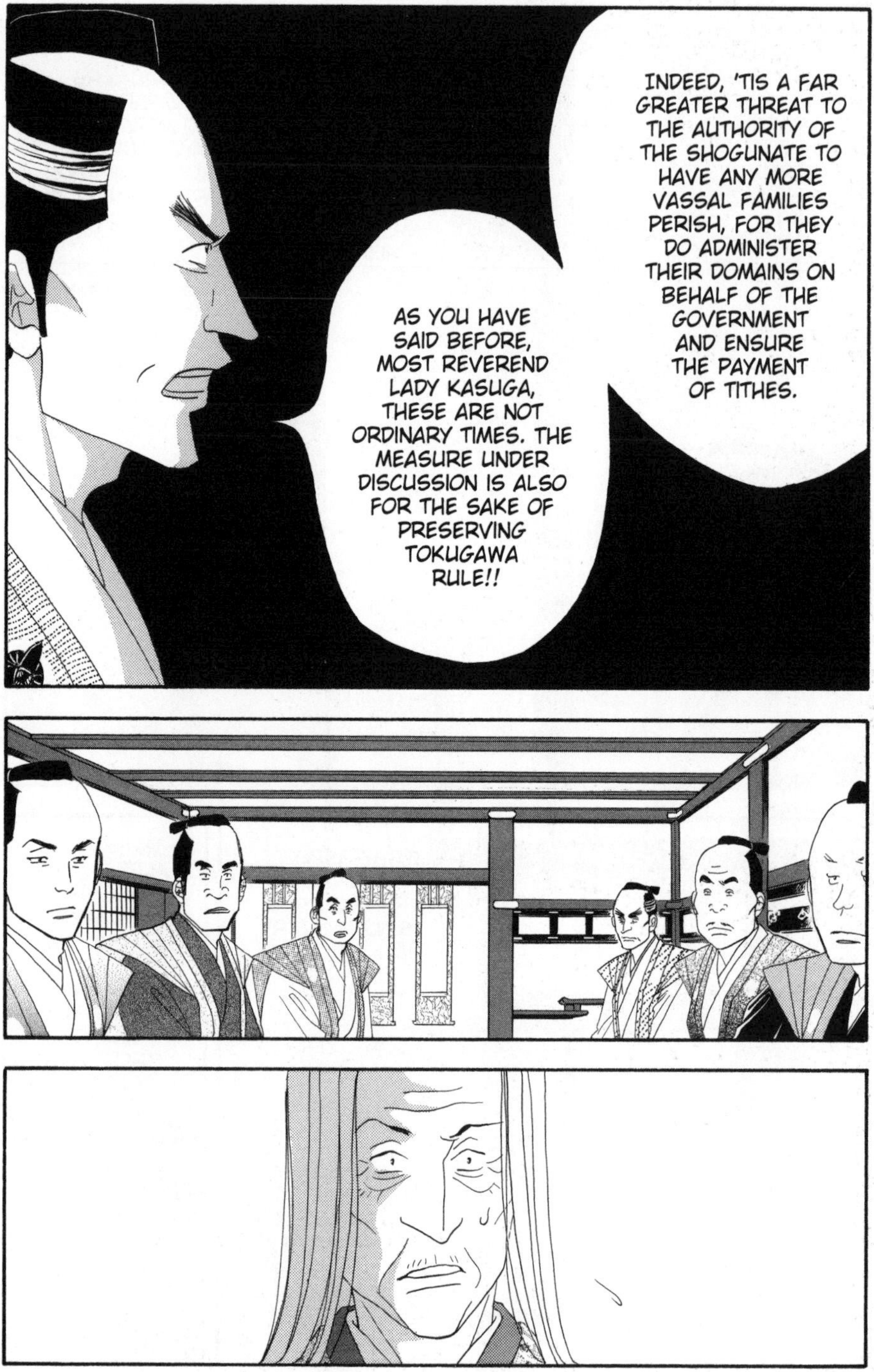
INDEED, 'TIS A FAR GREATER THREAT TO THE AUTHORITY OF THE SHOGUNATE TO HAVE ANY MORE VASSAL FAMILIES PERISH, FOR THEY DO ADMINISTER THEIR DOMAINS ON BEHALF OF THE GOVERNMENT AND ENSURE THE PAYMENT OF TITHES.
AS YOU HAVE SAID BEFORE, MOST REVEREND LADY KASUGA, THESE ARE NOT ORDINARY TIMES. THE MEASURE UNDER DISCUSSION IS ALSO FOR THE SAKE OF PRESERVING TOKUGAWA RULE!!

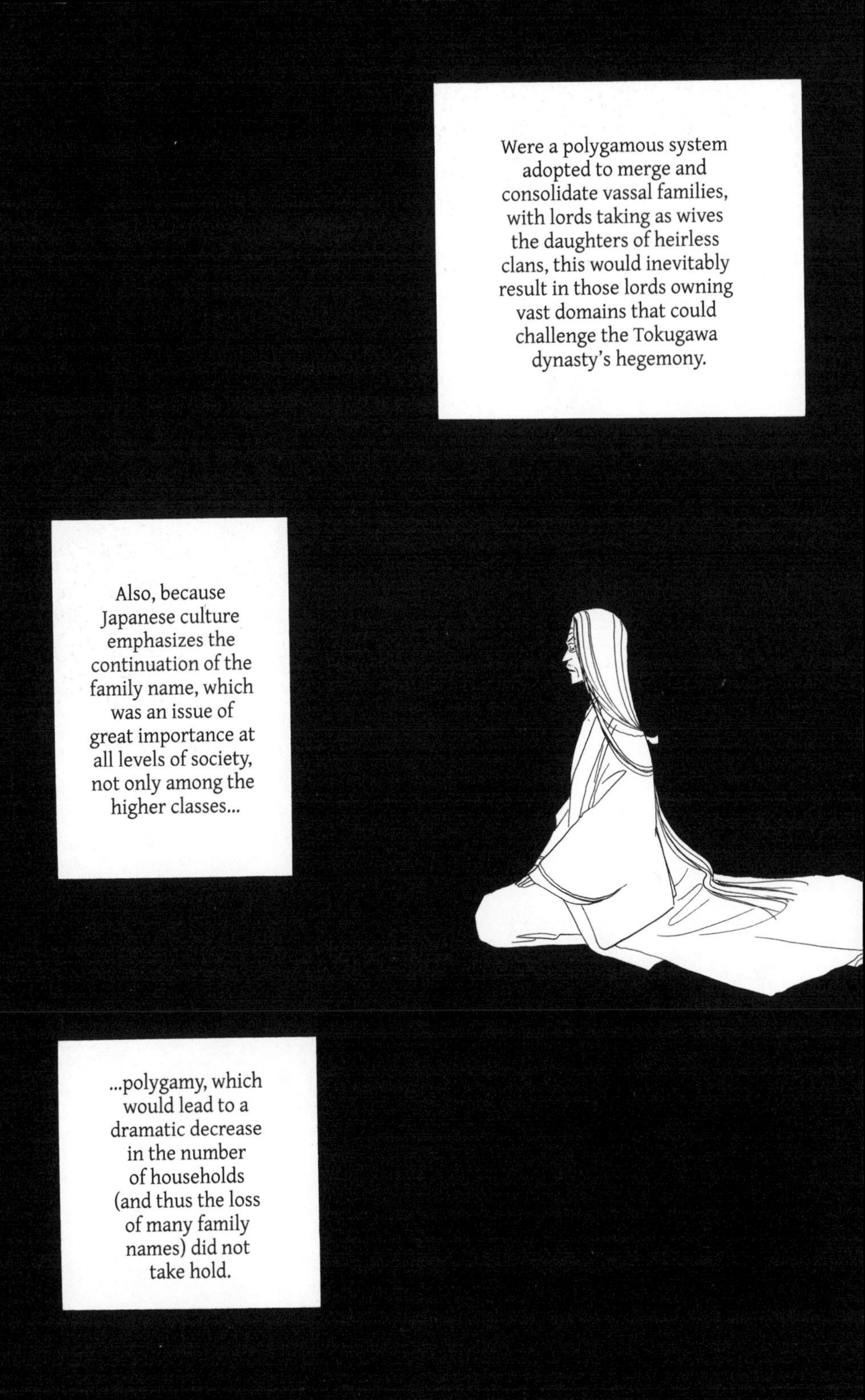
Were a polygamous system adopted to merge and consolidate vassal families, with lords taking as wives the daughters of heirless clans, this would inevitably result in those lords owning vast domains that could challenge the Tokugawa dynasty's hegemony.
Also, because Japanese culture emphasizes the continuation of the family name, which was an issue of great importance at all levels of society, not only among the higher classes...
...polygamy, which would lead to a dramatic decrease in the number of households (and thus the loss of many family names) did not take hold.

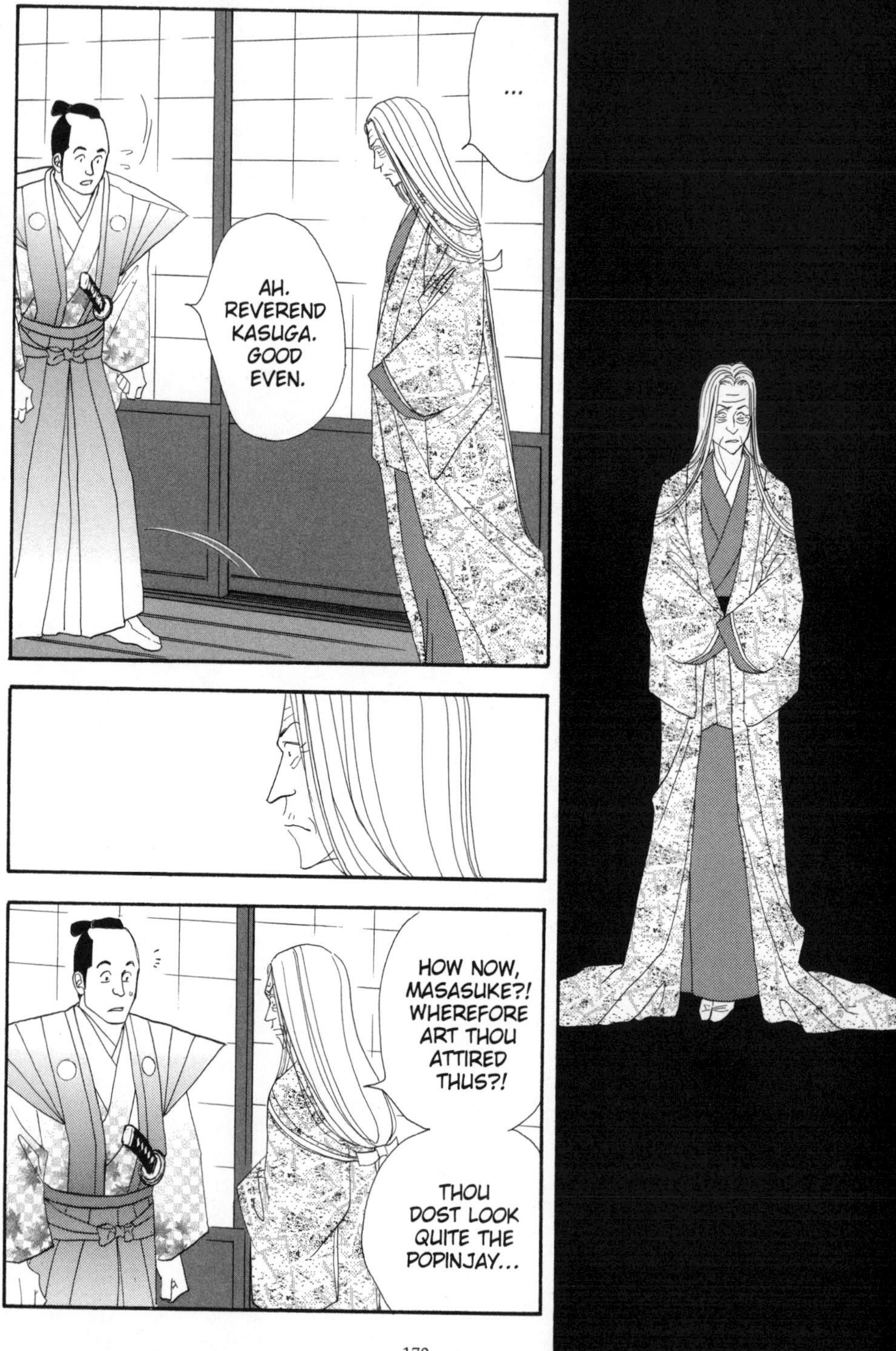
...
AH. REVEREND KASUGA. GOOD EVEN.
HOW NOW, MASASUKE?! WHEREFORE ART THOU ATTIRED THUS?!
THOU DOST LOOK QUITE THE POPINJAY...

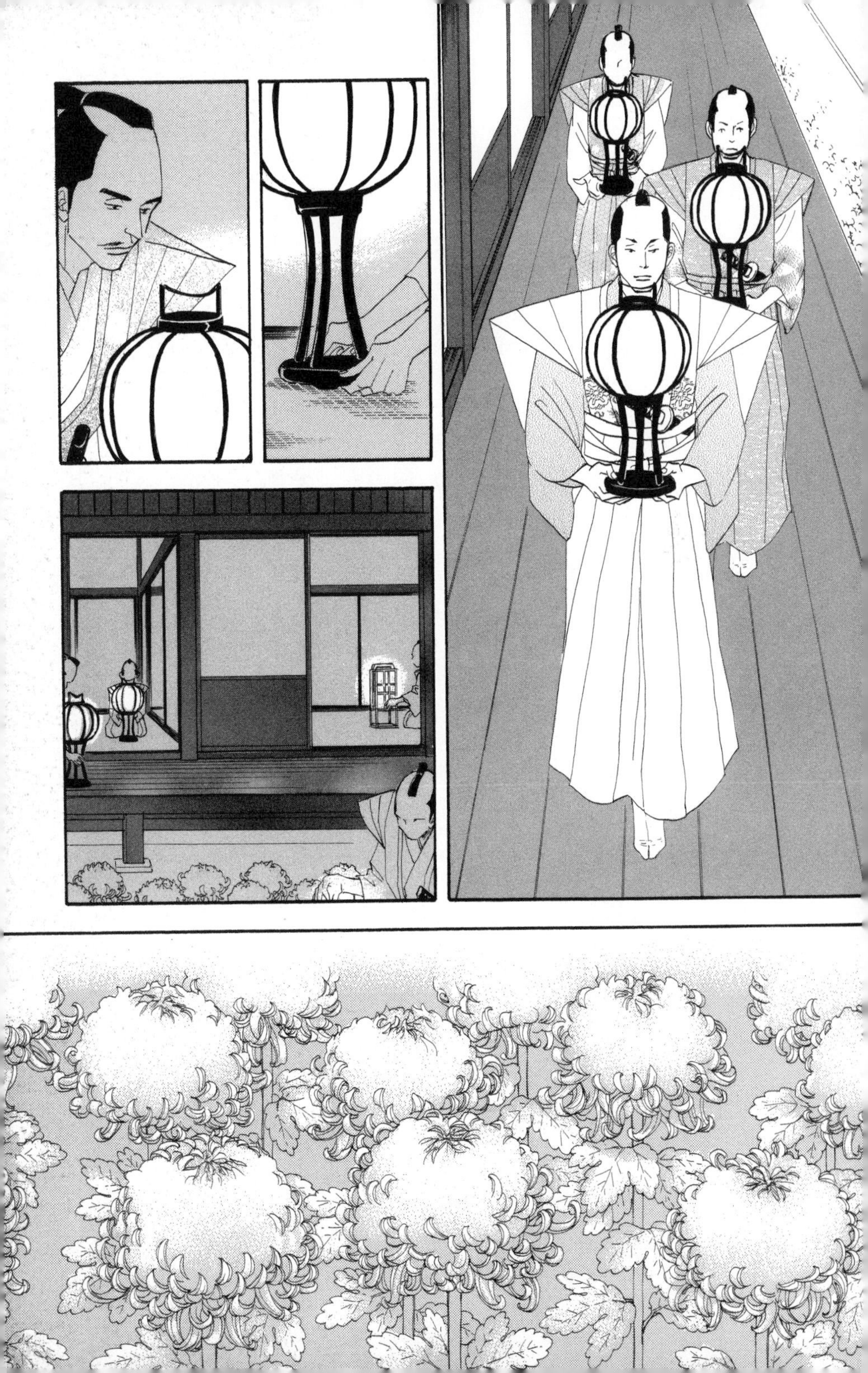

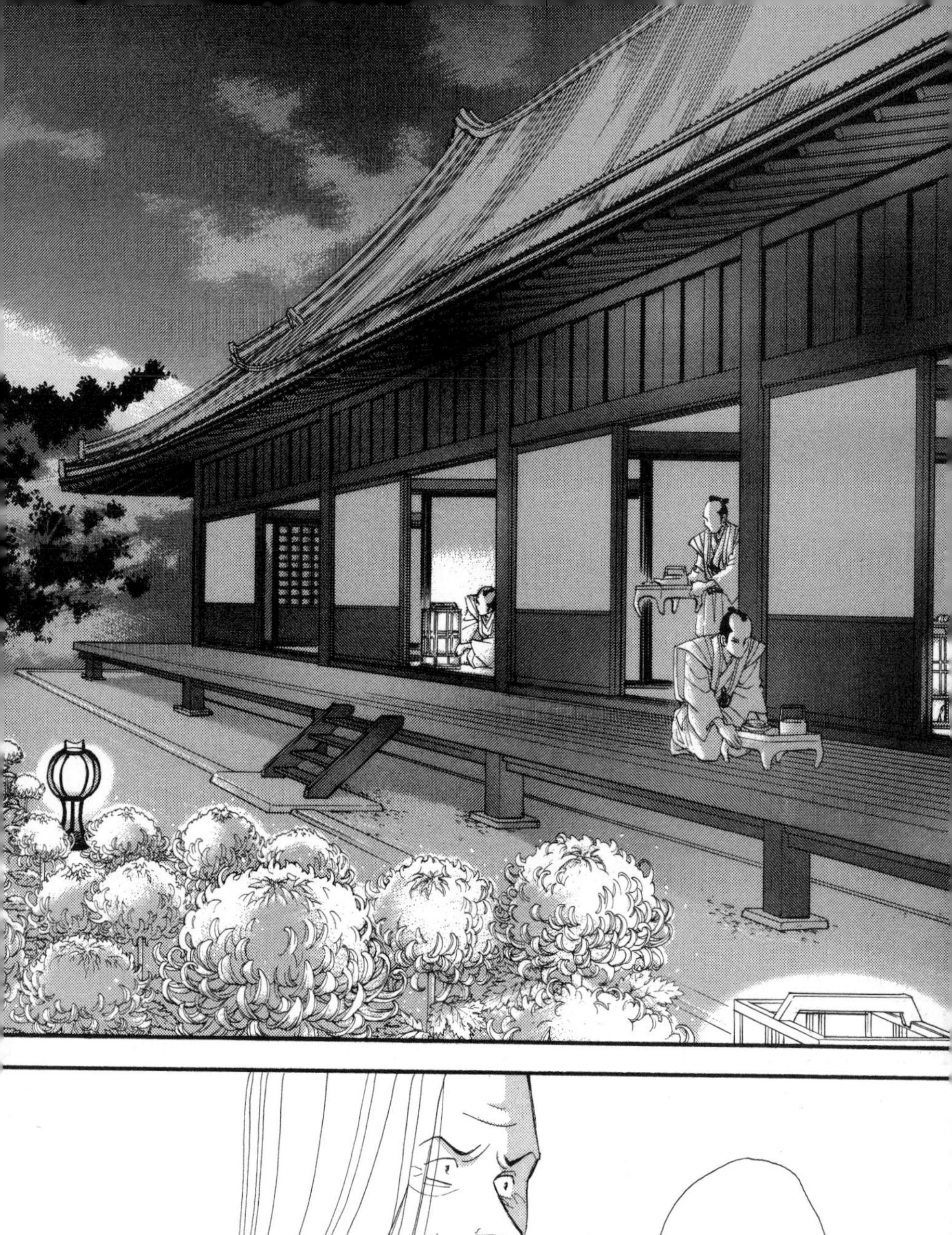

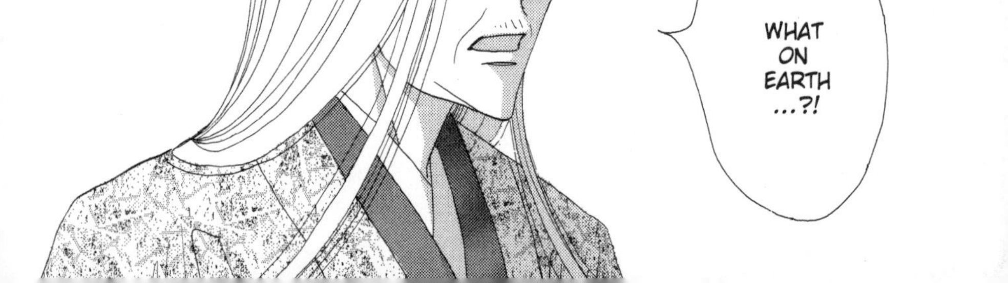
WHAT ON EARTH ...?!

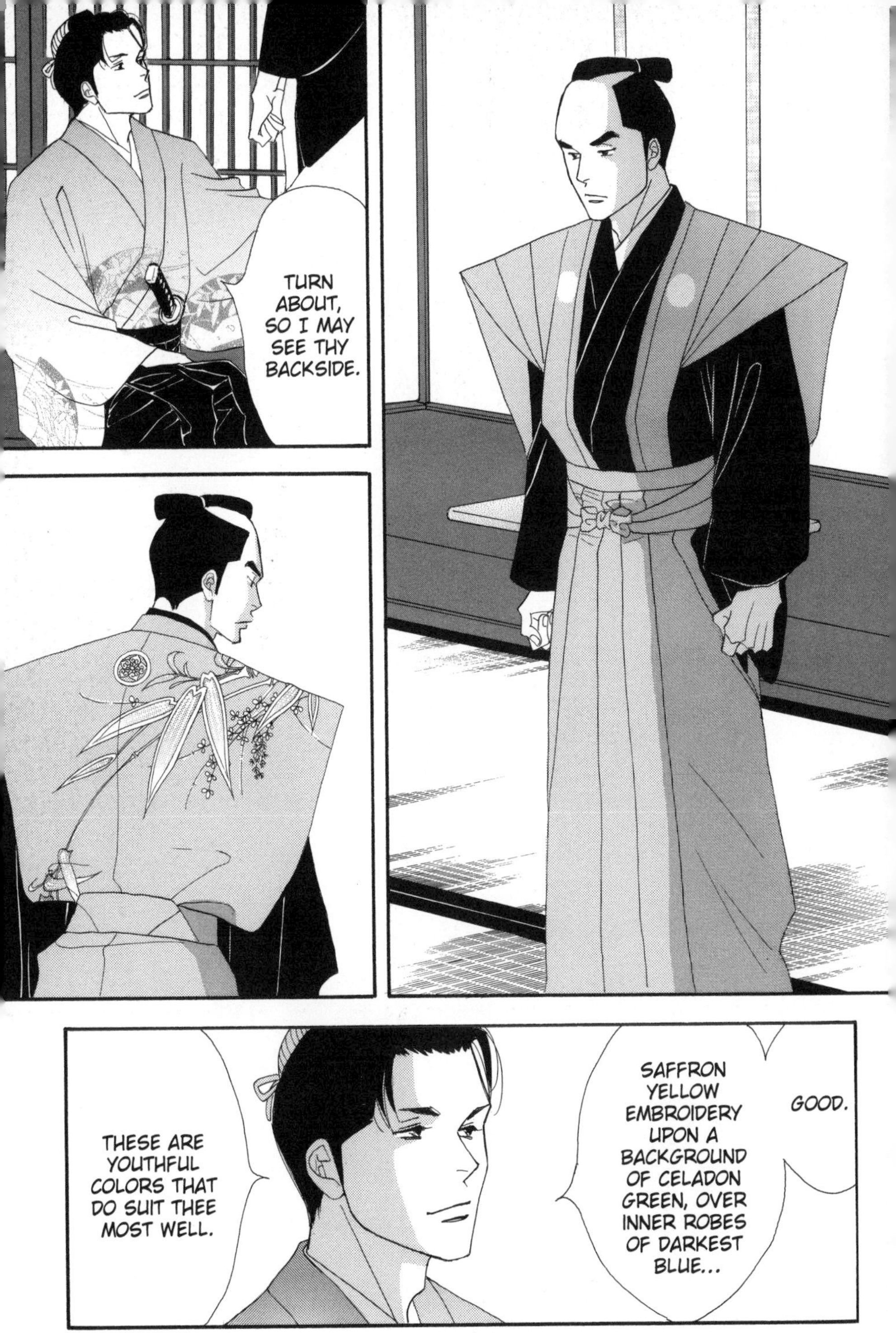
TURN ABOUT, SO I MAY SEE THY BACKSIDE.
GOOD.
SAFFRON YELLOW EMBROIDERY UPON A BACKGROUND OF CELADON GREEN, OVER INNER ROBES OF DARKEST BLUE...
THESE ARE YOUTHFUL COLORS THAT DO SUIT THEE MOST WELL.

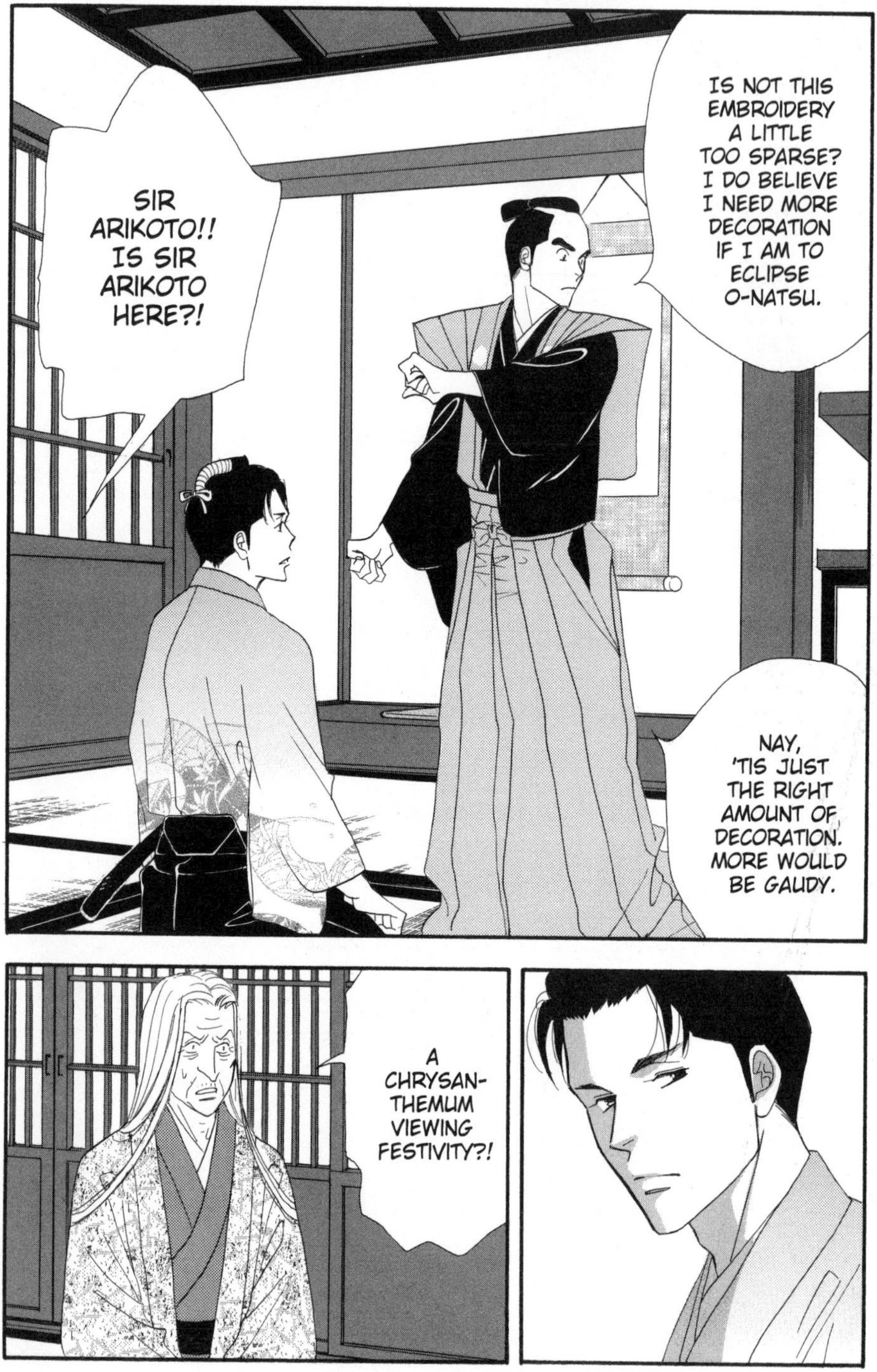
IS NOT THIS EMBROIDERY A LITTLE TOO SPARSE? I DO BELIEVE I NEED MORE DECORATION IF I AM TO ECLIPSE O-NATSU.
SIR ARIKOTO!! IS SIR ARIKOTO HERE?!
NAY, 'TIS JUST THE RIGHT AMOUNT OF DECORATION. MORE WOULD BE GAUDY.
A CHRYSAN-THEMUM VIEWING FESTIVITY?!

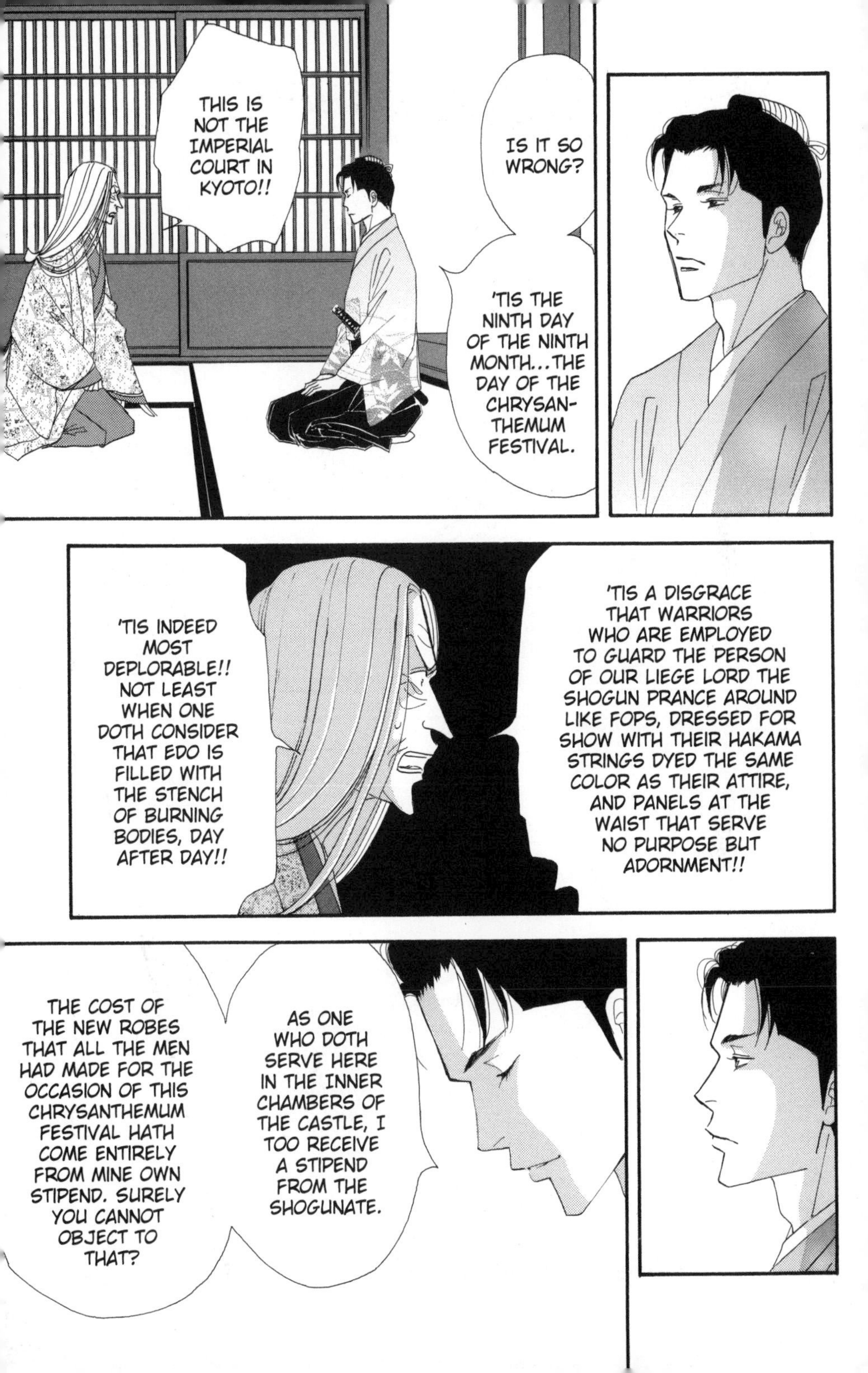
IS IT SO WRONG?
'TIS THE NINTH DAY OF THE NINTH MONTH...THE DAY OF THE CHRYSANTHEMUM FESTIVAL.
THIS IS NOT THE IMPERIAL COURT IN KYOTO!!
'TIS A DISGRACE THAT WARRIORS WHO ARE EMPLOYED TO GUARD THE PERSON OF OUR LIEGE LORD THE SHOGUN PRANCE AROUND LIKE FOPS, DRESSED FOR SHOW WITH THEIR HAKAMA STRINGS DYED THE SAME COLOR AS THEIR ATTIRE, AND PANELS AT THE WAIST THAT SERVE NO PURPOSE BUT ADORNMENT!!
'TIS INDEED MOST DEPLORABLE!! NOT LEAST WHEN ONE DOTH CONSIDER THAT EDO IS FILLED WITH THE STENCH OF BURNING BODIES, DAY AFTER DAY!!
AS ONE WHO DOTH SERVE HERE IN THE INNER CHAMBERS OF THE CASTLE, I TOO RECEIVE A STIPEND FROM THE SHOGUNATE.
THE COST OF THE NEW ROBES THAT ALL THE MEN HAD MADE FOR THE OCCASION OF THIS CHRYSANTHEMUM FESTIVAL HATH COME ENTIRELY FROM MINE OWN STIPEND. SURELY YOU CANNOT OBJECT TO THAT?

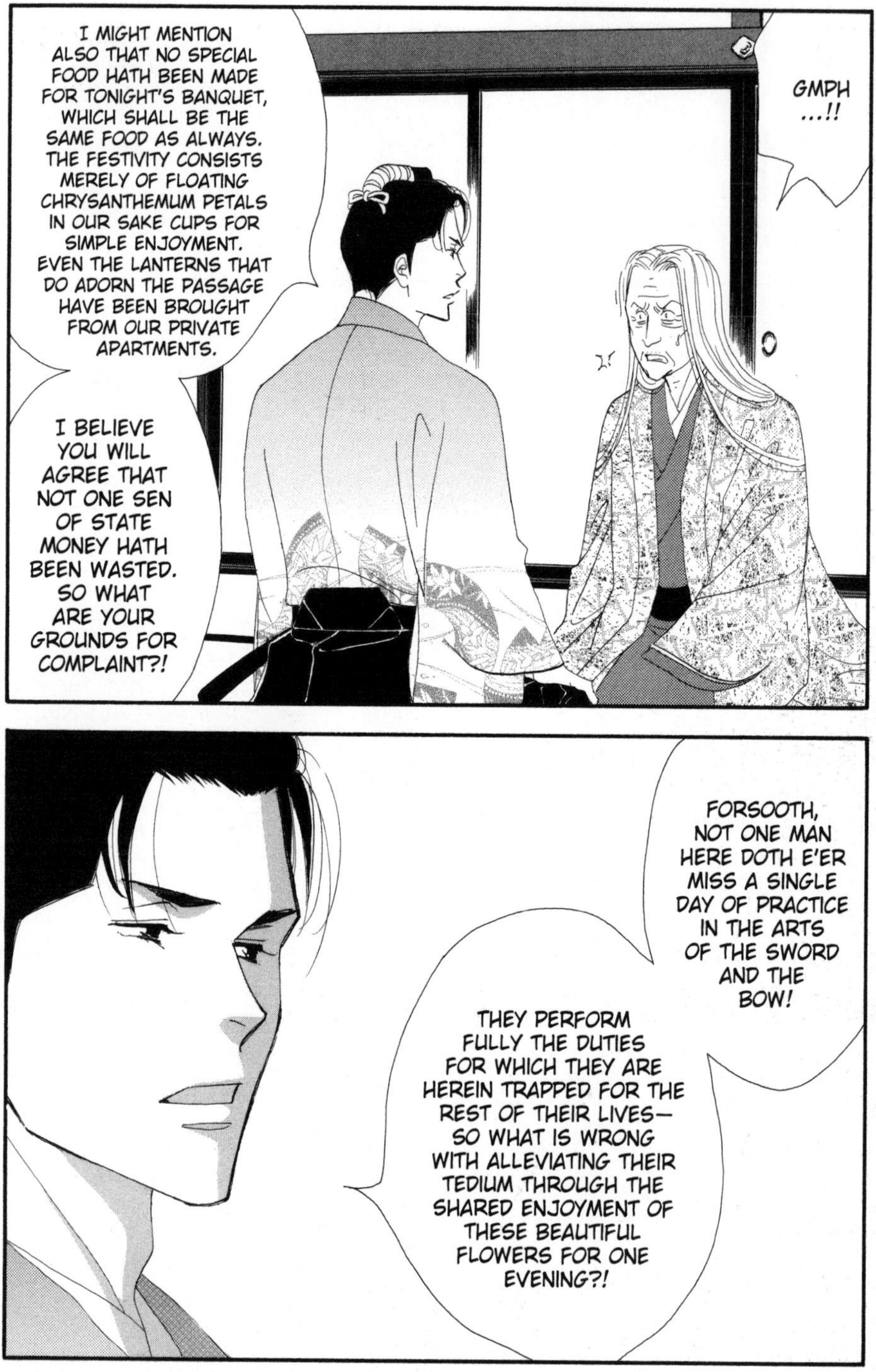
GMPH ...!!
I MIGHT MENTION ALSO THAT NO SPECIAL FOOD HATH BEEN MADE FOR TONIGHT'S BANQUET, WHICH SHALL BE THE SAME FOOD AS ALWAYS. THE FESTIVITY CONSISTS MERELY OF FLOATING CHRYSANTHEMUM PETALS IN OUR SAKE CUPS FOR SIMPLE ENJOYMENT. EVEN THE LANTERNS THAT DO ADORN THE PASSAGE HAVE BEEN BROUGHT FROM OUR PRIVATE APARTMENTS.
I BELIEVE YOU WILL AGREE THAT NOT ONE SEN OF STATE MONEY HATH BEEN WASTED. SO WHAT ARE YOUR GROUNDS FOR COMPLAINT?!
FORSOOTH, NOT ONE MAN HERE DOTH E'ER MISS A SINGLE DAY OF PRACTICE IN THE ARTS OF THE SWORD AND THE BOW!
THEY PERFORM FULLY THE DUTIES FOR WHICH THEY ARE HEREIN TRAPPED FOR THE REST OF THEIR LIVES—SO WHAT IS WRONG WITH ALLEVIATING THEIR TEDIUM THROUGH THE SHARED ENJOYMENT OF THESE BEAUTIFUL FLOWERS FOR ONE EVENING?!

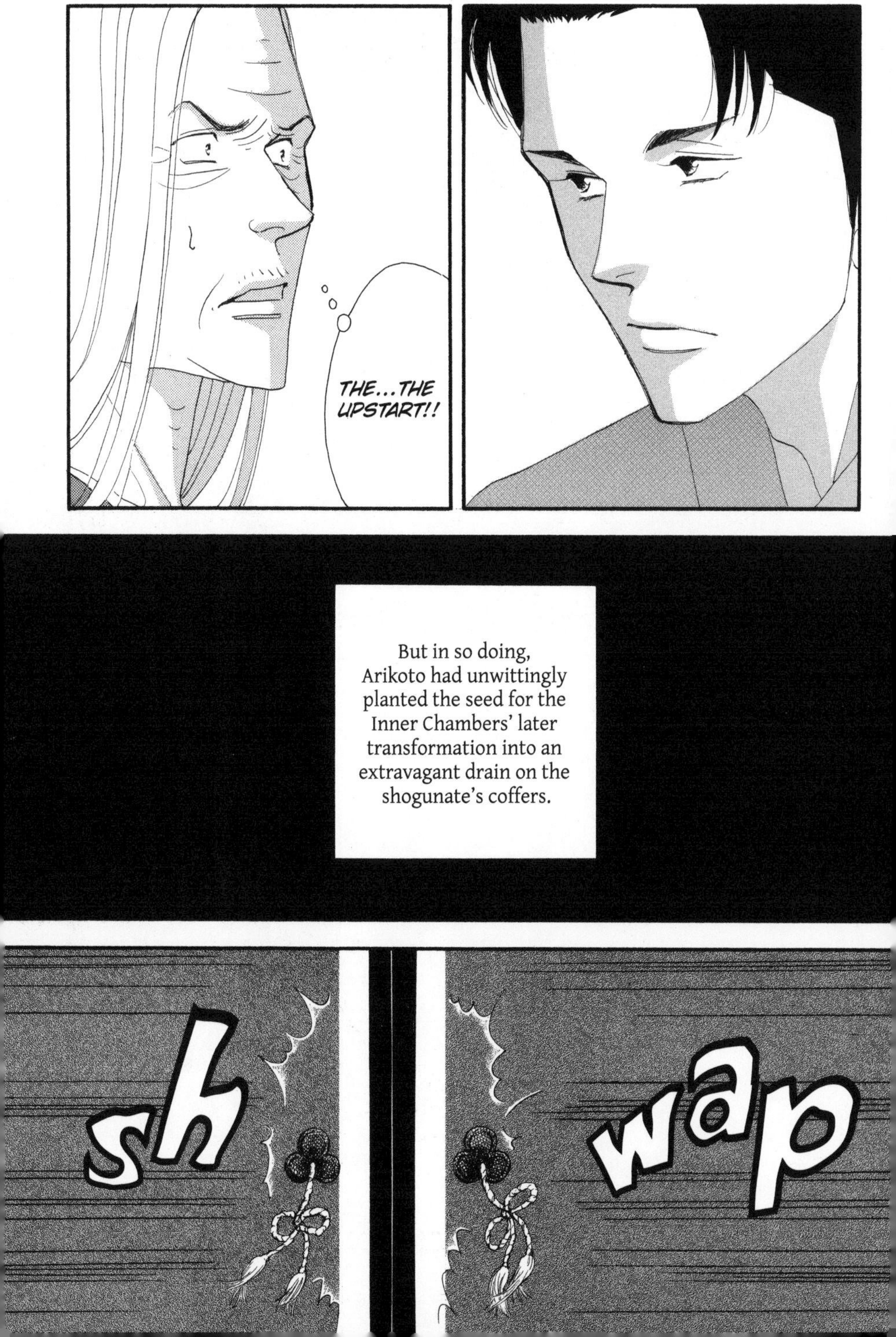
THE...THE UPSTART!!
But in so doing, Arikoto had unwittingly planted the seed for the Inner Chambers' later transformation into an extravagant drain on the shogunate's coffers.
sh
wap

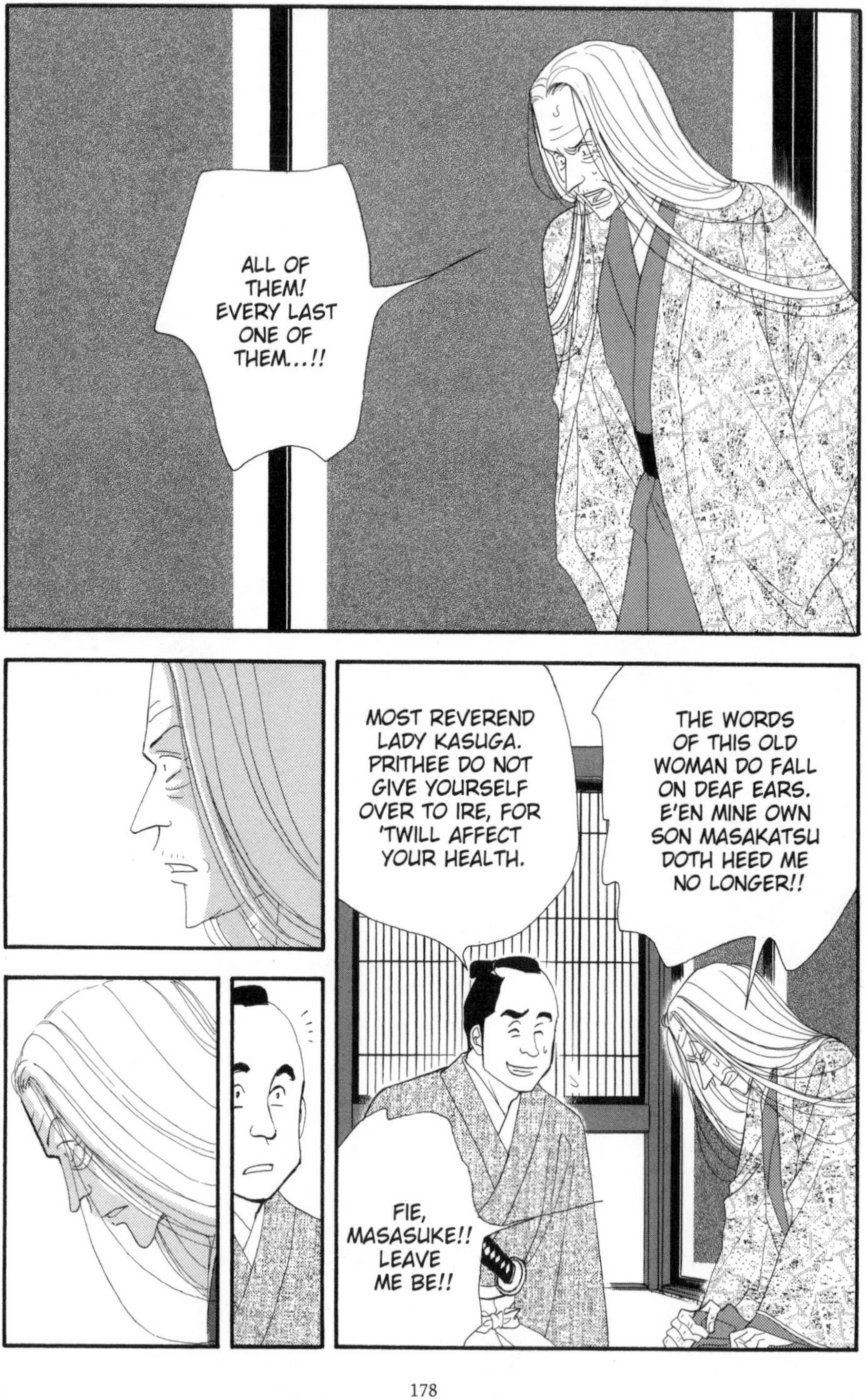
ALL OF THEM! EVERY LAST ONE OF THEM...!!
MOST REVEREND LADY KASUGA. PRITHEE DO NOT GIVE YOURSELF OVER TO IRE, FOR 'TWILL AFFECT YOUR HEALTH.
THE WORDS OF THIS OLD WOMAN DO FALL ON DEAF EARS. E'EN MINE OWN SON MASAKATSU DOTH HEED ME NO LONGER!!
FIE, MASASUKE!! LEAVE ME BE!!

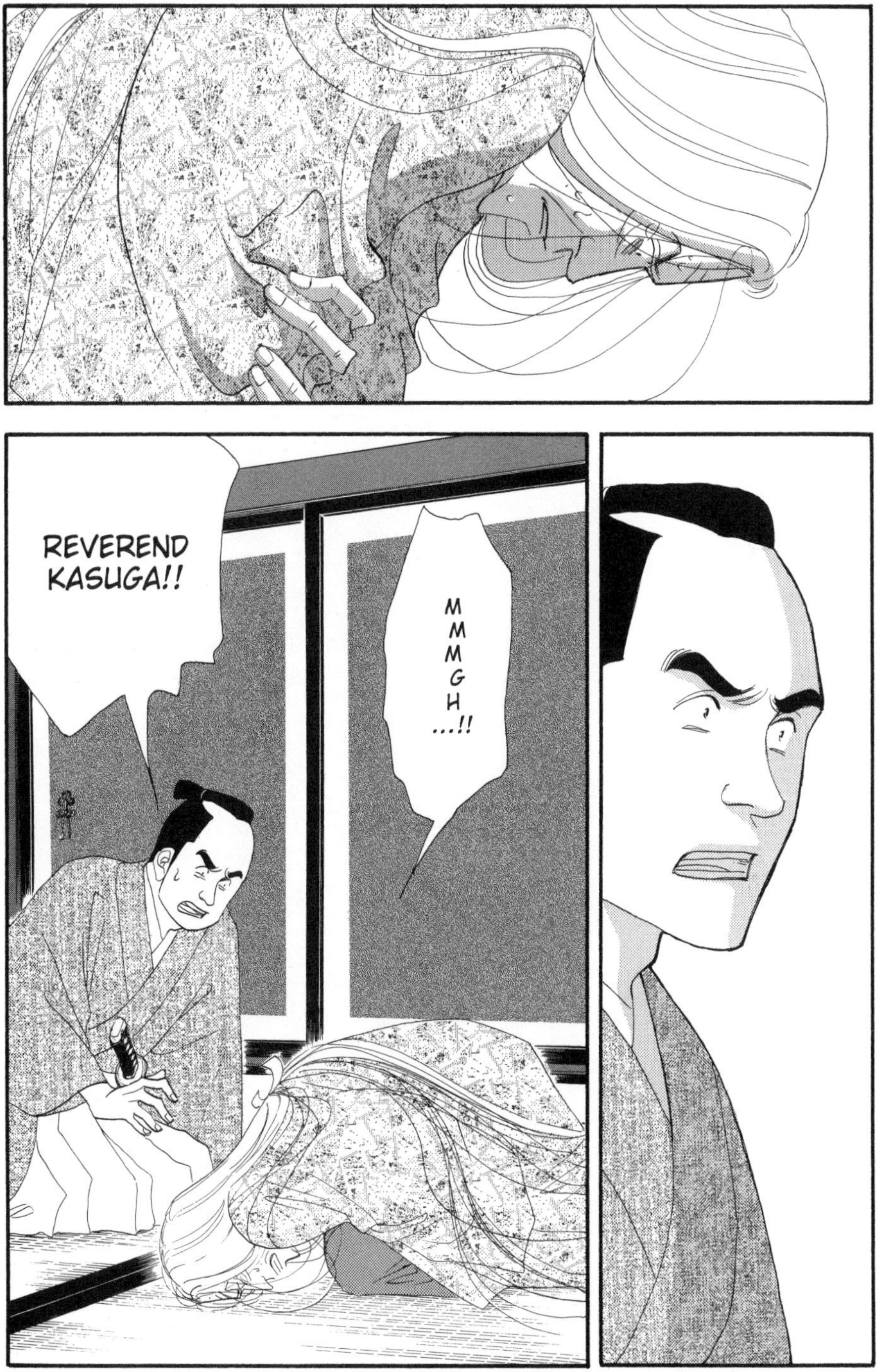
MMMGH...!!
REVEREND KASUGA!!

Ōoku
THE INNER CHAMBERS

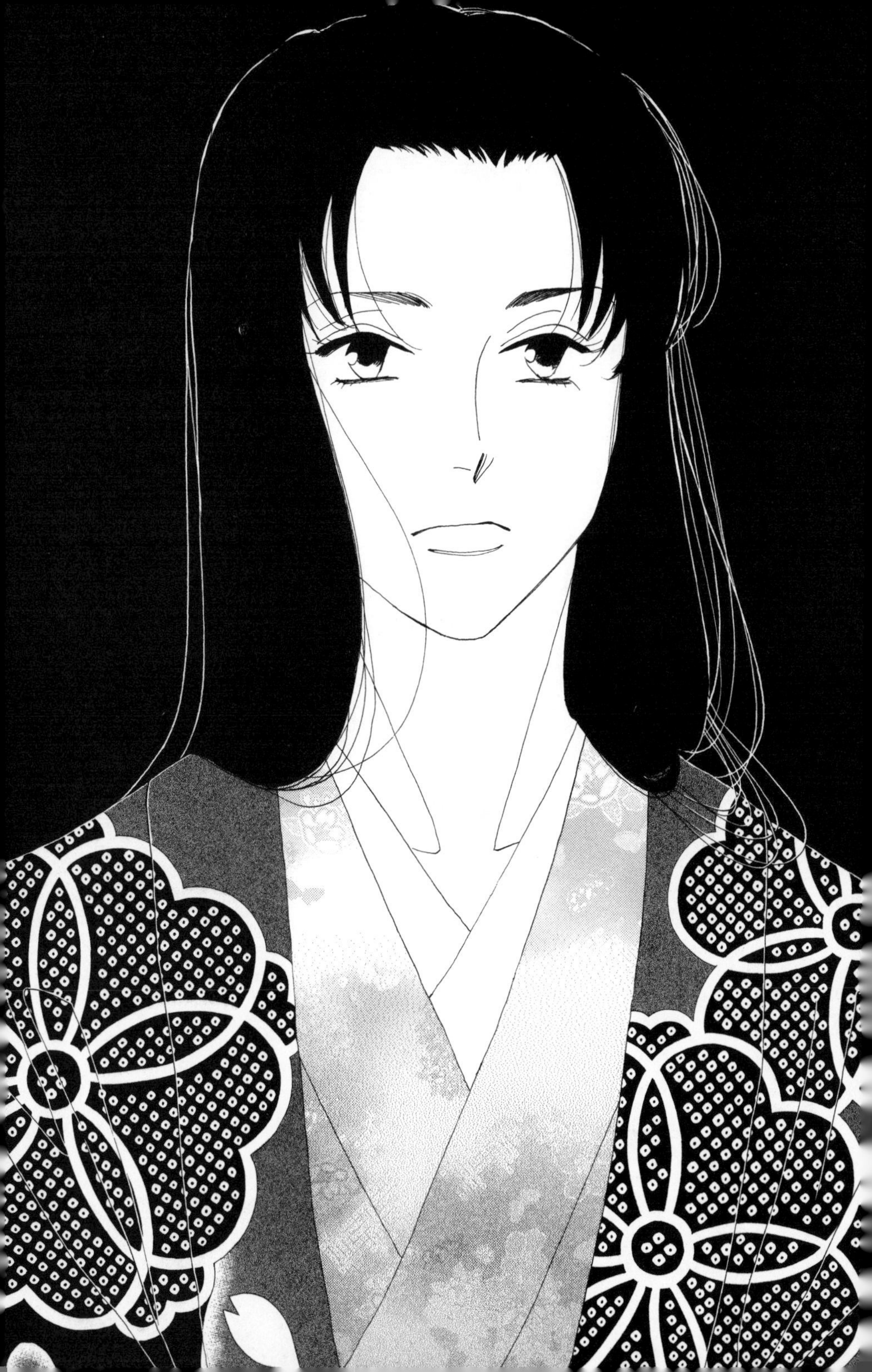

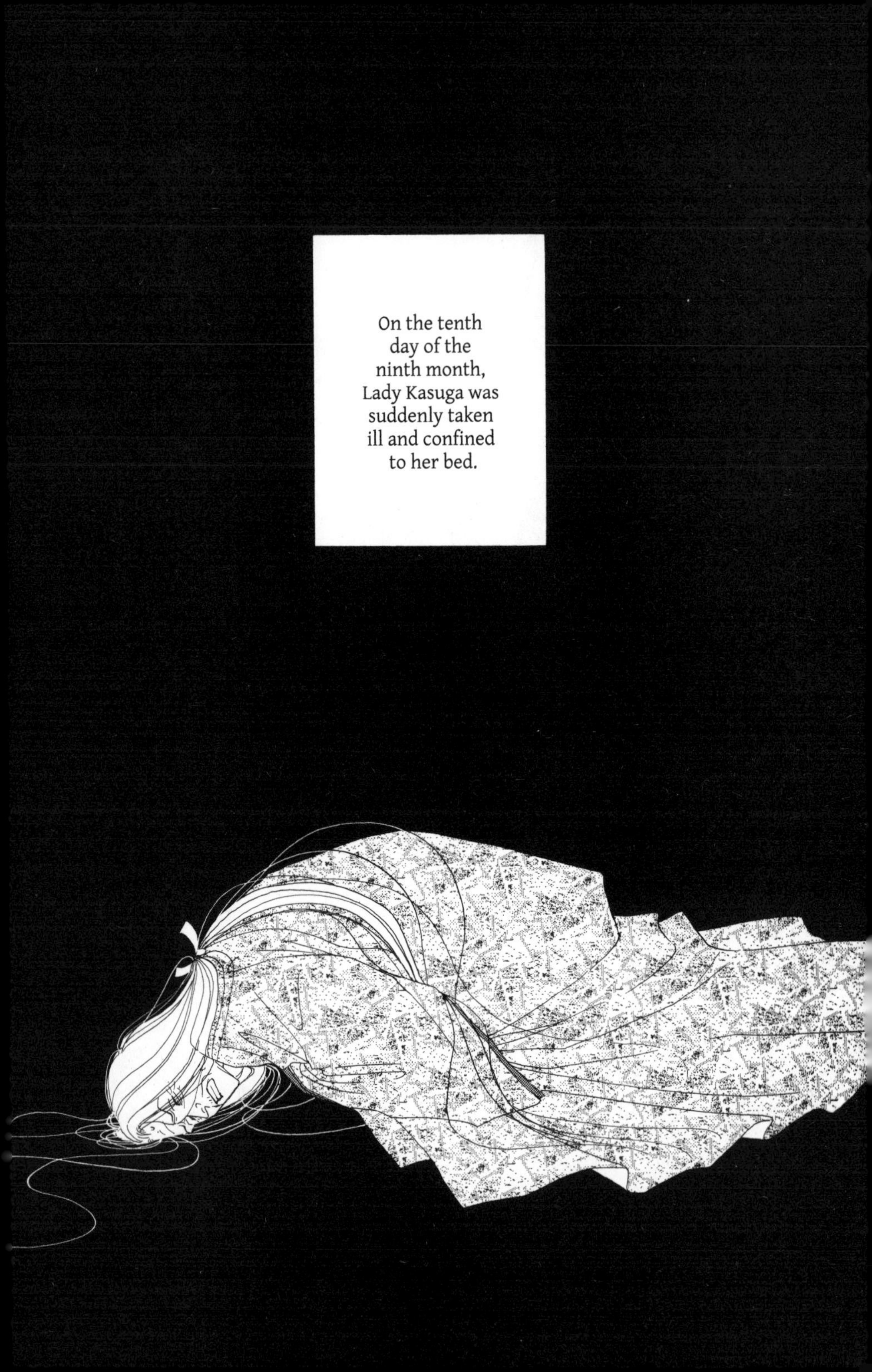
On the tenth day of the ninth month, Lady Kasuga was suddenly taken ill and confined to her bed.

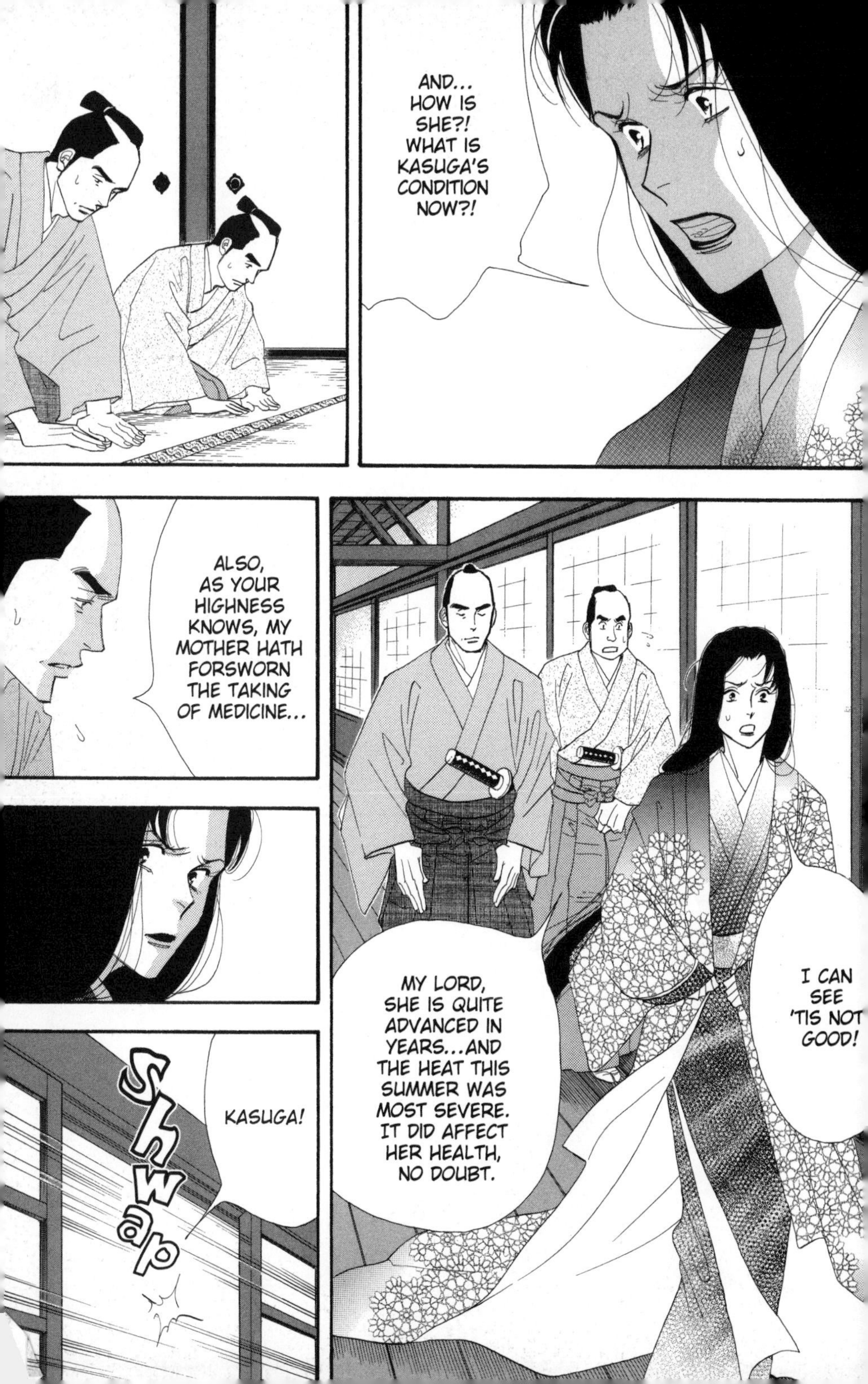
AND... HOW IS SHE?! WHAT IS KASUGA'S CONDITION NOW?!
I CAN SEE 'TIS NOT GOOD!
MY LORD, SHE IS QUITE ADVANCED IN YEARS...AND THE HEAT THIS SUMMER WAS MOST SEVERE. IT DID AFFECT HER HEALTH, NO DOUBT.
ALSO, AS YOUR HIGHNESS KNOWS, MY MOTHER HATH FORSWORN THE TAKING OF MEDICINE...
KASUGA!
Shwap

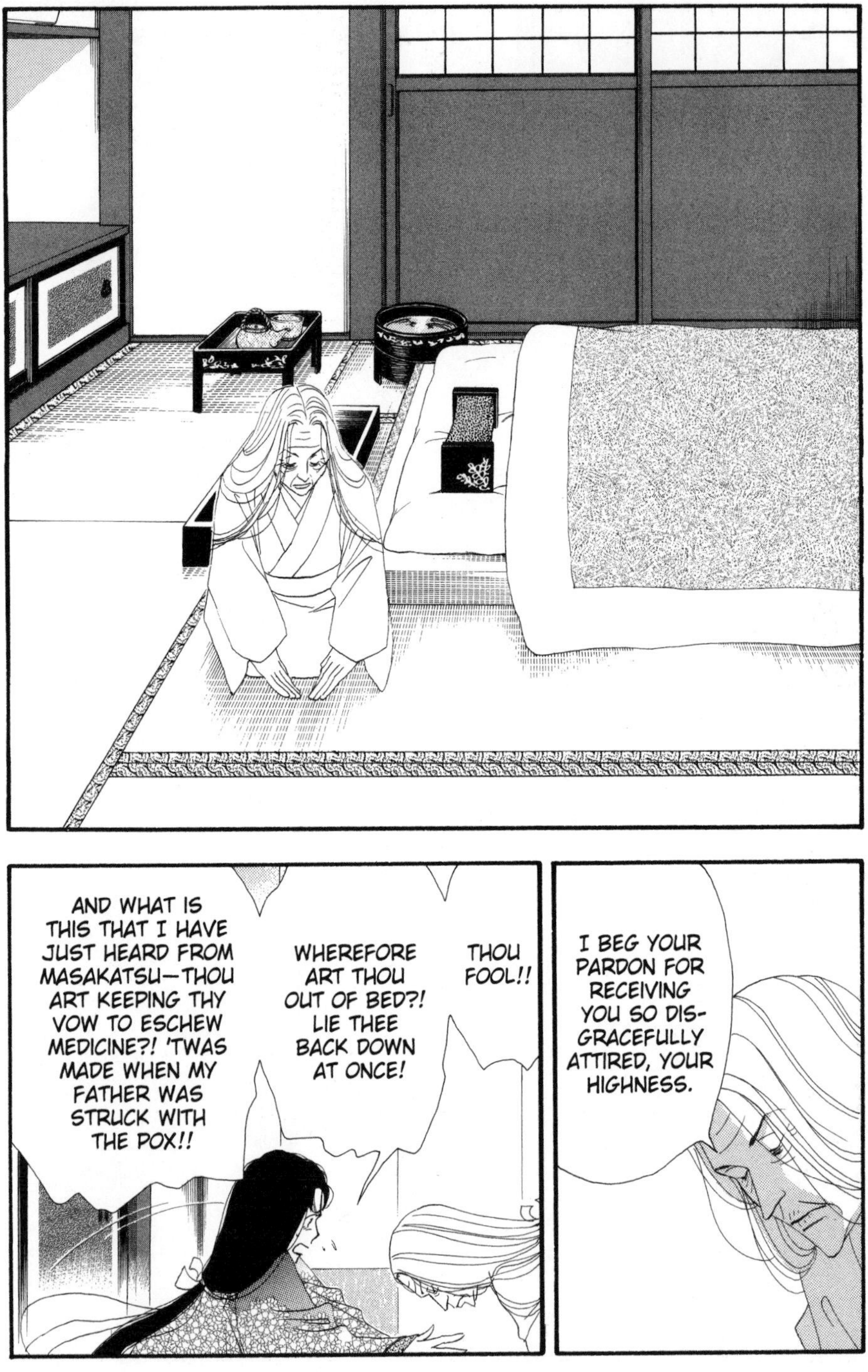
I BEG YOUR PARDON FOR RECEIVING YOU SO DIS-GRACEFULLY ATTIRED, YOUR HIGHNESS.
THOU FOOL!!
WHEREFORE ART THOU OUT OF BED?! LIE THEE BACK DOWN AT ONCE!
AND WHAT IS THIS THAT I HAVE JUST HEARD FROM MASAKATSU—THOU ART KEEPING THY VOW TO ESCHEW MEDICINE?! 'TWAS MADE WHEN MY FATHER WAS STRUCK WITH THE POX!!

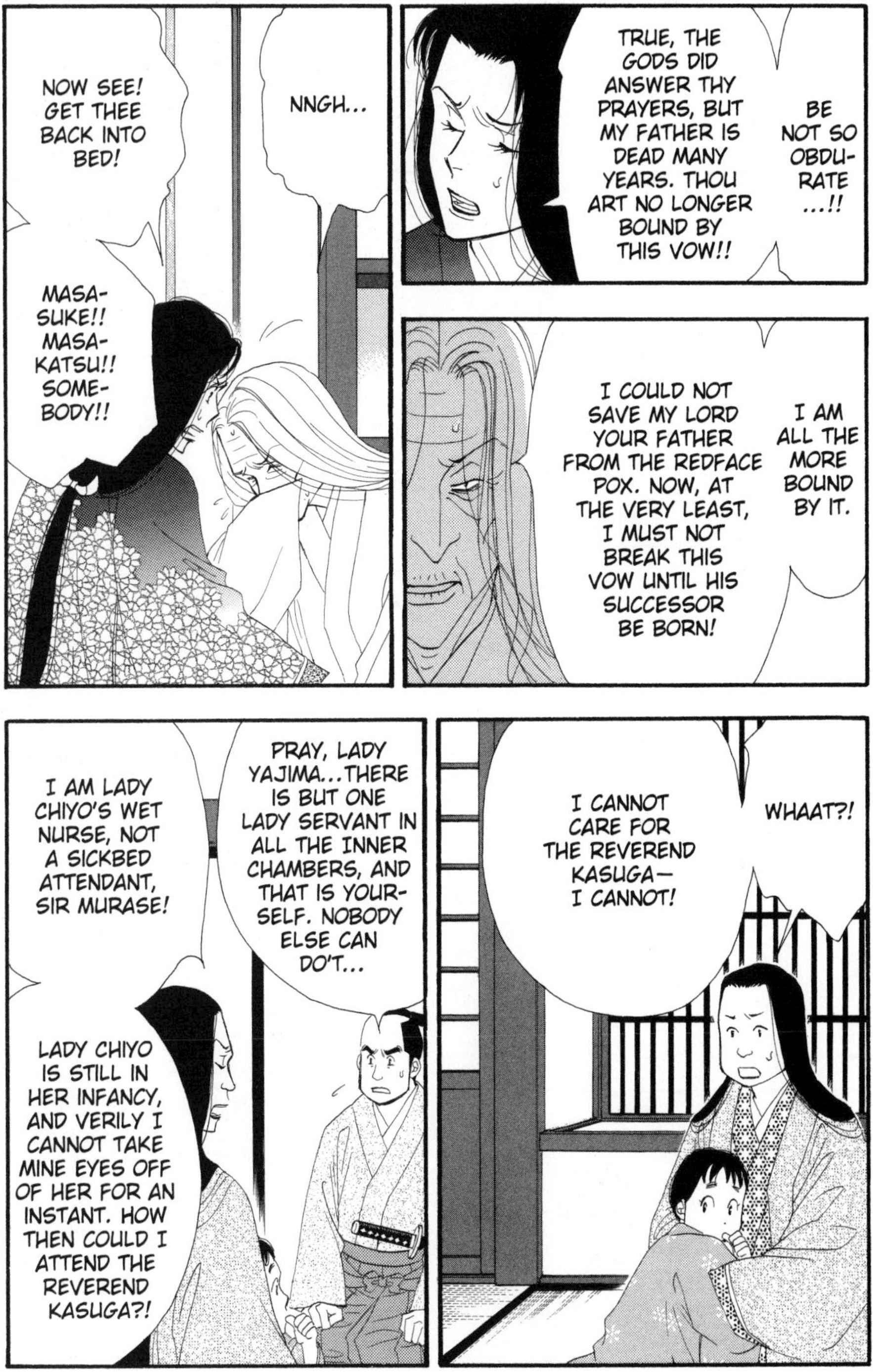
BE NOT SO OBDURATE ...!!
TRUE, THE GODS DID ANSWER THY PRAYERS, BUT MY FATHER IS DEAD MANY YEARS. THOU ART NO LONGER BOUND BY THIS VOW!!
I AM ALL THE MORE BOUND BY IT.
I COULD NOT SAVE MY LORD YOUR FATHER FROM THE REDFACE POX. NOW, AT THE VERY LEAST, I MUST NOT BREAK THIS VOW UNTIL HIS SUCCESSOR BE BORN!
NNGH...
NOW SEE! GET THEE BACK INTO BED!
MASA-SUKE!! MASA-KATSU!! SOME-BODY!!
WHAAT?!
I CANNOT CARE FOR THE REVEREND KASUGA— I CANNOT!
PRAY, LADY YAJIMA...THERE IS BUT ONE LADY SERVANT IN ALL THE INNER CHAMBERS, AND THAT IS YOUR-SELF. NOBODY ELSE CAN DO'T...
I AM LADY CHIYO'S WET NURSE, NOT A SICKBED ATTENDANT, SIR MURASE!
LADY CHIYO IS STILL IN HER INFANCY, AND VERILY I CANNOT TAKE MINE EYES OFF OF HER FOR AN INSTANT. HOW THEN COULD I ATTEND THE REVEREND KASUGA?!

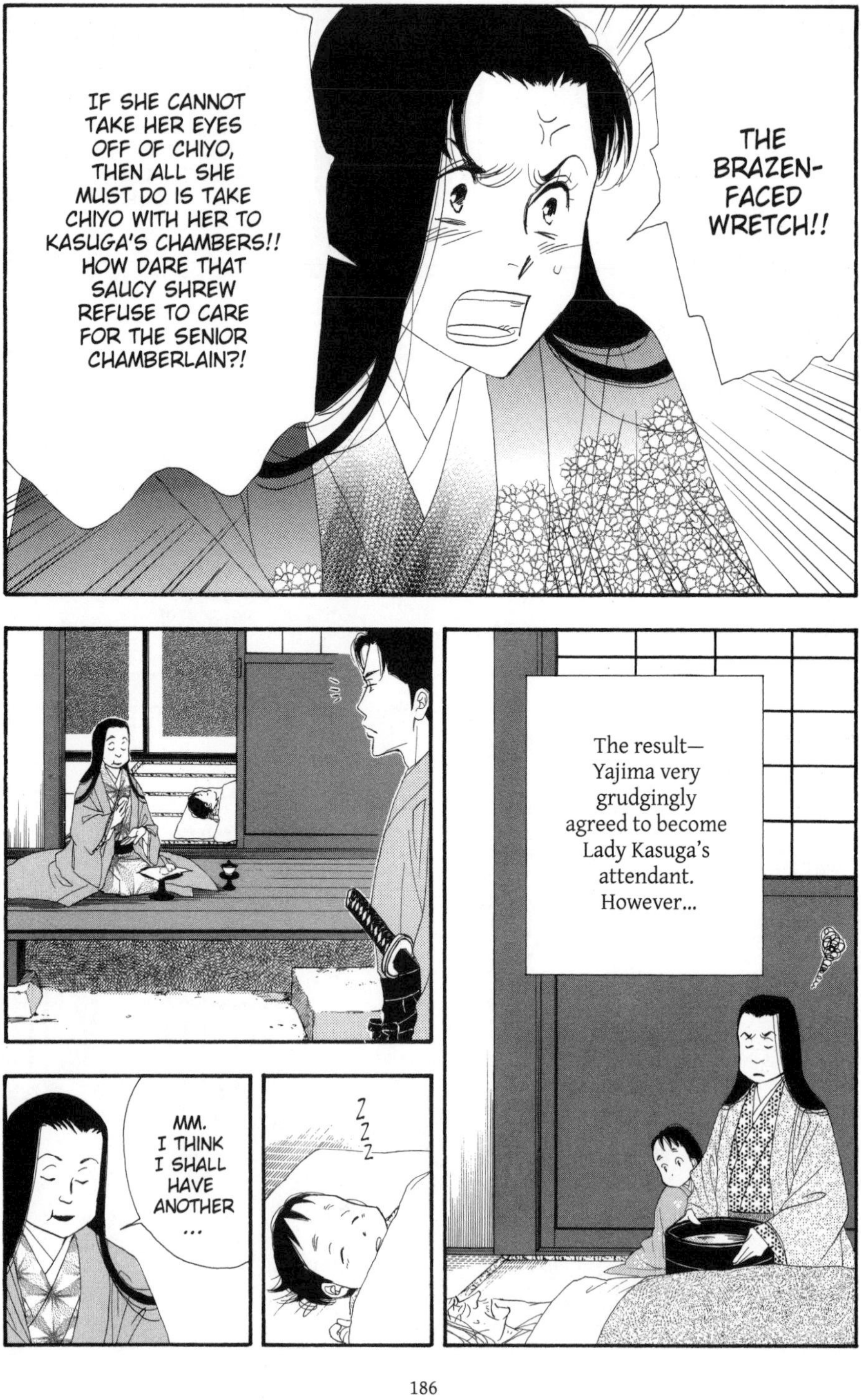
THE BRAZEN-FACED WRETCH!!
IF SHE CANNOT TAKE HER EYES OFF OF CHIYO, THEN ALL SHE MUST DO IS TAKE CHIYO WITH HER TO KASUGA'S CHAMBERS!! HOW DARE THAT SAUCY SHREW REFUSE TO CARE FOR THE SENIOR CHAMBERLAIN?!
The result—Yajima very grudgingly agreed to become Lady Kasuga's attendant. However...
ZZZ
MM. I THINK I SHALL HAVE ANOTHER ...

WATER...

I AM THIRSTY.

I HAVE NO MORE WATER.

YAJIMA!

YAJIMA...

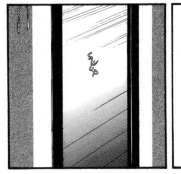

SWLIP

NOT HERE, AS USUAL... THE USELESS WOMAN.

HFF...

I HAVE BROUGHT YOU WATER, REVEREND KASUGA.

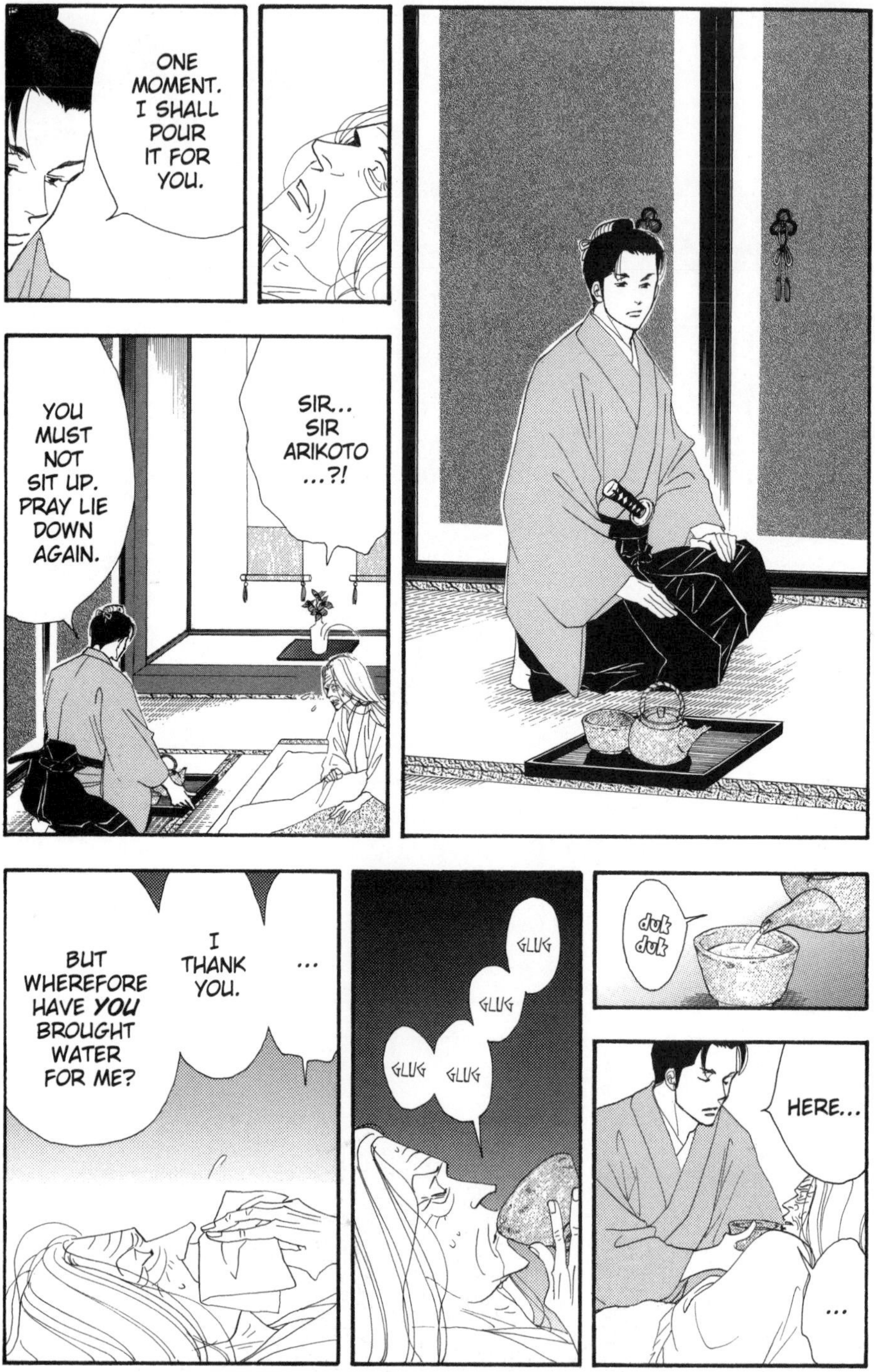
ONE MOMENT. I SHALL POUR IT FOR YOU.
SIR... SIR ARIKOTO ...?!
YOU MUST NOT SIT UP. PRAY LIE DOWN AGAIN.
duk duk
HERE...
...
GLUG
GLUG
GLUG
GLUG
...
I THANK YOU.
BUT WHEREFORE HAVE *YOU* BROUGHT WATER FOR ME?

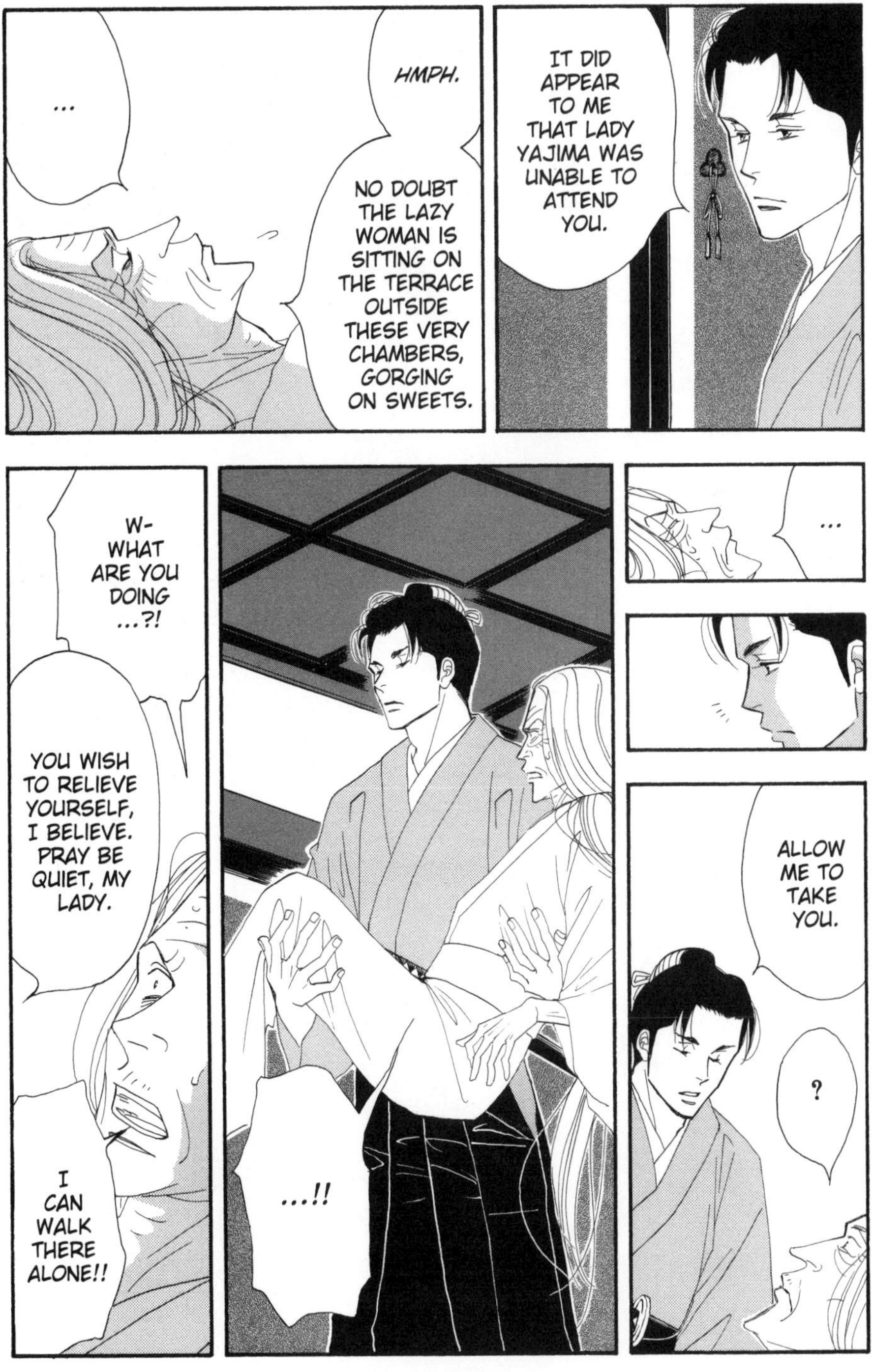
IT DID APPEAR TO ME THAT LADY YAJIMA WAS UNABLE TO ATTEND YOU.
HMPH.
NO DOUBT THE LAZY WOMAN IS SITTING ON THE TERRACE OUTSIDE THESE VERY CHAMBERS, GORGING ON SWEETS.
...
...
ALLOW ME TO TAKE YOU.
?
...!!
W- WHAT ARE YOU DOING ...?!
YOU WISH TO RELIEVE YOURSELF, I BELIEVE. PRAY BE QUIET, MY LADY.
I CAN WALK THERE ALONE!!

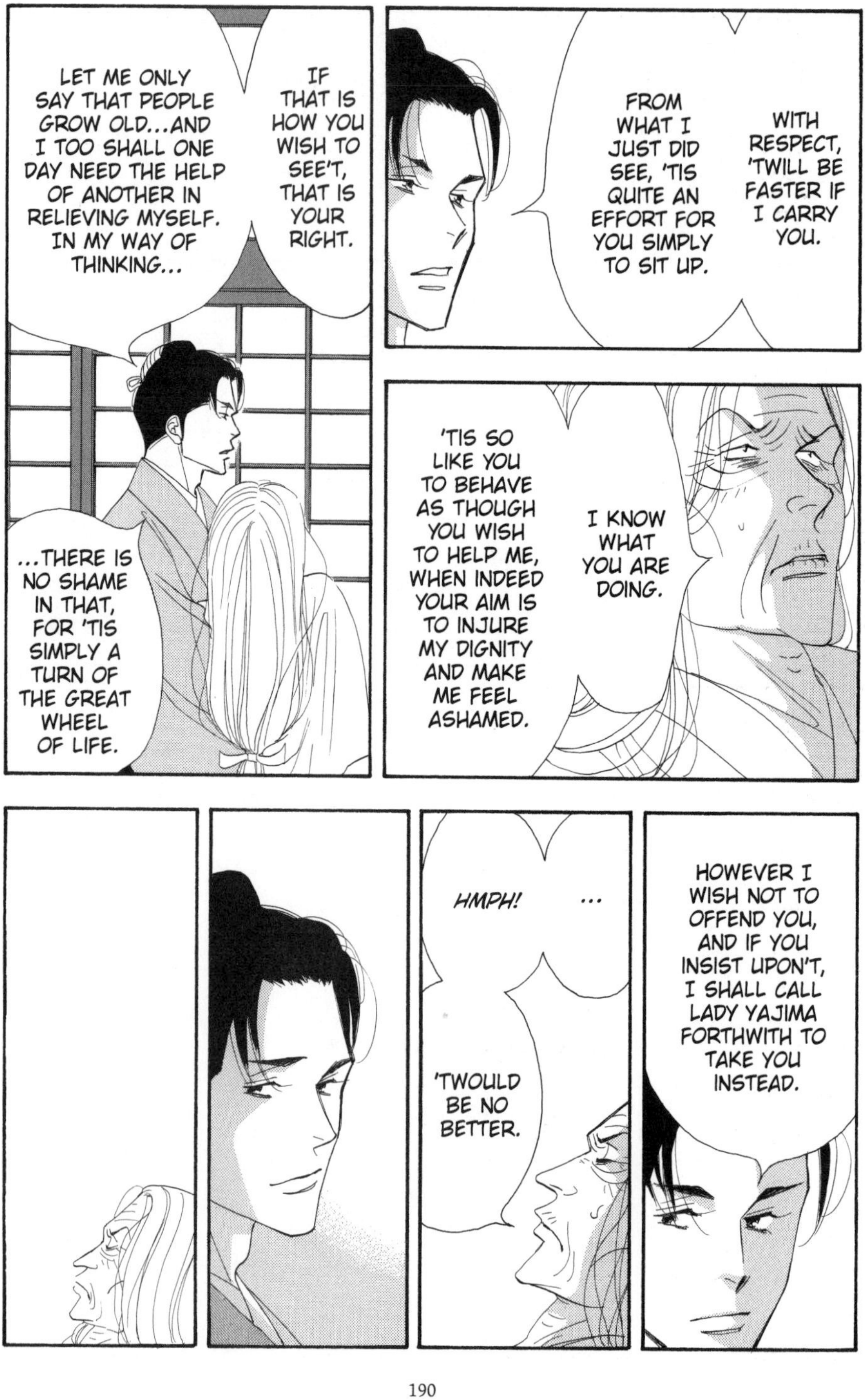
WITH RESPECT, 'TWILL BE FASTER IF I CARRY YOU.
FROM WHAT I JUST DID SEE, 'TIS QUITE AN EFFORT FOR YOU SIMPLY TO SIT UP.
I KNOW WHAT YOU ARE DOING.
'TIS SO LIKE YOU TO BEHAVE AS THOUGH YOU WISH TO HELP ME, WHEN INDEED YOUR AIM IS TO INJURE MY DIGNITY AND MAKE ME FEEL ASHAMED.
IF THAT IS HOW YOU WISH TO SEE'T, THAT IS YOUR RIGHT.
LET ME ONLY SAY THAT PEOPLE GROW OLD...AND I TOO SHALL ONE DAY NEED THE HELP OF ANOTHER IN RELIEVING MYSELF. IN MY WAY OF THINKING...
...THERE IS NO SHAME IN THAT, FOR 'TIS SIMPLY A TURN OF THE GREAT WHEEL OF LIFE.
HOWEVER I WISH NOT TO OFFEND YOU, AND IF YOU INSIST UPON'T, I SHALL CALL LADY YAJIMA FORTHWITH TO TAKE YOU INSTEAD.
...
HMPH!
'TWOULD BE NO BETTER.

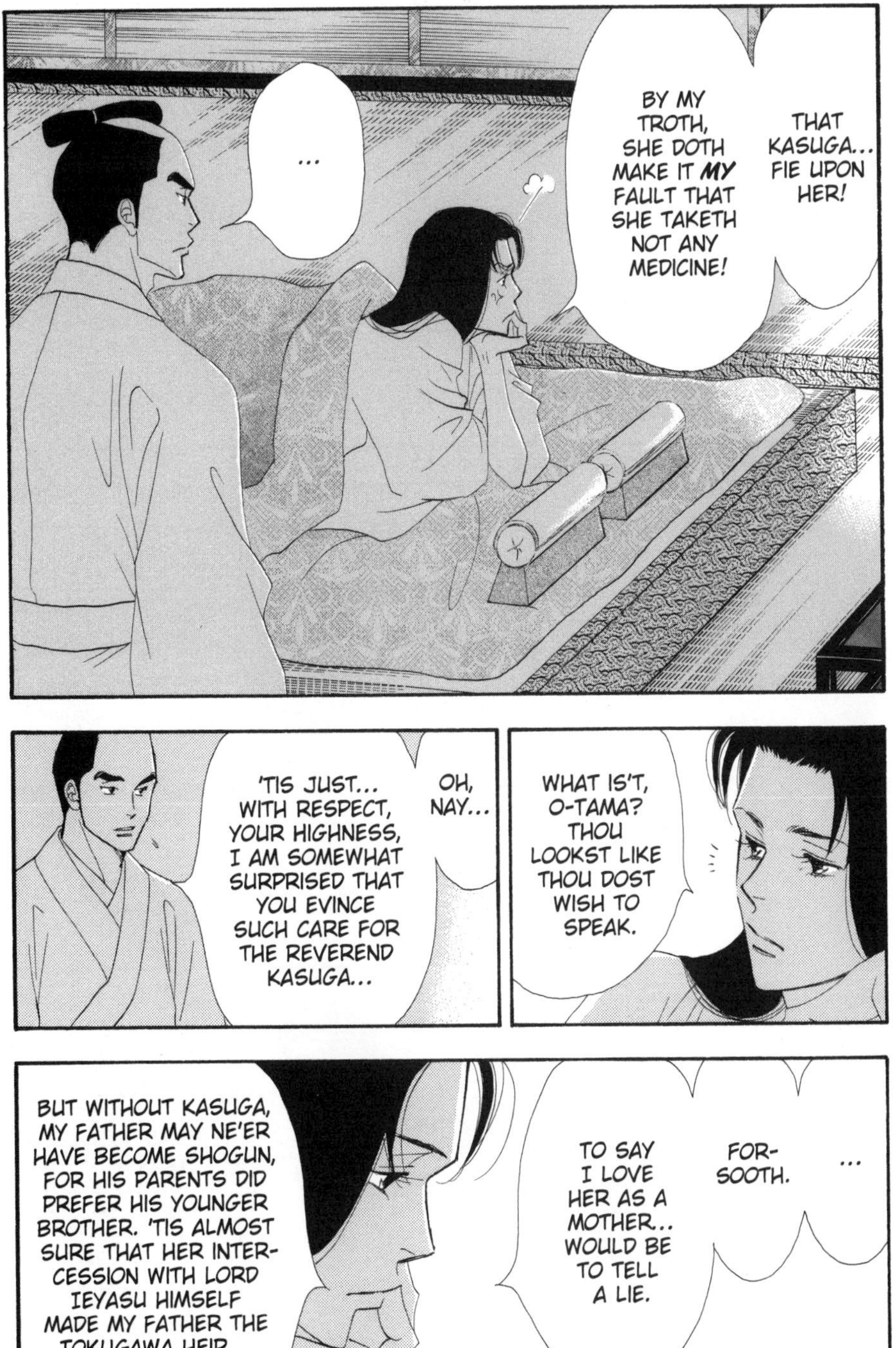
THAT KASUGA... FIE UPON HER!
BY MY TROTH, SHE DOTH MAKE IT **MY** FAULT THAT SHE TAKETH NOT ANY MEDICINE!
...
WHAT IS'T, O-TAMA? THOU LOOKST LIKE THOU DOST WISH TO SPEAK.
OH, NAY...
'TIS JUST... WITH RESPECT, YOUR HIGHNESS, I AM SOMEWHAT SURPRISED THAT YOU EVINCE SUCH CARE FOR THE REVEREND KASUGA...
...
FOR-SOOTH.
TO SAY I LOVE HER AS A MOTHER... WOULD BE TO TELL A LIE.
BUT WITHOUT KASUGA, MY FATHER MAY NE'ER HAVE BECOME SHOGUN, FOR HIS PARENTS DID PREFER HIS YOUNGER BROTHER. 'TIS ALMOST SURE THAT HER INTERCESSION WITH LORD IEYASU HIMSELF MADE MY FATHER THE TOKUGAWA HEIR...

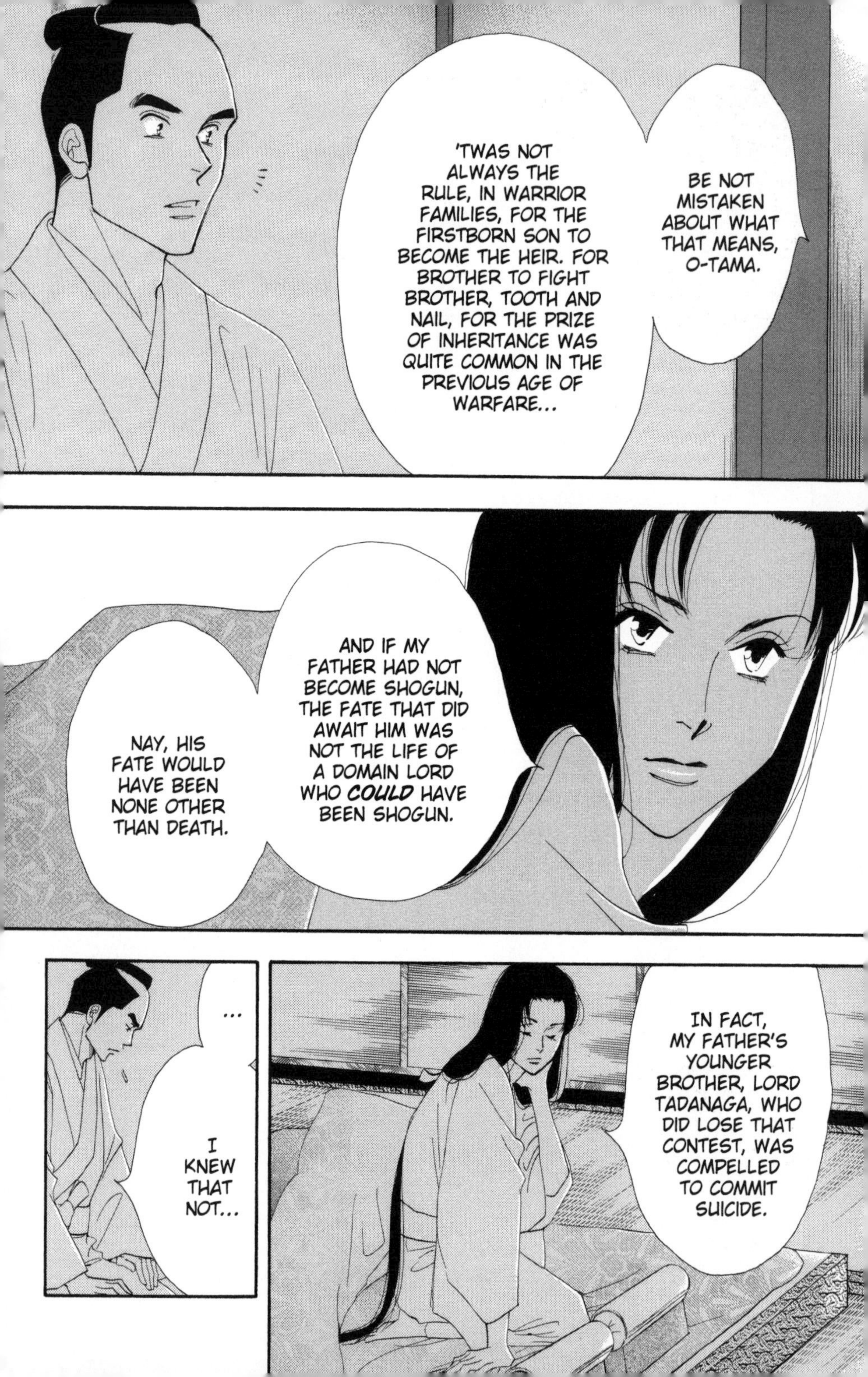
BE NOT MISTAKEN ABOUT WHAT THAT MEANS, O-TAMA.
'TWAS NOT ALWAYS THE RULE, IN WARRIOR FAMILIES, FOR THE FIRSTBORN SON TO BECOME THE HEIR. FOR BROTHER TO FIGHT BROTHER, TOOTH AND NAIL, FOR THE PRIZE OF INHERITANCE WAS QUITE COMMON IN THE PREVIOUS AGE OF WARFARE...
AND IF MY FATHER HAD NOT BECOME SHOGUN, THE FATE THAT DID AWAIT HIM WAS NOT THE LIFE OF A DOMAIN LORD WHO *COULD* HAVE BEEN SHOGUN.
NAY, HIS FATE WOULD HAVE BEEN NONE OTHER THAN DEATH.
IN FACT, MY FATHER'S YOUNGER BROTHER, LORD TADANAGA, WHO DID LOSE THAT CONTEST, WAS COMPELLED TO COMMIT SUICIDE.
...
I KNEW THAT NOT...

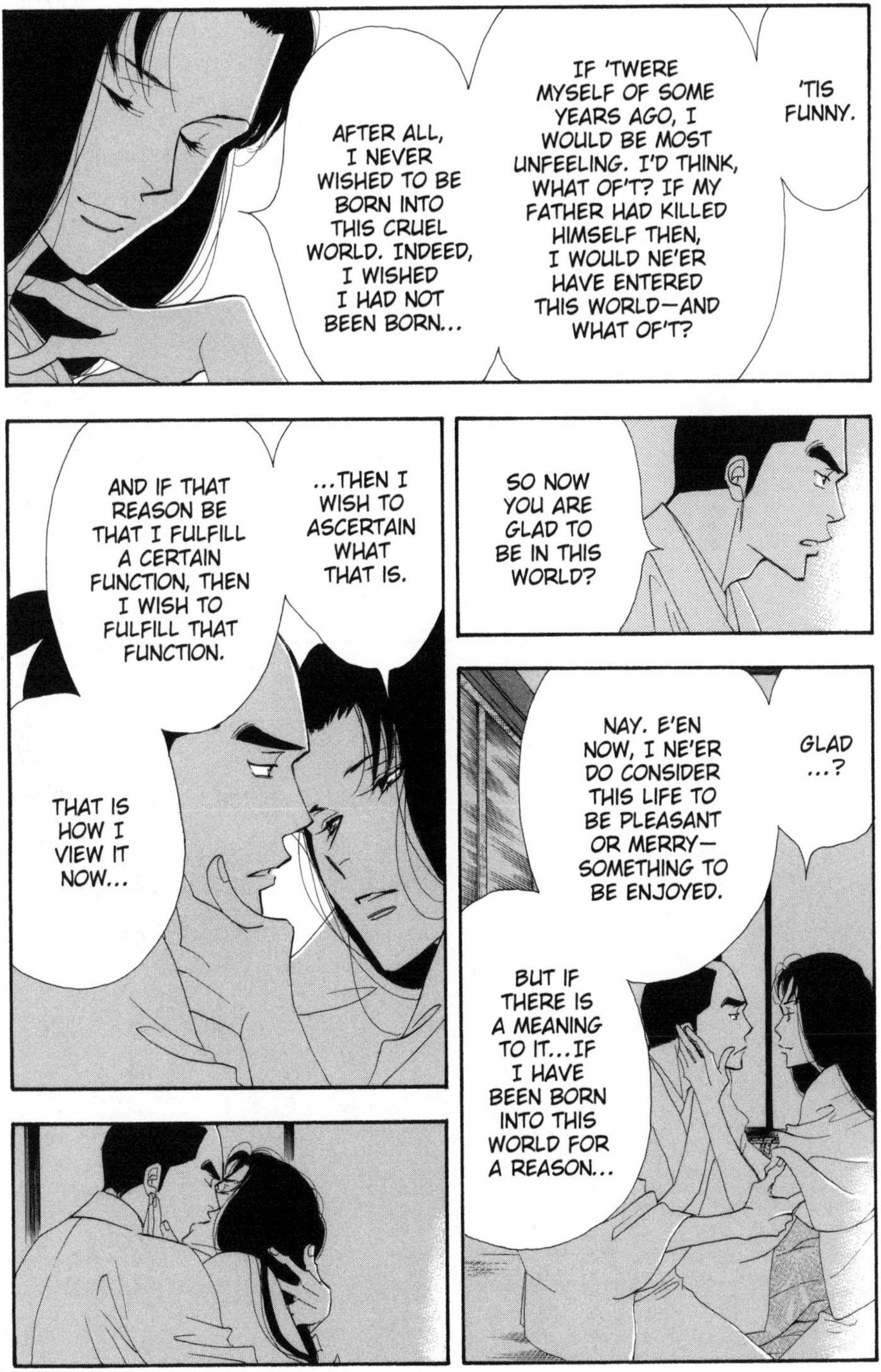
'TIS FUNNY.
IF 'TWERE MYSELF OF SOME YEARS AGO, I WOULD BE MOST UNFEELING. I'D THINK, WHAT OF'T? IF MY FATHER HAD KILLED HIMSELF THEN, I WOULD NE'ER HAVE ENTERED THIS WORLD—AND WHAT OF'T?
AFTER ALL, I NEVER WISHED TO BE BORN INTO THIS CRUEL WORLD. INDEED, I WISHED I HAD NOT BEEN BORN...
SO NOW YOU ARE GLAD TO BE IN THIS WORLD?
GLAD ...?
NAY. E'EN NOW, I NE'ER DO CONSIDER THIS LIFE TO BE PLEASANT OR MERRY—SOMETHING TO BE ENJOYED.
BUT IF THERE IS A MEANING TO IT...IF I HAVE BEEN BORN INTO THIS WORLD FOR A REASON...
...THEN I WISH TO ASCERTAIN WHAT THAT IS.
AND IF THAT REASON BE THAT I FULFILL A CERTAIN FUNCTION, THEN I WISH TO FULFILL THAT FUNCTION.
THAT IS HOW I VIEW IT NOW...

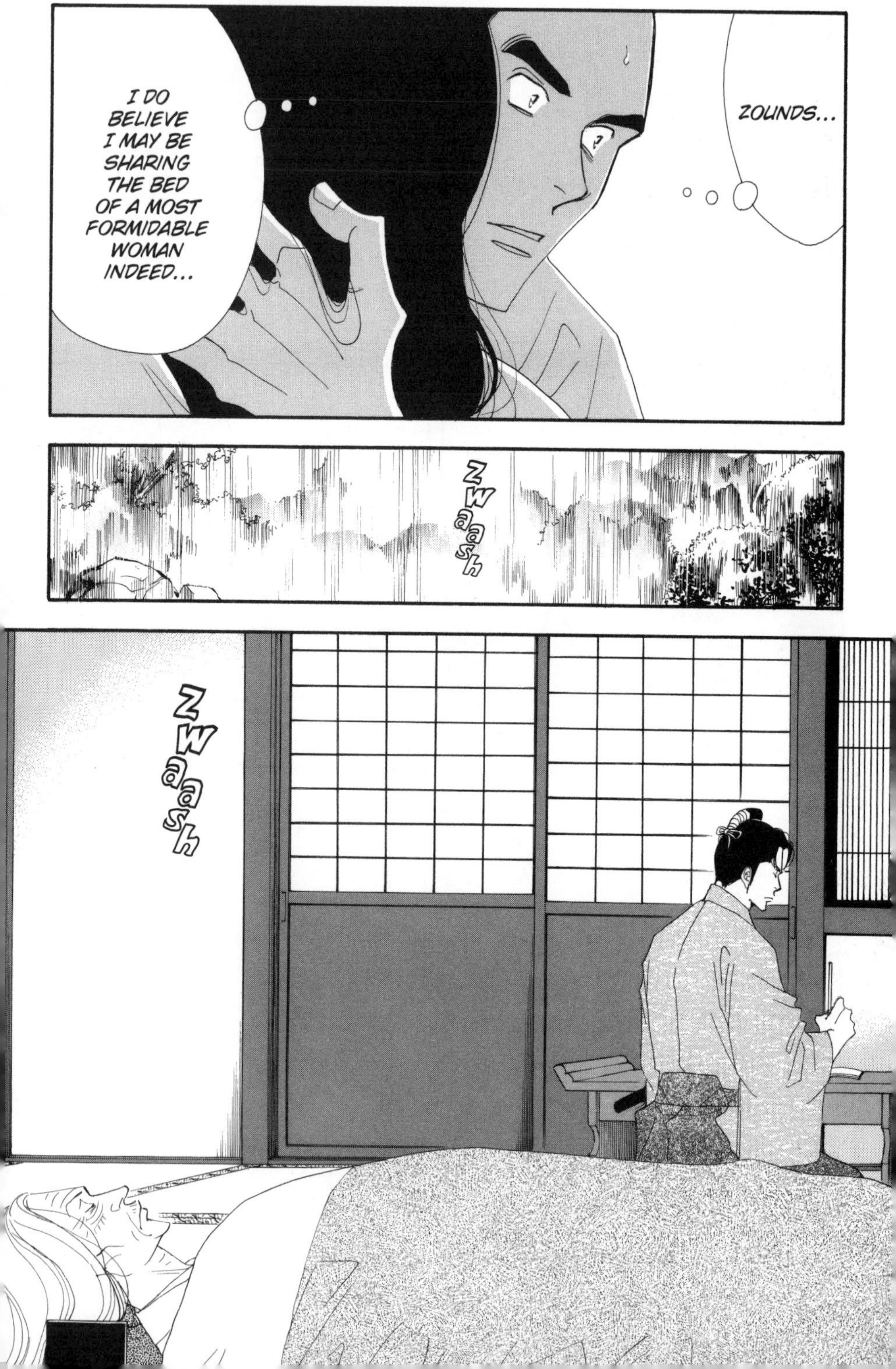
ZOUNDS...
I DO BELIEVE I MAY BE SHARING THE BED OF A MOST FORMIDABLE WOMAN INDEED...
ZWAASH
ZWAASH

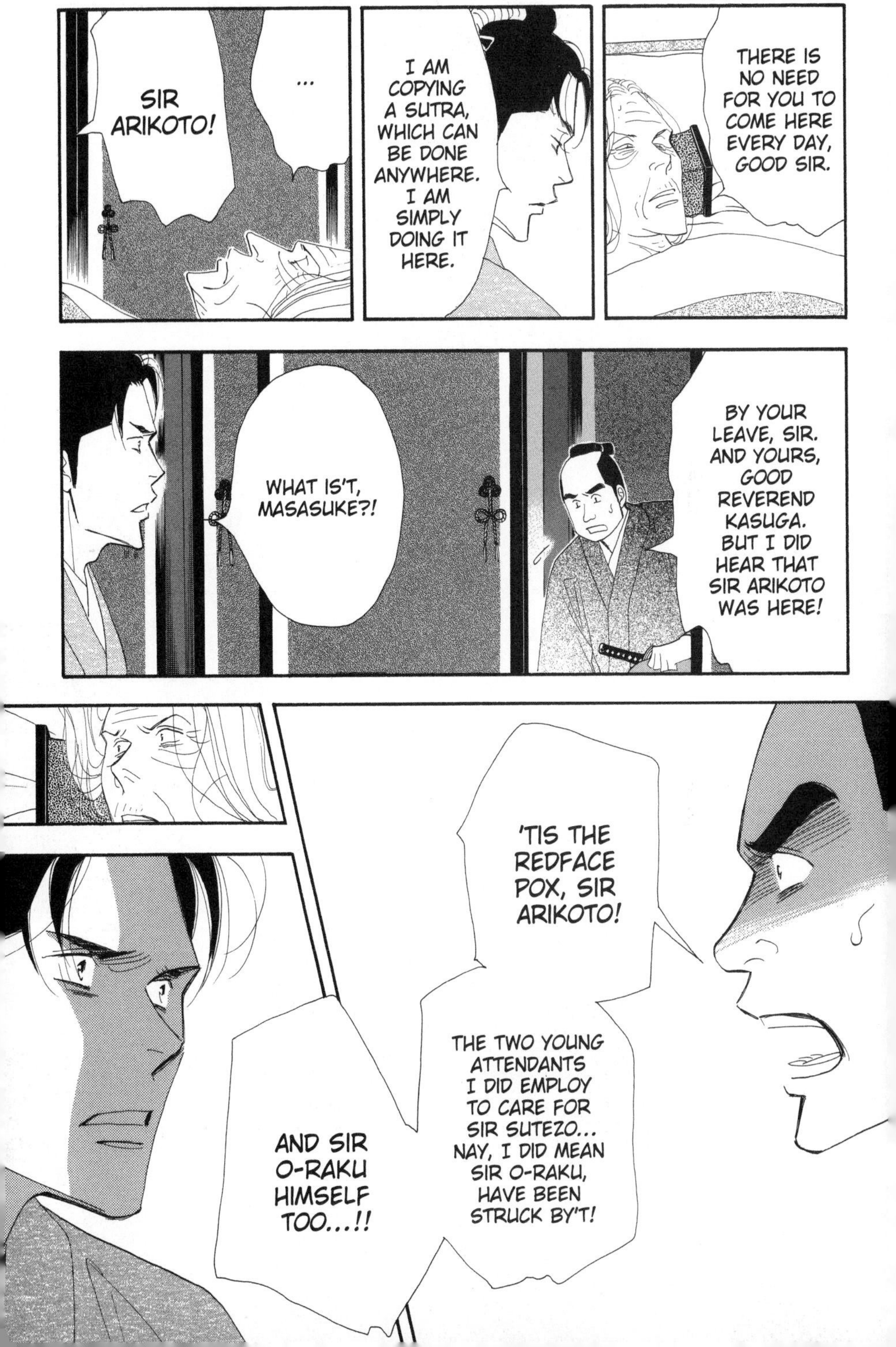
THERE IS NO NEED FOR YOU TO COME HERE EVERY DAY, GOOD SIR.
I AM COPYING A SUTRA, WHICH CAN BE DONE ANYWHERE. I AM SIMPLY DOING IT HERE.
...
SIR ARIKOTO!
BY YOUR LEAVE, SIR. AND YOURS, GOOD REVEREND KASUGA. BUT I DID HEAR THAT SIR ARIKOTO WAS HERE!
WHAT IS'T, MASASUKE?!
'TIS THE REDFACE POX, SIR ARIKOTO!
THE TWO YOUNG ATTENDANTS I DID EMPLOY TO CARE FOR SIR SUTEZO... NAY, I DID MEAN SIR O-RAKU, HAVE BEEN STRUCK BY'T!
AND SIR O-RAKU HIMSELF TOO...!!

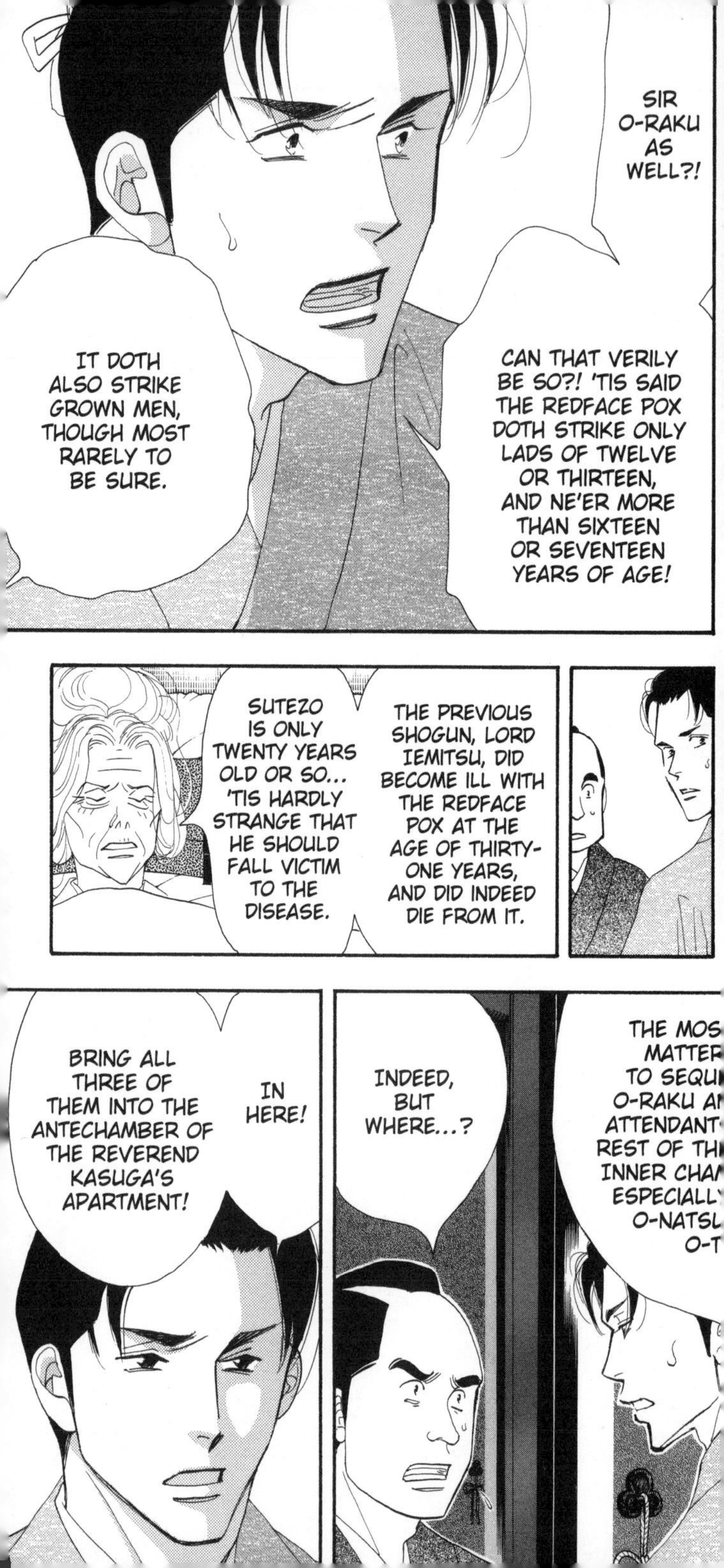
SIR O-RAKU AS WELL?!
CAN THAT VERILY BE SO?! 'TIS SAID THE REDFACE POX DOTH STRIKE ONLY LADS OF TWELVE OR THIRTEEN, AND NE'ER MORE THAN SIXTEEN OR SEVENTEEN YEARS OF AGE!
IT DOTH ALSO STRIKE GROWN MEN, THOUGH MOST RARELY TO BE SURE.
THE PREVIOUS SHOGUN, LORD IEMITSU, DID BECOME ILL WITH THE REDFACE POX AT THE AGE OF THIRTY-ONE YEARS, AND DID INDEED DIE FROM IT.
SUTEZO IS ONLY TWENTY YEARS OLD OR SO... 'TIS HARDLY STRANGE THAT HE SHOULD FALL VICTIM TO THE DISEASE.
THE MOS MATTER TO SEQU O-RAKU A ATTENDANT REST OF TH INNER CHA ESPECIALL O-NATS O-T
INDEED, BUT WHERE...?
IN HERE!
BRING ALL THREE OF THEM INTO THE ANTECHAMBER OF THE REVEREND KASUGA'S APARTMENT!

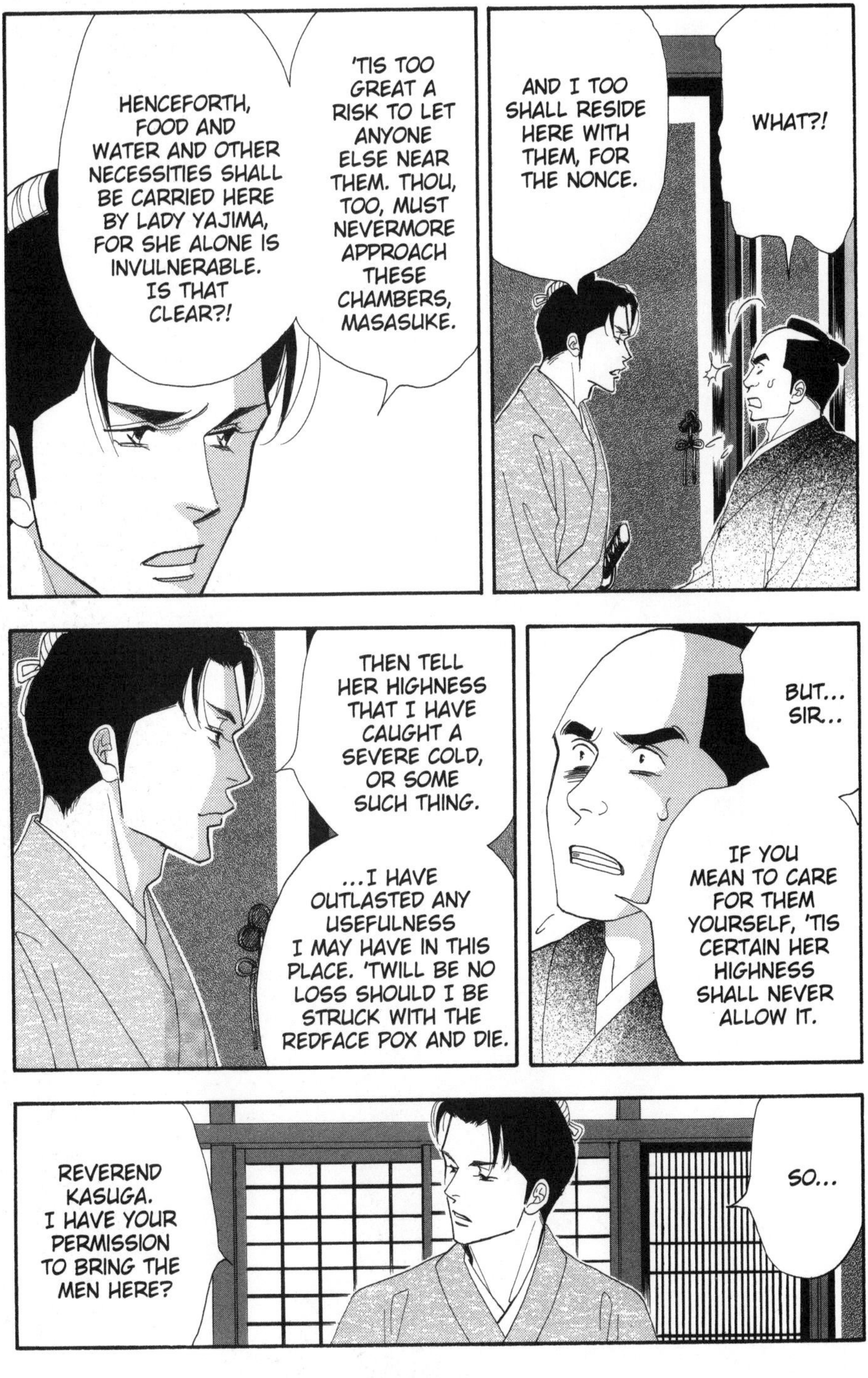
AND I TOO SHALL RESIDE HERE WITH THEM, FOR THE NONCE.
WHAT?!
HENCEFORTH, FOOD AND WATER AND OTHER NECESSITIES SHALL BE CARRIED HERE BY LADY YAJIMA, FOR SHE ALONE IS INVULNERABLE. IS THAT CLEAR?!
'TIS TOO GREAT A RISK TO LET ANYONE ELSE NEAR THEM. THOU, TOO, MUST NEVERMORE APPROACH THESE CHAMBERS, MASASUKE.
BUT... SIR...
IF YOU MEAN TO CARE FOR THEM YOURSELF, 'TIS CERTAIN HER HIGHNESS SHALL NEVER ALLOW IT.
THEN TELL HER HIGHNESS THAT I HAVE CAUGHT A SEVERE COLD, OR SOME SUCH THING.
...I HAVE OUTLASTED ANY USEFULNESS I MAY HAVE IN THIS PLACE. 'TWILL BE NO LOSS SHOULD I BE STRUCK WITH THE REDFACE POX AND DIE.
SO...
REVEREND KASUGA. I HAVE YOUR PERMISSION TO BRING THE MEN HERE?

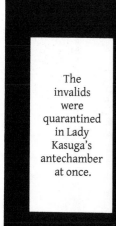

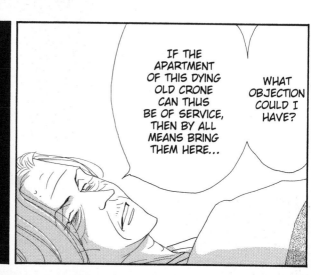

IF THE APARTMENT OF THIS DYING OLD CRONE CAN THUS BE OF SERVICE, THEN BY ALL MEANS BRING THEM HERE...
WHAT OBJECTION COULD I HAVE?
The invalids were quarantined in Lady Kasuga's antechamber at once.

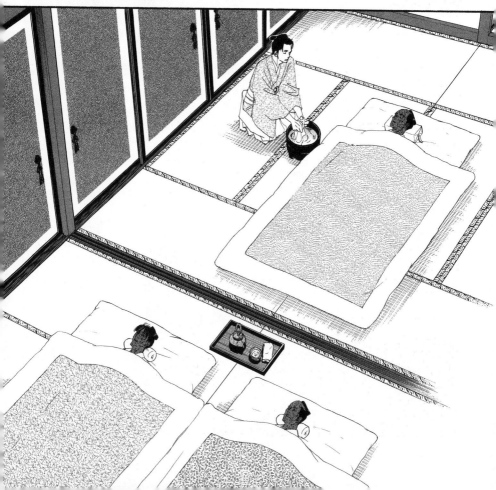

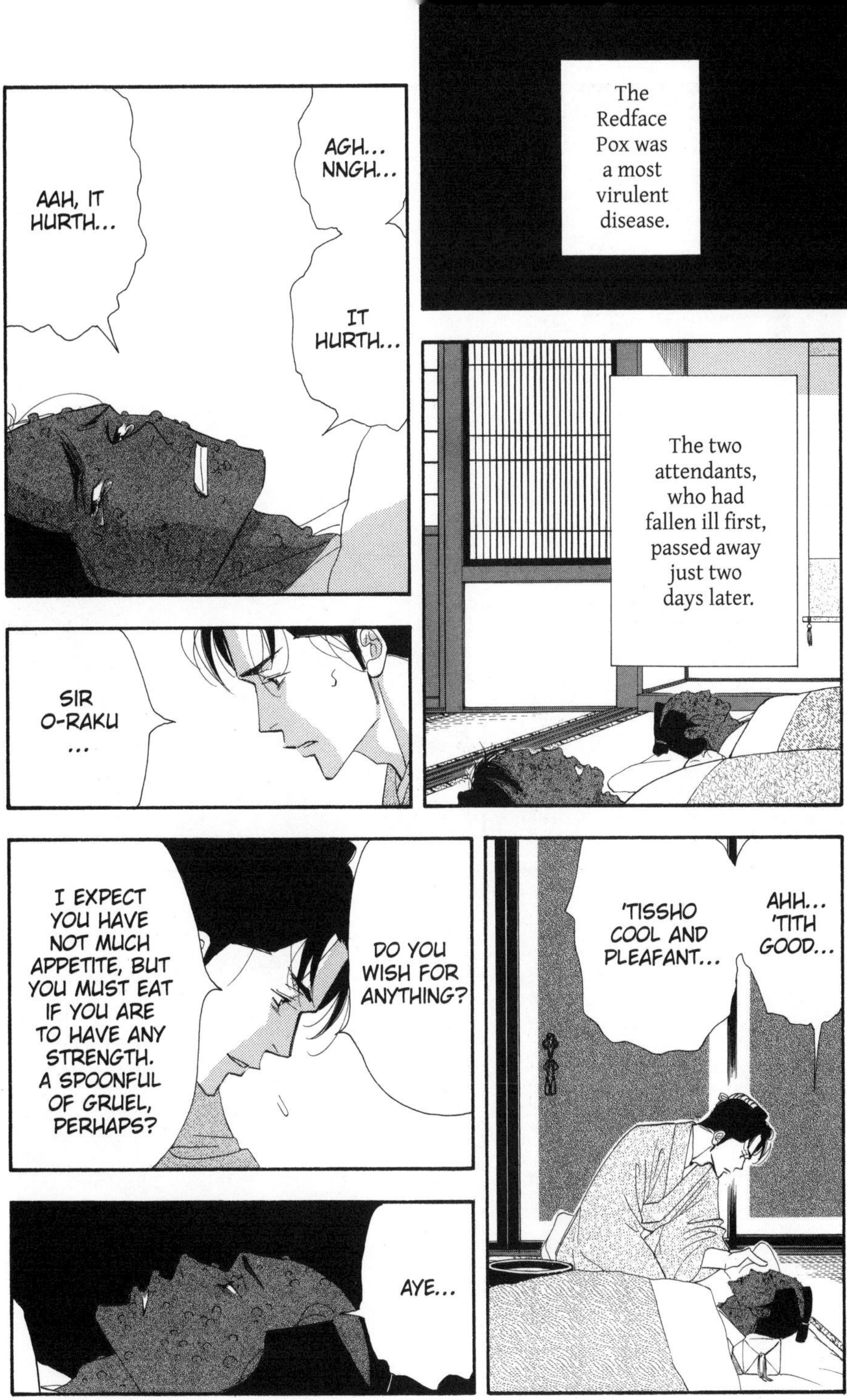
The Redface Pox was a most virulent disease.
AGH... NNGH...
AAH, IT HURTH...
IT HURTH...
The two attendants, who had fallen ill first, passed away just two days later.
SIR O-RAKU ...
AHH... 'TITH GOOD...
'TISSHO COOL AND PLEAFANT...
DO YOU WISH FOR ANYTHING?
I EXPECT YOU HAVE NOT MUCH APPETITE, BUT YOU MUST EAT IF YOU ARE TO HAVE ANY STRENGTH. A SPOONFUL OF GRUEL, PERHAPS?
AYE...

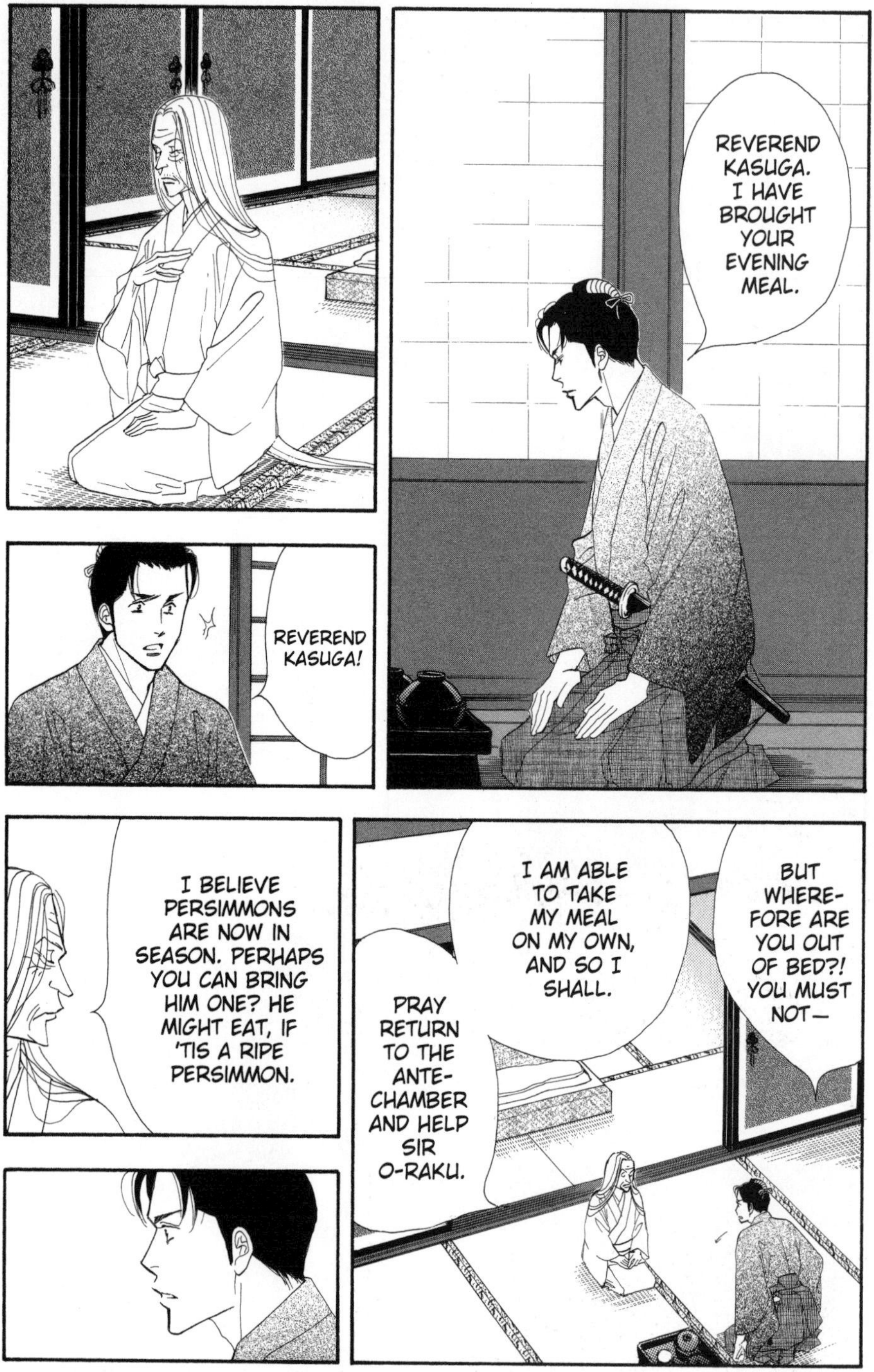
REVEREND KASUGA. I HAVE BROUGHT YOUR EVENING MEAL.
REVEREND KASUGA!
BUT WHEREFORE ARE YOU OUT OF BED?! YOU MUST NOT—
I AM ABLE TO TAKE MY MEAL ON MY OWN, AND SO I SHALL.
PRAY RETURN TO THE ANTE-CHAMBER AND HELP SIR O-RAKU.
I BELIEVE PERSIMMONS ARE NOW IN SEASON. PERHAPS YOU CAN BRING HIM ONE? HE MIGHT EAT, IF 'TIS A RIPE PERSIMMON.

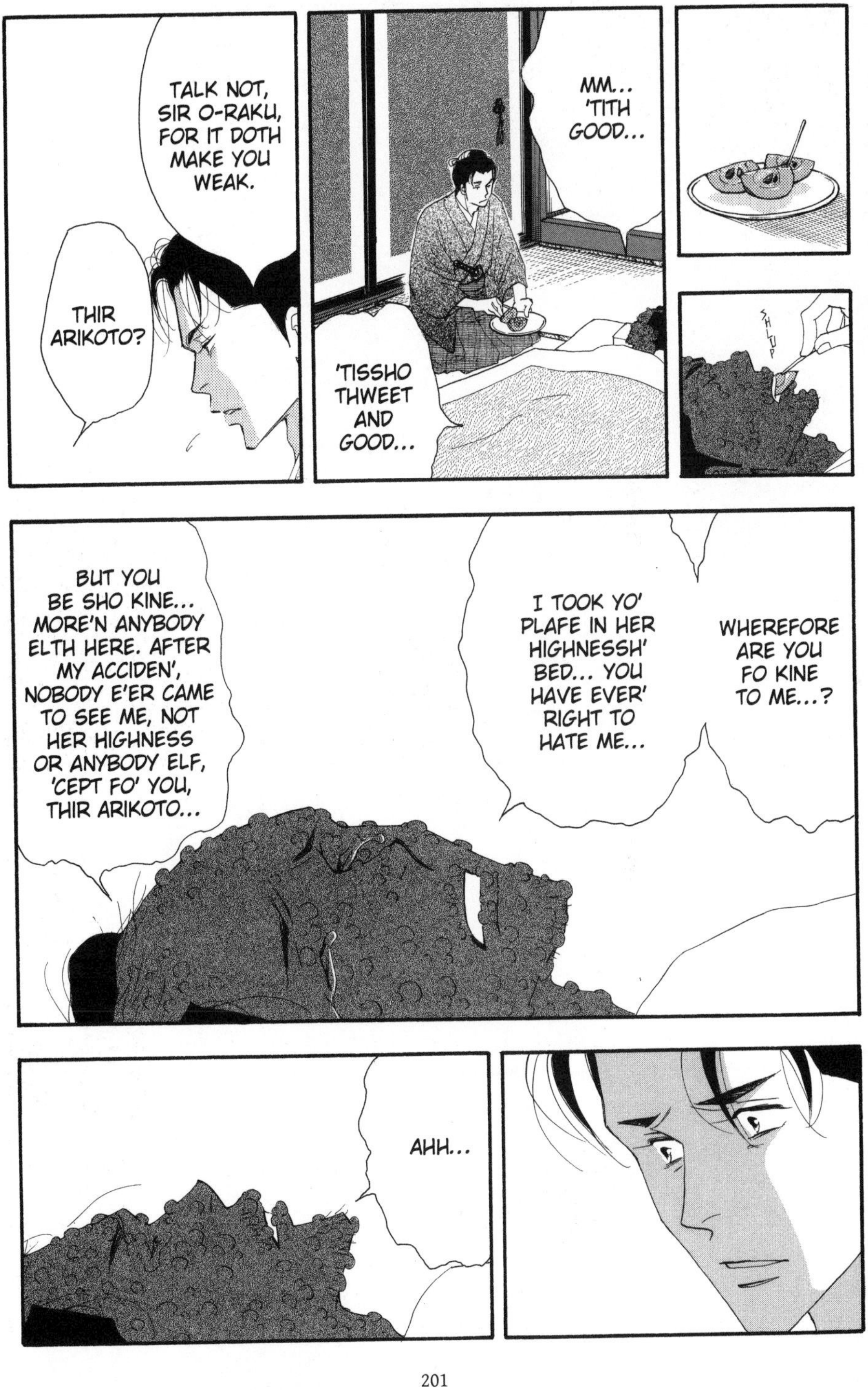
SHLUP
MM... 'TITH GOOD...
'TISSHO THWEET AND GOOD...
TALK NOT, SIR O-RAKU, FOR IT DOTH MAKE YOU WEAK.
THIR ARIKOTO?
WHEREFORE ARE YOU FO KINE TO ME...?
I TOOK YO' PLAFE IN HER HIGHNESSH' BED... YOU HAVE EVER' RIGHT TO HATE ME...
BUT YOU BE SHO KINE... MORE'N ANYBODY ELTH HERE. AFTER MY ACCIDEN', NOBODY E'ER CAME TO SEE ME, NOT HER HIGHNESS OR ANYBODY ELF, 'CEPT FO' YOU, THIR ARIKOTO...
AHH...

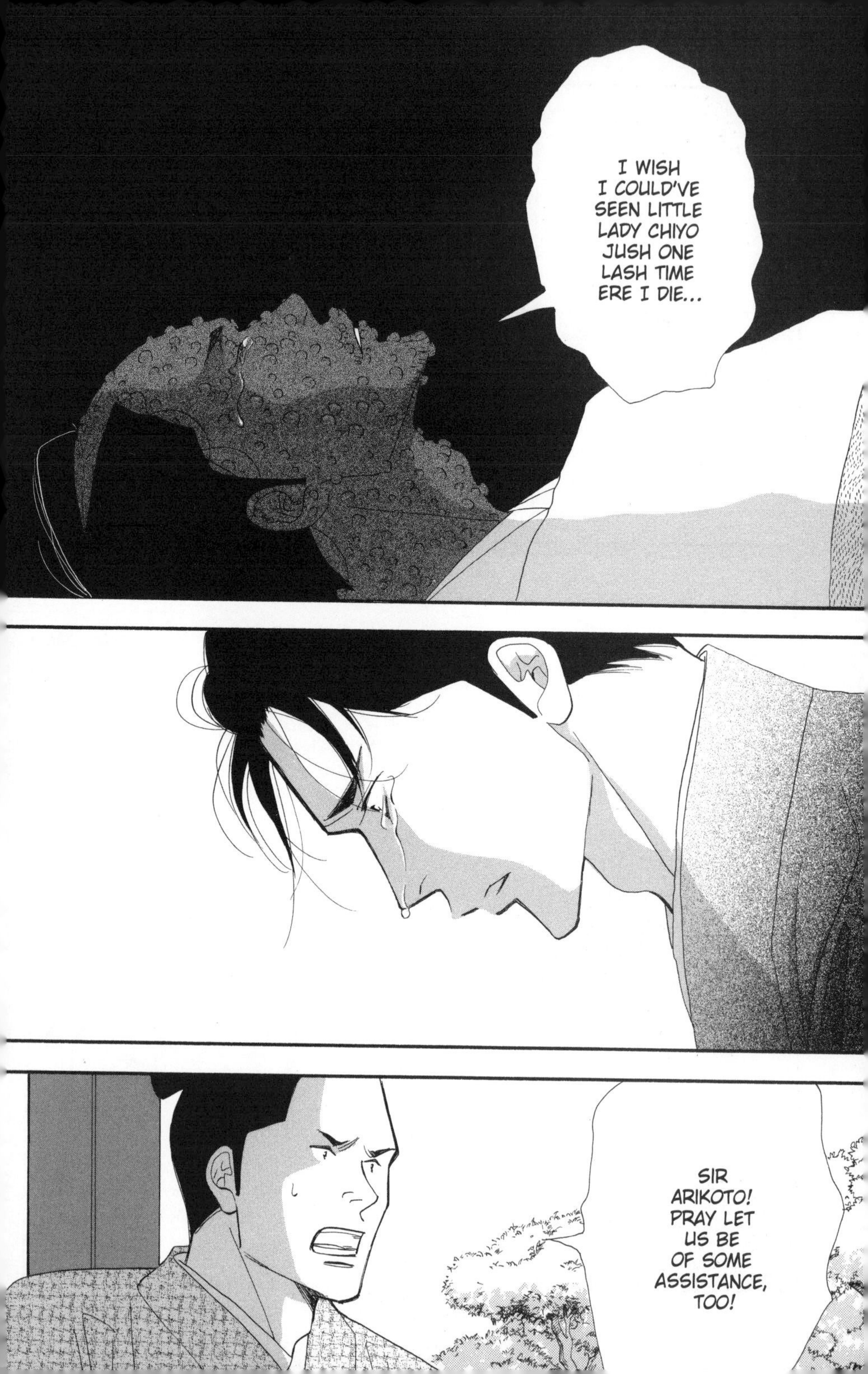
I WISH I COULD'VE SEEN LITTLE LADY CHIYO JUSH ONE LASH TIME ERE I DIE...
SIR ARIKOTO! PRAY LET US BE OF SOME ASSISTANCE, TOO!

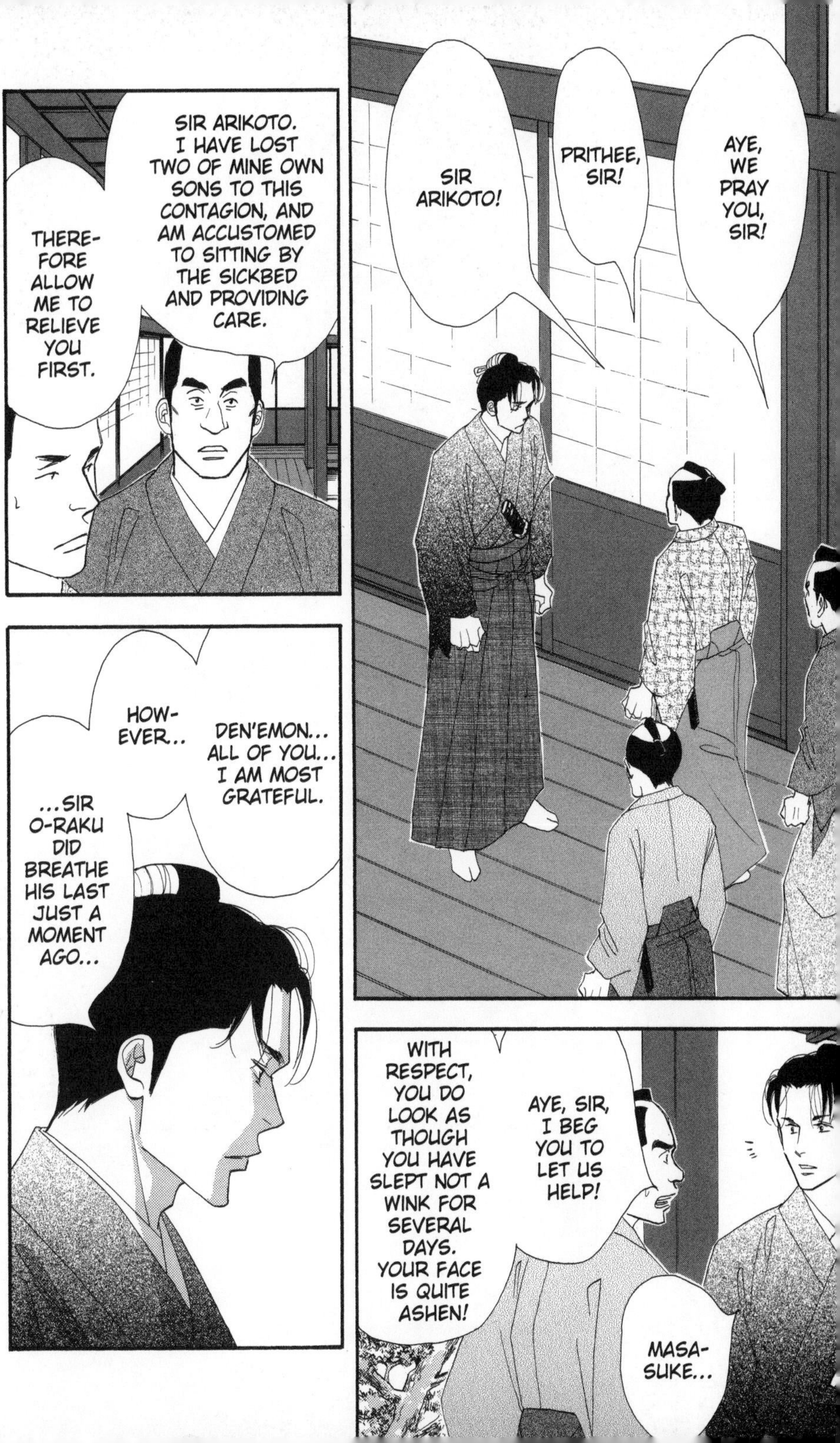
AYE, WE PRAY YOU, SIR!
PRITHEE, SIR!
SIR ARIKOTO!
SIR ARIKOTO. I HAVE LOST TWO OF MINE OWN SONS TO THIS CONTAGION, AND AM ACCUSTOMED TO SITTING BY THE SICKBED AND PROVIDING CARE.
THERE-FORE ALLOW ME TO RELIEVE YOU FIRST.
AYE, SIR, I BEG YOU TO LET US HELP!
WITH RESPECT, YOU DO LOOK AS THOUGH YOU HAVE SLEPT NOT A WINK FOR SEVERAL DAYS. YOUR FACE IS QUITE ASHEN!
MASA-SUKE...
DEN'EMON... ALL OF YOU... I AM MOST GRATEFUL.
HOW-EVER...
...SIR O-RAKU DID BREATHE HIS LAST JUST A MOMENT AGO...

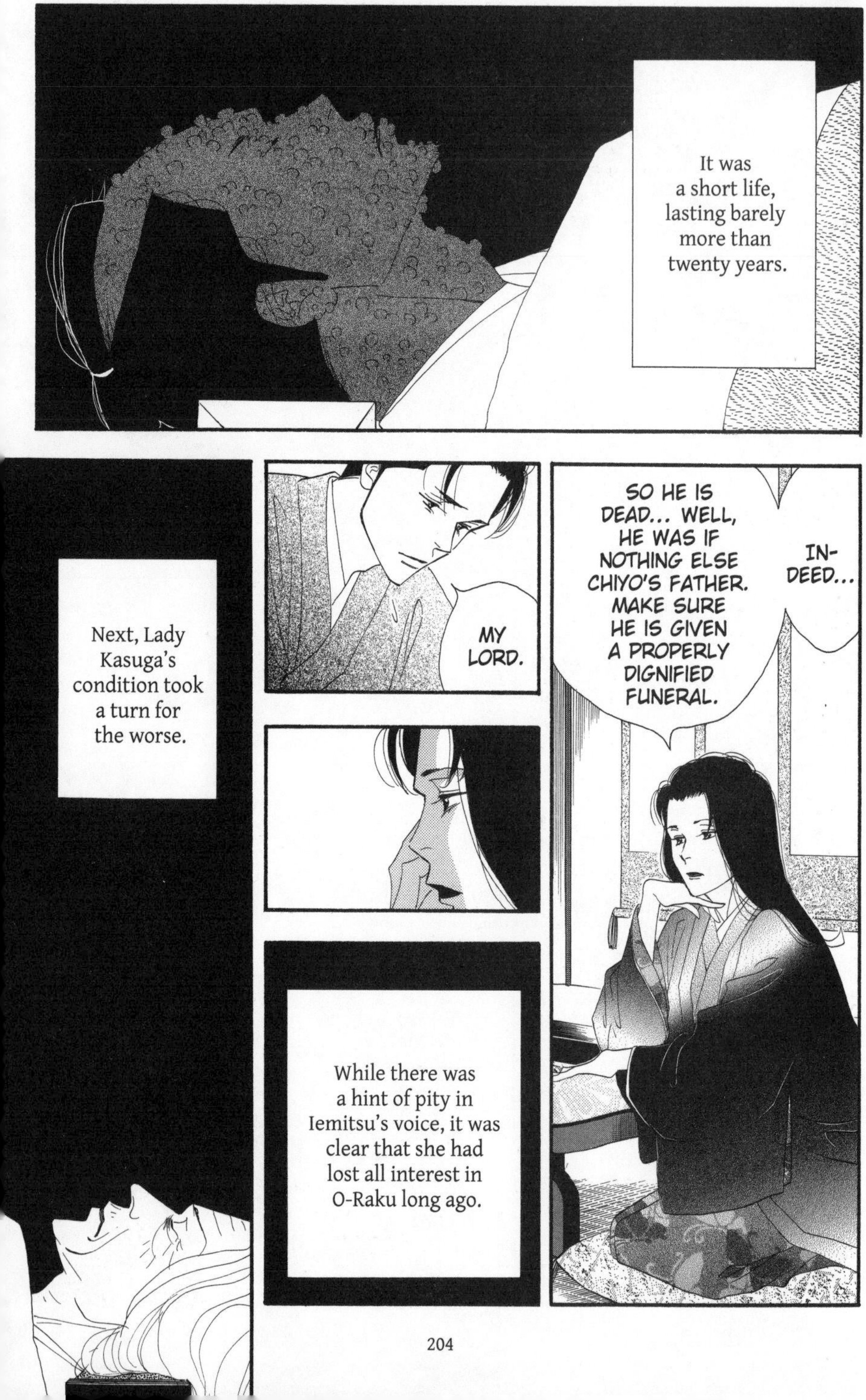
It was a short life, lasting barely more than twenty years.
SO HE IS DEAD... WELL, HE WAS IF NOTHING ELSE CHIYO'S FATHER. MAKE SURE HE IS GIVEN A PROPERLY DIGNIFIED FUNERAL.
IN-DEED...
MY LORD.
While there was a hint of pity in Iemitsu's voice, it was clear that she had lost all interest in O-Raku long ago.
Next, Lady Kasuga's condition took a turn for the worse.

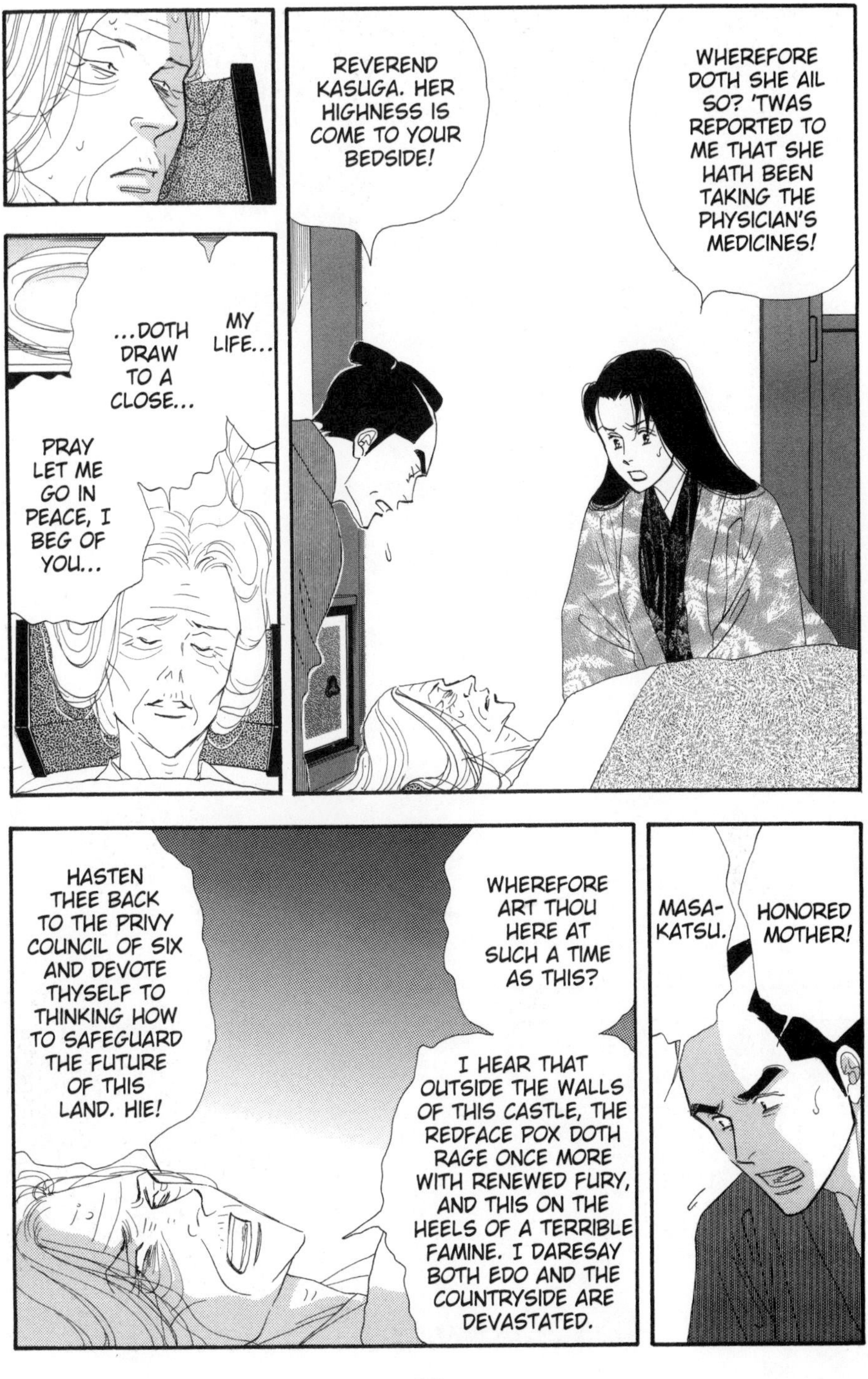

WHEREFORE DOTH SHE AIL SO? 'TWAS REPORTED TO ME THAT SHE HATH BEEN TAKING THE PHYSICIAN'S MEDICINES!
REVEREND KASUGA. HER HIGHNESS IS COME TO YOUR BEDSIDE!
MY LIFE...
...DOTH DRAW TO A CLOSE...
PRAY LET ME GO IN PEACE, I BEG OF YOU...
HONORED MOTHER!
MASA-KATSU.
WHEREFORE ART THOU HERE AT SUCH A TIME AS THIS?
I HEAR THAT OUTSIDE THE WALLS OF THIS CASTLE, THE REDFACE POX DOTH RAGE ONCE MORE WITH RENEWED FURY, AND THIS ON THE HEELS OF A TERRIBLE FAMINE. I DARESAY BOTH EDO AND THE COUNTRYSIDE ARE DEVASTATED.
HASTEN THEE BACK TO THE PRIVY COUNCIL OF SIX AND DEVOTE THYSELF TO THINKING HOW TO SAFEGUARD THE FUTURE OF THIS LAND. HIE!

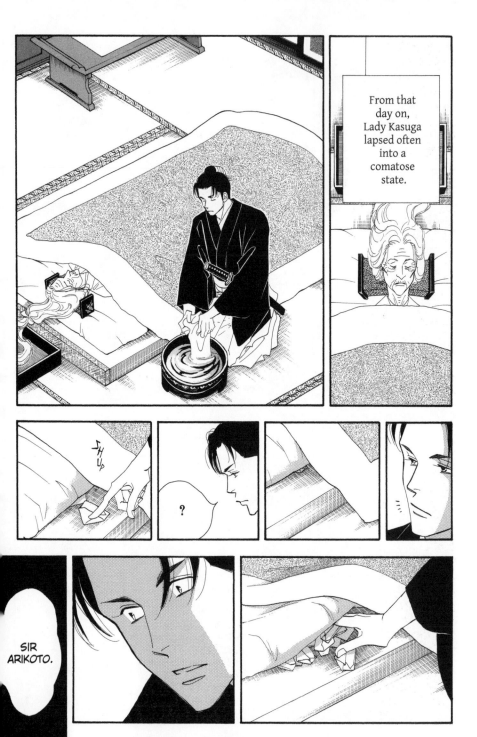

From that day on, Lady Kasuga lapsed often into a comatose state.

SIR ARIKOTO.

206

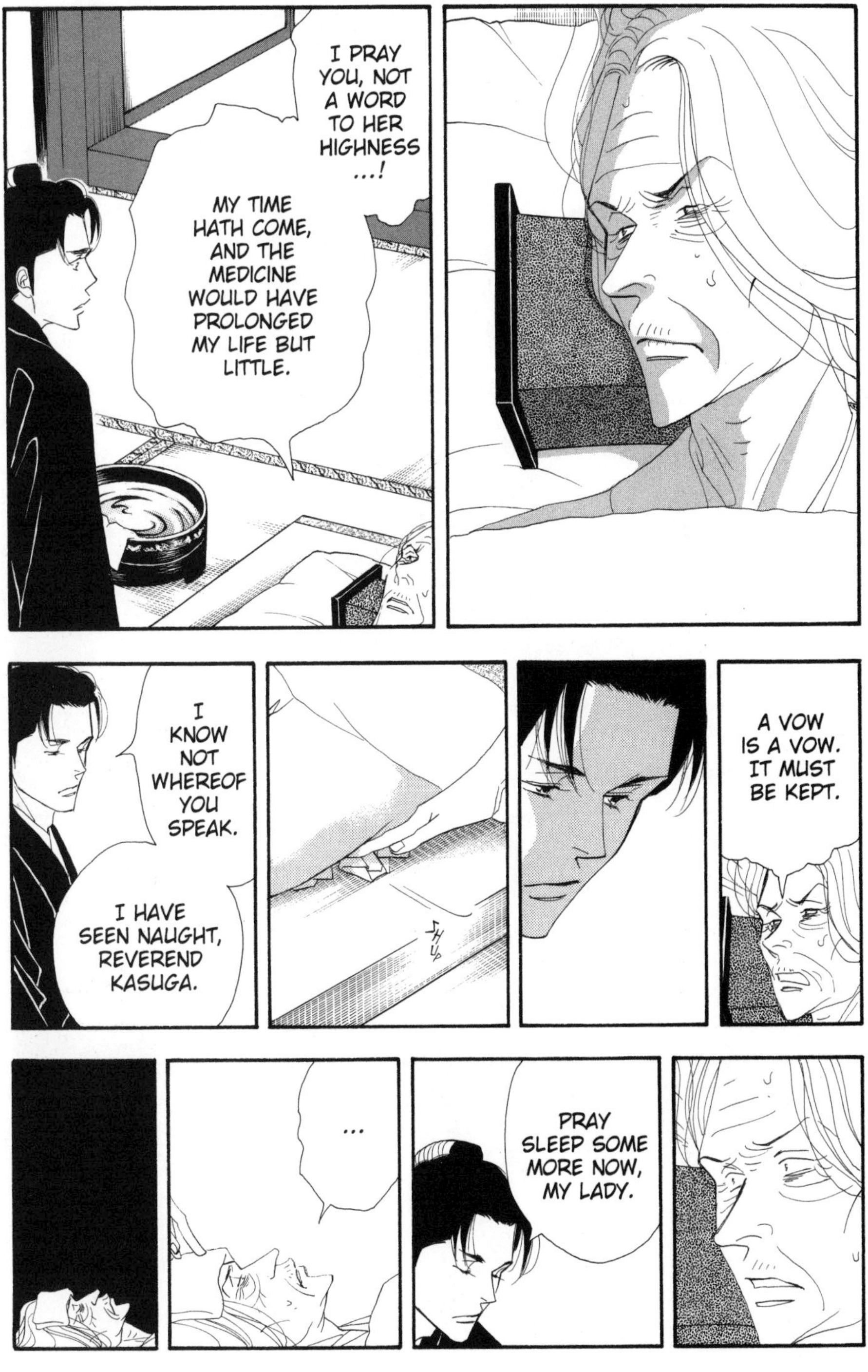
I PRAY YOU, NOT A WORD TO HER HIGHNESS ...!
MY TIME HATH COME, AND THE MEDICINE WOULD HAVE PROLONGED MY LIFE BUT LITTLE.
A VOW IS A VOW. IT MUST BE KEPT.
SHUP
I KNOW NOT WHEREOF YOU SPEAK.
I HAVE SEEN NAUGHT, REVEREND KASUGA.
PRAY SLEEP SOME MORE NOW, MY LADY.
...

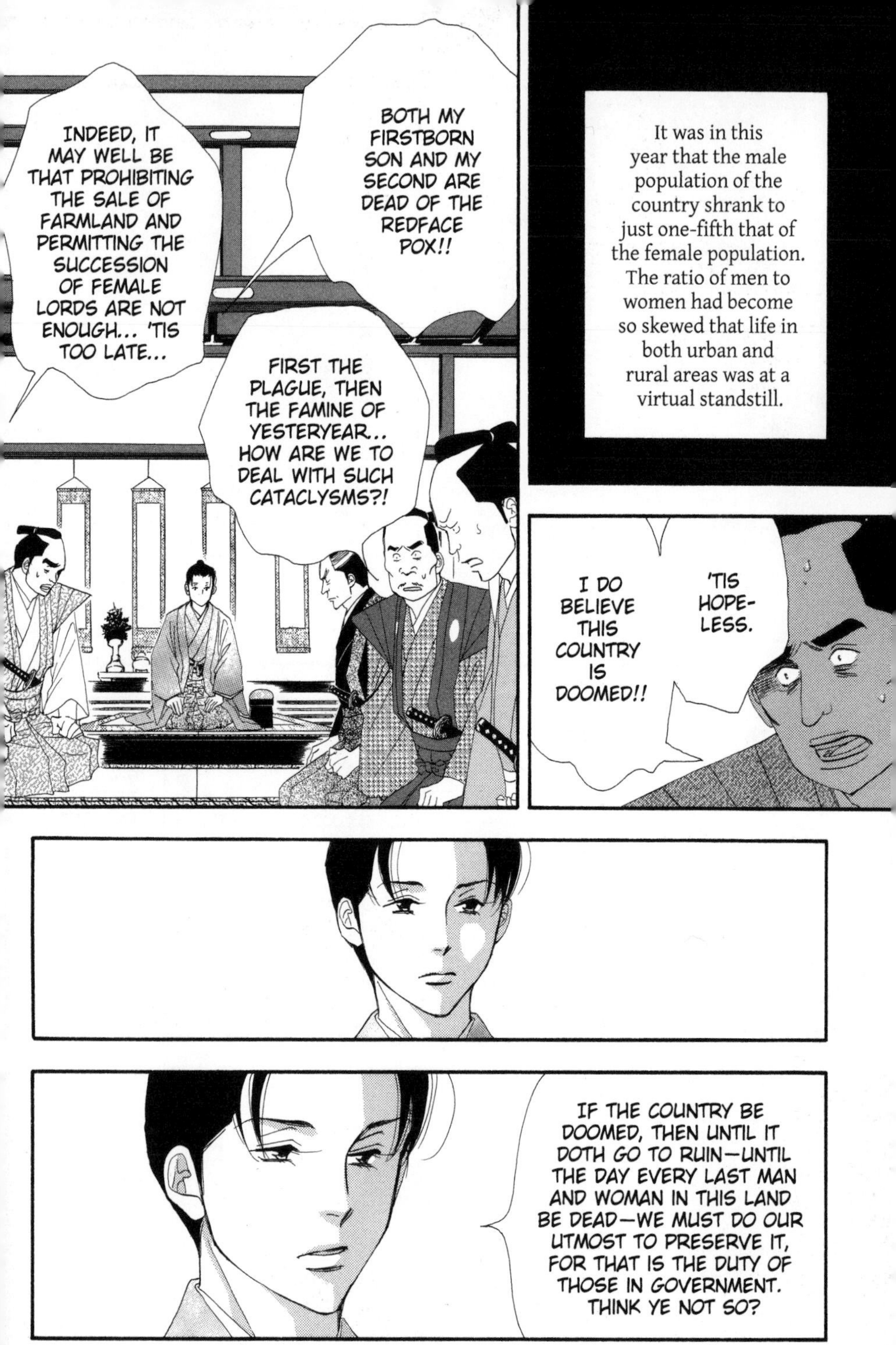
It was in this year that the male population of the country shrank to just one-fifth that of the female population. The ratio of men to women had become so skewed that life in both urban and rural areas was at a virtual standstill.
'TIS HOPE-LESS.
I DO BELIEVE THIS COUNTRY IS DOOMED!!
BOTH MY FIRSTBORN SON AND MY SECOND ARE DEAD OF THE REDFACE POX!!
INDEED, IT MAY WELL BE THAT PROHIBITING THE SALE OF FARMLAND AND PERMITTING THE SUCCESSION OF FEMALE LORDS ARE NOT ENOUGH... 'TIS TOO LATE...
FIRST THE PLAGUE, THEN THE FAMINE OF YESTERYEAR... HOW ARE WE TO DEAL WITH SUCH CATACLYSMS?!
IF THE COUNTRY BE DOOMED, THEN UNTIL IT DOTH GO TO RUIN—UNTIL THE DAY EVERY LAST MAN AND WOMAN IN THIS LAND BE DEAD—WE MUST DO OUR UTMOST TO PRESERVE IT, FOR THAT IS THE DUTY OF THOSE IN GOVERNMENT. THINK YE NOT SO?

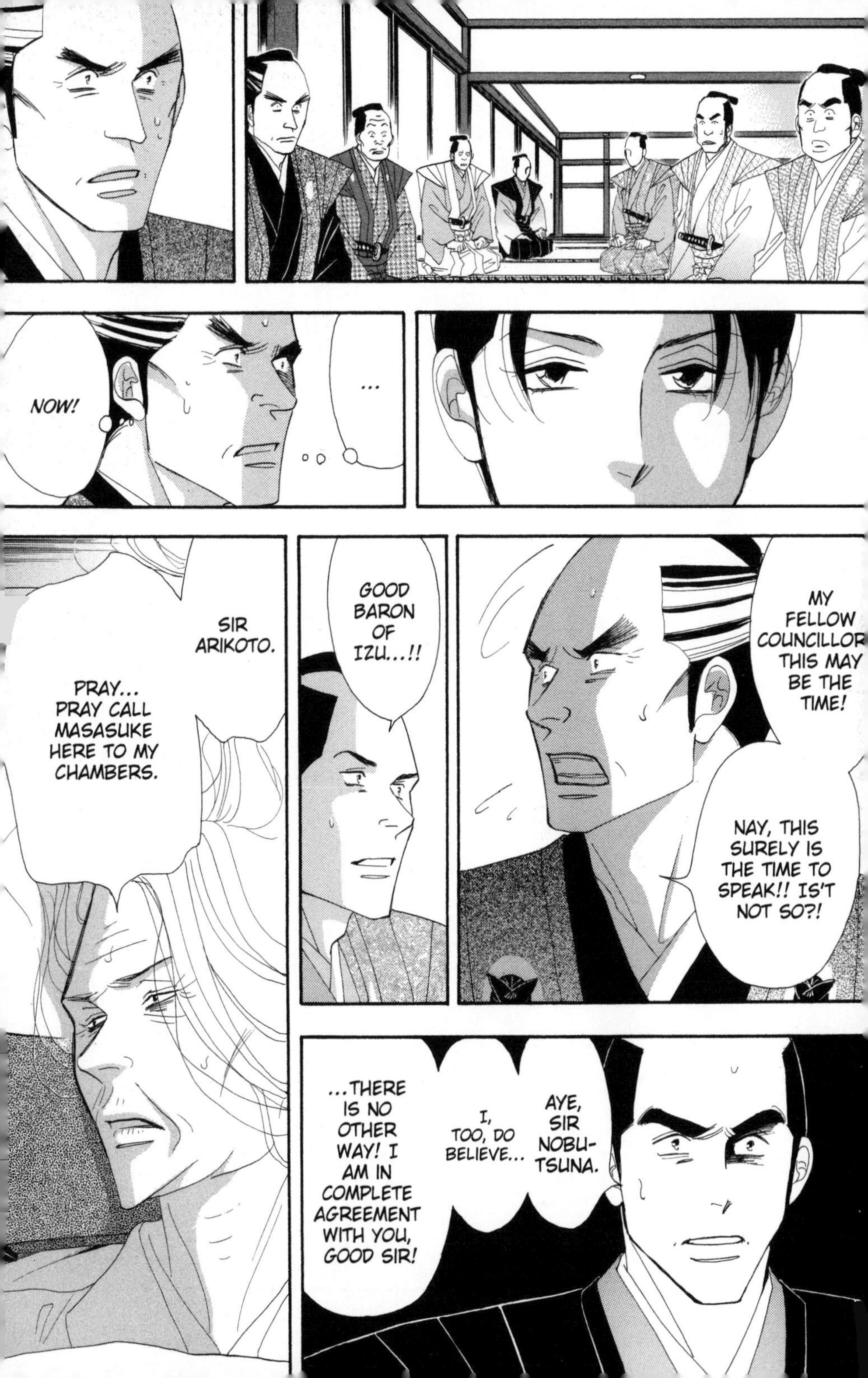
...
NOW!
MY FELLOW COUNCILLOR THIS MAY BE THE TIME!
NAY, THIS SURELY IS THE TIME TO SPEAK!! IS'T NOT SO?!
GOOD BARON OF IZU...!!
AYE, SIR NOBU-TSUNA.
I, TOO, DO BELIEVE...
...THERE IS NO OTHER WAY! I AM IN COMPLETE AGREEMENT WITH YOU, GOOD SIR!
SIR ARIKOTO.
PRAY... PRAY CALL MASASUKE HERE TO MY CHAMBERS.

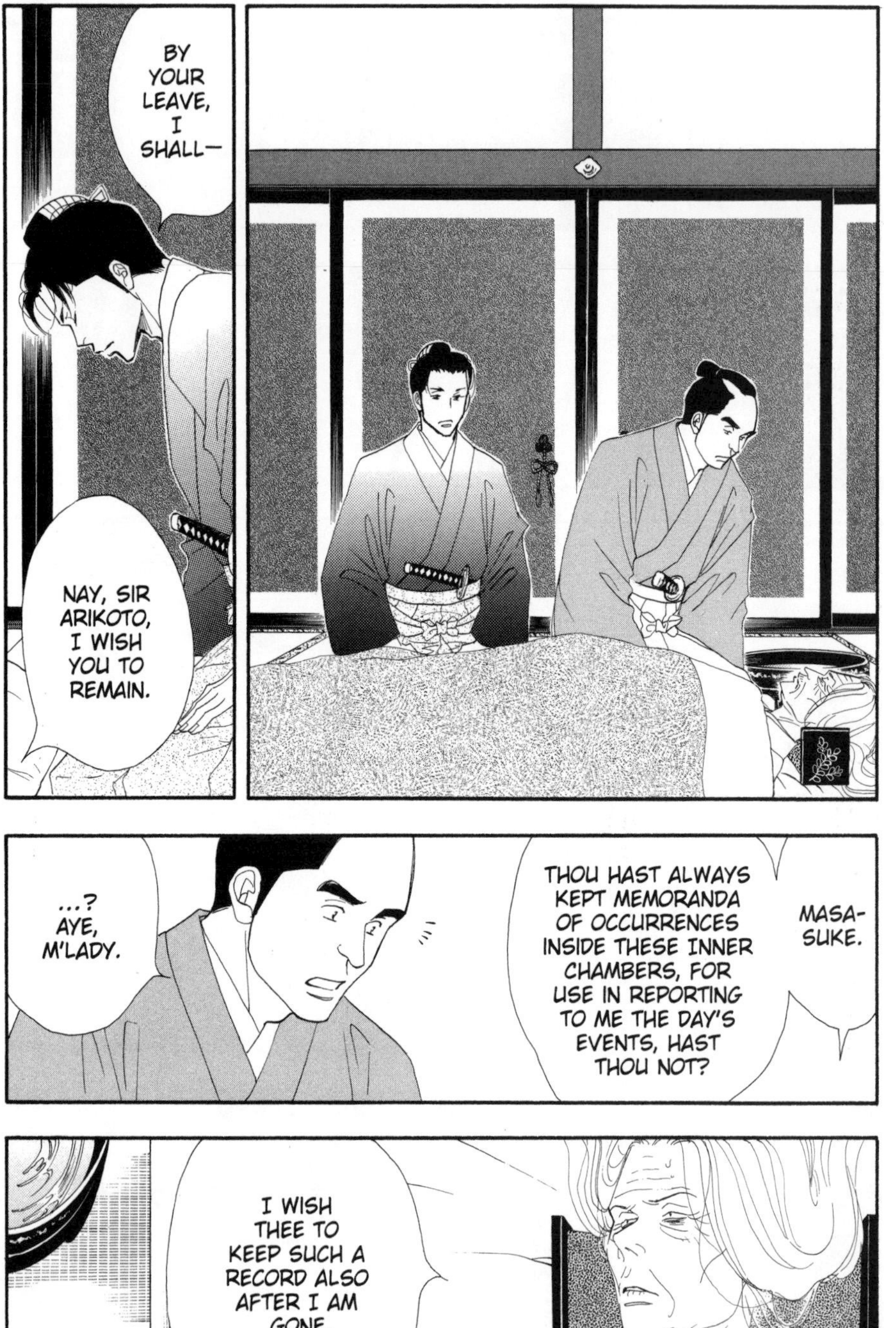
BY YOUR LEAVE, I SHALL—
NAY, SIR ARIKOTO, I WISH YOU TO REMAIN.
MASA-SUKE.
THOU HAST ALWAYS KEPT MEMORANDA OF OCCURRENCES INSIDE THESE INNER CHAMBERS, FOR USE IN REPORTING TO ME THE DAY'S EVENTS, HAST THOU NOT?
...? AYE, M'LADY.
I WISH THEE TO KEEP SUCH A RECORD ALSO AFTER I AM GONE.

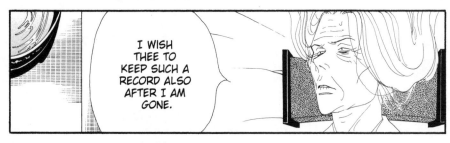

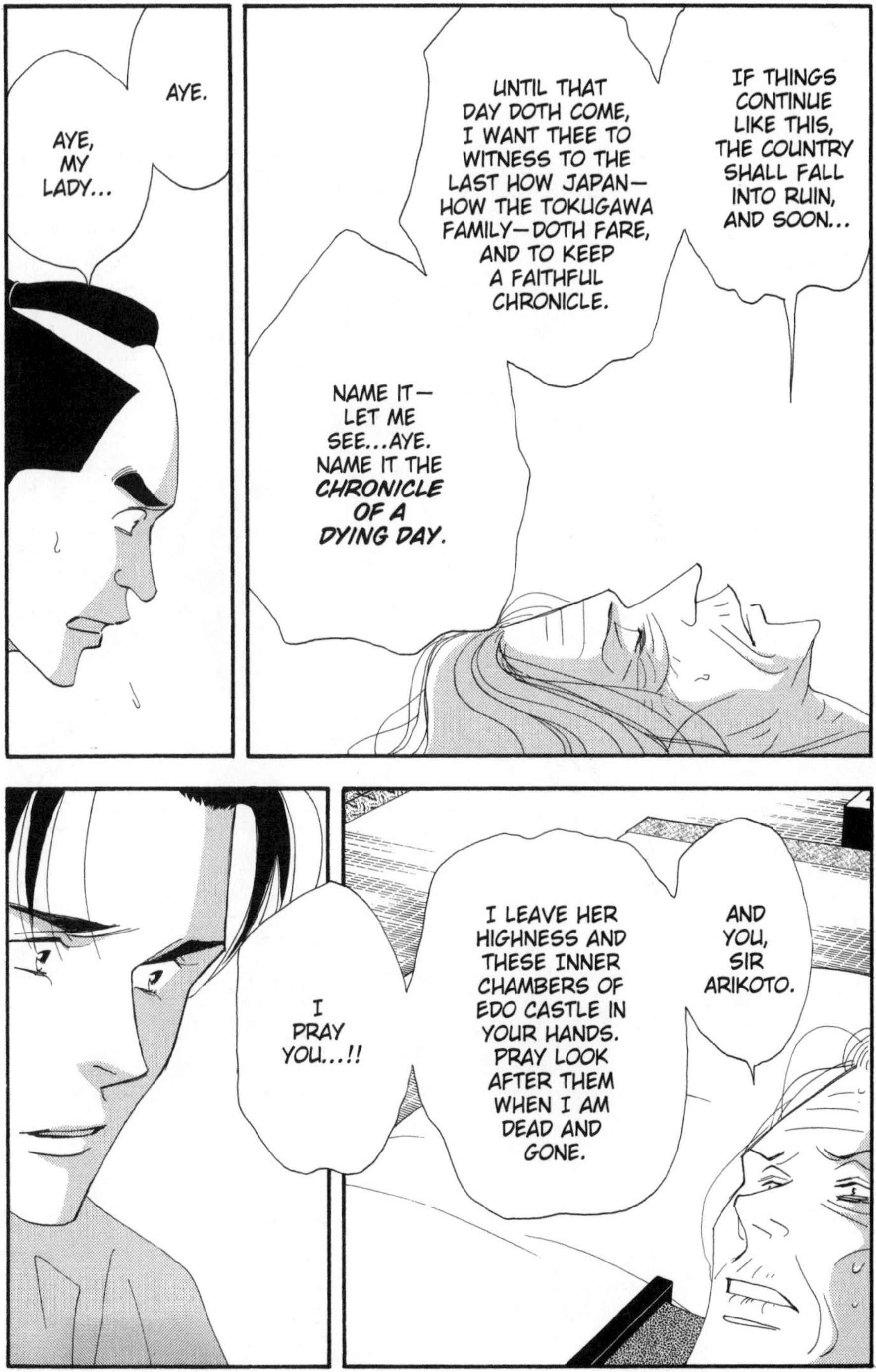
IF THINGS CONTINUE LIKE THIS, THE COUNTRY SHALL FALL INTO RUIN, AND SOON...
UNTIL THAT DAY DOTH COME, I WANT THEE TO WITNESS TO THE LAST HOW JAPAN—HOW THE TOKUGAWA FAMILY—DOTH FARE, AND TO KEEP A FAITHFUL CHRONICLE.
NAME IT—LET ME SEE...AYE. NAME IT THE *CHRONICLE OF A DYING DAY*.
AYE.
AYE, MY LADY...
AND YOU, SIR ARIKOTO.
I LEAVE HER HIGHNESS AND THESE INNER CHAMBERS OF EDO CASTLE IN YOUR HANDS. PRAY LOOK AFTER THEM WHEN I AM DEAD AND GONE.
I PRAY YOU...!!

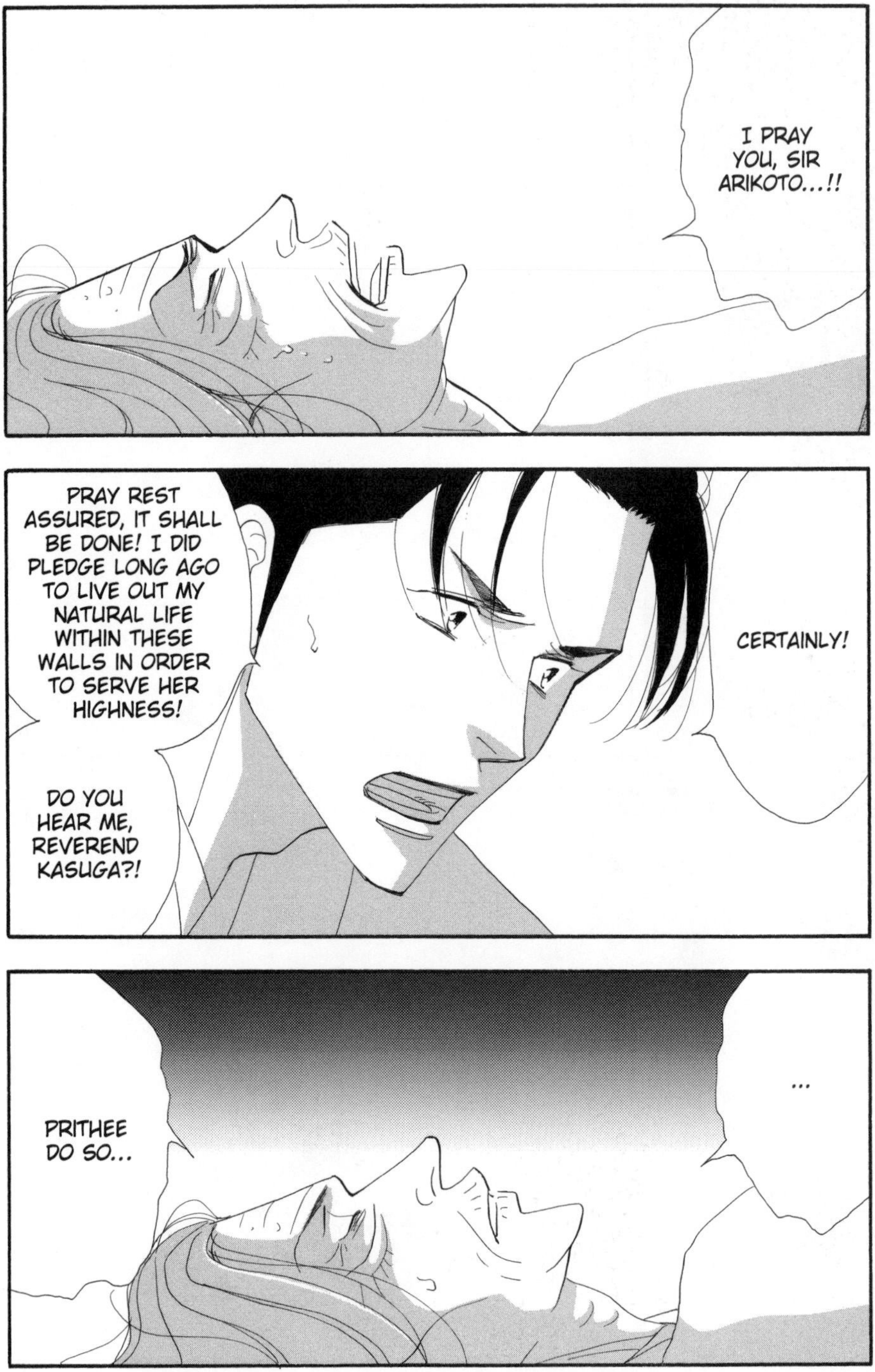
I PRAY YOU, SIR ARIKOTO...!!
CERTAINLY!
PRAY REST ASSURED, IT SHALL BE DONE! I DID PLEDGE LONG AGO TO LIVE OUT MY NATURAL LIFE WITHIN THESE WALLS IN ORDER TO SERVE HER HIGHNESS!
DO YOU HEAR ME, REVEREND KASUGA?!
...
PRITHEE DO SO...

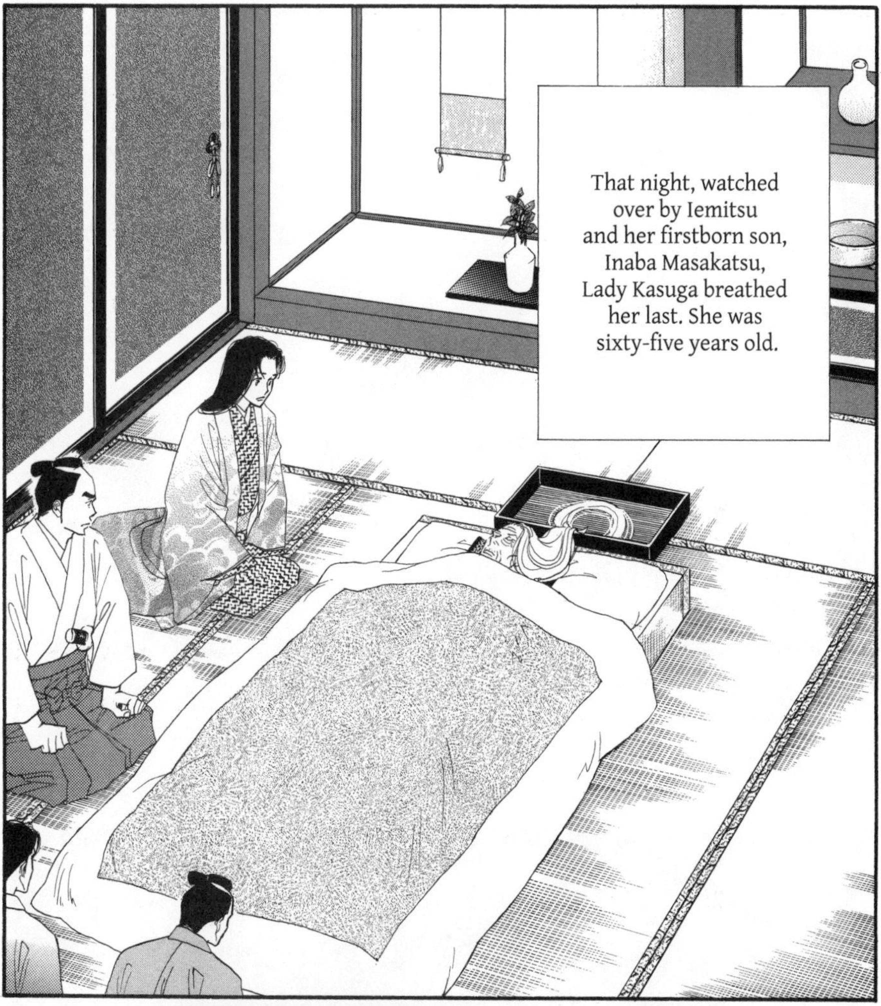
That night, watched over by Iemitsu and her firstborn son, Inaba Masakatsu, Lady Kasuga breathed her last. She was sixty-five years old.

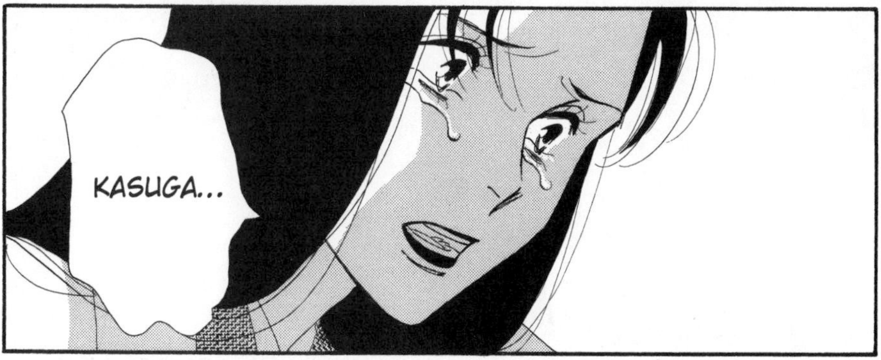
KASUGA...

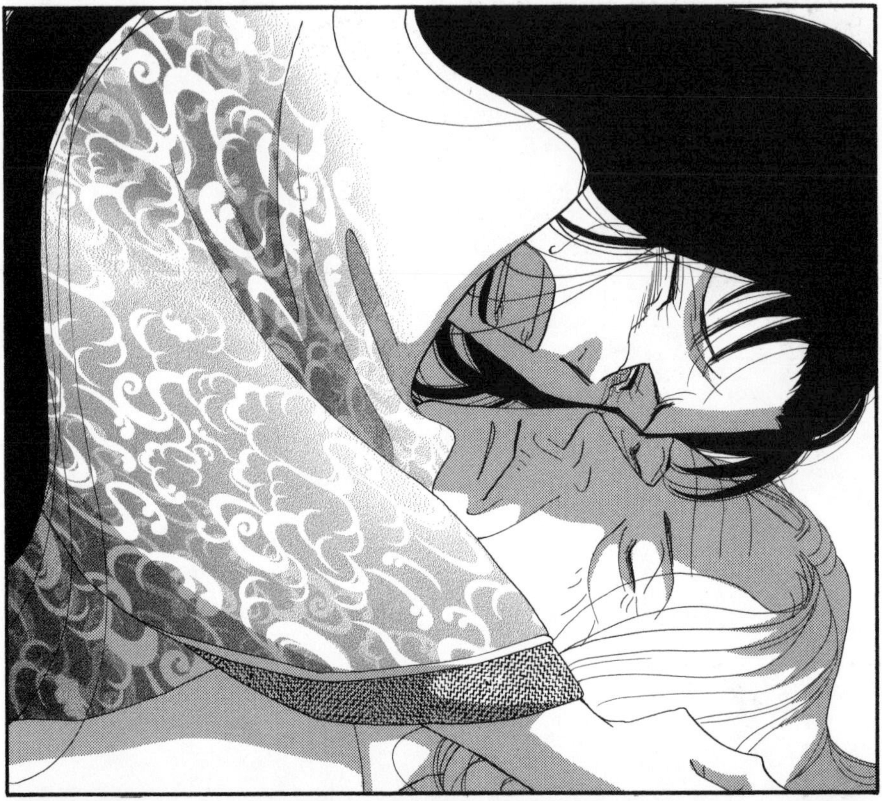
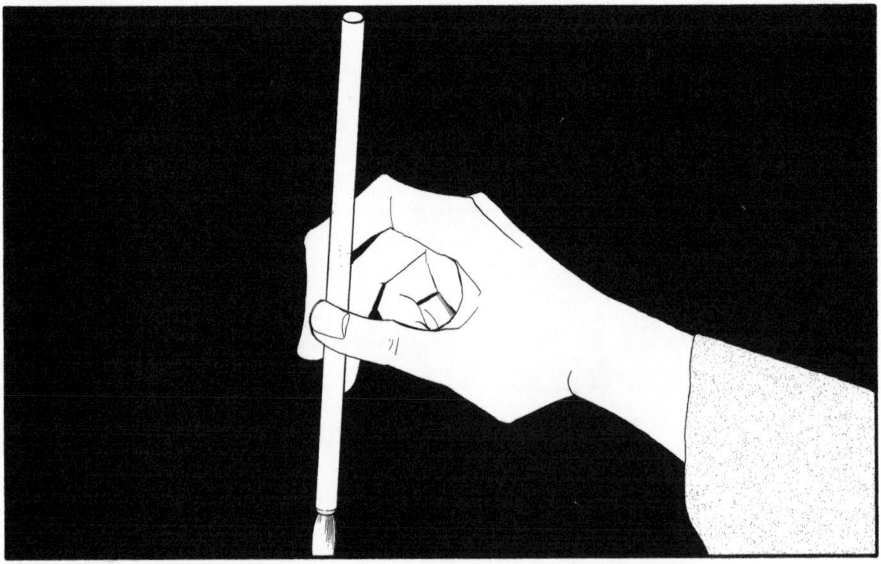

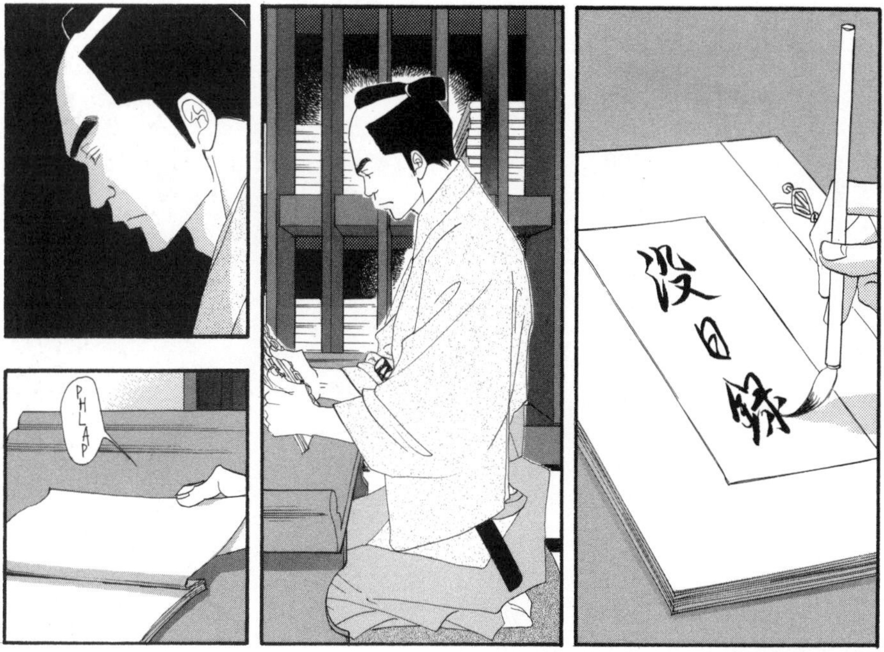
没日録
PHLAP

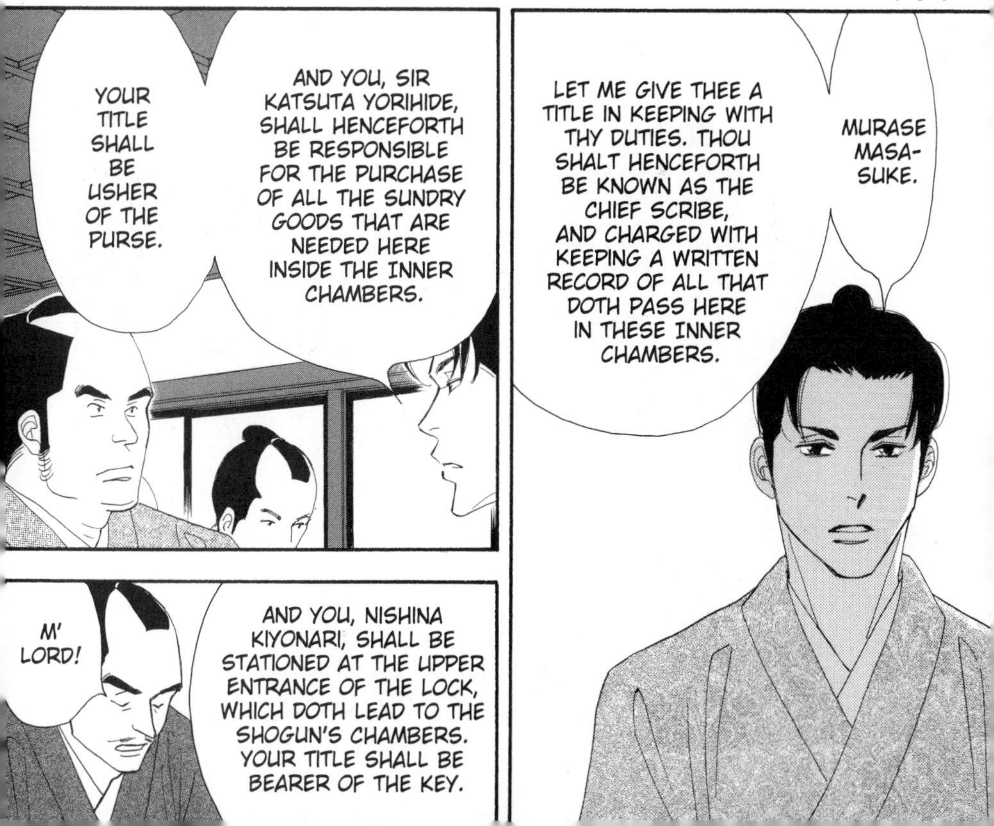
MURASE MASA-SUKE.
LET ME GIVE THEE A TITLE IN KEEPING WITH THY DUTIES. THOU SHALT HENCEFORTH BE KNOWN AS THE CHIEF SCRIBE, AND CHARGED WITH KEEPING A WRITTEN RECORD OF ALL THAT DOTH PASS HERE IN THESE INNER CHAMBERS.
AND YOU, SIR KATSUTA YORIHIDE, SHALL HENCEFORTH BE RESPONSIBLE FOR THE PURCHASE OF ALL THE SUNDRY GOODS THAT ARE NEEDED HERE INSIDE THE INNER CHAMBERS.
YOUR TITLE SHALL BE USHER OF THE PURSE.
AND YOU, NISHINA KIYONARI, SHALL BE STATIONED AT THE UPPER ENTRANCE OF THE LOCK, WHICH DOTH LEAD TO THE SHOGUN'S CHAMBERS. YOUR TITLE SHALL BE BEARER OF THE KEY.
M' LORD!

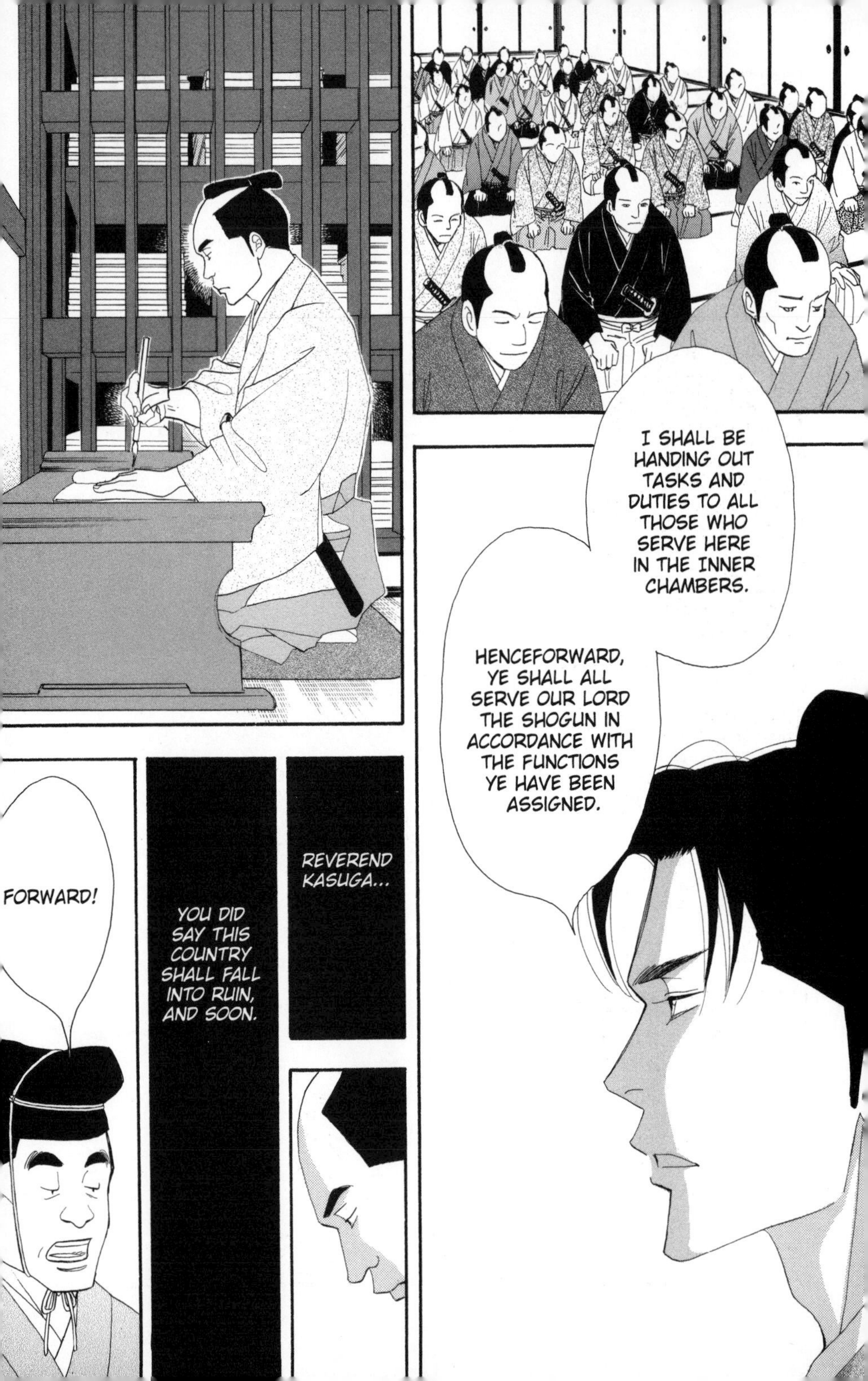
I SHALL BE HANDING OUT TASKS AND DUTIES TO ALL THOSE WHO SERVE HERE IN THE INNER CHAMBERS.
HENCEFORWARD, YE SHALL ALL SERVE OUR LORD THE SHOGUN IN ACCORDANCE WITH THE FUNCTIONS YE HAVE BEEN ASSIGNED.
REVEREND KASUGA...
YOU DID SAY THIS COUNTRY SHALL FALL INTO RUIN, AND SOON.
FORWARD!

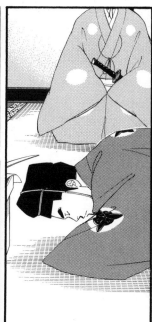

MATSUDAIRA TERUTSUNA, BARON OF KAI, DOTH WISH TO CONGRATULATE MY LORD ON THIS MOST AUSPICIOUS DAY!

HOWEVER, MOST HONORED REVEREND KASUGA...

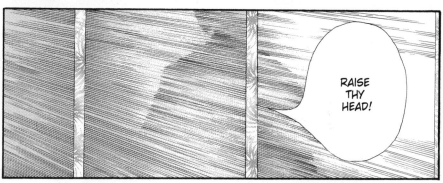

RAISE THY HEAD!

THIS DAY...

A WOMAN'S VOICE?

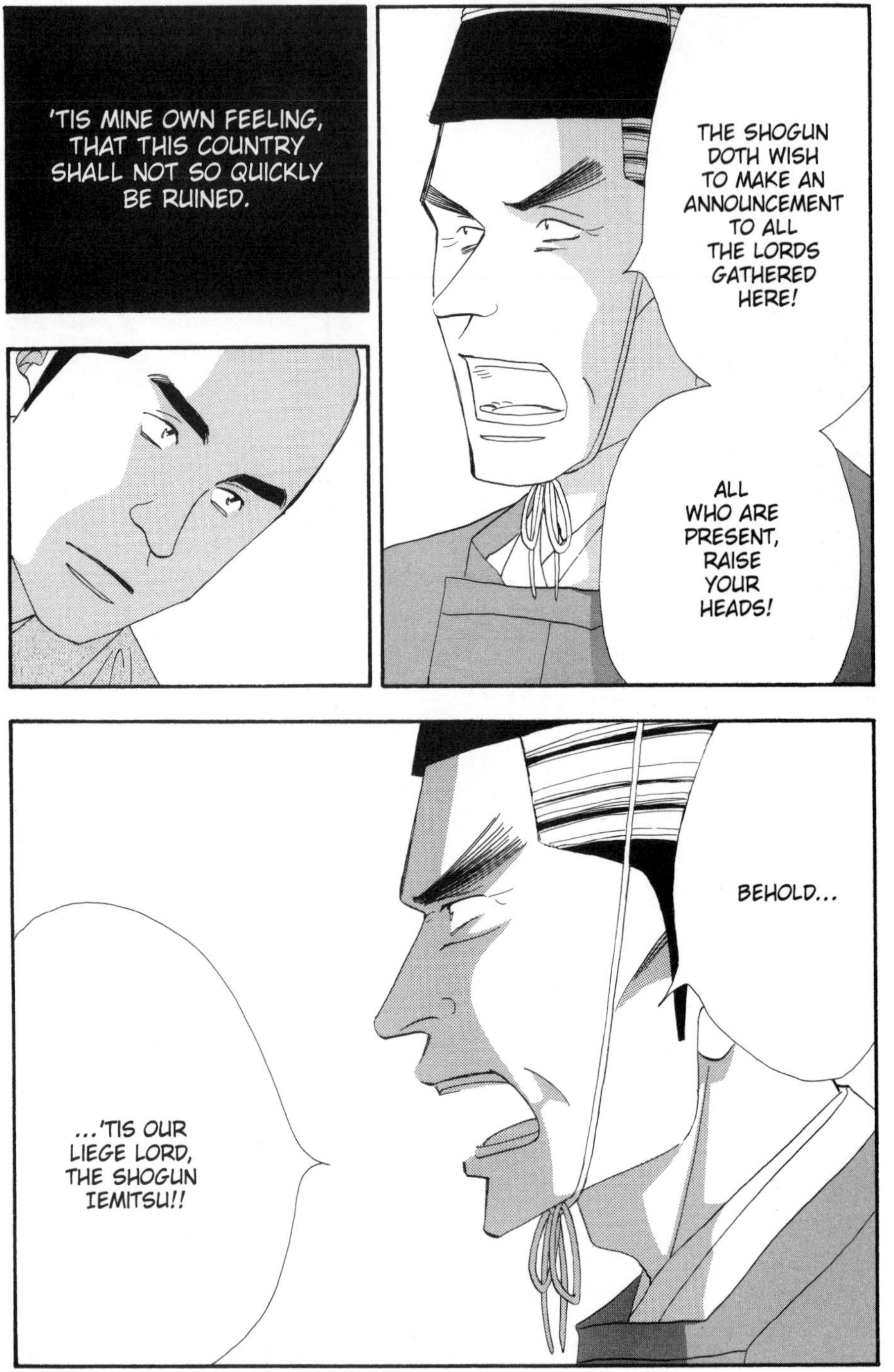
THE SHOGUN DOTH WISH TO MAKE AN ANNOUNCEMENT TO ALL THE LORDS GATHERED HERE!
ALL WHO ARE PRESENT, RAISE YOUR HEADS!
'TIS MINE OWN FEELING, THAT THIS COUNTRY SHALL NOT SO QUICKLY BE RUINED.
BEHOLD...
...'TIS OUR LIEGE LORD, THE SHOGUN IEMITSU!!

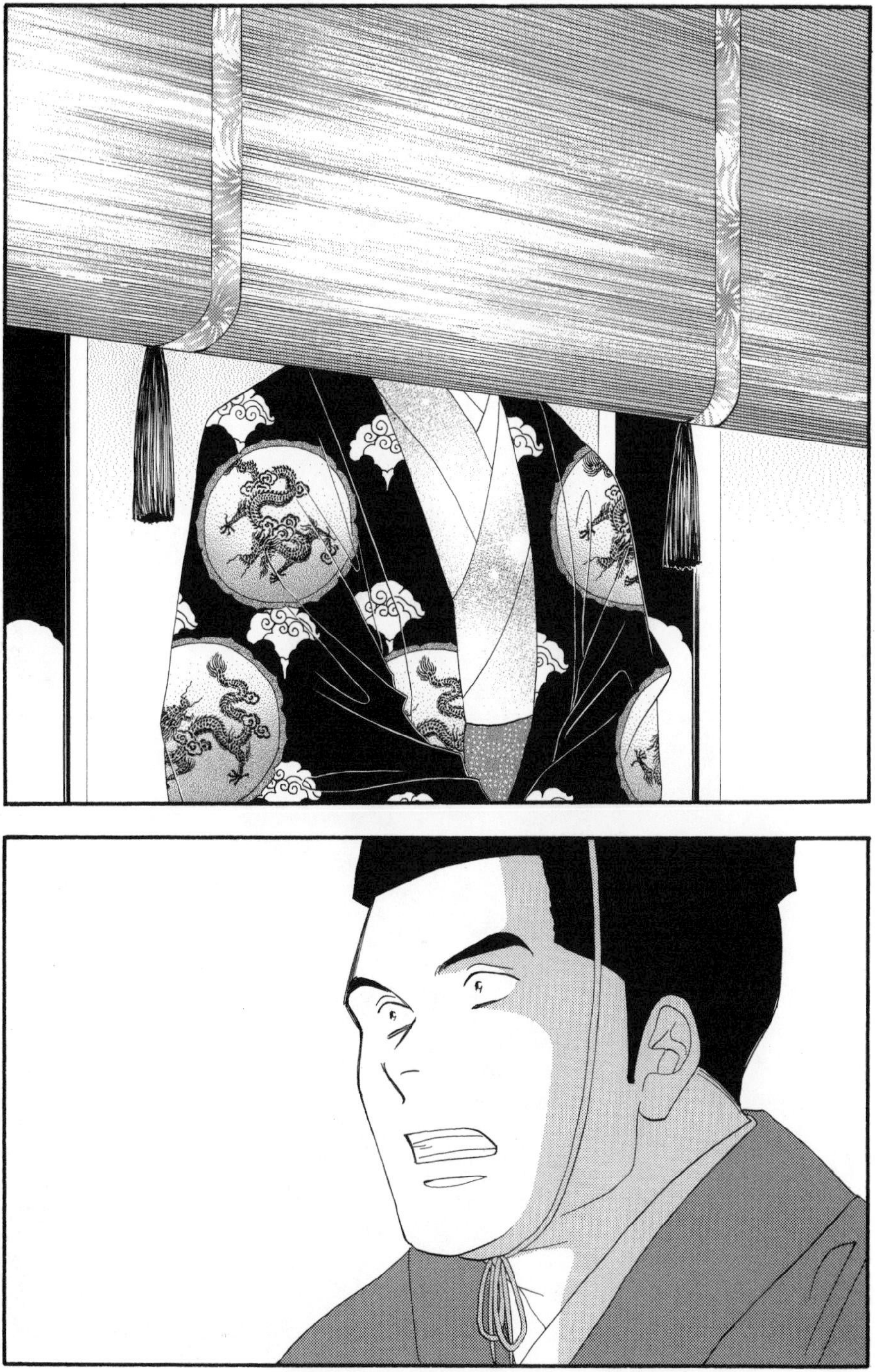

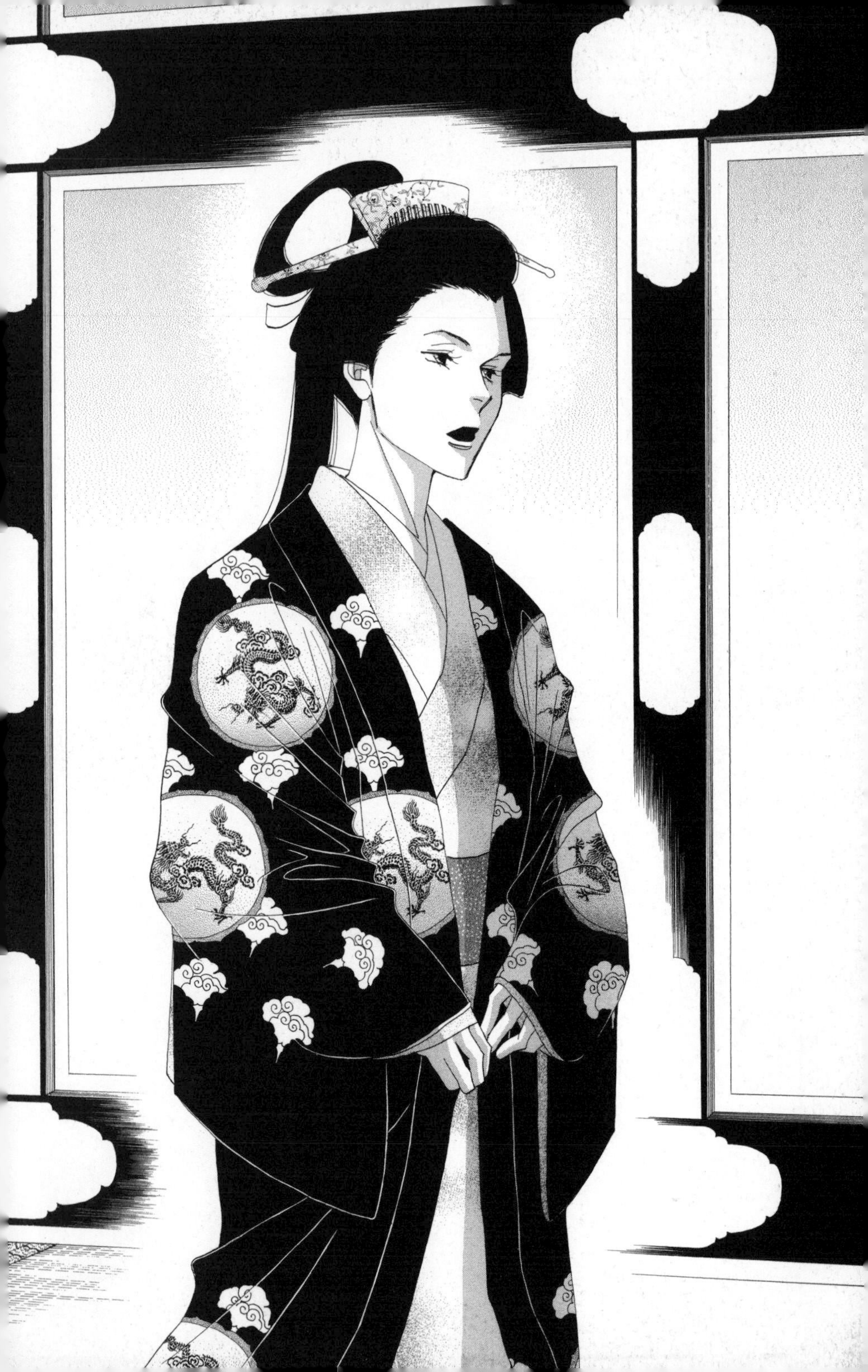

It was the
inauguration
of the
female shogun
Iemitsu.

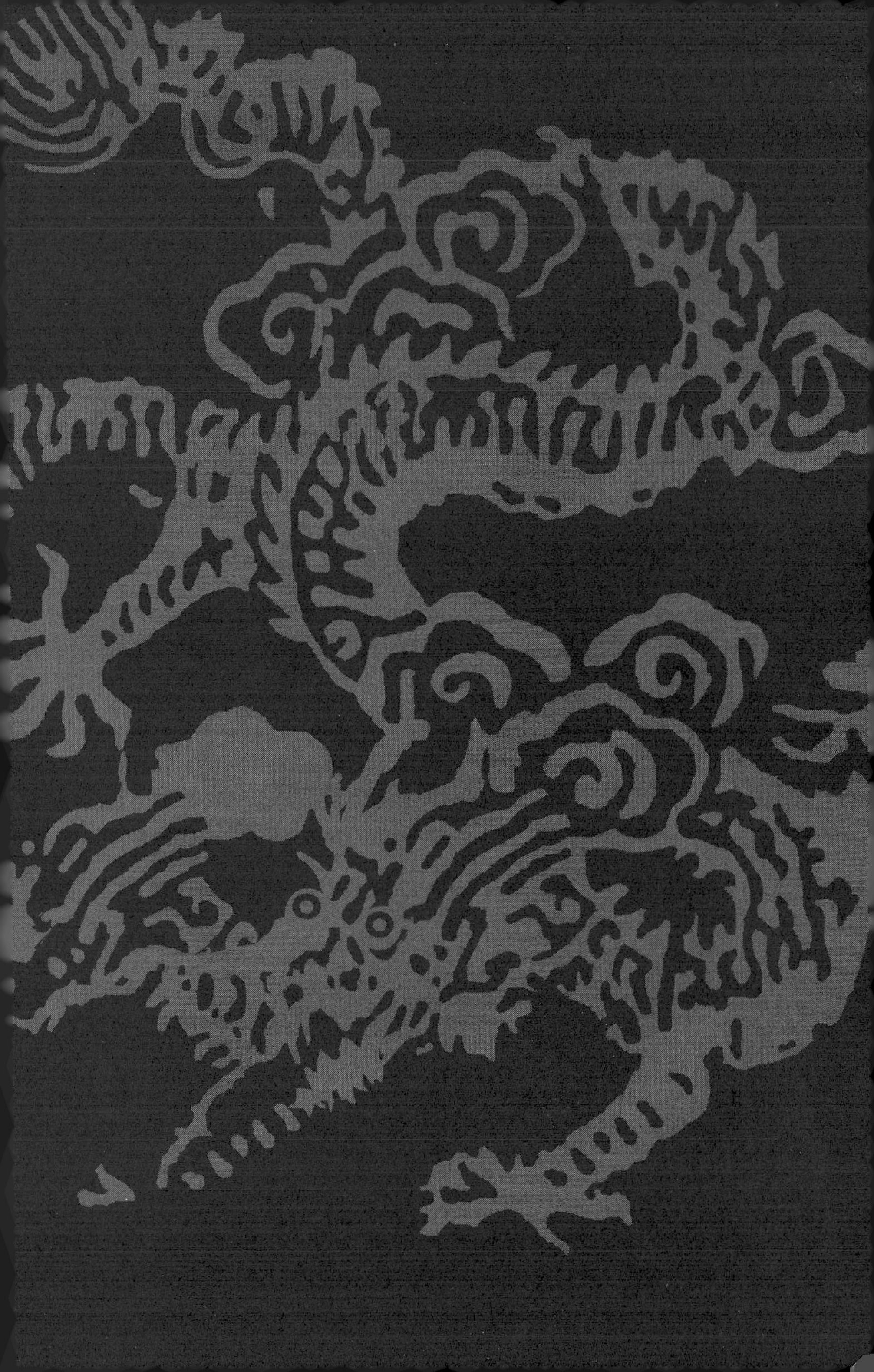